RACIAL BEACHHEAD

RACIAL BEACHHEAD

DIVERSITY AND DEMOCRACY IN A MILITARY TOWN

Seaside, California

Carol Lynn McKibben

STANFORD UNIVERSITY PRESS

Stanford, California

Stanford University Press
Stanford, California

Printed in the United States of America on acid-free,
archival-quality paper

Library of Congress Cataloging-in-Publication Data

McKibben, Carol Lynn, 1955– author.
Racial beachhead : diversity and democracy in a military town /
Carol Lynn McKibben.
pages cm
Includes bibliographical references and index.
ISBN 978-0-8047-7698-1 (cloth : alk. paper) —
ISBN 978-0-8047-7699-8 (pbk. : alk. paper)
1. Seaside (Calif.)—Race relations—History—20th century.
2. Fort Ord (Calif.)—Race relations—History—20th century.
3. African Americans—California—Seaside—History—20th century.
4. Minorities—California—Seaside—History—20th century.
5. Military towns—Social aspects—United States.
6. Military towns—United States—History—20th century.
7. Seaside (Calif.)—Social conditions—20th century. I. Title.
F869.S594M349 2012
305.896'073079476—dc23
2011027431

Typeset by Thompson Type in 10/15 Sabon

To my children, Andrew and Becky,
and to my dearest daughter-in-law, Diana

Contents

Acknowledgments

I AM HUMBLED by the people I met in Seaside. I learned so much from the women and men who lived this history. My understanding of race relations in America at midcentury and the full meaning of what the military embodies in American life became real to me in a way that I never expected when I began this project in the fall of 2005. At that time Seaside was in transition, from military town to resort community and tourist destination. I was in transition too. I had just published a book on Sicilian immigrants in Monterey and wanted to expand my work to include more comparative analyses of ethnic and race relations. With the help and guidance of Al Camarillo, Professor of History at Stanford University, Ray Corpuz, City Manager of Seaside, and historian Becky Nicolaides, I was able to do just that.

Professor Camarillo included me in a research project on minority majority cities in California that helped me put this history of Seaside into the broader perspective of urban California. He showed me the importance of writing histories of communities that had been dismissed as crime and drug ridden and unworthy of attention or economic investment, primarily because the majority of residents in these places were minorities and poor. His work proves there is more to these communities than crimes or drugs and sensational reporting in the media; his passion for his work was infectious and inspiring throughout the course of this project.

Ray Corpuz, who had been looking in vain for a history of the city he managed, was also incredibly supportive of the notion of writing a history of the town that would integrate Seaside alongside the history of the Monterey Peninsula and urban California and taught me so much about city government and good governance in the most challenging of circumstances.

Becky Nicolaides read early versions of this manuscript when it counted the most, and gave me critical feedback, from sharpening my argument to reorganizing the work. She has become a dear friend.

I began my research from scratch because historians of Monterey and its environs had long ignored the history of Seaside. The challenges were immense. There was no archive or local collection of history that served as a central place for research. Sources were scattered among residents, in their minds' eyes and in their garages, and casually collected but in disarray in bags and boxes in a dilapidated and mold-filled house in Seaside that served as headquarters for the Seaside Historical Commission, whose main function was to preserve the memory of its nineteenth-century founder Dr. John Roberts, and doing Christmas art projects to raise money. There was concern among the commissioners that any history of the city would expose racial tensions and the dark side of military town life and would be an embarrassment to the people of Seaside.

However, residents and former residents of Seaside—Richard Joyce, Lenora Bean, Don and Alice Jordan, William Meléndez, Ruthie Watts, Mel Mason, Ewalker James, Helen Rucker, Morris and Bobbie McDaniel, Jerry Smith, Brenda Thomas, Andy Yoshiyama, Emerson Reyes, Ralph Rubio, Al Glover, Estela and Patrick McKenzie, Nancy Towne, Rosa Sánchez, Sergio Rangel, Hector Azpilcueto, Sherman and Elizabeth Smith, former city council members and staff too numerous to mention, and so many, many others—thought otherwise. Besides sharing their stories, Seaside residents taught me how to navigate the political waters of their city, introduced me to friends and relatives who had stories to share, and encouraged me to complete this work wherever it might lead. I am immeasurably grateful to each one of them.

I am grateful for the support of the Seaside City Council, 2005–2009, Stanford University, the California Council for the Humanities, the Community Foundation for Monterey County, and the Monterey Peninsula Foundation. All provided much needed funding support to make this project possible. Because of their support, our history project was able to host a number of community events from "Speaking History" forums to photo days that were as critical to the history project as researching and writing this book. These events raised awareness about Seaside history throughout the Peninsula. It was because of these events that much of the archive now available through Oldemeyer Center was assembled.

No one could write anything without the help of research librarians and archivists. I am incredibly grateful for the research help, advice, critiques, and support Dennis Copeland, archivist and historian for the Monterey Public Library, has given to me over the years. The staff of librarians at the Monterey Public library are wonderful, especially Sarah Stewman, who patiently tracked down a source for me at the last minute. I am also grateful for research help from Kurt Kuss, California archivist, Defense Language Institute, Foreign Language Center, Historic Research Collection, Chamberlin Library.

My colleagues in the history department at Stanford University provided the most supportive and collegial environment imaginable, and many of them have become good friends as well. Al Camarillo, Zephyr Frank, Allyson Hobbs, and Gordon Chang read parts or all of the manuscript and gave me the most constructive feedback. I am thankful for the support and encouragement of, Paula Findlen, Richard White, Jim Campbell, Caroline Winterer, Richard Roberts, Estelle Freedman, and others who welcomed me into this extraordinary intellectual environment. I am also indebted to Quintard Taylor, Carl Abbott, Janet Bednarek, Lori Flores, and Shana Bernstein for reading my work and helping me refine the argument and organize the material better. Mark Wild and the anonymous reader at Stanford Press gave me invaluable feedback, which helped in the last stages of revisions and for which I am enormously grateful.

I thank my editors at Stanford Press, Kate Wahl and Joa Suorez, for sticking with me from the inception to the finish and seeing this project through. They have been a source of support throughout, but especially wonderful as this work neared completion. I also thank my editor, Margaret Pinette, whose work and support in the final stages was invaluable. I thank Chris Eberhart, Tracy Kegelman, and Lauren Wilkins for their incredible help with indexing.

I also thank my friends and family, with my whole heart, for their love and belief in me. Diane Belanger, Rachel Holz, Cindy Riebe, Paula Arnold, and Charlie Keeley provided welcome respite and much needed tea and glasses of wine throughout the years. I found such refuge in the love of the various members of the McKibben, Copelan, Caliri, Erekson,

Manwill, and Ernst families, particularly my sisters Laurie and Diane, and my brother David, and I am infinitely grateful to all of them.

Most of all I thank my family, my husband, Scott, who encouraged and supported and loved me every step of the way, and my unbelievably wonderful children, Andrew and Becky, and dearest daughter-in-law, Diana. In the preparation of the manuscript, Andrew patiently and lovingly helped me with all of the formatting that was causing me such frustration. I am so grateful to him, to Becky, and to Diana. My love for you is absolutely incalculable, and it is to you that I dedicate this book.

RACIAL BEACHHEAD

Introduction

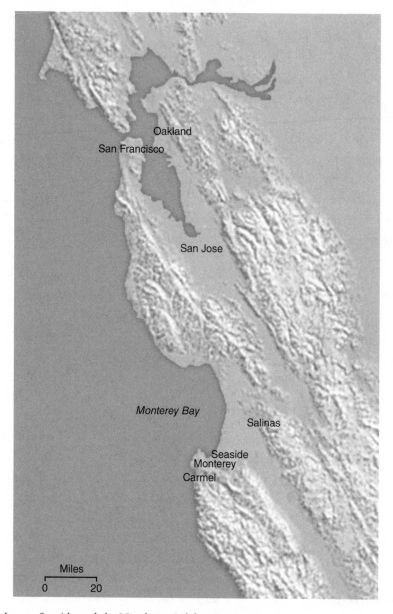

Oakland
San Francisco

San Jose

Monterey Bay

Salinas

Seaside
Monterey
Carmel

Miles
0   20

MAP 1. Seaside and the Northern California coastal cities.

ONE LONG-TIME RESIDENT of the Monterey Peninsula vividly recalled the first and now internationally famous Monterey Bay Blues Festival: "Those 14 men that started it were standing on that stage. Most were retired military. They looked so good in their uniforms. Those gentlemen looked like kings as they crossed that stage. The pride in giving that first festival you just knew they were going to succeed—to keep the blues alive means something about our history, our beginning. But from the first and through the years the festival wasn't just black. Martín Puentes and Sam Karas—they were a part of it from the beginning. What they wanted was to have a festival for scholarships, grants that helped the community. It was a joy to behold. It was military, civilians, locals, it was a community of people, there were Caucasians, blacks, Spanish—it is and was open."[1] This observer might have been describing the city of Seaside itself. In spite of enormous social and political pressure to separate by race in America at mid-twentieth century, Seaside, perhaps like many other military communities across the country, found a way to integrate peacefully. This book is the story of how, and why, that happened.

The story of Seaside, California, is entwined in the history of how World War II and developments in the postwar decades transformed much of California and the West. It is also a story of how a small California community, nestled between a massive military installation on one side and upscale resort destinations and historic Monterey on the other side, was reshaped by the U.S. Army at Fort Ord into a minority-majority, military community that struggled to incorporate the best ideals of the civil rights movement at midcentury. The story of Seaside is part and parcel of the story of the development of the American West, which was never the wild, independent frontier of American imagination but always dependent on, and an integral part of, federal investment and design.[2]

The forces that swept through California from the 1950s through the 1990s—significant growth of a diverse population and the consequences of social, economic, and cultural changes—manifested themselves in Seaside like so many other cities and suburbs in the Golden State. However, unlike other California cities during the second half of the twentieth century, the civil rights struggles, racialized local politics, and the movements of people in and out of Seaside were dramatically affected by the city's symbiotic relationship with the military, and by association with the federal government, which make it possible to understand race relations and urban/suburban development in new ways. The example of Seaside, and other military towns directly affected by federal mandates for integration, demonstrates that policies of contact, integration, and assimilation coupled with a vigorous civil rights movement in the civilian population, can indeed shape values and behavior in exceedingly positive ways, and do not necessarily lead to neoconservative backlash.[3] Seaside's history tests new racial formation theory, which attempts to explain the failures of decades of policies that attempted to rectify social and racial injustice.[4] Sometimes, as was the case in Seaside, and perhaps in other communities in the United States, both military and nonmilitary, those policies worked.[5]

Seaside is a community of about 35,000 people located on the Monterey Bay, but unlike the affluent communities of Pebble Beach, Carmel, and Monterey the presence of the huge military training base at Fort Ord altered the trajectory of its history in fundamental ways. Although Fort Ord was established adjacent to the tiny subdivision of Seaside in 1917, it was during the buildup to World War II and the impact of Fort Ord in the postwar era that changed everything about the character of the subdivision, from its incorporation as a city to its fundamental role in the civil rights movement. Yet, Seaside was among many places that have been overlooked by historians and other social scientists seeking to explain the complex history of the last half of the twentieth century in California. This book attempts to rectify that oversight.

On the one hand, as new scholarship on race and urbanization shows, the federal government actively colluded with cities to sustain inequality by refusing home loans to people of color generally and blacks in particular.[6] On the other hand, the military, an arm of the federal government, became the most progressive and integrated institution in the country after a series of policy decisions during and after World War II that culminated in the desegregation of the armed forces by the time of the Korean War.[7] Rank, not race, came to determine status within the military, unlike in American society generally. Moreover, policies about racial integration applied to life on and off base so that military families—black, white,

Hispanic and Asian—shared an experience far different than their civilian counterparts in the 1950s and 1960s, most of whom lived in isolation from one another in cities and suburbs throughout the country. For military personnel and their families, racial barriers were challenged head-on, which meant that military families, as well as those who lived alongside them in military towns across the country, experienced a new model of living and working together that showed integration working to the benefit of all, in spite of hysteria to the contrary. Although this may be harder to discern in huge metropolitan military centers such as San Diego, smaller towns such as Seaside offer a novel and more nuanced way of understanding the military impact on race relations in the development of town life at midcentury.

In California, institutionalized racial barriers to housing, marriage, and voting were already challenged successfully in the courts by the 1950s, although customized racial boundaries remained in place well into the twentieth century.[8] Still, California had a long history of diversity in its cities, suburbs, and rural areas that went beyond the boundaries of black and white. An enormous literature on the West and California emphasizes that above all, California cities and suburbs incorporated a jumble of people of color that included Asians, Mexicans, and Africans, along with Anglo Americans. Although the cities and towns of California and the West were often the sites of racial violence and conflict, they were also places where multiple communities of color lived side-by-side in ways that they did not in most eastern and midwestern cities and towns in the early half of the twentieth century. Sometimes but not always, these communities found ways to build coalitions with one another to achieve specific ends.[9]

What became the most progressive racial policy in the country under the auspices of the U.S. military had a much greater chance of success in California than at other bases and military towns in the United States because the civil rights movement in California was less focused on overturning restrictive Jim Crow legislation of the type that characterized the American South than with implementing laws that were already in place. The new military policy affecting race relations during the 1950s and 1960s was consistent with rather than in defiance of California law, which was increasingly liberalizing in favor of integration and fairer treatment of minorities.[10] Although there are plenty of studies on the economic impact of the military on large municipalities in California in the years during and after World War II, such as Roger Lotchin's work on San Diego, Los Angeles, and San Francisco, few studies look at smaller towns and cities attached to military bases, and fewer still analyze the impact of integration on military town development.[11]

Most importantly, the "long civil rights movement" that black women and men were engaged in throughout the country was bolstered by their association with the military at Fort Ord. Fort Ord gave black men secure employment, and as career officers or high-ranking enlisted men, they achieved a status that they could not have found in any other institution or organization in the country at that time.[12] Black women, who were traditionally the leaders in civil rights throughout the West, gained both prestige and security by association as officers' wives that enabled them to become even stronger and more successful as activists and leaders. Base life provided everything from affordable food, clothing, and other necessities through the commissary, to health care, giving African American military personnel advantages in daily life that African Americans not associated with the military simply did not have. Seaside was a poor community compared to other Monterey Peninsula towns, but its connection to the base gave its residents a measure of security that cushioned them from the harshest effects of economic racism.

I argue, first and foremost, that the military was responsible for the creation of the town of Seaside by fundamentally altering the demographics of Monterey County so that Seaside became home to a critical mass of soldier families, mostly black but also Asian, white, and multiracial, many of whom were career military personnel. Seaside became a minority-majority city on the Monterey Peninsula, amidst communities that were predominantly white, in a relatively brief period of time following World War II. Most importantly, these soldiers and families of all races had experienced the full impact of integration in their lives on base over time, and were poised to challenge segregation off base as well, not as racial blocs, but together, as an interracial community.[13] They shared values associated with being part of the military such as a high regard for authority, law and order, patriotism, and belief in family. According to one analysis of attitudes between soldiers, both careerists and those who served for only a short term and undergraduate students of the same age, "Whether black or white, soldiers are twice as likely as undergraduates to claim that they get along with other races . . . those in the military give more conservative responses than civilians . . . and are more likely to adhere to traditional family values."[14] However, the same studies showed that military people of all races had more liberal views when it came to issues such as poverty, viewing poor people as "victims of circumstance" rather than responsible for their own condition.[15] These and other attitudes characterized large numbers of Seasiders at midcentury. It was a population that was centrist, politically progressive, and family oriented, but also one primed to challenge racist practices at every level and to fight social inequality.[16] Most important, it was a population that included large numbers of career military people of all races, including whites and especially blacks, not just those who had served for the duration of World War II and then left for civilian life.

This work contributes to a small but growing literature on military towns, which rightly focuses on the twentieth century when the military challenged the edifice of American race relations. Two books on race relations and military towns—*Homefront* by Catherine Lutz and *Black, White and Olive Drab* by Andrew H. Myers—examine the impact of the military on town life in the years during and after World War II. Lutz argues that the impact of the military was overwhelmingly negative, especially for women living on and near bases, and had harmful repercussions for American society generally. Myers on the other hand, argues that the military was a mostly positive force, modeling equality for the citizens of Columbia, North Carolina, but also facing enormous resistance by a population determined to retain segregation and second-class status for blacks.[17] It is important to note that both Lutz and Myers focus on military towns located in the American South, a region most resistant to racial integration. There are no similar analyses of military communities in the American West.

Beth Bailey and David Farber looked at the ways that the military presence exacerbated an already complex racial dynamic in Hawaii, but they limited their study to a specific moment during World War II.[18] This book calls for a more nuanced view of the military that focuses on the context outside of large urban areas or the American South. The military certainly brought crime and drugs to its base towns and created a culture that was both violent and exploitive for women, both nationally and internationally. However, military life in the United States at midcentury offered people of color, particularly blacks, opportunities to participate as equals in American life. In terms of gender, the military bolstered and empowered black women who were wives of officers to leadership roles on and off base even more than their female counterparts elsewhere in the West. This is not to say that the military was the only factor in the way Seaside developed, but it is to argue that the common experience of long careers in the military among so many Seaside residents had a profound effect on the political evolution and cultural makeup of the town, leading to a political culture of inclusivity.

Military historians who analyze the history of blacks in the armed forces and the process of desegregation tend to juxtapose the experiences of military personnel in the urban North and South and have almost completely ignored installations in the West, even in California where a number of the most significant bases were located, and where race was not a simple divide between blacks and whites but also included Mexicans, other Hispanic peoples, and multiple Asian communities.[19] They also tended to focus either on the period before or immediately after World War II. Polly J. Smith studied the effects of desegregation in the 1960s in three military towns and argued that the policy of the military did indeed have a powerful effect on neighborhoods, creating far less segregated spaces than in nonmilitary towns within their respective regions.[20] She did not fully analyze the evolution of any one of these towns over time, however, nor did she expand her analysis into the later decades of the twentieth century. This study of Seaside traces its development over the entire course of the twentieth century and focuses on how diversity of population, influenced by military life, led to more than crime, drugs, and prostitution, but to a body politic that was remarkably inclusive.

This work on Seaside also contributes to emerging literatures on urban space and race relations, particularly in California. "Cities of Color," a term coined by Albert M. Camarillo in 2007 describes the outcome of urban segregation for people of color, including Mexicans, that forced communities of color into the least desirable areas of cities.[21] This phenomenon also is well documented in recent literature on racial segregation as it was embedded in both federal policy and in the American mind.[22]

This study takes that understanding a step further by showing how federal policy can also be used in powerful ways to effect change in exactly the opposite direction. Armed with a fiat from the highest levels of the military, base commanders not only integrated housing, schools, and all facilities on base, but were ordered to do the same off base as well.[23] Although this could not bring about major changes in restrictive housing or segregated schools in big municipalities like San Diego or San Francisco, for example, the power of the federal government at Fort Ord fundamentally (and rapidly) altered Seaside, and even the Monterey Peninsula as a whole.

New scholarship on race relations in urban California focuses as much on coalition building among groups as on the conflicts that ensued over other issues related to housing segregation, for example.[24] Most recently, Charlotte Brooks examined the two major metropolitan centers of Los Angeles and San Francisco in her analysis of the efforts of Asians and Asian Americans, once the most discriminated racial group in California, as they became, with the full complicity of whites, a middle-class "model minority." She demonstrated, through an analysis of housing issues, the pivotal role that Asian Americans played in challenging segregation, and the effects this had on civil rights for others, especially for blacks in California.[25] Shana Bernstein's analysis of the multiracial nature of the civil rights movement in Los Angeles also focuses on complex relationships among Jews, Mexicans, Asians, and blacks.[26] Yet, coalition building among minorities in the West could be difficult to achieve, as George Sánchez, Mark Brilliant, and Matthew Whitaker argue with regard to California and Arizona, respectively.[27]

The example of Seaside adds a new dimension to this literature by showing how the military policy of integration contributed to the weakening of group identity formed solely on the basis of race or ethnicity, and how it strengthened ties between individuals; in fact, in Seaside it was difficult to get racial or ethnic groups to vote together as a self-interested bloc. Even so-called well-organized black groups such as the Ministerial Alliance and the National Association for the Advancement of Colored People (NAACP) could not control their constituents, and almost every issue, large or small, contained individual members of all races and ethnicities, including many multiracial families. This was in stark contrast to civil rights efforts in other parts of California and the West.[28]

This work benefited from the substantial literature created by historians and sociologists of urban America who brought to light the "urban crisis" that characterized many eastern and midwestern American cities in the post-World War II period, which led to the establishment of an isolated "underclass" of mostly blacks "left behind" by the gains of the civil rights movement.[29] Foremost among historians, Thomas J. Sugrue demonstrated that once prosperous cities such as Detroit experienced severe decline in the form of high unemployment, poverty, and serious physical deterioration as early as the 1950s. Among the multiple causes for the increase in urban poverty and blight was the abandonment of cities by white and black elites who found jobs, homes, and opportunity in the emerging surrounding suburbs.[30] Sociologists such as William Julius Wilson focused on Chicago to demonstrate how and why the inner city became both impoverished economically and a center for drug use and crime. Like Sugrue, Wilson suggested multiple factors contributed to the problem, not the least of which was racism. However, he also emphasized the devastating impact in terms of loss of community spirit when more affluent African Americans moved out of the inner city in the 1960s. He attributed high crime; female-headed, fatherless households; and the prevalence of drugs to this exodus of middle-class blacks, as well as to businesses and industries increasingly relocating in suburbs, severely limiting employment opportunities for blacks who had no access to transportation systems.[31] The literature that explores where these black middle-class elites (and their white counterparts) fled *to* is mostly limited to examinations of all-black or all-white towns and suburbs.[32] However, this study of Seaside offers an alternative possibility. Seaside attracted people of all races who were striving toward middle-class life, who valued diversity, who had learned from military life that diversity and inclusion could be a good thing, not something to fear. These were also career military people, dependent on the base for everything from food to health care. It made no sense to leave when the base was literally next door.

Douglas Massey and Nancy Denton argued that it was the continuation of segregation in housing practices based on race, in spite of civil rights legislation that outlawed racially restrictive covenants in housing, which were as important as racism and class divisions in creating a black urban underclass, isolated from opportunities and values that characterized American life in the twentieth century.[33] Beryl Satter most recently has taken that argument further, suggesting that "contracts of sale" were routinely used to exploit blacks struggling to attain home ownership and middle-class status in Chicago. Contracts, or deeds of sale, were not mortgages, but only installment loans. They were used to finance homes for people who, because of their race, would not qualify for a regular mortgage. Those individuals may have believed they were paying off a mortgage, when actually they were only paying high interest, without receiving equity in their homes. They were also not protected from foreclosure if they missed a payment, which happened all too often.[34]

This analysis of Seaside provides a different view of the complexity of the story of black and minority communities. Seaside did not develop into an all-black ghetto like parts of Oakland, parts of Los Angeles, parts of southwestern cities such as Phoenix, or even northern urban centers such as Detroit, primarily because it was a place that middle-class blacks came to, rather than fled from, even when it was ravaged by the crack cocaine epidemic and the dark side of military life that included prostitution and the establishment of bars. Unlike other predominantly black suburbs and towns, Seaside boasts expansive ocean views and a climate warmer than neighboring communities. Black middle-class families (along with middle-class whites, Asians, and Latinos) stayed in Seaside and established many social organizations patterned after those both in predominantly black urban and suburban areas, and also in white, Asian, and Latino suburbs such as fraternities and sororities, celebrations of Mardi Gras and Debutante Balls, a tennis club, churches of every denomination, Latino dance, Buddhist festivals, and music festivals—famous ones such as the Monterey Blues and Jazz Festivals that began this book, which gave Seaside both stability and pride of place.[35]

Seaside, Carmel, Pebble Beach, Monterey, Carmel Valley, Marina, Sand City, and Del Rey Oaks, although distinctive communities, make up the mosaic that is the Monterey Peninsula in Monterey County. They share resources, government, history, and people. Seaside's story cannot be told outside of the context of its Peninsula neighbors, beginning with its native people and seventeenth-century Mexican roots, and extending through the twenty-first century. Chapter 1, explores Seaside's earliest history as part of the larger local and regional landscape and within the state and national context. It is an analysis of how and why Seaside's first residents and planners grappled with identity as chance and circumstance presented alternatives to the idea of Seaside as a resort destination adjacent to the famous Hotel Del Monte, and then as the poorer subdivision of the City of Monterey where the white working class and people of color began to make homes during the Great Depression.

Chapter 2 focuses on the demographic transformation of the 1930s and 1940s and how that regional identity broke down and became localized.[36] New populations of mostly military personnel drove Seaside residents to push to incorporate as a city with an identity intertwined with that of Fort Ord, and increasingly, with growing numbers of minorities, particularly African Americans. It was during this period that conflict arose between federal housing policies that specifically excluded all people of color and the military's need to invest in a town that was home to many of its new black officers and high-ranking enlisted men. The military population began to dominate Seaside in the wake of World War II and was, above all else, a diverse mixture of people. But unlike the other Peninsula cities whose populations were largely drawn from other parts of California, albeit by way of southern Europe, Asia, Mexico, and the Midwest, Seaside residents, both black and white, came mostly from the American South and Southwest. This gave Seaside a distinctive cultural affinity with these sections of the United States, expressed in everything from religion to culture and social life, but without the overt Jim Crow practices that affected nonmilitary towns settled by southern whites, such as Phoenix.[37] The city that emerged after World War II had the distinct stamp of both the military and the American South, and also incorporated new groups of Asians from the Philippines, China, and Japanese American returnees from American internment camps, as well as immigrants from Mexico.

Chapter 3 explores the consequences of city building in the context of socioeconomic marginalization and racial inequality that marked the state and the country at midcentury. In this era, 1956–1970, Seasiders felt the full effects of the policy to desegregate the military. It was also during this time that policy makers at the local level took full advantage of the federal government's efforts to rectify discrimination in housing and were able to utilize federal funding from the Kennedy and Johnson administrations to create infrastructure and to raze and redevelop large parts of the city. It was during this period that Seasiders also coped with the serious consequences of the Vietnam War. By the end of the decade of the 1970s, Seaside elected its first black mayor and would continue to elect blacks and Asians to the city council along with whites. They did this not as racially organized voting blocs but as an integrated citizenry.

Chapter 4 investigates Seaside's communities of color that included large numbers of middle-class officers and high-level enlisted men and their families. They were committed to life in Seaside, rather than abandoning the city when it was possible to do so as they achieved higher socioeconomic status. It was their leadership and dedication to Seaside that led to full integration in housing and neighborhoods, public spaces, businesses, and in the faculty of the public school system. Seaside women and men, white, black, Asian, and shades of brown, almost all of whom had military affiliations, worked together across racial lines to meet the highest goals of racial equality and inclusion at every level of economic, social, and political life. Their immense successes were based in no small part on their collective experience as middle-class military people who shared a common culture as part of Fort Ord.

In the decades of the 1980s and early 1990s, Seasiders coped with economic uncertainty and crisis, and the high crime that came with military life and the epidemic of crack cocaine into California, even as they continued the process of city building. Chapter 5 puts the issue of crime in perspective, as it was never as overwhelming as media reports presented. This chapter also traces the development of African American culture in Seaside that had an impact all over the region, and beyond. City events and celebrations that emerged from the black middle-class community of Seaside had the effect of defining Seaside as an African American enclave even though blacks never made up more than 29 percent of the city's population. The Monterey Bay Blues Festival, held in June, and the Monterey Jazz Festival, held in late September are examples of attractions that continue to draw the best musical talent and visitors from around the world. At the same time, Japanese, Filipinos, and Vietnamese contributed their own cultural events to Seaside city life. Numerous city events and activities initiated in these years served as the glue that held Seasiders of diverse nationalities and ethnicities together, all under the common bond of the military.

By the end of the 1990s, the direction that the city had been moving in for forty years abruptly shifted. Fort Ord closed as an active training base in 1994. Large numbers of Latinos without connection to the military settled in the city and changed the demographics overnight. Development took off as real estate formerly owned by the military and federal government became available for civilian use. Chapter 6 documents these changes and examines a significant identity shift as Seasiders struggled with the notion of what it meant to be a multicultural city without Fort Ord.

Seaside's relationship with the military makes it unusual, but at the same time, the story of Seaside is part and parcel of the story of American town life in the twentieth century and into the new millennium. The first Chairman of the Seaside Human Rights Commission, Sherman Smith, who was a former army officer, Tuskegee Airman, and a leader in the civil rights movement who helped desegregate the all-white Ord Terrace neighborhood in Seaside, and who was the first African American to serve on the Board of Monterey Peninsula College, had this to say about his city in an editorial for the newspaper, *Citizen Observer*, in 1968:

We here in California pride ourselves on our liberal and progressive attitudes, but every time a Negro-American or a Mexican American is refused a job because of his ancestry, every time a Japanese American is turned down in their attempts to move into a new neighborhood, we are as guilty of prejudice and discrimination as the Klan. The difference is one of degree, not of kind. We in Seaside have a special problem, and a special opportunity. Our population is one of the most cosmopolitan in the State, we have a tremendous variety of racial, ethnic and cultural strains, all of which have been woven into our way of life. When a newcomer arrives from the East or West, one of his first chores is to become accustomed to our street names, because so many of them are of Spanish derivation. Our challenge is to see that this new way of life [is] the truly American way of life . . . in which each man is accepted on his own merit . . . or rejected on his own shortcoming . . . not because of his color or his accent, or by the name he calls his God.[38]

With these words, Smith expressed the ideals of the early civil rights movement and the commonly shared sense of responsibility that African American residents of Seaside were committed to even as their counterparts in Chicago, Detroit, Los Angeles, Oakland, Phoenix, and elsewhere fled from black neighborhoods and cities. Middle-class blacks in Seaside together with other proponents of civil rights, most of whom had military ties, created a new politics of inclusion and a commitment to place that effectively shaped the city throughout the twentieth century and serves as a reminder that integration can work to make change in ideas about race.

CHAPTER I

Nineteenth-Century Visions, Twentieth-Century Realities

PHOTO I. The Seaside Post Office, founded by Dr. John "Doc" Roberts, 1889. Courtesy City of Seaside Archive, Seaside History Project.

IN 1910 MONTEREY COUNTY SUPERVISOR, Dr. John L. D. Roberts successfully lobbied President Theodore Roosevelt to locate Fort Ord in East Monterey, a community that was later incorporated as the City of Seaside. That decision altered the historical development of the entire region in profound and unexpected ways, one of which was Seaside's future as a minority-majority military town, distinct from all the other communities of the Monterey Peninsula.

It was never meant to be that way. When the subdivision of Seaside was first planned in 1888 on former Rancho Noche Buena land, it was an integral part of a region viewed by developers and common folk alike as brimming with possibilities for development. It was also an important part of the great vision of the Monterey Peninsula as a tourist destination. Yet, by the 1930s, this community called Seaside was completely set apart from the rest of Monterey as not only military but marginal, just as so many other poor and minority communities in the United States were defined as unworthy of federal investment and considered by all except those who lived in them as the least desirable places to live or to work.[1] Yet, unlike those communities, Seaside was a place with exquisite ocean views, and a warm climate, without the fog of Carmel, Monterey, or Pebble Beach.

The story of Seaside's first fifty years as a community and subdivision of the city of Monterey demonstrates that neither militarization nor marginalization was inevitable, but that once the process began both would come to define the city's identity throughout the remainder of the twentieth century and into the new millennium. Yet, there was always the essential reality of the beautiful environment, which presented constant possibility; an alternative to both militarization and marginalization.

ORIGINS: NATIVE AMERICANS
AND MEXICAN SETTLEMENT

The Americans who envisioned the development of Monterey County and specifically Seaside in the late nineteenth and early twentieth centuries had little understanding of what the region was like before they arrived. Like all of California and the western territories ceded to the United States after the war with Mexico, the Monterey Peninsula had been home to an indigenous population for over 10,000 years.[2] The members of the Ohlone, also referred to as Costanoan (including the Rumsien and Mutsun), together with Salinan, and Esselen tribes collectively numbered over 7,000 people. Each of these distinctive groups in Monterey County lived in communities related by language, family, and custom.[3] Pre-European Seaside was likely a site for temporary camps rather than a place of permanent settlement. The original inhabitants of Seaside were the Rumsien-speaking Ohlone who lived in permanent villages in present day Spreckles, Monterey, Castroville, Carmel Valley, and Moss Landing and used the area that is now Seaside as a hunting ground for deer and other game;

a place to gather shellfish, seeds, and berries; and as a base from which to fish.[4] The Rumsien-speaking people traveled back and forth through Seaside, a gateway from interior villages throughout Monterey County to the rich resources of the coast.[5]

The first Spanish settlements in the region were established in June 1770 when the Portolà expedition traveled from San Diego to establish the mission San Carlos Borromeo and the Presidio at Monterey on the edge of Monterey Bay. The mission was moved in 1771 to the mouth of the Carmel River in Carmel to ensure a better water supply and to separate the military establishment from the instruction of the mission Indians. The Carmel mission fluctuated considerably in population over time, but according to contemporary observers and scholars, the mission included approximately eight hundred local people—including the Rumsien and Esselen people, as well as Salinans brought in from the Salinas Valley, and people brought in from the Central Valley until Mexico's independence from Spain and the secularization of the mission system in 1834.[6]

The new Mexican government divided up former mission lands in California after independence from Spain. In 1835 Mexican Governor Juan Castro granted a tract of land that encompassed the area now designated as Seaside, the Rancho Noche Buena, to Juan Antonio Muñoz, a retired soldier, who came to Monterey to assume command of the Presidio in 1832. The ownership of the rancho subsequently passed through members of the Muñoz and Boronda families until it was sold to Jose Abrego in 1857.[7] As happened to so many Mexican landowners, the Abrego family was unable to retain their land in the aftermath of the war with Mexico. Eventually this part of the Noche Buena land grant was sold first to Anton Gigling in 1868 and then to the David Jack Corporation, which, along with the Del Monte Properties Company (which took over the Pacific Improvement Company's holdings), was one of the most powerful American developers in late-nineteenth-century Monterey County. Like so many other Mexican land grant holders in California, the families who once held powerful positions were gradually impoverished by Americans who used political power to create a new economy on former Mexican land.[8]

Monterey rapidly became both Anglo and urban in the aftermath of the Gold Rush at mid-nineteenth century and with the establishment of

American political hegemony. Former communal or pueblo land was divided up and sold into private hands throughout California, including in Monterey. Just like in every other Mexican community in California, mass migrations of Anglo Americans overwhelmed the Mexican population in Monterey and completely changed the socioeconomic and cultural landscape of the area. The population of Monterey increased 66 percent, from 707 to 1,176 between 1836 and 1850, with the foreign born increasing from a mere 15 percent in 1836 to 55 percent by 1850.[9]

PROGRESSIVE ERA SUBURB

As a satellite of Monterey, Seaside experienced a similar cultural and demographic transition as did its neighboring communities in the last twenty years of the nineteenth century. Monterey, Pacific Grove, Big Sur, Carmel, Seaside, and Pebble Beach all became Anglicized very quickly, sharing common goals, futures, and interests, even as they were each somewhat distinctive in the history of their settlement and community personality. Typical of the boosterism of the Progressive Era, regional newspapers of the time related gossip, news, farmer's reports, and current events all focused on the potential growth and development of the Monterey Peninsula. The *Monterey New Era*, the *Monterey Weekly and Monterey Daily Cypress*, and the *Monterey Peninsula Herald* reported every new addition to the area's railroad service, industrial growth, and connection to national and global trade and markets.[10] Real estate development was front-page news, especially on the part of the Del Monte Properties Company, descendant of the Pacific Improvement Company, the property arm of the Southern Pacific Company which had established the luxury resort, the Hotel Del Monte at Monterey and Pebble Beach. The *Monterey New Era* expanded its "Real Estate Transactions" column from a tiny notice on page 3 in 1896 to a full front page in length in 1904, and regularly published updates on "Our Progress" which included countywide real estate development, such as the expansion of the Monterey wharf that allowed steamships to connect the Peninsula to the world.[11]

In 1887, Dr. John Roberts, the ambitious physician from New York whose story opens this chapter, convinced his uncle in Pacific Grove to help him buy 160 acres from the Jacks Corporation, which he divided into 1,000 lots to create the town of Seaside. Roberts was determined, along with thousands of others of his generation of Progressives across the country, to create city spaces out of small settlements. That meant providing the infrastructure that would encourage both population growth and increasing tax revenues. Roberts founded the Seaside Post Office in 1889 and a school in the new district of Monterey. He also successfully lobbied the Pacific Improvement Company and David Jacks Corporation for better road access to the rest of the Peninsula communities in order to make Seaside as attractive as possible to potential home buyers. Roberts was elected to the Monterey County Board of Supervisors in 1908, and in this capacity he is credited for establishing several important roadways, including the portion of Highway 1 that linked Monterey north to Castroville. All of his efforts appear to be directed toward creating a residentially and commercially successful suburb to Monterey, a viable investment for himself and a beacon of civic pride in the Progressive Era.

Seaside was located just a mile to the northwest of the famous elite resort The Del Monte Hotel and consequently was conceived as an outgrowth of the resort community and identified as a tourist destination for the middle classes. First built in 1880 by railroad magnate Charles Crocker, the hotel was destroyed in a fire in 1887, rebuilt, and then was destroyed in a second fire in 1924 to be rebuilt once again in 1927. The earliest Seaside residents were white middle-class families, vacationers, and farmers. For example, the Henneken family arrived on the Monterey Peninsula in 1859 and first settled on land in Carmel Valley, bought at auction from the City of Monterey. They and twelve other homesteader families subsequently lost their property in a nasty lawsuit with the David Jacks Corporation. The Hennekens then settled in Seaside in 1903 as farmers and beekeepers. Kasper Henneken became county beekeeper and also established Seaside's first water works. The Bayliss family, also one of Seaside's earliest residents, built an impressive home in 1888 and remained as one of Seaside's important early families. These first families had migrated throughout the Midwest and California before settling in Seaside.

As Monterey became increasingly dependent on the fishing industry by the end of the nineteenth century, the surrounding communities, including Seaside, were developing into residential zones, just as happened across California and the rest of the United States.[12] Seaside in particular was singled out as one of the most desirable places to live during the period of early settlement in the 1890s. Developers large and small, from enterprising individuals such as Dr. John Roberts to the famous Del Monte Properties Company, enthusiastically sold plans for resorts, hotels, race tracks, casinos, theme parks, housing, and commercial developments both to the elite and to the middle class. Theirs was a typical nineteenth-century strategy according to historian Kenneth T. Jackson: "As has usually been the case in the United States, the distribution of population was governed primarily by the desire of property owners and builders to enhance their investments by attracting the wealthy and by excluding the poor."[13] Progressive Era planners envisioned Seaside as a vacation destination with an almost perfect climate and pristine environment in proximity to Monterey and the Monterey Bay.

The Monterey Realty Syndicate (MRS) developed a "colonization promotion" package specific to Seaside in 1910. According to the promotional report, Seaside had easy access to both the Southern Pacific Railroad line and the electric street car service, which connected Seaside to San Francisco and Oakland as well as to Monterey and other parts of the Peninsula. "Seaside is the recognized hub of Central California's scenic grandeur," the newsletter from the MRS claimed, "where new surprises await the tourist, or resident, with an inexhaustible fund of wholesome recreation and association with all life's fancies."[14] The MRS emphasized Seaside's low taxes (as a result of being part of the county rather than incorporated within the city of Monterey), low cost of living (because of abundant agriculture, fish and game, and nearness to dairies and poultry farms), and plenty of "pure" water. Numerous photographs and text emphasized Seaside's spectacular views and ocean beaches, connection to the famous Hotel Del Monte (only a 15-minute walk from Seaside), and "superb landscape." The pamphlet invited readers to imagine Seaside as home to the "captains of industry" sailing on Monterey Bay and to "observe the development of sturdy man and womanhood, strengthened by the outdoor life of Seaside surroundings."[15]

Seaside in 1910 was in the process of developing into a solid middle-class subdivision of Monterey with a "modern equipped school building that enjoys an enviable reputation for efficiency" and a post office of its own. Seaside was on its way to becoming a genuine community that would appeal to women as well as men who were interested in more than homes of their own but also schools, libraries, and organizations, or the "triple dream [of] house plus land plus community."[16] According to the promotional literature:

Seaside embraces the means of social life of an ideal family section. The Civic Club with a membership of 150, owning a most beautiful assembly building with a circulating library worthy of a metropolis, is the center of activity that follows the principals of American progress. The weekly meetings of the Noche Buena society are characteristic of a great family reunion that prevents the existence of catch penny commercialism. True to the principals of the American Woman's League, members of the organization residing at Seaside have commenced the erection of a Chapter House that bespeaks the worthy influence of this society in all American cities.[17]

By 1910, Seaside had a core of mostly white, middle-class permanent residents and a more transient population of middle-class white families who could not afford the opulent Del Monte Hotel but spent summer vacations in what was considered a "charming town" with "many advantages," such as "excellent bathing facilities . . . on a broad sand beach and a climate free from the harsh winds of the ocean." Seaside was described as a "gem of resorts," with a "beautiful lake and wonderful live-oak tree, said to be the largest of its species in the world."[18] Like most suburbs in the country, Seaside was envisioned as a white community where the idea of property value was based on race.[19] Developers were interested in middle-class whites as Seaside's most desirable residents. When a prominent Native American, Dr. White Wolf, grandson of Grey Eagle, chief of the Choctaw Nation, attempted to take advantage of inexpensive land in Seaside and build a home there, no contractor would agree to build it, even though he offered "$50,000 if [someone] will complete the house and furnish it, and lay out the lawns and garden according to my idea." He eventually gave up. By 1917, his six-acre Grey Eagle Terrace development was divided into lots and sold off.[20]

Yet, Seaside was not imagined as wholly residential. In the early decades of the twentieth century, plans for Seaside included commercial and industrial development on a grand scale. Like other "industrial gardens" in California, where the establishment of industry, commercial development, and housing was intended to complement each economically for the benefit of the whole, Seaside was a relatively sparsely settled area of Monterey that sought to incorporate both residential and industrial development.[21] According to an early historian of the Monterey Peninsula, Major Rolin C. Watkins, "Seaside . . . must be the future factory and industrial district of the Peninsula. When the projected harbor developments are matters of accomplishment, Seaside will be a hive of industry. Already far-visioned men have seen this and are planning for the culmination of such projects."[22]

The creation of transportation systems, such as the Del Monte Railway (which was completed in February 1912 and linked Seaside to Monterey), reinforced the idea of Seaside as a typical early-twentieth-century, white middle-class American subdivision where it was possible for families to own their own homes on single-family lots; share a sense of community through neighborhood, school, library, and church; and commute easily into the city of Monterey for work or shopping.[23] Seaside celebrated the new streetcar with a barbecue sponsored by the owner of Del Monte Heights, George W. Phelps, who "opened his home . . . with a fine lunch of beef, mutton, Spanish beans and mussels. Nearly three thousand Monterey area residents [came]. The Seaside Civic Club provided music by Mr. Torres' Spanish orchestra, with help from the Noche Buena Social Club."[24]

MILITARY AND MARGINALIZED

Dr. Roberts may have considered his drive to locate a new military base in Seaside as part and parcel of all of his other work and along the same lines as building roads for the new middle-class population of the community. He strenuously argued for establishing a new western military base in Seaside in several letters to President Theodore Roosevelt:

At one time it came to my attention that the United States Government was looking for three army camp sites, one in the East, one in the south, and one in the West . . . Immediately I wrote to President Theodore Roosevelt . . . I told him that I had seen the Jacks corporation and gotten from them an offer to sell to the government 15,609.5 acres of land for $385,000 . . . Things were held in abeyance for a time and in 1916 the government bought the Jacks property and subsequently Fort Ord was built.[25]

Roberts obviously believed that a military presence would make Seaside more valuable, but it is difficult to comprehend why the presence of the military would entice anyone to settle there. After the purchase of land from the Jacks Corporation by the federal government, the area adjacent to the community of Seaside that would become Fort Ord was initially used by the army as a training ground. According to historical archaeologist Keith Landreth, the area originally named the Gigling Reservation served as "a maneuver area and field artillery target range for the 76th Field Artillery, the 30th Infantry Regiment, and the 11th Cavalry, all of which were stationed at the Presidio of Monterey."[26] No real construction of a base occurred until 1940. The proximity to a military training ground suddenly altered Seaside's course of development from white subdivision to something far less desirable.

The years between 1917 and 1940 marked the first critical turning point for Seaside. Instead of fulfilling the dreams of nineteenth-century Progressives who sought to create a flourishing white community and vacation destination, such close proximity to a military training ground set this area of Monterey aside as the least desirable place to live, to work, or to vacation. No middle-class family (much less a wealthy one), wanted to invest in an area with soldiers marching through and conducting training and maneuvers. Development fell off in the 1920s. Instead of increasing population through neighborhood growth and capital investment, Seaside was settled in a helter-skelter manner in this period without the growing urban infrastructure or commercial and industrial development that benefited the neighboring community of Monterey. Thus, Pebble Beach and Carmel, not Seaside, became the destination for vacationers. Moreover, the burgeoning fishing industry gave Monterey's entire beach front, which was closest in proximity to Seaside, a working-class, immigrant, ethnic flavor that was vehemently contested by Samuel F. B. Morse, the head of the Del Monte Properties company who then moved his operations to Pebble Beach.[27]

The expansion of the Presidio in 1902, and the use of the Gigling Reservation as a training and maneuver range in 1916 through the 1930s set the stage for the army to take advantage of the expanse of land that would become Fort Ord in 1940.

FORT ORD: ITS BEGINNING

The army population of the Peninsula was located at the Presidio in Monterey. Collectively it included soldiers originally stationed on western outposts to fight Indian tribes, but who were subsequently deployed to the Philippines during the Spanish American War. Congress had significantly increased the standing army in these years as a response to a perceived Japanese threat to American hegemony in the Philippines. After the war, the soldiers returned to bases in San Francisco and Monterey and formed a population of only a few thousand at the Monterey Presidio. Most of the soldiers stationed at the Monterey Presidio in the period from 1902 to 1916 were Caucasian, but a significant contingent of African American Buffalo soldiers from the 1st Squadron, 9th Cavalry, then after 1904, the 3rd Squadron, 4th Cavalry, was also stationed there.[28]

By the turn of the twentieth century, race relations in the United States intensified, especially with regard to blacks, which was reflected in the armed forces that increasingly became more segregated and discriminatory through the period of World War I.[29] Enlisted men included ethnic immigrants and African Americans during World War I, but tight quotas were established and officers were uniformly white. The buildup to World War I did not make a significant impact on the demographic makeup of the Monterey Peninsula, however. Monterey felt some of the effects of its proximity to a military base, the Presidio, but Seaside, which was utilized for military maneuvers and training and as a space for target practice for the school of musketry located at the Presidio, was most affected.

Betty Dwyer Mahieu, age 92, remembered the communities of the Monterey Peninsula as "quiet" with the exception of Seaside by the 1920s and 1930s, which she described as being "full of soldiers:"

It was a horrible place. They were shooting guns on the beach. No one would want to go there . . . There was a pool where I took swimming lessons across the street from the Hotel Del Monte. As far as we were concerned, Monterey ended there. We didn't know anything about Seaside.[30]

As Mahieu observed, the fact that Seaside became a site of increasing military activity in the interwar years set it apart negatively from the other communities of the Peninsula. The 11th Cavalry arrived at the Presidio in 1919 and the 2nd Battalion, 76th Field Artillery came in 1922. Following World War I, soldiers regularly marched from the Presidio in Monterey to Seaside to use the area for target practice, both for small arms and for 75-mm howitzers and for training army reserves.[31] One writer for the *Carmel Pacific Spectator Journal*, writing in 1955, commented on this moment in Seaside history: "Before entering World War I, the U.S. Army held maneuvers in Seaside. They set up heavy machine guns on the corner of Broadway and Del Monte (already 'streets' at that time), and test fired them 2,000 yards up Broadway."[32]

Camp Gigling, which became Camp Ord in 1933, was undeveloped until the 1940s. Soldiers were housed in tent barracks, and all camp infrastructures, from hospital to commissary, were situated in large tents as well. The landscape was barren and dusty, susceptible to windstorms in the summer and swamps of mud in the winter. The winter rains even washed away tents, making Camp Ord notorious for its uncomfortable and unpleasant conditions. It must be kept in mind, however, that the landscape of Fort Ord still featured spectacular ocean views and a generally hospitable climate. It was the use being made of the land at this point that was the problem.

Soldiers from the Presidio of San Francisco traveled regularly to Seaside and to Camp Ord to conduct large-scale training and maneuvers. The Cavalry regiments were a notable feature of training at the Camp until after World War II. However, the soldiers were transitory and did not generate much concern among the populace or city officials of Monterey before 1940. The post-World War I years even saw a significant dip in the population of soldiers.

POPULATION CHANGES AND
DEPRESSION-ERA SEASIDE

By the 1930s when the Great Depression hit Monterey County, Seaside's image was much more closely tied to a place for training soldiers than to neighborhoods of white middle-class homeowners on the Monterey Peninsula. Indeed, many of the white middle-class families who had invested in homes in Seaside left during the 1930s. The hundreds of acres that had been snapped up by speculators at the turn of the century and into the 1910s went largely undeveloped. A local journalist who reflected on this stage of the community's development claimed that "Seaside grew with no sound guidance, without streets or improvements, growth was erratic. Speculators took their money and ran, leaving most of the land relatively untouched. As the years went by, an occasional owner or squatter would build a shack, drill a well and settle down in the sand or sagebrush."[33] Yet, oral histories and census data reflect a more nuanced view of the subdivision, one that suggests that although residents were increasingly marginalized and poor, they banded together in the midst of adversity. Seaside was a multiethnic, multiracial community that depended on neighborly support. And it was still a beautiful environment.

Increasingly the ethnic and social diversity of the Peninsula shifted to the Monterey waterfront and to Seaside.[34] In contrast to the earliest period of settlement, the Depression Era brought new working class and poor families and individuals into Seaside from the Dust Bowl and from southern Europe. A diverse population of Mexicans, Italians, Japanese, Portuguese, and a few African Americans began to settle in Seaside, which gradually gave Seaside a reputation both as a poorer subdivision of Monterey and a multicultural enclave, in spite of the continued presence of some of the original residents such as the Bayliss, Henneken, and Roberts families.[35]

Developers believed that settlement would solve the problem of a suddenly bad reputation for Seaside. After all, this was not an urban ghetto; the environment remained the same. They tried to overcome the loss of white, middle-class interest in Seaside by offering potential home buyers incentives such as free cars. In 1925, the Lakeside Realty Company, for example, "offered Hudsons, Dodges, Studebakers and Chevrolets free to buyers who bought certain lots in certain blocks" of the Lakeside Development tract, which was located just north of the Hotel Del Monte and Laguna Del Rey in Seaside.[36] During the Depression, *The San Francisco Examiner* offered a 75 x 25 foot parcel of land in exchange for a subscription to the paper, undoubtedly the easiest way to become a Seaside property owner. However, the surge of new poor and working-class people, both whites and racial minorities, desperately in need of scarce housing was too much for developers to withstand, much less control. Squatters appropriated space as needed in Seaside and created an altogether different socioeconomic and demographic environment than opportunistic developers imagined in 1900.

Deliberately or not, the grand nineteenth-century vision of the region overlooked the obvious. None of the promotional literature or brochures reflected the demographic reality of Monterey County, which was historically populated by Mexican people, Asians, and southern European ethnic immigrants. Monterey also included an African American population that began arriving in 1847, increasing when Buffalo soldiers were stationed at the Presidio in 1902.[37] The reality of the diverse population coupled with the impact of the Great Depression definitively ended residents' earliest aspirations of Seaside as a resort destination, in spite of its obvious natural beauty. Census data and oral history interviews show clearly how diverse the Monterey County population was at the turn of the century, a trend that increased significantly in the 1920s and 1930s; they also show how shifts in population coupled with new federal policies on zoning and housing segregation created an impoverished, heavily minority community in Seaside during the Depression years.

The census of 1900 divided Monterey into townships and designated only twenty-five people as permanent residents of the township of Seaside, all of whom had Anglo or German surnames. However, an analysis of what was considered the "outskirts of Monterey" in what is now called Seaside indicates that many Asians, Mexicans, and southern European ethnics lived there, even though census takers at the turn of the century labeled anyone who was not Chinese, Japanese, or African American as "white" obscuring ethnic differences that were becoming significant in terms of social change.[38]

Census takers one hundred years ago actually walked through every neighborhood in every town and city in America, recording information required by the census bureau. These people leave us with important profiles of neighborhoods such as those in Seaside. As the census taker walked the area which is currently Laguna Grande Park and Canyon Del Rey in Seaside, he noted that eighteen families lived in this mostly agricultural area and reported on their ethnic and racial composition. This included three families with Spanish surnames who were Mexican-origin/native Californios, two Portuguese families, and two lodging houses, one with twenty- seven Chinese and the other with nine Japanese—all men between the ages of eighteen and sixty. Nearby, another lodging house included fifty-three men—Anglos from the East, new immigrants from southern Europe, and native whites born in California. Within families and households there was evidence of diversity too. For example, L. Chayboya, a farmer, homeowner, and native Californio was married to Mary, an Irish immigrant. They had six children and lived next door to the Machado family, immigrants from Portugal and the Cook family, Anglo Americans, who came to California by way of Kansas and Illinois in 1891.

As the census takers in 1900 moved to the city of Monterey itself, they found more racial and ethnic mixing, with Chinese boarding houses located next to large families of Portuguese immigrants and Mexican people. In one neighborhood alone, the large Berwick and Meadows extended families, all originating from England, lived next to a Chinese boarding house lodging six men, a Portuguese family of five, and four members of the Díaz family, all native-born Californios, or Mexican Americans. Thus, even though Seaside contained a core white community, even as early as 1910 it was beginning to reflect the impact of racial minorities too.[39]

This pattern of racial and ethnic diversity was intensified by 1910, a trend reflective of California in general.[40] In Los Angeles, San Francisco, and San Jose distinctive ethnic enclaves of Chinese, Mexicans, whites, and some blacks were already well established.[41] Neighborhoods in Seaside and Monterey were mosaics of Japanese, Chinese, Italians, Portuguese, and Anglo Americans and, perhaps as a result of living and working so close together, intermarriage between ethnic and racial groups became even more common. Census takers began to have difficulty sorting everyone out, although they went to some lengths to do so in a period of American history when race was an important marker of character and class. They added "Mexican" to racial designations in this census although no such racial/ethnic label formally existed in census bureau instructions to enumerators. They also added descriptive identities to the category "place of birth of parents." For example, Andrew Gómez and Julia Díaz were among those who were designated by race as "Mexican" but were described as "Mexican-Spanish" and also "Part Portuguese" under the category of "Place of Birth of Parents." William Redbrook was described by race as Mexican, but gave his birthplace and that of his parents as Florida, an unlikely destination for Mexican immigrants who typically migrated to the American Southwest or California. His wife, Alice Redbrook, an African American, immigrated to California from Missouri where she and both of her parents were born.[42] By the time of the 1920 census, both William and Alice Redbrook were listed as "Negro."[43] Few African Americans were counted in the 1910 census for Monterey in the early decades of the twentieth century, but those that were lived among whites in these racially and ethnically mixed neighborhoods. John Simon, his wife Laura, and son James, for example, all three African American, lived between two white families in the city center.

What was actually emerging demographically was a multiethnic, multiracial population experiencing both racial tension and sometimes even racially charged violence. At the same time, the populations were shifting so that minority groups were slowly forced into the less desirable and less developed residential parts of the county, mainly Seaside. Here, at least, racial ideologies were less clear. The people of Seaside, mostly poor, paid far less attention to racial difference since most were focused on survival, in contrast to the Monterey area in general, which gradually became more racially segregated.

The population of Monterey County changed drastically in the period from 1915 to 1940, especially in Seaside. In 1920, the population of Monterey County was 27,980, of whom 5,479 lived in the city of Monterey, and 400 people resided in Seaside. By 1930 the county population almost doubled to 53,705, with 9,141 in Monterey and 800 in Seaside. Ten years later the county again showed a significant increase to 73,032. The city of Monterey's population rose by a smaller margin to 10,084, while Seaside the most affordable section of Monterey, more than doubled to 2,500.

The 1920 census provides a snapshot of Seaside neighborhoods that were increasingly ethnic working class and poor. For example, thirteen households in one block of the Oak Grove District of Monterey (which was adjacent to Seaside) included three Portuguese families, three Italian families, and two Mexican families. All the heads of households in this neighborhood listed occupations such as laborer, painter, contractor, butcher, farmer, fisherman, workers without any significant assets recorded. Newly arrived Italian, Japanese, and Portuguese immigrants, together with some Mexican immigrants, clearly dominated almost every Seaside neighborhood. Their occupations were all working-class fishermen, cannery workers, and laborers. The 1920 census also listed several African American families in Pacific Grove—all of whom lived in integrated neighborhoods and worked in the fish canneries. The new population reflected the increase in labor migrants who arrived to work in the fish canneries on the wharf in Monterey.[44]

According to the city directories in 1930, Monterey's population (which incorporated some outlying areas including Seaside and Del Rey Oaks) numbered about 9,500; of that number, 8,695 were designated as white, and 457 were described as colored. The "predominating nationalities" by 1930 were (in order) Italians, Spanish, Japanese, Mexicans, and Chinese.[45] The U.S. Census in 1930 specifically demarcated East Monterey (Seaside), as a separate subdivision. It revealed a marked shift in population. First, migrants from the American Southwest or the Dust Bowl were beginning to arrive in Monterey by 1930; many originating from Oklahoma, Texas, and Arkansas now lived in Seaside neighborhoods. They found employment in Monterey's new fishing industry and affordable housing in Seaside where they could build homes on the beach simply by constructing them. Unlike areas in central California such as Fresno and Bakersfield where Dust Bowl migrants settled, Seaside may have been less developed in terms of infrastructure, but it was still a beautiful environment with a hospitable climate and stunning ocean views.

At the same time, African Americans began moving into Seaside mostly from Pacific Grove to start businesses and buy property largely denied to them elsewhere on the Peninsula by 1930, as racially restrictive housing that privileged whites and banned minorities was enforced by realtors.[46] African Americans lived mostly in Pacific Grove from the turn of the twentieth century, but also began to build small-scale boarding houses and cafes in Seaside by the 1930s. Several African American residents of Seaside today, such as the Niblett family which included Jerry Smith (Seaside's mayor from 1998 to 2005), trace their roots to this period of settlement in Seaside. According to an article on the family matriarch, Mrs. Geraldine Niblett, who was interviewed in the *Monterey Peninsula Herald* in February, 1979:

"I came in 1939 and settled in Seaside from Texas. At that time there were seven black families and I had more children than anyone else." She recalled that most black people worked as domestics or in the fishing industry on Cannery Row. Mrs. Niblett owned and operated Fremont Inn for 16 years. "During that time I took in lots of black people who needed help. I was the mother of the all-black 47th Quartermaster Company that came here in 1942."[47]

Mrs. Niblett owned and operated the Fremont Inn, which was located at the corner of Harcourt and Fremont Avenue, and would eventually be part of the remodeled site for Victory Temple.[48] William and Mary Smith operated a laundry in East Monterey with their nine children and grand-children in the 1930s.[49] William McGary, age fifty, owned a rabbit farm in Seaside and property worth $10,000 in 1930.

Residents of Seaside in the 1930s also included Portuguese immigrants, mostly from the Azores, although Portuguese first arrived of Monterey in the 1880s to hunt whales around Point Lobos and later to establish dairy farms in Carmel Valley, Watsonville, and Castroville. The newest Portuguese arrivals, who worked mostly as fish canners, also found the cheapest housing in Seaside and established an ethnic enclave there beginning in the 1930s. The large, extended Souza family, prominent in Seaside today, is listed in the 1930 census as residing in the agricultural area of East Monterey. This included Manuel Souza, a dairy farmer, his wife Mary, and their five children; Constantine Souza, his wife Adelaide, and three sons; and two men surnamed Souza listed as boarders.[50] John Leandro, a laborer, his wife Angelina, and their six children all lived in East Monterey by 1930. According to oral histories, Mr. and Mrs. Manuel Freitas "lived in the 700 block of Fremont and Park Streets (Park renamed Trinity) in the 1920s and owned property all the way up to Fremont Street" and farmed strawberries.[51] Sara Souza, their daughter, recalled that "before Fort Ord was built . . . in that area were acres of peas," which she picked earning seven dollars per day.[52] She remembered dairy farms owned by the Souza and Avila families established by 1930.

Japanese Americans lived on the outskirts of Seaside beginning at the turn of the twentieth century; their numbers also increased significantly by 1930. Japanese fishermen and abalone divers originally migrated to the Peninsula in order to harvest the abundant abalone of the Monterey coast for market in the late nineteenth century, but they also worked as agriculturalists and landscapers for the Del Monte Hotel. According to Donald M. Howard who compiled a number of primary source documents related to Seaside history, a significant number of Japanese families had moved to Seaside from Monterey proper by 1910 and worked in landscaping for the hotel.[53]

Filipino laborers who migrated to Monterey County worked in the burgeoning service industries in Monterey, Carmel, and Pebble Beach at the turn of the twentieth century. They, too, were increasingly drawn to cheaper, available housing in the East Monterey subdivision. A large group of Filipino men who lived in Seaside, for example, worked at the Del Monte Hotel prior to 1940. The Filipino community of Monterey at the turn of the century largely came by way of Hawaii as agricultural workers. Many of these early migrants moved on to work in the fields of Salinas and became the backbone of the labor movement in the 1930s and 1940s. Though small in number until 1940, the Filipino community became an important group politically, socially, and economically in Seaside after the establishment of Fort Ord.

The Mexican population in the city of Monterey, which long preceded Anglo settlement, was increasingly forced out in the 1930s as Sicilian immigrants rushed in to buy up real estate closest to the wharf area, a neighborhood that was once made up predominantly composed of Californios.[54]

Several dozen Mexican families moved into Seaside from Monterey in the 1930s, forming the bulwark of a Mexican American community that continued to grow throughout the twentieth century. Ralph Rubio, former Seaside mayor, is the son and grandson of Seaside's earliest Mexican-origin families. Frank Soto, a laborer and woodcutter, was listed in the 1920 census as living in Monterey proper but by 1930 had moved to East Monterey with his wife Angelina and their five children.[55] Joe Pérez, a laborer and his wife, Helen, and their three daughters were among the Mexican Americans that moved to Seaside by 1930 along with the large families of John Muñoz and Manuel Cortéz, both railway workers. Although most Mexican Americans who lived in Seaside in 1930 were poor and working class, some had achieved middle-class status. For example, Frank Dondero, a building contractor who lived in East Monterey with his wife Carmen and three daughters, listed property worth $2,000. Orancio and Evangelina Pérez settled in Seaside in the 1930s and eventually became successful building contractors, forming the nucleus of a thriving Mexican American social group in the community.[56] According to Luis Pérez, Orancio's brother, who arrived from Texas in 1930, Seaside's diversity made for a rich cultural stew:

Right where we lived which was up the hill [on Luxton Avenue], there were no streets, only little paths. There were about 20, 30 Mexican families. There was Fernando Mata and his wife—they were Mexican. Next to him was his compadre, Enrique Chacón. On the corner of Luxton and San Pablo—these were the Mexican people—we called him Pipirin—his real name was Melquiades Paredes. I remember there were those people [a Mexican family] who lived way down below. They had a restaurant. The name was Apodaca. There were the Molinas—they lived way on top of Del Monte. At the corner which is San Pablo there was someone else—to me I think they were Gypsies or Arabs— they owned a little store. Mexicans, Portuguese and Italians were close. Let's face it we were all going to work. We used to get together at our fiestas—I don't remember anything bad about the Italians and the Portuguese. We were all together. At that time there were [few] blacks [in Seaside]. Blacks came maybe '48, '49. When Fort Ord got strong there were more blacks.[57]

Between the establishment of the Gigling Reservation as a military training ground and the Great Depression, Seaside increasingly came to be
known as a working-class community with a large population of whites
from the Dust Bowl, ethnic immigrants and their descendants from Monterey, and people of color. At the same time, as Luis Pérez suggested, this
collection of people was evolving into a community that was inclusive of
a variety of ethnic and racial groups.

RACIAL CONFLICT

Sprinkled through the news accounts in the decades of the 1890s and
early 1900s is evidence that although neighborhoods were racially and
ethnically mixed and intermarriage across ethnic and racial lines was
common, racism was as pervasive here as it was throughout California
and the nation. In Monterey, as elsewhere during the early years of the
twentieth century when Jim Crow was strongest, intergroup tensions
existed, sometimes erupting into violence. News reports rarely mentioned blacks or Mexican people except in connection to criminal activity. When Chinese, Japanese, African American, and Spanish-surnamed
people (who might have been either Mexican or Filipino) were reported
on, they were commonly referred to by race in demeaning ways, whereas
whites were not identified by race or disparaged by ethnicity.[58] This was
common practice in newspapers across the country during this period.
For example, on January 5, 1904, the *Salinas Weekly Journal* printed
a story about Amado Morales, describing him as "a drunken Mexican
who ran amok."[59] On August 26, 1909, an article described Jose Urdes
as "an ignorant Mexican [who] will serve 120 days in the county jail for
wife beating." A similar account in the same newspaper only one week
before reported the murder of a woman by a white man who was neither
identified by race nor referred to in a disparaging or damning manner.[60]
Mexican people in particular were referred to as "bandits," "drunken,"
and "bad men" whether or not they had been found guilty of crimes of
which they had been accused.[61]

Racial hatred against blacks intensified throughout the United States,
and California was no exception. In the Monterey region, discrimination
against African Americans was a given, and racially motivated acts of

violence occurred. For example, the *Monterey Daily Cypress* reported an attempted lynching of an African American man in January 1907. The victim was a soldier from the Presidio who was arrested apparently as a means of saving his life—a rope having already been tied around his neck.[62] There is no indication that the perpetrators were questioned much less prosecuted.

The most famous incidences of racial violence in Monterey County were directed against the Chinese in the early years of the twentieth century. Throughout California, a virulent anti-Chinese sentiment prevailed from the 1860s, coinciding with the migration of large numbers of Chinese labor migrants to the West to build railroads and mine for gold. Excluded from agricultural work in the late nineteenth century, the Chinese mostly settled in cities, most famously San Francisco.[63] Here they were segregated into restricted parts of the city, justified on the basis of race, much like Mexican people elsewhere in California in the mid and late nineteenth century.[64]

Chinese migrants had a long tradition on the Monterey Peninsula. They not only established themselves as the most successful fishermen, particularly as squid fishermen, but also founded their own village enclave near Pacific Grove. However, racial tensions exploded into violence, just as they did all over California in this period of virulent anti-Chinese sentiment, based in large part on the idea that Chinese people were a threat both to public health and to middle-class ideologies of behavior that condemned everything from Chinese practices of single-sex group living to prostitution and opium dens as anti-American.[65]

When fire broke out in Chinatown in 1906, it was not the first time. The Chinese experienced three earlier fires, in 1889, in 1898, and in 1902. The all black 9th Cavalry Unit stationed at the Presidio in Monterey, camped nearby (because they were not allowed to live with whites at the Presidio), helped the Chinese to contain the fire and damage to buildings. However, four years later, the mostly white spectators cheered as yet another fire finally destroyed Chinatown. Then, mobs of whites looted the remains of stores and homes belonging to Chinese residents. Rumors spread, but were never proven, that the Pacific Improvement Company, which wanted the Chinese out of Monterey and Pacific Grove, was actually responsible for starting the fire. The Chinese resisted efforts to abandon their homes and businesses as most wanted to rebuild one more time. But eventually they gave up and scattered to other parts of Monterey or left the area entirely. Many Chinese found refuge on the outskirts of Monterey, in Seaside.[66]

THE GREAT DEPRESSION

The Depression affected the state of California in peculiar ways, inspiring both innovation and radicalism. The Democratic Party became newly invigorated in the 1930s, but so did the Socialist Party and the Communist Party, all three of which found strong adherents in the new population of Seaside, which eventually became a stronghold for the Democrats in Monterey County.[67] Upton Sinclair, who had been a member of the Socialist Party, ran for governor as a Democrat in 1934, although Culbert L. Olson, a Democrat, was elected in 1938 and was responsible for California's benefiting from New Deal Programs that helped the economy of the state, generally, and regions such as Monterey County in particular.[68] Radical labor movements formed, most notably among longshoremen in San Francisco culminating in the general strike of 1934 led by Harry Bridges. Although the fish canneries of Monterey were far less impacted by radical labor, organizers were present, especially in the poorest communities such as Seaside.[69]

Residents of Seaside remembered fondly the presence of the Work Progress Administration (WPA) that provided jobs and food, and the Civilian Conservation Corps (CCC), which was located on the outskirts of Seaside in the area that would become Fort Ord. Vivian West recalled "treks to the W.P.A. Community wagon where corn meal, oats, flour, dried prunes were given away. We thought it was a lark, but I'm sure it was hard for Mom & Dad."[70]

Culturally Seaside felt the effects of utopian movements too. One of Aimee Semple McPherson's disciples founded a church in Seaside by the 1940s, but it was the arrival of tens of thousands of migrants from the Dust Bowl to work in the fish canneries in Monterey that had the most impact on Seaside's population. Dust Bowl immigrants lived in tents, in makeshift cottages, and anywhere they could in the least expensive, least regulated part of Monterey in the 1930s, which was the subdivision of

Seaside. Here they were not ostracized but incorporated in the diverse community that Seaside was in the process of becoming. Lois Bratt described the "dust bowl families" that settled in Seaside in the 1930s with a sense of admiration for their work ethic and for their sheer determination in the face of terrible adversity: "The Jenners . . . they had nothing. They came here in one car [with] stuff tied all over it. They were really workers. Mrs. Jenner and the kids went to Aromas, out in the fields. Anywhere they could get fruit that farmers were just gonna leave. They'd pick that, bring it home, and can it. She told me she had over nine hundred and some quarts . . . for the summer."[71]

Oral histories of residents who lived in Seaside during the 1920s and through the Depression years emphasize both diversity and poverty in the community, but also willingness, even an imperative to overlook racial barriers. For example, the West family moved to Seaside in 1926 and "lived in an old laundry" according to William A. "Tex" West and his daughter, Vivian. They soon moved "across the street to Mrs. Long's house . . . Mrs. Long was a Negro woman, a wonderful kind woman," who helped the family after Tex became seriously ill with lead poisoning and his wife Helen suffered a stillbirth with three young children to care for. Vivian West described the neighborhood as an eclectic ethnic mix of people in shared circumstances who helped one another when they could, regardless of race or ethnicity; "Our close neighbors were the Simas family up on the corner and the Moffetts and Ike Drakes next door . . . and the Castros down the street." Tex West remembered "about a hundred people in Seaside at that time [when he and his family first arrived from Monterey in 1926] . . . we come over to Seaside and went to work in Hovden's Cannery. And at that time everybody worked in the cannery . . . there wasn't much doing outside of the canneries, then the WPA came along. And people went to work on WPA and they certainly needed it . . . there were Okies and Arkies . . . there weren't too many colored people at that time. There were some Spanish people."[72] Their story evokes a sensibility that the poor in Seaside shared a sense of community that went beyond racial ideologies or racial boundaries; Seasiders also depended increasingly on cannery work in Monterey for employment.[73]

Oral accounts emphasize that at the same time the fishing industry contributed to the urbanization of Monterey, Seaside retained a rural, agricultural flavor. Families in Seaside included many small farmers such as the McGuires who had a small farm just above Lorenzo Court. "They killed and sold poultry in their store, Mac's Poultry, in New Monterey."[74] Vi Drake moved to Seaside in 1929 when she married. She recalled using "a little ole kerosene lamp until power lines went up . . . [There was] nothing, see, nothing whatsoever back there clear up to the Burns just fields, empty fields . . . we had chickens and rabbits [and drew water from] a hand pump well . . . a little house here and there . . . and sagebrush."[75] Adeline DeSilva remembered the pig farm located "down the hill on the way back to Monterey" where the intersection of Canyon Del Rey and Fremont Avenue now stands. She remembered the "beautiful home of Dr. Roberts" perched above the city near the lake. The area around the lake was called Lakeside, while the area near Del Monte Boulevard was called Seaside, she recalled. "As far as the eye could see," she remembered "there was Manzanita bush and not a house in sight."[76] This landscape most resembles areas outside of Los Angeles in the 1920s and 1930s, rather than segregated minority communities of the urban northeast. However, in contrast to subdivisions of Los Angeles or even Oakland or San Francisco, this poor, increasingly minority population occupied beachfront land.

Beginning in the teens and 1920s, racially restrictive clauses in real estate deeds that did not allow particular minority groups from owning or renting property, together with less formal but equally effective customary exclusions, slowly forced Mexicans, Filipinos, and many Asians, and African Americans out of Monterey proper, out of Carmel, Pebble Beach and even Pacific Grove and into what was becoming, for many reasons, the less developed margins of the city—Seaside.[77] Poverty and color became intertwined in the minds of many Monterey Peninsula residents in the years between 1915 and 1940. "Because of its diversity Seaside has sometimes been referred to as 'Little Chicago.'"[78] Yet, in every possible environmental way, Seaside could not have been more different.

The idea of Seaside as a marginal part of the city was reinforced by federal policy with regard to home loans in the wake of the Depression and resulting foreclosure crisis of the late 1920s and 1930s. In 1933 alone, half of all homes in the United States were in default and foreclosing at the rate of one thousand per day.[79] President Franklin D. Roosevelt created the Home Owners Loan Corporation (HOLC) in June 1933 to supply long-term, low-interest loans to urban home owners in danger of losing their property—but there was a catch. The HOLC appraisers who determined which homes were deemed worthy of government support created a ratings system based explicitly on the ethnicity and race of the home owner and only secondarily on the condition of the property.[80] They were not inventing a new concept for determining housing values; race and ethnicity had long been used to segregate city spaces. But the HOLC ratings system (in numerical and alphabetical categories) reified those customs and practices, now known as "redlining." This had the effect of excluding women as well as everyone deemed a person of color, but especially blacks, even entire sections of cities, from eligibility for desperately needed home loans and other federal investment during the Depression and thereafter.[81] Seaside was one of those places that were redlined and its residents denied federal funds for home mortgages because it contained a population of people designated as nonwhite. The fact that it was part of a region designated as one of the most beautiful areas of California did not affect federal policy.

CONCLUSION

All of the factors that eventually defined Seaside as lower class and ethnic were in place by the end of the 1930s. When the military established a training ground in 1917 it effectively marginalized the area. The combination of a racial ideology that grew increasingly hostile toward minorities, especially blacks, and was supported fully by federal policy, created a minority enclave out of the new training area. By World War II, Seaside was transformed from its earliest incarnation as a Progressive Era, middle-class, white community into an underdeveloped and undesirable one, and also increasingly as an appendage of Fort Ord. The establishment of Fort Ord as a critical training center in 1940, however, expedited the change in Seaside, both in terms of its identity as a military town and in cementing its character as a "City of Color," as a new population of military migrants and their families came to live there.[82]

The early story of Seaside suggests that in spite of other possibilities for development at the end of the nineteenth century, the power of the federal government, and by extension the military was truly remarkable. The establishment of the Gigling Camp and eventually Fort Ord on Seaside land as training zones for the army effectively ended any chance for Seaside to receive private investment for growth and development, in spite of its obviously attractive natural environment. The result by 1930 was that Seaside was a community, like so many others in the country, redlined by the HOLC.

Seaside residents spent the remaining decades of the twentieth century and the first years of the twenty-first coping with the reality and irony of being a multiracial military town that was every bit as beautiful as the rest of the more demographically homogenous Peninsula. This diverse, multiracial community of increasingly working-class people came together in neighborhoods that depended on everyone to survive, just like other California suburbs and towns similarly marginalized by restrictive housing practices.[83] Unlike these other places however, Seaside was positioned to absorb a huge new population of military personnel and their families as the country prepared for war, adding a whole new complexity to its population and identity. It was the best and worst that could happen to this supposed "little Chicago."

CHAPTER 2

From Subdivision to City: The War Years

PHOTO 2. April 1940, ten thousand soldiers from Fort Ord on parade, Alvarado Street, Monterey, California. Courtesy City of Monterey Public Library, California Room.

RICHARD WOODS A RESIDENT of Seaside since the early 1940s recalled Seaside just before World War II: "This area up here was next to the base. It was sagebrush, sand, jackrabbits, cactus and black folks."[1] The changes came with the war, Woods remembered:

There were a lot of soldiers, but the military was really strict in those days. You had to wear your uniform if you went off base. It wasn't so much that you saw soldiers roaming around, but you heard them. You could hear the troops—you could hear them marching—there was always military vehicles moving in and out. It was more like you FELT the military everywhere.[2]

The U.S. military, prior to and during World War II, was largely responsible for one of the most spectacular population shifts in American history as people of all races and ethnicities flocked to cities and towns to work on expanded military bases and in the new defense industries developing on a massive scale as America girded for war.[3] The one state most affected by this huge demographic change was California, whose population increased by 55.3 percent, four times that of the rest of the United States in the decade between 1940 and 1950, almost all of which was due to migration as a result of the war effort.[4] Although most migrants settled in large urban centers that were also centers for the defense industry such as Richmond, Los Angeles, San Francisco, and Oakland, Monterey County had the fifth greatest population gain in the state of California, increasing 54 percent between 1940 and 1949. Monterey County was ranked eighteenth among the state's fifty-eight counties in terms of population by 1949.[5] Within the county, the city of Monterey experienced a 60 percent increase in population, but the subdivision of Seaside quadrupled between 1940 and 1950, from 2,500 to 10,226, setting the stage for Seaside for incorporation as a municipality by 1954.[6]

The preparation for war stimulated an economy in California towns and cities exhausted by the Great Depression.[7] Fort Ord, built in 1940 on 28,514 acres, with an additional government purchase of 100,000 acres at that time to be used for large-scale maneuvers and training was located immediately to the north and northwest of Seaside. Suddenly money poured into Monterey County too and, because of its location adjacent to the military base, Seaside benefited the most from development projects ranging from new residential housing to commercial enterprises and light industry. For African Americans in particular, who faced discrimination in civilian and military life, Seaside offered hope for prosperity and place.

Areas in and around Oakland, San Francisco, San Jose, Los Angeles, San Diego, and nearby Salinas all experienced population growth and diversity due to mass migrations of people seeking work in the new industries, and for Salinas, the agricultural development that supported the war effort.[8] The difference was that in both large metropolitan centers and in smaller towns, those multicultural neighborhoods remained minority-majority enclaves, located in the least desirable parts of towns.

Residents usually could not directly challenge, much less overcome, the power of long-established political regimes made up mostly of elite Anglo Americans. The subdivision of Monterey known as Seaside, on the other hand, with its still spectacular ocean views, became an incorporated town separate from the town of Monterey by 1954 because the sudden influx of people, mostly new minorities and especially blacks connected to Fort Ord, provided an opportunity for the invention of a new town altogether.

Throughout the war years Seaside shared characteristics with other towns and cities in California experiencing explosive growth, but it was in the aftermath of World War II that Seaside diverged from them and began to resemble other American military towns in its social and cultural character far more than it resembled its counterparts of Monterey, Pacific Grove, or Carmel on the Monterey Peninsula or Salinas and San Jose to the north.

The mixed ethnic and racial population of soldiers, veterans, and their families permanently altered the demographic landscape of Seaside. However, unlike Salinas, San Jose, Oakland, or Los Angeles, which also experienced incredible diversity in the population surges from the war effort, the postwar military gave Seaside's residents a strong common bond and a foundation for working together. Seaside experienced clashes among ethnic groups and between white southern soldiers and people of color, during the war years, but nothing like the Zoot Suit riots of 1942 in urban areas such as Los Angeles and in nearby Salinas.[9]

Cities such as Oakland, Richmond, San Francisco, San Jose, Los Angeles, and San Diego, and their suburbs, all depended on the defense industry to drive their economies.[10] All of these large urban centers had far more diverse economies than Monterey County. Whites in these cities coped with increases in the numbers of blacks, Hispanics, and Asians by isolating them into clearly designated residential enclaves, prompting a new era of civil rights activism in California in the postwar years.[11] Whites either fled or became the political adversaries of minority groups in these cities, although some liberal whites, particularly Jews in Los Angeles, joined forces with minority groups to advocate for civil rights.[12]

Monterey and other Peninsula cities grew increasingly racially homogenous during this period too, as the new influx of minorities were forced into Seaside or Salinas, just as minority groups, particularly blacks, were restricted into residentially specific areas of Oakland, Los Angeles, or San Francisco.[13] By the 1940s, Seaside had become an extension of the part of the city of Monterey housing the workers in the canneries who were too poor to live near the wharf on Cannery Row; it was home to a diverse population of whites, Mexican Americans, Italian Americans, Japanese Americans, Portuguese Americans, and a few African Americans, although the Mexican American population was largely centered in Salinas, not Seaside, reflecting a dependence on the agricultural economy of that area. At the same time, Seaside was gradually taking on the character of a military town. Unlike its neighbors, Salinas or Monterey or other towns and cities in California, Seaside was following a different political trajectory, one that incorporated minorities into its body politic rather than ostracizing them. Much like other military towns of the era, Seaside was notable for its multiracial neighborhoods and political cooperation among minorities, and whites.[14] Yet, as in every other community in the United States, whites had enacted racially restrictive covenants as early as 1941 to keep black residents from renting or buying homes in certain neighborhoods in Seaside, a restriction that became indefensible after *Shelly v. Kraemer*, the Supreme Court decision that outlawed those covenants in 1948.[15]

Seasiders increasingly utilized the common denominator of the military as a basis for building political coalitions across racial and ethnic lines on everything from incorporation to economic development as Seaside evolved from subdivision to city. Its residents may have had differences among themselves but in the aftermath of war, they shared the trials, travails, and tribulations of military life, many of them firsthand, as they reshaped this community at mid-century.

WORLD WAR II AND SEASIDE

The military conducted exercises at Fort Ord that can only be described as massive as America prepared for war. "The War Games of 1940" was the most important of the large-scale maneuvers that occurred in the prelude to war. The event was described in *The Monterey Peninsula Herald* as "the Battle of the Century . . . Mighty Armada Enters Bay at

Dawn." This included four days of maneuvers with "Battleships, cruisers, destroyers, 'mosquito' boats and transports, plus dozens of low and high flying airplanes."[16] The army, navy, air force, and National Guard were all involved, as well as local police, the forestry service, and civilian employees. The entire Third Division, with all of their artillery, arrived from Olympia and Tacoma, Washington. Three months later, in April 1940, ten thousand soldiers marched in review in Monterey, demonstrating with live ammunition.[17] It was an impressive show of force.

Fort Ord became the regional reception and training center for an enormous influx of soldiers in the early 1940s as the United States mobilized for World War II. Many of these soldiers were nonwhite, in contrast to the predominantly Caucasian makeup of all the armed services in the 1910s and 1920s. After 1940, the 3rd, 27th, 35th, and 43rd Infantry divisions trained at Fort Ord, and a prisoner of war camp for Italian and German soldiers was located there during World War II. According to one observer, "At one time [during the war years] there were more than 50,000 troops [stationed at Fort Ord] although the average was about 35,000."[18]

The 7th Infantry Division, which included a sizeable number of African Americans and "an unusually large percentage of Mexicans and Indians," was the largest and perhaps most significant example of an expanded and diverse new military, according to Major Park Wollam's analysis of the history of Fort Ord.[19] The 1st Filipino Infantry Regiment was trained and organized at Fort Ord in 1942, and included by war's end survivors of the "Bataan Death March."[20] Fort Ord also became home base for the 2nd Filipino Infantry Regiment.[21]

Although most of these soldiers were transient trainees destined for war zones in the Pacific, Fort Ord contained a population of soldiers, particularly higher ranking enlisted men and officers, who were assigned to train soldiers and to stay for longer tours of duty.[22] This group of military personnel often came with families and extended families who settled on base when possible, but just as often off base in Seaside, adding a critical component to the area's demographic makeup. Although all military bases were generally diverse, Seaside stood out as particularly so for its position as a center for mixed-race military families, especially in the post-World War II era.[23]

TABLE I
Total population of Monterey County, Seaside, and City of Monterey,
1920–1960.

	Year				
	1920	1930	1940	1950	1960
Monterey County	27,980	53,705	73,032	130,498	198,351
Monterey City	5,479	9,141	10,084	16,120	22,618
Seaside*	400	800	2,500	10,226	19,353

Source: Report on the United States Census, City of Monterey, Population Folder Two, Verticle File, California Room, Monterey Public Library, Monterey, California.
*Seaside was an unincorporated area of the City of Monterey until 1954.

Between 1940 and 1946 Seaside's population nearly doubled.[24] Prior to the war, Seaside was mostly a poor and ethnically mixed working-class community. However, a confluence of events and circumstances during and after World War II made possible Seaside's incorporation as a city in 1954 that first and foremost depended on a critical mass of people settling there. Seaside had the youngest, most dynamic, most diverse population in Monterey County by the time it incorporated in 1954. It was also the poorest in the county.[25] Seaside grew from a population of only 800 in 1930 to over 10,000 by 1940, and its population doubled again in the next decade.

One-quarter of Monterey County's ethnic and racial minorities lived in Seaside, and fully one-third of Seaside's population was composed of people of color by 1960.[26] Seventeen percent of Seaside's population was black and 7 percent Asian in 1960; by 1970, those percentages had increased to 21 percent and 10 percent, respectively.[27] Although the U.S. Census routinely enumerated African Americans and Asian Americans, the Hispanic population was not counted as a separate ethnic group until 1980. Consequently, the total number of Hispanics in Seaside in 1960 was undercounted at about 300.[28] However, the Hispanic population, which was almost exclusively Mexican in origin, was consolidated in the agricultural center of Salinas nearby and included a new population of over 4,000 braceros by 1942.[29]

Seaside shared many problems with other military towns that experienced explosive growth in the World War II era. The influx of soldiers and military families into Fayetteville, North Carolina, which was at-tached to Fort Bragg in the 1940s, produced a booming economy too, but also almost entirely negative consequences for the town. It was de-scribed by residents in the harshest terms as "squalid" and "tawdry" because of the new military presence.[30] The expansion of bases around Columbia, South Carolina, also meant a surge in growth of the economy of the city, which included bars catering to soldiers. The economies of military towns throughout the nation expanded rapidly, as Seaside did, and also in a helter-skelter manner.[31] Honolulu, Hawaii, unusual in its diversity of population before the war, was overwhelmed by the mostly transient military population during the war years that saw a prolifera-tion of bars, brothels, and dance halls and new business enterprises cater-ing to soldiers. One navy flier, Samuel Hynes, described the city during the war years: "It looked . . . like a set from a war movie. It looked like any other Navy town . . . Nothin' but Amarillo with a beach."[32] In her excellent analysis of Salinas, Lori Flores described Salinas as similarly richly diverse during the war years, with "interracial meeting grounds" that ranged from neighborhoods such as Alisal, to Salinas's notorious Chinatown, which was filled with brothels and bars catering to soldiers on leave from Fort Ord.[33]

Although Seaside was completely transformed by the military, the impact of World War II affected life in the entire Peninsula. As early as 1940 Montereyans noted an "appalling increase in crime in Monterey County since the new army cantonment's 'camp followers' have begun arriving."[34] Defense Secretary Leon Panetta recalled the clear military presence in Monterey when he was a child, "Lower Alvarado Street [clos-est to the wharf area] was so packed with soldiers there were MPs down there all the time."[35] The small area of the Monterey Peninsula, compared to greater metropolitan regions in Southern California such as San Diego or Los Angeles and the San Francisco Bay area to the north, made the convergence of soldiers and military support personnel all the more con-spicuous and significant.

Disorder, lack of regulation, and lack of enforcement of building codes made Seaside appear hazardous to residents and visitors alike during the war years. A report by the Seaside Historical Commission described the city and the early effects of Fort Ord:

There was no industry, streets were unpaved, no storm drainage, substandard shacks, septic tanks, twenty-five foot lots bisected by thirty foot streets, and with helter-skelter fashion of undeveloped land. With no code restrictions, giant slum areas [developed]. World War II and Fort Ord [brought] thousands of soldiers and workers descending on the area. Substandard construction was the order of the day without plans, codes or ordinances.[36]

One journalist described Seaside in the context of the rest of the Peninsula in 1950:

While the Peninsula's other communities were terraced levels of society . . . Seaside was new homes, board and bat sometimes redwood and glass—and the trees hadn't even been planted yet. Seaside in early 1950 was the sleek packaged evanescent luxury of motels along Fremont, a sign 'Jesus Saves,' a liquor store across the street, a little bit of Chicago and a lot of frontier . . . It was a town where muscle, brawn, and mechanical skills prevailed. But it was a warm town . . . a town where faith was demonstrated in a big way, but in small frame churches . . . where the New Years Eve celebrants in a neon-streaked barn of a bar fought four carloads of sheriff's deputies rather than give up their drinking.[37]

The "Jesus Saves" red neon sign that this writer referred to was positioned at the top of the first Victory Temple Church on the corner of Harcourt and Fremont next to Mrs. Geraldine Niblett's Fremont Inn and across from Max Reed's "26" Club and Fred Mitchell's pharmacy.[38] Seaside's town center included everything from small stores to bars. Ira Beverly described Seaside in 1945 as "nothing like it is now. [People] were living in tents. [Seaside] didn't hardly look like nothing. It was sandy. We stayed out of the way because . . . there were rattlesnakes [and] soldiers."[39] Yet, even with all of this disorder and ramshackle housing, Seaside still had gorgeous ocean views and potential for development on the scale of Carmel, Pebble Beach, or Monterey.

Like all other military training bases in the United States, war meant expansion. By 1942, one observer commented on the development of the base: "Miles of paved street replace the dust laden lanes, and a panoramic view reveals a great and complete army encampment, a solid example of American Can Do. Today construction continues apace to meet still greater needs."[40] The *Seaside News-Graphic* in August, 1941 claimed that "The biggest breadbasket the Peninsula has ever had is Fort Ord . . . and we in [Seaside] are the nearest [to] the head of the table where that bread is coming from."[41] Largely because of the influx of soldiers and their families, Seaside experienced explosive economic growth in the 1940s. In an article looking back on Seaside development, one Carmel writer put it this way: "Fort Ord did the trick for Seaside. It helped the rest of the Peninsula too, but it pushed Seaside into prominence."[42] The *Carmel Pacific Spectator Journal* enthused about the impact of Fort Ord on Seaside, "The thunder of guns resounds in Seaside's city streets; but this is fine, each shot is like money clanking in the till,"[43] During the debates over incorporation, some Seasiders even considered changing the name of the city to "Ord City."[44]

Fort Ord attracted the usual bars, gambling operations, prostitution, and drugs that typically locate in military towns.[45] Although Seaside, Salinas, and Monterey teemed with soldiers in the late 1940s, Seaside was the most directly affected. According to the local police department, "Military personnel and itinerant workers at Fort Ord use Seaside as their recreation headquarters. They do a lot of drinking and fighting and we get about a dozen 'family trouble' calls a week. Also there are a lot of young fellows in the service who escaped going to jail only by enlisting."[46]

Residents of Monterey County generally, and Seasiders in particular, were mostly proud of their close association with the military especially in the wake of Pearl Harbor. The buildup to war fueled the proliferation of new businesses and residences that sprang up in Seaside between 1940 and 1950. Suddenly Seaside was beginning to look far more like a municipality rather than the rural subdivision of Monterey that it was in the 1930s.

It was during this period that the federal government actively supported racial segregation as a means to protect property values. Only white neighborhoods and cities could qualify for federal mortgage loans or federal investment. As a result, it was in the economic interest of the rest of the residents of the Monterey Peninsula to isolate, residentially, minorities in Seaside in order to protect their own property values from declining or being "redlined," the practice used by the Federal Housing Administration to demarcate areas deemed unqualified for mortgage financing.[47] When the Monterey County Board of Supervisors made the decision to locate the county dump in Seaside in 1947, Seaside residents realized that unless they protected themselves from further incursions by some county officials who viewed the area as a virtual dumping ground for the county and as the least valuable part of it, their investments were in real jeopardy.[48] As early as 1941, it appeared that real estate in the Seaside subdivision of Monterey County was going to be worth much less than that elsewhere on the Peninsula, even though it retained all of the environmental attributes developers were so enthusiastic about in the early years of settlement, as discussed in Chapter 1. "Seaside has always been a dumping ground for Monterey," complained one Seaside resident.[49] Seaside was always commonly considered "the other side of the tracks" by Peninsula residents, even as it was the site of spectacular growth, great ocean views, and warmer weather than its neighbors.

Despite its increasingly unsavory reputation, the federal government needed communities that were geographically connected to its bases to be able to serve its personnel, and this became the most critical factor that drove Seaside toward incorporation. An important military community, Seaside received special attention and study from the federal government, which concluded after lengthy review in 1941 that Seaside was first on a list of California defense communities for federal aid in the millions of dollars for the development of schools, housing, sanitation, and water systems. However, because it was an unincorporated place, Seaside was unable to apply for the funds. It had no agency that the federal government could recognize as formally representing the community. An editorial in the local newspaper lamented the situation: "Having no legal status, being an unincorporated area, there is no chance of obtaining any of the funds proposed for the area until this status is obtained."[50] This was a bad enough situation, but the editor of the newspaper followed up with inquiries to government officials and concluded that without incorporation the future of Seaside was grave indeed.

The editor was told that the government would solve the problem of health hazard [in Seaside] the way . . . they would have done elsewhere with the liquor and prostitution problem, Seaside would be out of bounds [for all military personnel]. There would be a blackout of business from the government . . . neither soldiers nor civilian employees would be allowed to live or do business in the blighted area; Nuf sed [sic].[51]

Incorporation gained popularity in Seaside and also served as an issue that politicized Seasiders, regardless of race. The fight for incorporation as documented in newspaper accounts and, after incorporation, minutes from city council meetings, show that politics in Seaside was always a multiracial mix, with blacks and Spanish-surnamed people (who might be either Filipino or Mexican American), as members of the city council and as citizens with a vocal presence in city affairs at every level. Unlike its counterparts in Salinas or parts of Los Angeles, or even military municipalities like Oakland, Richmond, or San Francisco, the war years gave Seaside residents a chance to veer off from other multiracial communities and re-invent themselves as an incorporated town of their own design. There was no entrenched white elite in Seaside to control the shape of development or the politics of the emerging town. Partisanship was not defined by race in Seaside. For example, one Republican group of seven people who flew to Los Angeles to hear President Eisenhower speak in September 1954 included four whites, one African American, and a Mexican American couple.[52] Many black ministers became particularly vocal proponents of the effort to incorporate.

As a result of the action by the federal government to deny Seaside badly needed development funds in 1941, a cadre of business men and some women that included a variety of ethnic and racial group members extended an open invitation for Seasiders to begin working toward incorporation. According to a local newspaper, a meeting was scheduled for August 8, 1941, at the "Business Men's Association" with "the purpose of the meeting . . . to organize a committee of workers who can help with the passing around of petitions and information."[53] A letter to the editor in the same edition of the newspaper stated "Of the hundreds of people to whom we . . . have the opportunity of talking, we have only two who have been against [incorporation] and one of these raises hogs in the midst of the proposed area for incorporation."[54] The meeting was followed by a series of articles directed at homeowners, business people and the community at large strenuously urging incorporation. The East Monterey Businessmen's Association, organized in 1941, became the Seaside Chamber of Commerce (COC) by 1943.

The COC continued to campaign for incorporation. To convince other Seasiders that incorporation was needed, necessary, and economically feasible, James Patton, one of the COC members, conducted a poll in September 1947 that showed 79 percent of Seasiders favored incorporation.[55] The COC also debated a name change from Seaside to Del Monte, with the hope of recalling more prestigious days and altering popular perceptions of Seaside as multiracial and working class. One COC member, James Mays, tried to convince others of the name change because "It would mean millions of dollars of free advertisement, since the Hotel Del Monte and Del Monte are known throughout the world." Others argued that changing the name would encourage Seasiders who opposed incorporation to support it: "the name [Del Monte] would do much to bring harmony to opposing groups, who especially object to incorporating the area fearing that a new city would be called Seaside," a name that already had negative connotations for Peninsula residents due to its associations with blacks and with the military.[56]

The major objection to incorporation for Seasiders had to do with tax increases and costs of operating a city government. Thomas Twohig suggested property taxes would go up from $100 a year to $160 and also indicated that Seaside's estimated assessed valuation was $8 million. This was contested by George Pollack, labor rights attorney, owner of the water company in Seaside and former president of the COC who argued that $4 million was more likely.[57] He stood to lose his business if the city incorporated and water systems were publicly owned. Mr. Pollack led the fight against incorporation, but when petitions were passed to put incorporation on the ballot, he ran and won a seat on the first Seaside City Council.

The location of the county dump in Seaside was insult enough, but the annexation of the Del Monte subdivision to Monterey in 1948 finally convinced a majority of Seasiders to actively support incorporation as a way to keep federal funds in Seaside rather than become even more dependent on the county or city of Monterey for infrastructure and development. The local Seaside newspaper, *Monterey Bay News*, whose motto was, "If It Will Help Seaside The Bay News Is For It," featured weekly articles arguing for incorporation in great detail, and almost nothing against the idea. It featured interviews with every prominent business and property owner in its editorial section, *Seaside Forum*.

In the midst of World War II, Seaside, like every other multiracial community in California, simultaneously experienced explosive population growth, chaos, and interracial engagement. However, as we have seen, in becoming a military town supported by federal dollars, Seasiders had a chance to incorporate as a city in their own right and, at the same time, to challenge the way politics was practiced in more established cities by creating a town based on a multiracial community of equals.

FORT ORD: FROM SEGREGATION TO INTEGRATION

Fort Ord was one of the largest and most vital training centers in the United States from 1945 until the mid 1990s. Importantly, it was the first base in the country to undergo complete integration.[58] Throughout the war years, the military maintained strict segregation in training, housing, and combat as in keeping with the racial segregation practiced in American society. Although challenged head-on by civil rights activists before the war and especially during the war years, the military resisted integration in favor of making separate facilities more equal.[59] On December 1, 1941, the Adjutant General's Department of the United States Army released a statement that reflected the department's frustration with demands from black activists to integrate the armed services: "The Army is not a social laboratory . . . Experiments to meet the wishes and demands of the champions of every race and creed for the solution of their problems are a danger to efficiency, discipline and morale and would result in ultimate defeat."[60] Enlistment quotas based on race were strictly enforced, as were job placements that kept blacks in the least desirable and lowest skilled positions in all the services.[61] At the same time, numerous research studies conducted by the military showed that black soldiers were every bit as competent as their white counterparts. Furthermore, the studies showed that the military policy of segregation and quotas was inefficient at best and even harmful to the war effort.[62]

The civil rights movement of the 1930s and 1940s focused in large part on segregated practices and put continuous pressure on the government to do something about a segregated and discriminatory military.[63] The Roosevelt administration had already demonstrated the power of government to make transformative social change, which black leaders such as William H. Hastie embraced. Hastie served as civilian aide to the War Department and although he left in frustration, he worked tirelessly to change military policy with regard to racial segregation.[64] In spite of pressure from activists and the black press, every branch of the armed services resisted integration throughout the war and made no effort to alter formal policy.[65]

The ethnic stew that embodied Fort Ord was a microcosm of America at midcentury and offers a glimpse into a momentous beginning to a period of great change in race relations throughout the country. Like most institutions throughout the nation in the 1940s, the military reflected the racism (and sexism) of American society, most especially with regard to black soldiers. Black servicemen had little choice but to conform to military rules and regulations. Besides being treated as second-class soldiers, African Americans, no matter how well educated or qualified, could not rise to the rank of commissioned officers until after 1947 when integration policies were put in place.

The *Fort Ord Panorama*, the official newspaper for the base, revealed just how racism played out for African Americans and other soldiers of color in the 1940s. With the notable exception of Filipino soldiers, the newspaper paid little attention to soldiers of color. Photographs showing soldiers and officers engaging in a wide variety of activities focused almost entirely on whites, even though there were large numbers of Mexican American and African American soldiers at the base. Mexican American soldiers were almost completely absent from the pages of the newspapers during the 1940s. Women appeared predominantly as pin-up girls although women, including married women and mothers, worked in administrative, nursing, food, and laundry services and as critical support personnel throughout the war, as they did in every military installation in the country.[66] Employment at the base gave women in Monterey County and the female members of military families generally, a much needed source of income for their families, however. Until the 1960s, black women, no matter how well educated, could find work only in the laundry, as they were excluded from the mainstream economy.[67]

The African American troops stationed at Fort Ord were segregated into "colored" units and were required to use only the "colored" United Service Organizations (USO), unlike their Mexican American and other ethnic counterparts who were officially deemed "white" for the purposes of the military.[68] According to a description of the African American barracks, their living quarters were clearly substandard: "These boys came to Fort Ord and established themselves at the former location of a CCC camp called the "Dust Bowl. They love it though. Frankly speaking, they began with almost nothing, but through the untiring efforts of their officers they have been made comfortable enough."[69]

Family housing was segregated too. In September 1942, the military announced "many choice apartments" available in Fort Ord Village for families of servicemen on a sliding scale depending on rank. This list of requirements for eligibility indicated that black families were given a token number of living spaces, as it was reported that "There are 20 apartments now open for colored tenants."[70] More serious was the inequality in terms of training soldiers about to enter war zones. An article in the *Fort Ord Panorama* in late October 1942 praised a "Colored Unit" for "cramming 13-weeks training into four," denying blacks the requisite training needed for the field.[71] Although this abbreviated training schedule might have become more common for everyone as the war wore on and replacement troops were needed in the field, it is important to note that this practice was the norm for blacks from the beginning.

Conforming to racial stereotypes and representative of segregated recreational events, when black soldiers are featured in the *Fort Ord Panorama* they are usually shown dancing, such as in a photograph with the explanation that "the Conga Line seems to be part of every dance attended by soldiers, and Sunday night's hop for Negro troops . . . was no exception."[72] Another example of the way blacks were commonly portrayed in the newspaper featured a photograph of a young black couple,

"Jam and Jive was the keynote of a dance given in the Sports Arena recently for colored troops stationed at Fort Ord. Here a happy pair knock themselves out over a hot number."[73] In addition, black minstrel shows for white audiences were also common as indicated in an October 1942 minstrel show "staged by the colored hospital unit" for a capacity audience.[74] This demeaning public portrayal of black soldiers lasted through the war years, in stark contrast to the way other American soldiers were depicted. Yet, it was typical of the way blacks were treated elsewhere. Military policy during the early 1940s conformed to American social and political norms of segregation and discrimination.[75]

By contrast, whites were consistently described with respect, even when in play, and are shown in a wide variety of social activities and work, although women faced the usual sexism of the times. Every edition of the *Fort Ord Panorama* during the war years began with a full page display of the latest pin-up girl, and every single one of them was white, scantily dressed, and placed in provocative poses. Occasionally, women are featured in regular articles, but almost always in secondary roles, even though there were women's divisions of each of the services in the war years stationed at Fort Ord as nurses and as military personnel.[76]

Not all people of color at Fort Ord were treated with the same degree of inequality as were blacks. Although Mexican American soldiers were routinely ignored by the newspaper, Italian Americans, Greek Americans, and other European-origin Americans soldiers were regularly mentioned in articles about sports, training, and events at the base. Although Filipinos were segregated into their own units at the base during World War II, they were privileged in ways that African Americans were not.[77]

By the end of May 1942, the 1st Filipino Infantry Regiment was formed in Salinas. That same month the Philippine Naturalization Bill was passed, and Filipinos were sworn in en mass as U.S. citizens. In September 1942 the first Filipino officers graduated from training at Fort Benning, Georgia. The 1st and 2nd Filipino regiments trained at Fort Ord, and subsequently distinguished themselves in the Battle of Leyte and the Bataan Peninsula.[78]

In contrast to African American soldiers and families who were denigrated and demeaned in the newspapers, the *Fort Ord Panorama* portrayed Filipino soldiers with approval and respect as valiant fighters. For example, in October 1942, the newspaper described General Valdez of the Philippines, who had recently escaped from Corregidor, as a hero and his treatment at Fort Ord as that of "a distinguished visitor." An article reported "A 13 gun salute was fired in honor of the visiting dignitary after which the band of the field Artillery Unit stationed here played the Philippine National Anthem."[79] The newspaper even contained a special "FILIPINOTES" section, which contained humor and announcements specific to Filipino soldiers and regularly featured individuals in news stories that emphasized their bravery and expertise as soldiers. One article about the Battle of Luzon, for example, emphasized the camaraderie between American and Filipino soldiers fighting side by side: "The battles in Luzon . . . have amply demonstrated that American and Filipino soldiers . . . fight better than the Japs." The contrast was clear. Filipino soldiers were treated with serious esteem and blacks were tolerated only as long as they conformed to racial stereotypes. The Filipino families who settled Seaside as part of the military in the 1940s and 1950s then had much less experience of racism directed at them than did blacks.

African American troops were never given the kind of positive press for their heroism in the field that other groups, particularly the Filipinos, received. Yet, the military, for all of its racism, was also the first American institution to be fully integrated in 1948. It was a moment in time when the early civil rights movement was beginning to force some changes in longstanding practices and policies of exclusion.

In the aftermath of World War II, Harry Truman won a close election in part because of support from African Americans and civil rights advocates. Postwar America was still deeply tied to segregation, but the racist policies of Germany and the need for moral high ground at the beginning of the Cold War infused the civil rights movement with new energy and also forced many white Americans to question hierarchy based on race, though a majority still believed in segregation. Secretary of State and former Army Chief of Staff George C. Marshall argued before the President's Committee on Civil Rights that American practices of segregation and discrimination based on race weakened its standing in the eyes of other nations: "The moral influence of the United States is weakened to the extent that the civil rights proclaimed by our Constitution are not fully confirmed in actual practice."[80]

Two weeks after the Democratic Party convention of 1948, President Truman issued two executive orders. The first, Executive Order 9980 prohibited discrimination based on race and ethnicity in the civil service and established the Fair Employment Board. Executive Order 9981 established as presidential policy that "there shall be equality of treatment and opportunity in the armed services without regard to race, color, religion, or national origin," and also that this policy was to be put in place "as rapidly as possible."[81] Most importantly, Executive Order 9981 ended the quota system that kept African Americans in the armed services at 9 percent, opening the way for new minority enlistments.

On July 31, 1948, three days after Truman's executive order, Monterey Mayor Hugh F. Dormody, together with the mayors of Pacific Grove and Carmel, sent a jointly signed telegram to California's United States Senator William F. Knowland contesting the Truman Order, insisting that the Monterey Peninsula was a tourist area that could not absorb thousands of black soldiers "without serious threat of racial conflict."[82] At the time, however, the Peninsula was known far more for its fishing industry than its tourism, and it had already absorbed a wave of immigrants from southern Europe, Japan, Mexico, the Philippines, and American Dust Bowl migrants of the American heartland without incident. Nonetheless, the mayors were terrified at the prospect of the influx of African Americans at Fort Ord spilling over into the communities on the Peninsula. This was, after all, a moment in time when African American migration had completely altered the demographic landscape of the American West generally and California in particular. In 1940, California's African American population totaled 124,306, but by 1950 it had increased to 462,172, an increase of 272 percent, almost all of which was centered in urban California, in cities such as Los Angeles, San Francisco, Oakland, and Richmond.[83]

Senator Knowland sent the mayors' telegram to the Secretary of the Army, Kenneth C. Royall, who responded to Knowland that "Fort Ord, California is the most favorable location west of the Mississippi river where both white and Negro personnel coming into the Army from the western part of the United States can be trained. It has accordingly been designated as a Replacement Training Center for white and Negro Personnel."[84] Black soldiers arrived at Fort Ord in October 1949, with little incident; certainly nothing occurred in the way of large-scale racial violence that the mayors feared and predicted. It is not known exactly how many black soldiers came to the Monterey Peninsula after 1949, but population figures for Seaside indicate that this migration was large enough to mark a significant demographic shift that affected the political, economic, social, and cultural landscape of the city for the next fifty years. By the 1950s, as African American soldiers returned from tours of duty in Europe and from the Korean War with European and Asian brides, Fort Ord was declared one of three "compassionate duty" bases in the United States, along with Fort Dix in New Jersey and Fort Bliss in Texas, where multiracial families were deliberately stationed under the assumption that they would be more comfortable among populations such as in California that were already ethnically and racially more diverse than the rest of the country, although the choice of Fort Bliss, Texas, appears counterintuitive.[85]

The order to integrate, in and of itself, would usher in dramatic change for black soldiers and officers who would now live, work, and train side by side with whites as regular soldiers. This included being featured together in numerous Fort Ord yearbooks and in the pages of the *Fort Ord Panorama*.

By the end of the Korean War and throughout the 1960s, Seaside's population continued to increase, and by the time parts of Fort Ord were annexed in 1968 Seaside became the largest city, 35,940 people, and most diverse on the Monterey Peninsula. By 1968, sociologist Elaine Johnson noted that "Seaside is unique in that it has the largest number of non-whites of any community between San Francisco and Los Angeles."[86]

CRITICAL MASS, THE ARMY POPULATION, AND COMMUNITIES OF COLOR

Seaside emerged from World War II and the postwar decade as one of the most diverse cities, not only in Monterey County but also in California in general. The Japanese who settled Seaside after World War II are a good example of the new minority communities that formed in the postwar years. From the earliest years of the Issei migration (the immigrant first generation) between 1898 (after the annexation of Hawaii) and the 1920s, the Japanese community on the Peninsula lived in Monterey in multiethnic neighborhoods of Sicilian Americans and Mexican Americans. The Japanese were mostly fishermen and small business owners. They also resided in Salinas where they worked as farmers and intermingled with white, Sicilian, Filipino, Portuguese, and Mexican American neighbors. Some filtered into Carmel Valley and Seaside as farmers, landscapers, and gardeners but, for the most part, the Japanese population in the prewar years was centered in Monterey and Salinas. [87] The Japanese Association Hall, built in 1925 in Monterey, became the center for community activity and is still used today for community meetings and events. [88] It was also used for Buddhist temple worship until the first Buddhist Temple was built in Seaside in 1965. [89]

In the aftermath of the internment experience and the end of World War II, former Japanese American residents of the Peninsula returned, as they did to other areas of California. [90] Those Japanese Americans who originated from Salinas found that their farmlands had already been appropriated by former neighbors. Many who originated in Monterey found themselves without property as well. The internment order was implemented so quickly that most Japanese were forced either to abandon property such as fishing boats or sell them for a fraction of their value to Sicilians and other fishermen who rarely gave them back when the Japanese returned. [91]

The Japanese immigrant and Japanese American (the Nisei generation) survivors of the internment camps had to start over, and without question the most affordable, promising place to do so on the Peninsula was Seaside. The new Japanese American community established in Seaside after 1945 included residents formerly from Monterey and Salinas. The Japanese American community increasingly centered in Seaside was not part of a military migration, but many Japanese wives of American soldiers—the so-called "war brides"—connected the community to Fort Ord. Moreover, unlike their counterparts from the migrations of the early twentieth century, these women were mostly urban and middle class and not from farming or fishing communities. They altered the character of the postwar Japanese American community by incorporating both a military culture and a teaching and promotion of Japanese visual and performing arts.[92] In this way, women of Japanese descent married to U.S. servicemen of various races and ethnicities, including blacks, not only changed the culture of Seaside's Japanese American community in Seaside but, more importantly, created a critical link between the Japanese American community in Seaside and other minority groups connected to Fort Ord.

Like the Japanese, Filipinos re-formed in the years following World War II into a visible community that was both military oriented and centered in Seaside. During the postwar years the Filipino community became active in the Catholic Church and in the military as a new Filipino American cultural identity was shaped. Unlike Filipinos, all of whom originated as immigrants, the postwar Hispanic community of Seaside was made up mostly of Mexican American families that had historic roots on the Monterey Peninsula, in Monterey rather than in nearby Salinas, which had a far more important and substantial Mexican community.[93] Mexican Americans lived in Monterey and Carmel Valley as well as Seaside and formed a community that was not specific to one city. Many Mexican Americans in Seaside had roots as agricultural workers and shared a culture and identity shaped by Catholicism and a long history as one of California's largest ethnic minority groups. Mexican Americans in Seaside organized barbecues and city events such as Cinco de Mayo that drew thousands of residents throughout the 1960s and into the 1980s.[94] It was not until well into the 1970s and 1980s that Guatemalan political refugees and immigrants from Peru and El Salvador added to the composition of the Hispanic community in the city. Not until the 1970s did new populations of Vietnamese refugees arrive in Seaside.[95]

The major difference between Hispanics, including Mexican Americans, and later Salvadorans and other Central Americans and every other immigrant group in Seaside was that most did not arrive as part of the military migration to Fort Ord. Hispanics were the only prominent minority community in Seaside with few ties to the military, despite their important role in American wars, especially since World War II.

Although Mexican Americans and Asians contributed to the diversity of the city, it was the emergent African American community of Seaside more than any other minority group that redefined the city. Unlike other municipalities in California, the black community of Seaside derived from the military. A San Francisco guest journalist wrote in the *Monterey Peninsula Herald* in 1968, "Seaside, primarily a residential community, has more Negro residents than any other city between Los Angeles and San Francisco . . . most authorities agree that some 6,000 Negroes live in the town . . . this figure was slightly higher than San Jose's . . . Almost half of the Negro male labor force is on active military duty, while a sizeable segment of the rest of the workforce is on civilian payrolls on military installations."[96] Also important, the Seaside African American community included significant numbers of German, French, and Asian women who had intermarried with African American soldiers in the immediate postwar years and during the Korean War, while on tours of duty in Europe, Korea, and Vietnam, creating the most intimate links between groups and adding a level of complexity to black community life in Seaside.[97]

By 1948 the army had reduced its population from 8 million in 1945 to 600,000; importantly, Fort Ord was used as a major demobilization center, making it easy for retired and newly released military personnel to stay.[98] In the aftermath of demobilization, approximately 6,000 retired military personnel and their families settled on the Peninsula. Although many whites settled in Carmel, Pebble Beach, and Monterey, and blacks, Asians, and Mexican Americans were concentrated in Seaside, many other white former military personnel settled in Seaside too, which remained the most affordable housing market in the county throughout the period from 1940 to 1990, and also with its sweeping ocean views, one of the most beautiful military towns in the country.[99]

It is important to keep in mind that Seaside's population always included whites, who remained in Seaside even though it clearly became a destination for many minority groups, particularly blacks. At the same time that a racially mixed population of soldiers and their families were pouring into Seaside in the postwar years because of their connections to Fort Ord, whites originating from the Dust Bowl and white veterans-turned-business owners who could not afford to live elsewhere settled in Seaside. These people, the Oldemeyers, Andersons, Cunninghams, Dolans, and others formed themselves into an interest group that helped drive the community toward incorporation as a city in its own right by 1954 and also helped steer the political and economic life of Seaside until the mid-1960s. One writer acknowledged the unusual mix of Southern whites and blacks in Seaside: "A quarter to a third Negro population and a great many whites talk with a Mason-Dixon drawl, there is no racial problem in Seaside. It is the problem of mixed neighborhoods, however, that is keeping a good many people from buying homes in Seaside."[100] It is intriguing to consider what this writer meant by "no racial problem" in Seaside. Certainly Americans in the postwar decades shared a deeply ingrained racist ideology that privileged whites. However, Seaside residents exhibited a sense of inclusiveness that accepted, even assumed, that everyone would participate in city life, regardless of race or ethnicity, and regardless of their own personal racist beliefs.

Mixed neighborhoods, on the other hand, were highly unusual in postwar America, except in military towns. The interracial neighborhoods of the war years increasingly gave way to rigid and restricted housing practices until successfully challenged by civil rights advocates in *Shelly v. Kraemer* in 1947. However, multiracial neighborhoods characterized even southern military towns during this period.[101] Not only were military towns less segregated than towns of comparable size nationally, but military towns stood out regionally for being centers of diversity with multiracial neighborhoods in direct correlation to Truman's 1948 directive to integrate the military. Like Seaside, other military towns throughout the United States experienced enormous expansion associated with military bases in the postwar period.[102] This is not to say that multiracial neighborhoods or multiracial families prevailed in the city, but that there were enough examples of them to make a difference in perceptions of race and in city life, as Seaside's economy continued to be bolstered by the federal investment in Fort Ord in the aftermath of World War II.

POSTWAR EXPANSION

Fort Ord committed to hiring local labor for its 500-unit housing project proposed in 1951, which provided much needed employment opportunities for Seaside residents, women and men alike. Retail stores, beauty and barber shops, restaurants, real estate and insurance firms, banks, three major grocery stores, medical and dentist clinics, and light industry sprang up. Ninety-two business licenses were issued in one year alone. A national moving company, Pyramid National Van Lines Inc., located its headquarters in Seaside in 1948, and the Greyhound Bus Company announced a new terminal and bus station in Seaside the same year.[103] Industries included a pottery-making plant, a plastic tray manufacturer (which moved locations from Monterey to Seaside), and an auto parts manufacturer. In 1952, the local *Seaside News Sentinel* announced "Seaside's greatest step and continued climb toward a modern city" with the building of a "gigantic sewage system . . . the largest project of its kind in the county of Monterey."[104] It was sorely needed as the population increased and pressure built on basic county services.

A glance through the city directories of the 1950s through the 1970s and interviews with longtime residents show just how the face of the city underwent transformation during these decades of increasing population. One newspaper article written in 1950 described Seaside as a community expanding so rapidly that "its physical appearance changes from week to week."[105] Polk's County Directory described Seaside in 1955 as "potentially the greatest district on the Monterey Peninsula for industrial development." The short description of the city emphasized Seaside's proximity to recreation areas and its "considerable vacant property," suggesting opportunity for development. The residents included "thousands of Army and Navy personnel" stationed at Ford Ord, the Navy General Line School (later named the Navy Post-Graduate School), and the Defense Language Institute (both located in Monterey). In addition to a "new modern theater" (the Del Rey Theatre) Seaside also had "many modern buildings" according to the Directory.[106] Joe Cortéz, Seaside postmaster, recalled Seaside in the 1940s and 1950s in vivid detail:

[In the 1940s] Fremont was just a two lane street . . . In 1948 they widened it to a four lane highway . . . [it] had very little traffic on it . . . we would play out in the middle of it . . . by the 726 Club. I think at that time it was known as the 26 Club, Nelsons Emporium . . . Mann's little grocery store at the corner of Hamilton and Fremont . . . I used to venture down Broadway because the Del Rey Theatre was there . . . I used to sneak down Olympia and play with Tommy

Neilson [son of Herman and Ruth who owned Neilson's Plumbing] . . . and very seldom ventured any further north than that . . . it was just sagebrush . . . looking in that direction. Looking towards Noche Buena it was very little activity. Most of the concentrated housing was from Fremont running towards what is now Sand City which was also part of Seaside at that time. Sand City and right around the Seaside School and that area down there between Fremont, Canyon Del Rey, West of Fremont is where all the population was . . . [but] very little business or shopping . . . [by the 1950s] the house where we lived in sat across the street almost where Sprouse Reitz is and they moved it clear across Fremont. They moved all the houses to the right . . . it was a long process but it employed a lot of people.[107]

Cortéz's narrative describes Seaside as it emerged from the tiny subdivision of the 1940s to a growing town in the 1950s, including the structural changes he mentioned such as the widening of Fremont Street, the moving of houses around, and the outcomes of a large population surge.

According to city directories and maps of the time, if one were to drive south on the county road (renamed Highway 1 in 1957) to reach the Monterey Peninsula in 1955 one would see the big sign welcoming visitors to Seaside, the "Gateway to the Monterey Peninsula," at the crossroads of Fremont and Del Monte, both main avenues that meandered first through Seaside, then through the tiny community of Ord Grove, and finally into Monterey, Carmel, Big Sur and down the coast. Barely noticeable from the highway and partially hidden by sand dunes was the Monterey County Dump. On the East side of the highway was a towering grove of Eucalyptus trees. There were a few houses creeping into the Eucalyptus grove, but for the most part as you headed down Fremont Avenue and into Seaside, you would see a sprinkling of small businesses along Fremont and lots of empty space in the hills—it was sand dunes and brush for as far as the eye could see, just as Joe Cortéz remembered.

The picture of Seaside that emerges from city directories, contemporary observations, and reflections of longtime residents is one of a small community that changes significantly over time. These depictions of Seaside capture a town in the throes of transformation. Former sections of the town that were relatively undeveloped began to fill in. The scattered business along Del Monte, Fremont, and Broadway were joined by new retail establishments. More noticeable still were the numerous churches that were formed in Seaside to serve the expanding population of new residents, most of them migrants associated in some way with Fort Ord.

SEASIDE CHURCHES: A MILITARY TOWN

The proliferation of churches provides some of the strongest evidence for Seaside's change in character from small community to multiracial military town. In 1930 the Monterey city directory listed only one church located in Seaside, the Methodist Episcopal Church, which traced its roots to 1899, serving the local white community since the earliest years of the twentieth century. By 1951 there were fourteen different congregations listed in Seaside's city directory. By 1964, there were twenty-three different churches in Seaside and thirty-five by the 1980s.[108]

One of the most prominent of the black churches in Seaside remains Greater Victory Temple, Church of God in Christ, and a Pentecostal denomination, which was founded by Elder S. R. Martin in a small building next to Geraldine Niblett's boarding house at 724 Harcourt Avenue in 1943. Later, the church moved to a prominent location on the corner of Yosemite and Broadway in Seaside. Elder Martin led Greater Victory Temple for thirty-seven years, and was one of the founding members of The Ministerial Alliance which became an important political organization in Seaside in the decades between 1948 and the 1990s. After Elder Martin's death in 1980, Elder Wilburn Hamilton negotiated for the purchase of land and supervised the building of the new church site in Seaside.

The Hays Colored Methodist Episcopal Church, organized in 1940, increased its membership from 12 to 150 by 1946. Its members renovated a former cabinet shop into a permanent church building with the leadership of the pastor Reverend T. C. Broach, who also happened to be a building contractor. In addition to its role as the spiritual home of the congregation, it served as a vital center of organization and social activity for its members.

The Friendship Baptist Church was organized in 1945 and first met in the firehouse in Seaside before the congregation constructed a building in 1946, where it was reported "The members laid the foundation with their own hands and each contributed two sacks of cement." In 1953, the church announced a plan to raise a projected $40,000 for a new building in response to a swelling membership. The Friendship Church was described as "a patch of Texas on the Peninsula" with a congregation of 150 that was "predominantly Negro, [but] with two white members. Six other white people attend services regularly and a number more attend them occasionally." Like so many other churches on the Peninsula, this church was formed on the basis of region as much as race and was a reflection of the city's demographic link to the military. According to an interview with the pastor, Reverend Joseph S. Sutton, "Folk just seemed to gravitate to a church where the preacher and parishioners were from their own home state . . . There are other congregations on the Peninsula the majority of its members which are predominantly from Louisiana and from Arkansas and the respective pastors are from those states."[109] Eight African Americans from Tennessee founded the Church of God in Christ in 1945. By 1948 the membership rose to seventy-one, and a new church building was constructed to accommodate the small but growing congregation.[110]

St. Francis Xavier Catholic Church was established in 1950 as a parish and represented most clearly Seaside's immense diversity. St. Francis Xavier served a wide racial and ethnic mix of Catholics in Seaside throughout the 1950s, including blacks, Mexican Americans, Filipinos, and southern Europeans (Portuguese and Italians) comprised most of the congregation. St. Francis met the social as well as spiritual needs of its parishioners. St. Francis was far more diverse than either the white or the black Protestant churches in Seaside in the war years and through the early years of incorporation. According to the Catholic Church newspaper, *The Observer*, "[St. Francis] is both Catholic and 'catholic' with worshippers of all races and colors, bearing prayer books in many languages. The priests themselves are from opposite ends of the world: one speaks English with a Northern Irish accent, the other with a Northern Chinese accent." By 1958 the church had such a large congregation that "there was standing room only at four of the five Sunday masses."[111]

In addition to mainstream Protestant and Catholic churches in Seaside and in addition to the Pentecostal Victory Temple, there were also a variety of other Pentecostal sects, a Mormon temple, an Eastern Orthodox Church, and a Buddhist Temple by the end of the 1950s. The International Church of Foursquare Gospel, originally founded by the popular Aimee Semple McPherson in the 1920s, also had a congregation in Seaside, which was headed almost exclusively by a succession of women pastors. The Reverend Inez Arnes founded the church in 1941, and the Reverend Viola Davis took control of the congregation by 1945.

The military population was responsible for sustaining a strikingly large variety of churches in Seaside. The proliferation of churches and especially the abundance of churches with specific, regionally based congregations show just how important numerically the military became to community life. Ministers from those churches, particularly from the mostly black congregations, would play an enormously important role in Seaside politics in the decades to come, first and foremost, in the drive to incorporate.

Spectacular population growth spurred by the military challenged Seaside residents to maintain a sense of community. Suburbs such as South Gate in Los Angeles, according to historian Becky Nicolaides, saw their sense of community undermined by the "convulsive population boom during the war years."[112] San Francisco East Bay cities such as San Leandro, Milpitas, and Fremont developed as independent and homogenous white municipalities as a response to the influx of blacks, Mexicans, Asians, and other nonwhite workers in the war industries who arrived in Oakland in the same period.[113] In San Jose, race divided groups as well. Instead of coming together as a community, Mexican American San Joseans were forced into East San Jose barrios as a result of their increasing numbers.[114]

Although, as Mark Brilliant demonstrated in his analysis of California civil rights activism, racial and ethnic groups pursued very different agendas in the postwar years, groups also came together to form coalitions, create community, and actively and collectively fight for civil rights.[115] Mark Wild emphasized the common ground Los Angeles residents found at church, at school, in the context of labor unions and politics, and most importantly, in mixed marriages and at play in dance clubs and concerts.[116] In her analysis of restrictive housing practices in San Francisco and Los Angeles during the 1940s and 1950s, Charlotte Brooks stressed the importance of interracial coalitions that ended discrimination in neighborhoods in both cities. Shana Bernstein credited New Deal policies and programs for bringing disparate ethnic and racial groups together to work for the common purpose of civil rights in the postwar period.

Yet, the military component in Seaside adds a new dimension to our understanding of how and why some racial and ethnic groups who may have been competitors for privilege in American society came together in common purpose. People who served in the military and their families along with them experienced integration for themselves. Bases after 1948 were segregation-free zones that incorporated diverse people, with less conflict than was expected by anyone. When these individuals and family members came to Seaside they formed a critical mass of people who had become accustomed to sharing space with people different from them. For military families, unlike Americans generally, it was not abnormal for whites, blacks, Filipinos, Japanese, and Hispanics in Seaside to envision a city that included all groups in its body politic, regardless of one's racial views.[117]

TOWARD INCORPORATION

In the early 1950s, Seasiders organized local clubs and organizations that brought together a clearly defined community, an important step leading to incorporation. In 1947, the Seaside Fire Department, Juan Cabrillo Elementary School, the Del Monte PTA, the Seaside Lions Club, and the Seaside Sewing Club represented the Seaside subdivision in Monterey's school bond parade, with G. T. "Sarge" Cunningham representing the Seaside Chamber of Commerce. Seasiders were also active in organizing programs for young people. In 1947 the public schools recreation program formed a Juvenile Orchestra, with instruments provided by the school. In a special section titled "Travels With Seaside" in the *Monterey Peninsula Herald* on June 4, 1951, Seasiders explained that they wanted to incorporate rather than become formally annexed to Monterey in order to "retain [their] own identity." "Identity" was both military and multiracial by 1951. However, photographs of these events and in the multiple news and feature story articles documenting Seaside's history, the faces of Seaside are depicted as predominantly white. Business, shopping, and real

estate development were featured as white enterprises as Seasiders advertised themselves as just another white American suburb, indicating a clear
consciousness among residents that perceptions of whiteness were integral
to successful development, and more importantly, that even though the
city was multiracial, whites remained in large enough numbers to create
the perception of homogeneity, even when the reality was far different.

Edwin Hawes who had lived in Seaside since 1907 and who was a
"property owner" warned Seaside residents that Monterey was poised
to annex Seaside, to use the area for its growing population in ways that
would harm property values in the city: "We missed the boat ten years
ago on the sanitation system. We're paying through the nose for that . . .
But it is not too late for incorporation. It will be, if we don't act. We let
Del Monte get away. If we do nothing Monterey will step in and take
bigger chunks."[118]

The COC formed multiracial committees to study the costs and benefits of incorporation and sent members into the field throughout the late
1940s and early 1950s. In 1951, committee member Pat Patterson (who
would emerge as a vigorous opponent of urban renewal in Seaside later
in the 1950s and 1960s) reported "overwhelming sentiment in favor of
incorporation . . . and a unanimous vote of the Ord Terrace Property
Owners Association meeting for incorporation."[119] Thomas Twohig
chaired a fact-finding committee and reported that "The chief idea that
the Chamber of Commerce is interested in is assembling of facts for the
benefit of the public at large."[120]

By April 1951 all reports proclaimed incorporation "feasible." However, the COC understood that incorporation would not be possible
without the support of the multiple communities that made up Seaside.
Instead of making a formal statement on incorporation as representatives of Seaside, the COC made arrangements to meet collectively with
"all other civic organizations in the area to make the movement more inclusive." Jack Simon, president of the local chapter of the NAACP was a
member of the Seaside Council who focused on voter registration in the
black community to support incorporation. The Reverend Joseph S. Sutton, pastor of the Friendship Baptist Church, was included in the COC.
Homer Spann, who owned much real estate in Seaside and was known

as the first black millionaire in Monterey County, chaired the committee that circulated petitions for an election of city officers that would be part of the incorporation vote. Richard Joyce moved to Seaside in 1952 and eventually owned a successful custodial business. He worked actively to generate support for incorporation. He, along with Jack Simon, formed the all black Seaside Civic Voters League in 1953 (Jack Simon was elected president) which met once a week at Noche Buena School auditorium to develop political strategy for African American Seasiders:

I was for incorporation. I saw great things that could happen if [Seaside] was under local control as opposed to the county coming over here whenever they felt like it. We all thought it would be best to do so. I know we [African Americans] were instrumental in the success of incorporation. I organized [the campaign to incorporate] along with Jack Simon. We were trying to get people who were trying to advance themselves. I saw great potential here in this community for black people. White groups came to us.[121]

Joyce's comments and the experiences of other black activists in Seaside in the postwar period are in stark contrast to the experiences of black activists in California and throughout the western United States. In Phoenix, for example, blacks dedicated to civil rights and "race work" struggled for decades with political marginalization. White elites, part of entrenched political establishments in cities whose corporate histories go back for decades, effectively kept blacks from holding power until well into the 1970s.[122]

The COC succeeded in convincing most Seaside residents that incorporation was the right step. "I remember that there wasn't too much resistance to become a city. People wanted to be incorporated because we didn't have fire departments, nothing like that. We had to depend on the county,"[123] recalled Luis Pérez, seventeen years old at the time.

The Seaside COC moved ahead, forming committees on incorporation that would allow for the election of a city council. Seasiders discontent with the site of the county dump finally led to an action by the newly formed Monterey County Garbage board to "remove the infamous dump from Seaside."[124] This success allowed civic leaders to concentrate on deciding city boundaries and infrastructure such as water service, which was deemed "inadequate" throughout the city, and to build an urgently needed sewage system in response to unprecedented growth.

By November 1951, Seasiders agreed to city boundaries that included whites in Ord Terrace but excluded the all white neighborhoods nearby in Del Monte Beach, Del Rey Terrace, and Del Rey Woods. The residents of these areas succeeded in convincing the City of Monterey to annex their neighborhoods in order to prevent them from becoming part of Seaside.[125] More importantly, there was no annexation of Fort Ord.[126] On January 16, 1952, Seasiders packed the Seaside COC meeting to begin petitioning for incorporation. As incorporation became a reality for Seaside residents, it also became more contentious. George Pollack, who led the fight against incorporation, was careful to avoid the public perception of conflict of interest. Mr. Pollack expressed fears that incorporation would allow business people to exploit the community, drive up taxes and exclude the poorest residents from future economic development.[127] In any case, the idea of incorporation generated widespread interest in Seaside. Seasiders were involved and politicized. At one debate over incorporation, the local newspaper reported that "Old-timers declared that the Seaside Council audience [at a meeting February 6, 1952] was the largest ever gathered at a public meeting in this area . . . 200 people were present. Every chair was occupied and the crowd stood two deep on three sides of the hall overflowing into a second room."[128]

On March 5, 1953, COC Vice President Homer Spann delivered 1,914 signatures for incorporation to the Monterey County Board of Supervisors—only 1,500 signatures were needed. Mr. Spann collected 642 of the signatures himself. However, white homeowners in the Del Rey Oaks and Ord Terrace area disputed city boundaries, delaying the vote for another year. The boundaries were redrawn to exclude Del Rey Oaks, which itself incorporated as a separate city in April 1954. The predominantly white residents of Ord Terrace attempted a counterpetition to create their own city, no doubt realizing that the racially segregated zone they created in the 1940s would not be sustained in an incorporated, multiracial Seaside. They failed, but only because of filing irregularities. By April 1954, a committee of local business owners that included John Bean, an African American real estate broker, hired a municipal engineer, a municipal finance advisor, and a legal expert to push incorporation to a vote once and for all.[129] On July 15, 1954, the Monterey County Board of Supervisors scheduled an election for October 4, 1954, to decide incorporation. They did so over the protests of Bessie Kramer, spokesperson for the Ord Terrace group, who asked that their subdivision be withdrawn from Seaside.[130] Their efforts conformed to white responses throughout California during the postwar period when the influx of people of color, especially African Americans, threatened white hegemony.[131]

Concerted voter registration drives began in late July led by John Watson, Homer Spann, Joe Cota, Sam DeMello, Al Underwood, John Pattulo, and John Bean. According to John Bean, "stimulating voter registration" was the most important factor in determining the success of incorporation.[132] The filing deadline for city council was August 11. By August 5, eight Seaside leaders had registered including two African Americans, Homer Spann and Jack Simon.[133]

Out of the twenty-two candidates for city council on the 1954 ballot to incorporate, one was a woman, business owner Bessie Kramer, and three were African Americans (Homer Spann, John Simon, and John Bean). Spann had moved with his family from his native Florida to Los Angeles in 1909 when he was nine years old. He lived in Carmel for six years before moving to Seaside in 1933 and began buying property and developing the city. A strong advocate of incorporation, he was quoted as saying "We are going to have a city whether I'm elected councilman or not. All you people have to do to try to make this a city is to outdo me." In his campaign he emphasized his role in the church and that he was a self-made man. According to Mr. Spann, "Seaside is not only the gateway to the Monterey Peninsula, but the power of the Peninsula."[134]

John Bean came to Seaside as part of the 7th Infantry Regiment in 1943; in retirement he became the first African American realtor in Seaside. His wife, Lenora Bean, who still lives in Seaside, remembered him as an active participant in Seaside politics, "but only so far," she recalled, emphasizing the racism of the times. Mr. Bean was also a strong advocate for incorporation and made it a centerpiece of his campaign.[135]

Jack Simon, also an army veteran, barber, president of the NAACP, and vice president of the Seaside Council, had the support of "many business and several ministers," according to the *Seaside Post-News Sentinel*. He was also described as an official of the Ocean View Baptist Church. "The goal for Seaside lies ahead," he said at a meeting of candidates in October 1954, "just open the door."[136] The comments of Joyce, Spann, Simon, and Bean clearly suggest something more than incorporation was going to give African Americans a real chance to create the kind of community where they could participate and prosper, but they hardly represented a unified voting bloc and were running against one another as much as they ran against any of the other nonblack candidates.

Of the sixteen Caucasian men who ran for office, none had deep roots in Seaside and most arrived sometime in the 1940s and most by way of the military. Jack Oldemeyer, later elected Seaside's first mayor, was an automobile mechanic who came to Seaside in 1928 and became actively involved with establishing a fire district in Seaside, an issue that generated great support among Seaside residents who felt neglected by the county. He described himself as "100 per cent American." G. T. "Sarge" Cunningham managed The Del Rey Theatre (Seaside's only theater); he was an army veteran who had lived in Seaside for fourteen years. Joe Cota came from Salinas to Seaside in 1948 and owned a moving and storage company. He had been actively involved in everything from the local Lions Club to the Seaside COC and would also take a turn at mayor. Beauford T. "Andy" Anderson, grew up on a Wisconsin farm and became a war hero during World War II, earning a Medal of Honor. He reenlisted and was stationed at Fort Ord, where he remained after leaving the service in 1952. He established a floor covering and linoleum business in Seaside. "I was one of the few businessmen in town who lived in town," said Mr. Anderson in 1989, "I guess that's what got me into politics." John Pattulo was an insurance and real estate agent and former civil engineer who arrived in Seaside in 1948 from Nebraska. He was elected to the city council and appointed mayor in 1964. The municipal pool in Seaside was later named after him. None of these men, who would all spend several terms each on the Seaside City Council and who took turns as mayor, were experienced at governance and, with the exception of John Pattulo, were not as well educated as their black counterparts. What they did have in common, however, was either their military backgrounds or their connection to the Fort Ord economy, which they shared with African Americans and everyone else in Seaside. Those who ran for political office in Seaside were roughly equals in terms of length of residence and strength of political base, with black activists having an edge in terms of status in the military and educational attainment.

The effort to incorporate proved successful in 1954, with 50 percent of the city turning out to vote.[137] The predominantly black Noche Buena neighborhoods supported Simon and Spann but did not show the same support for the third candidate, John Bean. None of these African American candidates won election. An all male, all white city council was elected in 1954, and because there were so many more white males who ran for office the result was unsurprising. The three black candidates split the African American vote. Joe Cota, who was Portuguese, Jack Oldemeyer, Sarge Cunningham, George Pollack, and army veterinarian Dr. John Craige were elected to Seaside's first city council. The council voted 3–2 to elect Jack Oldemeyer Seaside's first mayor.

CONCLUSION

In slightly more than a decade, between World War II and 1954, Seaside was transformed from a neglected but still awesomely beautiful subdivision of Monterey to a town defined both by the military and by its racially diverse population, most especially by its new population of blacks. The majority of Seasiders had some connection to Fort Ord, either as military personnel, civilian employees, or business owners who depended on the military population for economic survival. In fact, the military largely was responsible for all of the elements that led to Seaside becoming the City of Seaside—the surge of population, the influx of minorities, particularly blacks, but also Asians and Hispanics, and the promise of federal dollars that depended on Seaside's attachment to Fort Ord, which made incorporation economically feasible. However, it was the effect of military policy of integration that would eventually matter the most.

The struggles over incorporation show the importance and activism of minorities who organized into political groups, but these groups were not strictly race-based organizations. Minorities united for common cause elsewhere in California towns and cities too, but most often they were organized along racial lines, and it was predominantly in the name of civil rights rather than in the more race neutral work of creating a city.[138] Most importantly, minorities in other towns and cities in California and the West typically faced off against a long-established white political elite, which sometimes (though rarely) offered support for their inclusion in city government. Not so for Seaside. This town was brand new, and everyone in it was roughly equal in terms of residence and socioeconomic status.

The multiple controversies that challenged Seasiders in the years to come were shaped by the common denominators of race and the military. As residents focused their energies on creating infrastructure and developing their city, it became clear that interpretations of city identity were based on the twin notions of multiracialism and the military. Seasiders had to build coalitions and work together, regardless of their racial feelings, because no one group was so numerically dominant or so homogenous that it could exercise power at will. As members of military families, Seaside residents in the postwar years accepted a new racial reality that assumed everyone ought to be included in city life. Seaside became a military town, but one that was notable for its multiracial, multiethnic coalitions in politics, economic development, and community life. Yet, in the years after incorporation, simmering differences over economic opportunity and housing based on racial ideologies that privileged whites came to the fore, adding a new challenge to the formation of the city.

CHAPTER 3

Creating an Integrated Seaside After the War

PHOTO 3. Three soldiers sharing beers in postwar Fort Ord. Courtesy of Elizabeth and Sherman Smith, City of Seaside Archive.

RICHARD JOYCE, prominent Seaside community activist and political leader, described Seaside as a "utopia for black people" when he arrived in 1952. Unlike Chicago, Boston, New York, or cities in the West, or even in California, he explained, "everything was open in Seaside for young, enterprising black people. Things weren't fixed. The city was unincorporated. There was tremendous opportunity for us to create something new."[1] The "something new" that he and other activists envisioned was a town without the racial barriers that were fixed elsewhere, in places such as Oakland or Los Angeles where minorities fought hard, even with one another, for inclusion into neighborhoods, schools, and public places, but most especially with established white political elites for inclusion into city governments.[2]

The civil rights movements that emerged in the aftermath of World War II would permanently alter American society, but not without great effort by the women and men whose "race work" finally overcame racial barriers in everything from housing to schools.[3] This important work took place all over the country, but was most successful in the West and in California.[4] In Seaside it was further bolstered by the very obvious presence of Fort Ord and a new model of inclusion.

African American residents of Seaside were deeply aware of, and involved in, the multiple civil rights movements of the 1950s and 1960s, and many had close connections to its leadership, including with Dr. Martin Luther King Jr. who visited Seaside in 1962. Importantly, they were also closely connected to Fort Ord. As shown in Chapter 2, by the time of the important 1968 Civil Rights Act, "Seaside, primarily a residential community, has more Negro residents than any other city between Los Angeles and San Francisco . . . most authorities agree that some 6,000 Negroes live in the town . . . this figure was slightly higher than San Jose's . . . Almost half of the Negro male labor force is on active military duty, while a sizeable segment of the rest of the workforce is on civilian payrolls on military installations."[5] Seasiders, and most especially African American Seasiders, were deeply embedded in military culture as well as in the civil rights movement.

In the aftermath of World War II, the military challenged one of the most fundamental characteristics of American society—racial segregation. In fact, it was the first institution in society to force integration. Eventually, the military went so far as to create a culture of integration far surpassing anything that was going on in the rest of America. Although all branches of the military fiercely resisted efforts by the federal government to desegregate during the war, once President Harry Truman issued his executive order in 1948, the military became the only institution to mandate that "getting along" was a requirement on base; it also became a basis for interracial cooperation off base. Military bases after 1948 were segregation-free zones that incorporated all sorts of people with some racial conflict, but much less than might be expected in the context of a deeply racist and segregated country. When military personnel and family members came to Seaside they helped form a more racially tolerant community than their fellow Americans at midcentury, even though many held on to ingrained racial prejudice. Their city mirrored what was happening next door at Fort Ord. According to historian James McNaughton, "The Army tried to replicate the suburbs that were springing up everywhere in post-war America, with schools, playgrounds and swimming pools for soldiers' families . . . [Fort Ord] built a golf course in 1954 and an airfield on the north side of the post . . . The only difference at military bases like Ford Ord was that special facilities were built for officers and their families, thus separating people by rank, rather than [by] race."[6] The spatial divides within the military based on rank rather than race forced interaction between people who might otherwise never encounter someone of another race in a civilian community.

It would be useful to be able to compare the experience of city politics in other military towns across the nation, especially because Seaside's location in the West and particularly in California makes its multicultural, egalitarian character less unusual than a military town located in the South or eastern part of the United States or in a different country.[7] In *Homefront*, Catherine Lutz investigates the mostly negative effects of a nearby military base, both for minorities and women, but not on the workings of city politics in Fayetteville.[8] In his analysis of Columbia, South Carolina, and the bases surrounding this city, Andrew Myers focuses more on the interplay of the military and the city over integration rather than on city government itself.[9] Polly Smith studied segregation practices and racial attitudes in a comparative sociological study of Colorado Springs, New London, and Fayetteville without delving into the day-to-day workings of their respective city governments to see if integrated neighborhoods also led to integrated city councils.[10] There is also a great deal of scholarship on the effects of American military bases on communities internationally, beginning with Cynthia Enloe's excellent work in 1990, *Bananas, Beaches, and Bases*, and on racial intermarriage between soldiers and so-called war brides, but these literatures mostly tell a story of exploitation or conflict, rather than the individual histories of the military-related towns and communities themselves.[11] This chapter addresses that process and illustrates how integration on base played out in city life and politics in Seaside in the 1950s.

CHANGING IDEOLOGIES OF RACE
IN THE POSTWAR MILITARY

Analyses both in military-sponsored studies and independent academic work indicate that the military policy of integration may have affected military towns in important ways. For example, in 1966 noted sociologist Charles C. Moskos Jr. compared two military studies about the attitudes of soldiers with regard to race and integration. One study, reported in *The American Soldier*, was conducted in 1943 and the other, Project Clear, was conducted in 1951. Both studies were carried out within a racially segregated military in the throes of desegregation. He compared these findings to his own studies in 1965 regarding racial attitudes. What he found was startling. According to Moskos, in a few years (1943–1951), integration alone had a powerfully positive impact on all soldiers, blacks and whites (which included everyone not designated as black). This result, he argued, was even more dramatic by 1965. Moskos concluded that the example of the military showed how easily whites and blacks can adjust to "egalitarian race relations with surprisingly little strain." He described the shift in attitude to be "massive," and argued further "That such a change could occur in less than a decade counters viewpoints that see basic social attitudes in large populations being prone to glacial-like changes." Moreover, the official military policy of integrating everything on base from swimming pools to theaters gave all personnel, and especially their families, many opportunities to interact, which he argued, had the effect of changing attitudes about other races even more quickly.[12] Moskos clearly overemphasized the positive effects of mandated integration and minimized the racial tensions and conflicts that continued to occur in the military despite integration orders. He also does not consider that people may hold racist attitudes, but behave otherwise when they are in a situation, such as part of the military organization, that requires tolerance. However, his conclusion that military personnel and their families were generally more tolerant of racial and cultural difference than the rest of

American society is intriguing, and it is also supported by numerous other studies and this analysis of Seaside.[13]

Military towns throughout the country were models of how people of different races can live and work together without this diversity always leading to open conflict. Colorado Springs, Colorado; Fayetteville, South Carolina; New London, Connecticut; and Seaside, California, were all places, and there were many others, where a critical mass of military families infused their respective communities with the attitudes and values that were part of military life.[14] Military families were deeply patriotic, respectful of authority, advocates of family values, but tended to be liberal in their views on racial equality and social justice. For example, according to Moskos, they were more likely than other Americans to consider poor people the victims of circumstance rather than wholly responsible for their condition. This description could also be applied to African American and other activists in the civil rights movement of the 1950s and early 1960s, whose ranks were filled mostly with middle-class blacks, whites, Mexican Americans, and Asian Americans.[15]

Military people, on the other hand, tended also to be people who were used to forming relationships quickly and had traveled extensively, both in the United States and in Europe and Asia. As experienced travelers, they tended not to view cultural or racial differences as problematic, but as the norm. Although they shared with other Americans racial ideologies that privileged whiteness, they were thrust into a completely integrated world on base by the 1950s, an environment that challenged those ideologies head-on.[16] Ruthie Watts, a prominent civil rights activist in Seaside who was born and raised in the Jim Crow South, first expressed a sense of wonderment when she and her husband were stationed in Japan in the mid-1950s. Wonderment soon gave way to acceptance of integrated life as the new normal, however, as white, Asian, and black wives of military personnel came together for social events, family dinners, and both formal and casual get-togethers.[17]

Seaside, along with every other military town in the country, experienced this radical shift toward integration firsthand. Military towns throughout the United States mirrored the bases they were attached to, and as a result, set an example for the ways in which integration could work to create community, not chaos, as so many Americans had feared in the early days the of civil rights movement.[18] One did not have to look to the South or to northern cities such as Chicago for evidence of fierce resistance and violence on the part of whites when black families committed the simple act of moving into an all white neighborhood. In areas such as Phoenix, for example, Lincoln and Eleanor Ragsdale and their children experienced terrible threats, open hostility, and ostracism simply for wanting to leave the poorer (and black) part of the city for a nicer neighborhood and better schools in the white area. Josh Sides and others who studied the experience of African Americans in post–World War II Los Angeles found similar instances of violence when blacks challenged racial segregation in neighborhoods and schools.[19]

According to multiple studies on military life, integration itself allowed for better understanding across racial lines. Blacks began to express more understanding about class disparities among whites and to feel a confidence about their own abilities that most of their peers outside the military could not, given the highly discriminatory nature of postwar America, which effectively kept most African Americans out of the mainstream economy.[20] In spite of continued racial prejudice within the military, African Americans after 1948 now had an opportunity to rise in the ranks according to their respective abilities, as barriers to success based solely on race were systematically eliminated.[21] White enlisted soldiers had to accept black officers as well as black comrades in war zones like Korea.[22] They did not always do so willingly, especially soldiers from the south, even finding clever ways to avoid saluting black officers. However, interviews with white former military personnel uniformly suggested acceptance rather than resistance:

I'm white and observed no conflict between races at Ft Ord or any other military installations on which I served: Ft Leonard Wood, MO, Ft. Gordon, GA, Lackland AFB, TX and Ft Richardson, AK. Many NCO's and a few officers were black and we got along fine. Some of the best drill instructors were of minority races. I agree with your statement that the Army model of integration was ahead of American society as a whole . . . In the stateside Army of the late '60's, race did not matter.[23]

Of course race always mattered, but the point made by Tom Namvedt cited here and other military people of all races is that the remarkable aspect of military life in the 1950s through the 1970s is that race became less and less a barrier that separated whites and nonwhites. For Seasiders with military backgrounds, which included almost all of the city's population, interacting across racial divides was a norm they learned in the military and an expectation many carried out in politics and in daily contact within their multiracial city, whatever their personal racial beliefs or values. The integrationist mandate of military life manifested in the civilian life of Seaside was often confronted and contested by the long held racial attitudes of some city leaders and residents, especially in the rest of the Monterey Peninsula. Yet these tensions between racial exclusion and integration were ameliorated as the forces of inclusion won out over time.

Although there were opportunities for interracial social activity in Seaside, this did not mean that blacks, whites, Asian Americans, or Latinos always socialized together, or even liked one another, although they certainly did interact more than was common at the time in most communities. Groups continued to form race-based and ethnic clubs and organizations. However, in this multiracial, multicultural environment, they also demonstrated, both in politics and in social life, that they saw each other as roughly equal members of society and not as racially defined groups. The political battles fought in the construction of the city had advocates of all races on all sides, with an expectation of equality and participation across racial lines that was striking. Most importantly, the lack of strong racial identity politics did not preclude the formation of city identity. In fact, it enhanced it.

POSTWAR SEASIDE

In stark contrast to Seaside, cities elsewhere in California in the postwar period were racially segregated. Albert Broussard, Quintard Taylor, Richard White, Mark Wild, and many other scholars have described how segregation of minorities throughout California in the early part of the twentieth century resulted in multicultural neighborhoods, which contained several different racial minority groups as most whites lived in their homogenous enclaves.[24] The multiracial spaces that developed in the early part of the century took a sharp turn toward separatism after World War II when the mass migration of new minorities, especially blacks from the South, created communities that were all-black or all-Asian. Groups formed racially based organizations to combat increasing discrimination and hostility by whites fearful of the new population of minorities. Sometimes blacks and Asians worked together to overturn a specific piece of discriminatory legislation through the courts, but it was through racially based organizations such as the Japanese American Citizens League (JACL) and the NAACP rather than free-flowing and constantly fluctuating coalitions based on ideology or policy, which were the norm in Seaside in the postwar years.[25]

In Seaside, because of its close connection and proximity to Fort Ord, racially diverse neighborhoods that were common everywhere in the 1920s and 1930s persisted and even increased throughout the twentieth century. Moreover, Seaside's diversity also included multiracial families, many of which were white (or Asian) and black. The military families that continued to arrive in the decades after World War II included a variety of ethnicities and racial groups as well as multiracial families, replenishing a diverse community. These families were far less likely to identify with one racial group to the exclusion of others. Their presence in Seaside, in and of itself, ran counter to the formation of a strong racial identity politics.

As Seaside organized into an incorporated city, it was natural for its residents to assume that everyone wanted to be included in the process of governing regardless of race. This is not to suggest that there was no racism. Racist attitudes and practices of segregation were prevalent in Monterey County and in Seaside, but racial ideologies were constantly challenged by both the vigorous work of national civil rights actions well publicized throughout the country and the weight of integration and equality at Fort Ord. Even when people held fast to racist beliefs, it did not prevent different people in Seaside from working together in the common purpose of creating a functional, modern city. The same sensibility that allowed white enlisted men to accept the authority of black officers in this period also allowed a still substantial white population in Seaside to accept black leadership on the city council and on important commissions.

Military towns such as Seaside had the best chance of making integration work.

Bolstered as they were by the new power of the civil rights movement nationally, the integration of military bases and the insistence of fair treatment for black soldiers on base made it that much easier to drive integration and civil rights efforts off base. As Moskos and so many others have found, integration itself may have helped change attitudes because individual relationships softened rigid group identities across color lines.[26]

Bursting with possibilities in 1954, the new city of Seaside was, in many ways, like other California municipalities that were transformed in the post-World War II decades. The postwar years in the "Golden State" brought new prosperity and spurred tremendous growth in cities while attracting a new stream of people seeking sunshine, jobs, and a better way of life in California's expanding suburbs. The changes in the local population of Seaside from the mid-1950s through the mid-1970s also reflected some of the demographic changes affecting other California cities such as San Jose, Oakland, San Francisco and its East Bay suburbs, and Los Angeles and its suburbs. The war and its aftermath ushered in, among other developments, a significant increase in the number of ethnic and racial minorities, a trend that accelerated after 1970, leading eventually to the formation of many "minority-majority" cities by the late twentieth century. Seaside by the late 1970s had joined the ranks of these so-called "Cities of Color." In a 1981 article in the *Seaside Post-News Sentinel*, community development director Harold Comacho announced that based on new 1980 census data Seaside's combined minority population had surpassed whites.[27]

The critical difference between Seaside and most other emerging minority-majority cities and towns in California, however, besides the profound influence of the military, was that it was multiracial in the fullest sense. By contrast, in Oakland, for example, white elites had been entrenched for decades, and African Americans, Mexican Americans, and other minorities had to organize within powerful racial and ethnic organizations in order to enter the local political arena.[28] In a different example, the fragile coalitions built by blacks, Jews, Mexicans, and Asians in the postwar and Cold War eras in Los Angeles had broken down by the time of the Watts riots in 1965 and quickly transformed many central Los

Angeles suburbs, such as Compton, Lynwood, South Gate, and Monterey Park into cities of color with sharply divided communities of blacks and Latinos in Compton, Lynnwood, and South Gate, and Asians and Latinos in Monterey Park.[29] Newly arriving white San Joseans determined to fuel the economic boom of new industry in the emerging Silicon Valley pushed Mexicans out of the city altogether and into a segregated section of East San Jose, maintaining white hegemony. Mexican Americans there formed themselves into organizations such as the Community Service Organization (CSO) to gain political power and to give their community the social services that they needed.[30] In nearby Salinas during the same period, Mexican Americans conflicted with wealthy growers over labor issues and political inclusion and were also restricted in housing to the least desirable neighborhoods of East Salinas.[31]

Although the history of Seaside shares common features with these and other California cities and towns in the post-World War II era, it stands out from the larger patterns of suburban development because whites, blacks, Mexican Americans, and Asian Americans always had to work closely with one another or little could get accomplished in the city, politically or otherwise. Although racial politics played a critical role in the history of the city, it never defined boundaries in the absolute way it did in most other places. Multiracial coalitions existed in Seaside since the 1950s and in ways that were quite different from other municipalities. Also important, Seasiders were always keenly aware of the natural beauty of their community, the ocean views, and weather that surpassed that of the other Peninsula towns, thus offering great potential for development. This is very different from the squalid areas of cities where blacks and other minorities had to live in Oakland, Salinas, San Jose, Los Angeles, or San Francisco, or even in other parts of the West, such as in Phoenix, for example, places where the middle class and upper class among them could not wait to escape when civil rights legislation made it possible to do so.[32]

OPPORTUNITY FOR CHANGE

Seaside's relationship with Fort Ord was always ambiguous, especially after the end of World War II. Although Seasiders shared a common bond with the military installation and generally viewed it as an asset, they also resented almost everything that came with being so closely associated with a huge army base. Early on, Seasiders were torn between contesting the new military population and embracing it. There were repeated efforts by the city over time to outlaw gambling, get tough on prostitution, close bars that soldiers frequented, and generally eliminate everything negatively associated with the army population, even as Seasiders incorporated the military into parades, clubs, and events in the city.[33] The Municipal Code for the City of Seaside enacted in 1958 included an entire chapter of fifty rules on "Morals and Conduct," fifteen of which addressed the issue of prostitution alone.[34]

These negative aspects of being an army town were noticeable in other military towns across the country. But what was less obvious was the transformation in racial interactions that were quickly taking place on base and that had repercussions off base as well. In a vivid account of his life as the son of a military officer who became actively involved in redevelopment issues in Seaside, Carl Williams, a staff member for Seaside Redevelopment Agency in 1965, recalled the effect of the integration order on military bases in the 1950s:

My Dad was a career army person called into service during the Korean Conflict . . . He decided to remain in the service because, as he told me, there were more opportunities in the military [for African Americans] . . . This was in the '50s. My Dad was stationed at that time at Fort Lee Virginia in Petersburg. When Dad got transferred to Fort Lee we lived in town in Petersburg—segregation was the rule of the day there—the schools were segregated even after Brown vs. Board of Education . . . Eventually we were able to live on the military base. There was no segregation by race on the military base. Swimming pools. All . . . facilities were available on an equal, nondiscriminatory basis since Truman's edict. But there were no schools on a military base so when we went to the schools in town—we would be bused to the black school and the white students would be bused to the white schools. In terms of social activities— I would invite my friends to come to the military base to see movies, go swimming. I didn't make a big deal of it. But I can remember getting out of the car and my friends said "Wait a minute there are white people swimming!" I do remember having a lot of conversations with my white and black friends—the whites said "This [segregation] is really stupid. Why do we have to do this?"

Carl Williams was also actively involved in the civil rights movement of midcentury. As a young man, he climbed out of his bedroom window in the middle of the night to join civil rights actions in the South, much to his mother's dismay. His parents had forbidden him from going to the South, insisting that they came to Seaside purposefully to avoid the dangers of life in the South for blacks during the civil rights era.[35]

In another example of the ways in which an integrated army bolstered the civil rights movement, Pearl Carey, whom Carl Williams described as "Seaside's Rosa Parks, Martin Luther King—everyone was embodied in that woman," struggled to find housing in Seaside after her arrival in 1952 as a military wife.[36] On the base, however, this was not an issue, as Carey lived among whites. "My husband was a Master Sergeant," she recalled, "We lived in an apartment complex with officers. Of course many of them were white. There was a white family that lived right upstairs from us."[37] The stark difference between equality on base and segregation in town inspired her, and many others, to work for change. "It made me determined to live where I wanted to live, to change things," she said.[38]

Morris and Bobbie McDaniel first came to Seaside in 1959 when he was a Second Lieutenant stationed at Fort Ord. "I was partial to living on military installations," McDaniels reflected, "It's a different world unto itself. It's a protected world. To a large extent it was protected from racism—it wasn't tolerated. People could hold whatever feelings they wanted but their actions were subject to review."[39] Here McDaniels expressed the basic truth about the impact of the military on the civil rights movement at midcentury. The military was not attempting to change hearts and minds so much as rules and behavior. However, there was great power in changed rules and behavior in and of itself that may have led more quickly to changes in hearts and minds as a result. For example, the McDaniels had trouble finding an apartment to rent off base. McDaniel recalled, "It was the first incidence of discrimination I felt here." They were finally able to move into an apartment in Monterey with the help of a fellow lieutenant who was white and who, the McDaniel's remembered, "had heard we were having trouble." This was one of many instances of white military personnel stepping in to help a fellow soldier overcome discrimination, just as many white liberals assisted blacks overcome housing discrimination in civilian life.

Many African Americans like Carl Williams and Pearl Carey, as well as whites who experienced integrated life at Fort Ord and other military bases across the country, began to question and contest the discriminatory practices they experienced in civilian life. Of course, the national civil rights movement was in full force in the 1950s, and the important "race work" that black women and men were carrying on would soon result in legislation that changed race relations in this country in a fundamental way. The landmark *Brown v. Board of Education* outlawed school segregation. One year later, Rosa Parks's refusal to sit at the back of the bus initiated the famous Montgomery Bus Boycotts. College students began lunch counter sit-ins in Greensboro, North Carolina, which led to the formation of the Student Nonviolent Coordinating Committee (SNCC) in 1960. And in 1961, SNCC and the Congress of Racial Equality (CORE) began Freedom Rides throughout the South. Like Carl Williams and Pearl Carey, Seasiders were bolstered and emboldened on the twin fronts of the national civil rights movement and their life experiences in an integrated military. They strengthened the civil rights movement in places like the Monterey Peninsula, particularly in Seaside, when the sheer number of soldiers and families affected by the Truman order became a force to be reckoned with. Their views collided head-on with life in Monterey County, which was, like most of California and the nation in the 1950s, a region that reflected exclusions based on race, including segregated neighborhoods.

RACE AND SPACE IN MONTEREY COUNTY

According to Nellie Parker Lewis, the Pacific Grove Branch of the NAACP was formed at the First Baptist Church of Pacific Grove in February 1927. This chapter later became known as the Monterey Peninsula Branch of the NAACP, located in Seaside. Evelyn Smith remembered that her husband, Reverend Wellington Smith, was a strong proponent of the NAACP. She stated that sometime in the early 1930s, her husband and a "white politician went to a diner on Tyler Street [Monterey] to remove a sign prohibiting service to blacks . . . the local NAACP included white members . . . there was prejudice here that needed attending to."[40]

The African Americans who settled in Monterey County in the 1950s not only experienced painful consequences of racism, but also had first-hand evidence of the possibilities of racial equality. As black veterans and their families settled in Seaside, they began to push the boundaries of the "color line" throughout the county. By the late1950s, the NAACP in Seaside was already actively challenging hiring practices by white business owners and discrimination in the educational system and, most importantly, influencing politics throughout the region.[41] African Americans in Seaside were generally well educated, well traveled, and in a position to create an environment that allowed them to be fully vested as citizens, just like other African Americans who were engaged in "race work" throughout the West.[42] The difference was that Seaside was brand new and military. Challenging discrimination was never an easy task, anywhere, but the expansion of Seaside and its struggle to incorporate offered black activists far more opportunity to make change than if they had lived in long-established towns or cities, where exclusionary politics based on race were firmly established.

Racism was insidious, omnipresent, and institutionalized at the national, state, and local levels in the United States in the first half of the twentieth century, at least until unprecedented civil rights era legislation ended the worst forms of public discrimination in schools, housing, and employment in the mid-1960s. Race relations in California went beyond black and white; Mexicans and also Asians were subject to discriminatory practices.[43] The color line often determined where (and if), you could buy or rent a home, where you went to school, where you attended church, where you were employed, and which public accommodations you were allowed to enter. In a letter to the editor of the *Salinas Californian* in October 1943, Manuel C. Jímenez described how he and his friends were consistently denied service in restaurants and bars in Monterey County: "If a Latin American asks for a 7-Up or a bottle of pop [restaurant owners and patrons] will bark at you: 'We don't serve Mexicans and don't ask why.'" Mr. Jímenez condemned this behavior as "Hitlerism" adding

"If you were an American of Mexican descent you'd wonder about many things, yes even about democracy." He traced his lineage to the Aztecs: "My father is of Aztec blood, and my Aztec ancestors were in this country long before any European landed at Plymouth Rock. And now I am told I am not an American. [Racial] discrimination is all right in a Nazi country, but not in democratic America."[44]

Filipinos also experienced racial discrimination, and their prevalence in California made them targets of violence. Emerson Reyes, past president of the Fil-Am Club of Seaside remembered that "Filipinos were not allowed to own property or marry whites through the 1950s. There were even some riots. When a Filipino boy tried to court a white girl [during the 1950s], the whites from Monterey came to the Filipino Clubhouse on El Estero Street in Monterey and started a fight with Filipino men. In Watsonville [in the same decade], the Fil-Am Club was bombed by the whites who disapproved the relationship between a Filipino boy and a white girl . . . but in Seaside because it was a military community these things didn't happen."[45] Clearly, Reyes, himself an army veteran and political activist in Seaside, saw the direct impact of military racial values in Seaside, which accepted racial difference as normal, in stark contrast elsewhere in Monterey county, such as in Salinas which experienced racial violence between whites and Mexicans during this period.

When Ralph Carey was assigned to Fort Ord in 1952, as part of the newly integrated United States army, Pearl Carey remembered:

We were very excited to know that we were going to be stationed in California, thinking that we would not face any more racism or unfair treatment. To our amazement, I found that [people in California, especially employers] were illiberal, closed minded and intolerant to minorities, most especially to black people . . . during this period of time there were very, very few hotels or motels that were user friendly to black people so we had no choice but to sleep in our car as we had done in the 1940s in the South. We were very surprised because we had heard that California had no racial barriers. Not So![46]

She, like so many other African American residents of Seaside who were part of the civil rights movement and also part of the military migration, had high hopes that the inequality and discrimination so prevalent throughout the country was coming to an end. They were poised to make that dream a reality in Seaside.

"I can say there is less racial prejudice on the Peninsula [than in Texas]," claimed Reverend Joseph S. Sutton, who first came to California in 1948 to conduct revival meetings and stayed to become pastor of the Friendship Baptist Church. "But there is some. It is felt especially in real estate—in trying to rent houses. People will say that they personally don't object, but that they don't believe that their neighbors would like a Negro family on the block."[47] Reverend Nance, who arrived in Pacific Grove in 1956, recalled, "I know blacks who moved to Seaside in the 1950s because in Monterey, Carmel, Pacific Grove they were BLOCKED. Seaside was surrounded by people who had fences up as far as blacks were concerned. Here in Pacific Grove nonwhites were blocked into an area. You hardly got closer to the beach than Lighthouse and you couldn't live beyond Congress Avenue."[48]

Racially restrictive covenants were commonly used in Monterey County and even in Seaside by the time of incorporation in 1954. They were supported by white homeowners and realtors who held fast to them in spite of new federal policy and the Supreme Court ruling in *Shelley v. Kraemer* that rendered their enforcement illegal after 1948. Frank Eubanks arrived at Fort Ord in 1953 to enroll in Arabic at the Defense Language School in Monterey. He wanted very much to live in Monterey but discovered that the entire Peninsula was rigidly segregated. "I found that the Real Estate Board of Monterey County controlled where you lived" he remembered and, "I tried to find realtors to sell me a house in Monterey and nobody would show me anything outside of Seaside between Military Avenue and Ord Grove." By the time Mr. Eubanks finally bought a home in Monterey (with the surreptitious help of a white Seaside realtor, Adeline DiLorenzo), he claimed that "There were only four other black families in Monterey. Everyone else was in Seaside."[49] In fact, Monterey (and Pacific Grove) included more than just four black families, but his perception that blacks had centered in Seaside in this period was accurate.

According to one observer in the mid-1950s, "New subdivisions coming into Seaside have safe-guarded themselves as much as possible with deed restrictions, and 143 homes soon to be built around Kimball Avenue in various tracts will be a far cry from Seaside's traditional mixed atmosphere."[50] More generally on the Monterey Peninsula, title company records consistently show evidence of deed restrictions through 1964 that excluded everyone considered nonwhite. Under the heading "Covenants and Conditions," for example, the Del Monte Properties company routinely included the following clause, "Said premises shall not, nor shall any part thereof, or any improvements thereon at any time be occupied or used by Asiatics, Negroes, or any person born in the Turkish Empire, nor any lineal descendant of such person, except that persons of said races may be employed as household servants."[51] This boilerplate restriction by race in real estate deeds excluded Jews and Asians (including Filipinos) as well as African Americans by race from all of Pebble Beach and Carmel, most of Monterey, and some parts of Pacific Grove, as well as in specific neighborhoods in Seaside. For example, Bessie Kramer, a white woman who ran unsuccessfully for city council in 1954, described Ord Terrace, a subdivision located in the Seaside highlands adjacent to Fort Ord:

[Developers of Ord Terrace] found ready buyers. With each lot went a copy of the deed restrictions to which the property is subject. A most attractive community was planned if these deed restrictions were respected . . . Of course there are always the recalcitrant few who like to break the rules just to see if they can be done. Then there are those who do not know them or do not quite understand them. To see that the deed restrictions were carried out and to do everything possible for the betterment of the community, the Ord Terrace Property Owners Association was formed. The first official meeting was held May 4, 1948 . . . Ord Terrace is a pleasant community, a part of Seaside, yet a little off to itself on its clean gently sloping hill out in the sunshine.[52]

The "Declaration of Establishment of Protective Restrictions" for Ord Terrace that Kramer referred to included sixteen different restrictions. Number eight applied to race.[53] This Seaside-specific restrictive covenant apparently opened Ord Terrace to Jews and southern Europeans, while the countywide covenants included Jews together with blacks as excluded races. This conformed to new alliances between Asians and whites in the 1950s and 1960s intended to open up formerly white neighborhoods to Asians at the expense of blacks.[54] By 1959, when the Lee family moved

to Seaside, Asians lived in mostly white communities, but blacks continued to be excluded from some neighborhoods. According to Anna and
Charles Lee:

We bought our house in Seaside in 1959. It took us a whole year to decide where
to live—here or Salinas. Salinas had a big population of Cantonese whereas in
Monterey it was Mandarin. We had to think of the school, the weather. Seaside
was a small town in 1959. It was convenient for the kids' schools. They were
all different ages and all of their schools were nearby. There were lots of blacks
in the schools then. The weather was better and for us and my front door was
never locked. I felt we were safe. There were mostly blacks but there were probably more Filipinos than Chinese and Japanese. There were lots of war brides.
Mostly our friends were Caucasian. This was a white neighborhood with us and
the Filipinos. From San Pablo and over were more blacks.[55]

Her comment is striking because most observers would not view her
neighborhood as "white" if it included Filipinos and Chinese, but as multiracial. In Seaside, however, even neighborhoods that included several
white families also included people who would be considered nonwhite.
Estela McKenzie, who is Filipino, remembered real estate agents showing
houses to Filipino families in all areas of Seaside, including neighborhoods
designated for whites only. "We were free to choose to live wherever we
wanted," stated Estela and Patrick McKenzie, "It wasn't racial. It was
whatever we could afford."[56]

Restrictive covenants and deeds that regulated sales of property by race
were hardly unique to Monterey County. Throughout America, almost
everywhere minorities came to settle, white homeowners associations, real
estate boards, and residents worked to exclude them and to force them
into specific residential areas. In some cases minorities were excluded
from certain cities altogether.[57] The federal government was complicit in
maintaining racial exclusions when in 1938, the Homeowners Loan Corporation (HOLC), later known as the Federal Housing Authority (FHA)
sent staff to major metropolitan areas in order to determine the suitabil-
ity of locations where government loans were made to individuals. Field
workers used race even more than economic factors as markers to decide
which cities and neighborhoods would be rated most favorably to receive

home loans and which would be "redlined." Redlined areas were usually excluded from the government funding that gave millions of families access to middle-class life through home ownership.[58]

However, in Seaside, redlining and segregation were practices in direct conflict with the integration that occurred on base and were challenged by military people of all races, especially during the 1960s when the civil rights movement reinforced the integration model that the military had established, leading to federal legislation mandating integration and equal rights. The policies that the military created regarding integration and civil rights was in support of and consistent with the goals of national civil rights movements. In communities throughout the country, and especially in the West, housing discrimination was one of the first and most important battles those civil rights activists, who had no connection to the military at all, fought and won.[59] Seaside civil rights activists had a formidable ally and model in their close association with an integrated military that their counterparts in other towns and cities did not have. The first step in breaking down racial barriers in Seaside, however, was not in demonstrations against housing restrictions but in making sure that city government was truly representative of its multiracial population.

CITY POLITICS 1954–1976

The army's decision to make Fort Ord the center of its policy of racial integration occurred during the years when Seaside was being transformed from subdivision to city. These two simultaneous developments created the perfect opportunity for proponents of civil rights to fulfill the ideal of equal representation in government that the movement promised. Fort Ord gave Seaside a continuing stream of well-educated, worldly, and sophisticated people, particularly of African Americans, who were closely connected to the national civil rights movement and greatly influenced by all that was going on in the country at the time. These were people who had experienced instant integration firsthand. They were prepared to enter local politics and to create a new kind of local government based on principles of integration and fairness but also dependent on coalition building among various groups. Seaside's sizeable population of diverse whites and Asian Americans were less tolerant of racism than the general civilian population at this time, going so far as to elect blacks and other minorities to the city council and mayor's office, hire blacks and other minorities in staff positions in city government, and support the appointment of blacks and other minorities to powerful commissions. Most importantly, when whites—and sometimes Filipinos—did express a sense of privilege or superiority in governing, they were met with loud and effective resistance by blacks, other whites, and other minority groups who did not allow the ideology of white superiority to persist.

Seaside was officially recognized as a city on October 13, 1954. On the same day, the new all-white city council—including George T. (Sarge) Cunningham, Joe Cota, Jack Oldemeyer, George Pollack, and Dr. John Craige—met "before a capacity audience" at the Seaside Youth Center to choose a mayor, showing that the new citizens of Seaside were active and passionately interested in politics.[60] Oldemeyer was elected with a 3–2 margin. The composition of the first city council, which did not include any minority members stimulated the emerging population of African Americans to form organizations with others and mobilize for the next election scheduled for 1956 to ensure that minorities would be represented in city government. There was no question that Seasiders were not going to continue to accept a city council that did not reflect the realities of the multiracial and ethnic composition of the city.

The years 1955 and 1956 were fraught with controversy on the city council and, according to an analysis by the *Seaside Post-News Sentinel*, "political turmoil . . . and continuous uproar" characterized council proceedings.[61] City council members "Sarge" Cunningham, Joe Cota, and Jack Oldemeyer with the backing of City Attorney Saul Weingarten, who was Jewish, and African Americans such as Homer Spann, John Bean, and Richard Joyce, were eager to begin the process of transforming Seaside from "a shack town" into a proper city with housing developments and commercial growth that would attract a new middle class and catapult Seaside into prominence, equal to if not surpassing the economies of the other Peninsula cities, especially rival Monterey.[62] Black ministers in Seaside also supported the effort to build the city, as they expanded congregations and came together as a political force in the form of the Ministerial Alliance organized in 1948. Seaside became a city in the con-

CREATING AN INTEGRATED SEASIDE AFTER THE WAR

text of huge civil rights gains in the country, as shown earlier. In addition, the farmworkers movement in nearby Salinas was gearing up in the early 1960s, especially with the 1965 Delano grape strike that involved many Filipino Seaside residents.

All of the promotional literature about Seaside in this era depicts Seaside residents as white, a community of small families and homeowners rather than as a military town of multiracial families who were largely transitory residents. However, for these leaders to have done anything else would have been economic suicide. Investment money, from the federal government as well as local developers, depended upon a perception of white homogeneity. There were enough whites in Seaside to make that argument and to resist the characterization of the city as a multiracial military town.[63] Blacks objected, but did not openly confront whites on the issue. Lenora Bean recounted, "We weren't too happy about that because we lived here too. My husband didn't like it. But there was so much going on in those days."[64]

The city council also needed the economic boost that Fort Ord gave them, so city council members could never go too far in condemning it, and usually worked with, rather than in opposition to, military personnel to control crime and drugs. Almost all of the politicians in Seaside, like the rest of the community, had some connection to Fort Ord, a relationship that increased in the next two decades. "The army is pretty important to us around here," said John Landis, Seaside's Chief of Police in 1956, in something of an understatement. "I think we ought to do everything we can to work with them." With that he initiated a program to include military police on city patrols.[65]

An examination of city council meeting minutes for the 1950s and 1960s showed increasing bitterness over the way the city council operated as well as tension over the policy disputes about development, demonstrating that Seaside residents were not going to tolerate politics as usual. The council in these years seemed to be more of an "old boys club" rather than a serious political entity. Robert's Rules of Order were routinely ignored, and city council members met out of chambers regularly, even daily, to make decisions about all aspects of city government. Former Mayor Lou

Haddad, who was eventually recalled and ostracized in Seaside, remembered the "coffee club," which never included minorities:

We had a group that met at the 726 Club on Fremont [now the site of a Mexican Restaurant, La Tortuga] for coffee every morning at 10:00 o'clock . . . the coffee club was made up of council members, former council members, the mayor, former mayors, planning commissioners and others who apparently ran the town to decide policy.[66]

The 726 Club was a curious choice of locale for policy meetings. It was a nightclub, not a restaurant or coffee house. Nonetheless, the behind the scenes meetings reflected some of the Seaside City Council's casual and covert approach to city government, which was challenged directly by council member George Pollack who was recalled in a special election one year later.

The conflicts at city hall came to a head in 1955 as Mayor Oldemeyer and Police Chief John S. Davis clashed in an episode that revealed a new racial climate emerging in Seaside. Mayor Oldemeyer had long accused Police Chief Davis of corruption. Mayor Oldemeyer claimed that the police chief allowed and even promoted vice in Seaside. According to Oldemeyer there was "an effort underway to bring organized vice and gambling into Seaside . . . an underworld group manipulated the appointment of the present chief of police in order to protect gambling interests and 'open up' Seaside."[67] For his part, Chief Davis was "in possession of an affidavit accusing Oldemeyer of making anti-Negro remarks."[68] This was in reference to Clayton Mosely, the first African American police officer hired in the entire Monterey Peninsula area. Cecil Bindel, a white business owner in Seaside and labor chairman for the NAACP, approached Chief Davis in 1955 and recalled: "I told him I felt it would make things nicer if there were black police officers on the force. He agreed and asked me if I knew of any qualified blacks. I recommended Clayton Mosely."[69] Mosely served on the Seaside police force from 1955 until his death in 1964.

During the November 3, 1955, meeting of the city council, African American ministers in Seaside weighed in on the debate over the police department and sent a collective letter "commending [both] the Councilmen and the Seaside Police Department." It was signed by the first members of the Alliance, Reverends Ş. R. Martin, W. W. Wells, J. J. Tyler, Marvin D. Slade, J. W. Paige, G. E. Ellis, and T. C. Broach.[70] Although the ministers did not take sides (despite Oldemeyer's racist views), their cautious response was in keeping with the general pragmatism and centrism in Seaside that was part and parcel of black middle-class political sensibilities of the times and of a military point of view that did not challenge authority directly.[71] Their statement also showed that they viewed themselves as important actors in Seaside politics, even placing themselves above the political fray. On January 19, Mayor Oldemeyer dismissed Davis, two police sergeants, and Georgia Robinson, the police department secretary. Patrolman Harry Landis was immediately named the new Seaside Police Chief. Landis served as police chief for five months and was replaced by Raymond R. Rude (1956–1959). Lee Pilcher, who served as Chief from 1959 to 1964, hired the first African American woman, Ira Threadgill Lively, as a juvenile officer who went on to become a city council member herself.[72]

In any other city in California or in the country in 1955, "anti-Negro remarks" by a mayor may have been tolerable, perhaps even acceptable to residents, even though the civil rights movement was coming into its own throughout California and the nation.[73] In Seaside, however, the response to Davis's accusation of racial bias on the mayor's part was immediate and focused the attention of the entire community on the machinations of city government. Oldemeyer lost the next election and retired from politics. Ironically, in the 1980s, when Seasiders built a community center and were deciding on a name for it, they chose Oldemeyer because he had been the city's first mayor. "We weren't aware of his history," said E. Walker James, a Seaside African American community activist and leader.[74]

The 1956 election was pivotal for Seaside because it was a moment when effective organization based on a commitment to fulfill the promises of integration succeeded. No one group could elect representatives without support from the multiracial populace. There at least had to be tacit agreement that elected officials should look like the people they represented and that all people deserved a place in city government.

According to Reverend Welton McGee who came to Seaside in 1949, "That's when the black ministers were beginning to organize and get the black folks together and vote. That's when we put Monroe Jones on the city council."[75] As a forum for minorities, African Americans formed the Civic Voters League under the leadership of Richard Joyce and Jack Simon on November 12, 1954. Their efforts to elect a black city councilman failed in the 1954 election because, according to Joyce, there were too many blacks running. He argued in 1956 that "if there were two Negro candidates they would split each other's vote and neither would be elected. It happened in 1954 during the incorporation and [the League] wanted to make sure it didn't happen again."[76] However, by 1955 there were not enough black people in Seaside to elect a representative on race alone. Even as late as the 1980s, Mayor Lance McClair insisted, "You can't run for office in Seaside as a black candidate. You've got to represent everybody because there are so many different groups here."[77]

The Civic Voters League elected Richard Joyce as its president in February 1956 and began to prepare for the next election in which all city councilmen, including the mayor, were up for reelection.[78] Three African Americans decided to run for city council. John Bean was a planning commissioner and a member of the conservative Seaside Citizens' Committee for Good Government, which supported the mayor and was responsible for the recall of George Pollack.[79] The Reverend G. E. Ellis, pastor of the Ocean View Baptist Church and resident of Seaside since 1948, also filed for election to city council and vied for the support of the League. Reverend Ellis had supported Pollack in the recall election.[80] Finally, Monroe Jones, a 29-year-old former boxer and head custodian for Del Rey School, also filed to run for the council. He shared a background as an army veteran with the rest of the candidates for city council. He was described as a "soft-voiced man with a talent for political oratory."[81]

More than one hundred members of the mostly black Civic Voters League (CVL), the multiracial women's group, Crusaders for Democracy (CFD), and the mostly white Seaside Democratic Club (SDC) met at Noche Buena School on February 14, 1956. According to SDC President George Pollack, "We want to run three candidates against [Oldemeyer, Craige, and Hambrook] . . . One of them should certainly be a Negro."[82] Although John Bean was the most well known of the candidates and the logical choice, Pollack threatened to withdraw support of the SDC if the

League endorsed him because Bean "circulated a recall petition against me."[83] Yet Pollack's comment dramatically illustrated a new concept in city politics in 1956, when the national civil rights movement was struggling with basic issues like voting rights in most parts of the country. In Seaside, whites, other minorities, women, and blacks expressed a collective belief that city government should not be a white male club but should necessarily include all groups as equal partners on the city council, including blacks and women. This forward thinking view of politics reflected three realities in Seaside. First, its diversity required cooperation and coalition building. Second, the rhetoric and power of the national civil rights movement resonated deeply among a population already accustomed to practicing integration and seeing it modeled successfully at Fort Ord. Finally, Seaside was a new place for all of its residents. No one could claim a powerful or long-established political base. There was no white elite to square off against.

The combined political organizations (CVL, SDC, and CFD) voted to endorse Jones. This was not a bloc of black organizations, nor was it a coalition of minority groups alone. It was a political coalition that included multiple groups of like-minded people who were Asian American (Filipino and Japanese), Hispanic American (Mexican origin), black, and white.

The Citizens Committee for Good Government endorsed Oldemeyer, Craige, and Hambrook at which point John Bean and Reverend Herman Jeffries, pastor of the Lighthouse Full Gospel Church, both charter members of the organization and both African American, resigned in protest. Bean went on to organize the moderate and multiracial Seaside Democrats with a membership of sixty-four.[84] Again, both of these organizations in opposition to CVL, SDC, CFD, and the League were comprised of people of different ethnicities and racial groups who were united in their more conservative political views and support for the mayor.

Most African Americans in Seaside rallied around Jones as a candidate, but as is clear, whites and other minority groups supported him as well. League President Richard Joyce stated forcefully at the February meeting that "[the League] should work to elect a Negro to the council because we make up one third of the city's population . . . this is not a racial issue and we don't want a councilman for the Negroes. We want a councilman

for Seaside who will be concerned about the welfare of all our people."
This statement reflected a clearly defined sense on the part of African
American political activists that Seaside was a community that stood for
fair representation and equality, rather than a community in which one
racial group vied for power at the expense of everyone else. Moreover,
it reflected the military model of equal treatment and full integration.

The African American-led coalition prevailed in 1956 and established
a political benchmark in Seaside history. Joe Cota and "Sarge" Cunningham were returned to the city council, but Oldemeyer, Hambrook, and
Craige were not. Monroe Jones won a city council seat with the fourth
highest number of votes. An article in the *Seaside Call-Bulletin* stated that
Monroe Jones was "one of only two or three Negroes to hold such office
in California, and ran a good fourth against a field of 13 candidates."[85]
Clearly, Seaside voters, whites and minorities together, disapproved of a
city council made up only of white men who had behaved as though they
should govern exclusively.

Two years later, the election results were even more dramatic. By 1958
Jones not only won reelection to the city council but also won with the
highest number of votes and, according to the *Seaside News Sentinel's*
front page headline, "Swept the Field":

Monroe Jones marched to an impressive victory at the polls last night. He ran
almost 150 votes ahead of his nearest competitor, Mrs. Bessie Kramer, and
racked up commanding leads in virtually all of Seaside's 11 voting districts.
Jones, a Negro . . . drew heavy support from all racial and nationality segments
of the community.[86]

Again the emphasis here is that Jones had the support of people who came
from a variety of ethnic and racial groups. Although there were pointed
efforts to organize black people, for example, it was done with a sense
of inclusiveness that was rare in the 1950s. Although Jones remained the
only black member of the city council, his election showed what could
be accomplished when citizens, whites as well as minorities, embraced a
view of politics that was based on integration and egalitarianism rather
than white privilege. This was a sensibility diametrically opposed to racial ideology everywhere else in the nation, or even in California, at the

time, but was clearly the hallmark of the civil rights movement led by Dr. Martin Luther King Jr. This is not to argue that racism evaporated in Seaside. It is to contend that from its inception, the political battles in Seaside showed that this city was moving quickly into a world that looked a lot more like the world of the present in race relations than the one in other urban and suburban communities in California or the rest of the country of the 1950s.

Given that he received the most votes, Jones might have been appointed mayor by the other council members, but according to a contemporary and friend, Reverend Welton McGee, he did not take advantage of it:

Bessie Kramer and [Thomas G.] Dorney [both newly elected to the Council in 1958] offered Monroe the [position of] mayor but he refused. He said it's really Cota's turn. Monroe said that. He refused to be the mayor. But Monroe could've been the mayor back then. That was the worst thing he could've done. They elected Joe Cota mayor.[87]

McGee's extreme disappointment was a testament to an environment in Seaside that gave blacks the highest expectations of representation in government that went far beyond voting rights. Richard Joyce, who acted as campaign manager both times Jones ran for city council, claimed that the other city council members objected to the possibility of a black mayor. Unbeknown to them, Joyce overheard their discussion: "I was in one room listening to Joe Cota, Sarge Cunningham, and Anderson—Monroe Jones name came into play. 'We can't make Monroe Jones mayor pro tem,' [they said]—it's too close to being mayor of the city. What if the mayor should get sick or something—we cannot make him [Monroe Jones] mayor.' That's when they decided the mayor would be elected [separately]. It stayed with me. I'll never forget [their conversation] as long as I live."[88] As in the example of Reverend McGee, the fact that Richard Joyce was appalled, rather than accepting of such values (he was from Texas after all), is noteworthy because it suggests that in Seaside there was an expectation of equality of treatment and fairness that even civil rights advocates in California may not have envisaged in the 1950s.

What is even more interesting is that the two council members advocating Jones for mayor pro tem, Kramer and Dorney, were considered part of a radical fringe centered in the mostly white neighborhood of Ord Terrace. These two individuals opposed the redevelopment projects that the mayor and most people in Seaside supported. On the one hand, racism was blatantly expressed in conversation, as Joyce attested to, and in petitions by Kramer and Dorney to keep parts of Seaside segregated. On the other hand, there was an expectation that everyone, black, white, Latino or Asian, should be part of the city council and able to work together to achieve the city's goals without an underlying racial focal point or purpose. Kramer and Dorney might be racist, but they lobbied Jones to become part of their coalition opposing development and expected to work with him as partners on the city council. This is in stark contrast to what was happening in large metropolitan centers at this time that included a new migration of blacks. These once multiracial urban areas such as Los Angeles and Oakland began to look a lot more like segregated eastern cities by the 1950s. Their city governments tended to exclude minorities, especially blacks, until a decade or two later.[89]

Jones supported the mayor on the issue of urban renewal and redevelopment in Seaside, however, and soon made enemies of both Kramer and Dornan. Jones stood with the rest of the more conservative city council members on most issues. When Pat Patterson came before the city council and accused the planning commissioners of not knowing any more about Seaside "than a pig does about astronomy" and claiming to speak "for the people of Seaside," Jones, not the mayor, spoke for the city council: "Patterson can't speak for the people. They won't have him. Twice the people of Seaside have refused to elect him to the city council." At which point, Jones threatened to walk out of the meeting if Patterson did not sit down. "This is not Little Rock," Patterson blurted out in a strange reference to the famous civil rights action in Arkansas. Mayor Cota had Patterson ejected by Police Chief Rude at Jones's behest and over the objections of Kramer and Dorney.[90] The following summer in 1959 both Kramer and Dorney were recalled from the city council and replaced by white conservative army veteran and Medal of Honor winner Beauford "Andy" Anderson (who was Seaside's mayor from 1960 to 1964).[91] Anderson was followed in office by John Pattulo (1964–1966) and Lou Haddad (1966–1972), a Lebanese immigrant. All were army veterans who had once been stationed at Fort Ord.

COMMUNITY IDENTITY

The politics of inclusion that Seaside citizens demanded from the very first years of incorporation was reinforced by a variety of city events, clubs, and organizations that reflected both the values of the military and a multiracial and multicultural spirit of the new city. The Seaside Arts Commission, organized in 1956, promoted culture in Seaside, organizing awards competitions for arts and crafts throughout the year. Amy Stuart, one of the first presidents of the ArtsCommission, was responsible for collecting historical documents, photographs, and artifacts for display, encouraging civic pride and community activism. Her collection, which spans the 1940s through the 1980s, is a treasure and includes her own opinions on the tumultuous politics of the city, especially in the early years of incorporation.[92]

The local newspapers reported Red Cross drives and a variety of fundraisers to benefit everything from schools to after school youth programs, the library, and the beautification of the community. The Kiwanis, Lions, Jaycees, and Rotary Club all formed chapters in Seaside dedicated to the betterment of the community. They raised money to support beautifying their community, including a "Welcome to Seaside" sign. The American Legion had a post in Seaside as did the Veterans of Foreign Wars. Many other less well-known clubs were also organized, including the Quota Club and the Whiskerinos (a social organization common in California communities organized around people with beards and facial hair). The clubs came together to organize Seaside's biggest event of the year—the Fourth of July parade. Floats, bands, drill teams, and large numbers of people from Fort Ord made up crowds of as many as 20,000 people to watch and celebrate Independence Day in Seaside. Seaside participated as a community in other Peninsula area events as well. In 1954, the Seaside float won grand prize in Monterey's Santa Rosalia Fisherman's Festival.[93] Santa Rosalia was celebrated by the Sicilian community in Monterey beginning in the 1930s. This ethnic group dominated the fishing industry in Monterey and was a predominant social force in the city. Over 50,000 people came to Monterey from as far north as San Francisco during the Santa Rosalia Festivals of the 1940s through the 1960s, so it was indeed a coup for Seaside to create the winning float for the parade.[94]

Seasiders were also active in organizing programs for young people. Local newspapers were filled with news about youth sports programs, particularly baseball; even Little League teams made front page news in the local sports section.[95] By 1964 the Seaside Chamber of Commerce had two hundred members and a vision of the city with Fremont Avenue as "a boulevard with a shoppers park . . . a gentle curving street with diagonal parking bordered by planter boxes, trees, flowers and benches."[96] The Chamber continued to promote the city through its sponsorship of floats, both in the signature Fourth of July parade and in other community parades throughout Monterey, Santa Cruz, and San Benito Counties. Seaside's annual Fourth of July parade was also one of the year's highlights on all of the Monterey Peninsula, a testament to Seaside's military population, which was deeply patriotic. In January 1956, an ethnically diverse committee was organized to plan the parade.[97]

The media reports of these events show mostly white faces in the county newspaper, the *Monterey Peninsula Herald*. But in the local Seaside newspapers, the racial and ethnic mix of club membership and event participation is clearly apparent. It shows that Seaside residents accepted the reality of their diversity almost as a matter of course. The local Lions, Kiwanis, Rotary, Business and Professional Women's Club (BPW), and the Democratic Women's Club thrived with new membership that included minorities. In 1964, African American realtor John Bean was elected as commander of American Legion Post 591, perhaps, according to Mrs. Bean, as a token representative of the black community.[98] Nonetheless, this American Legion position was an important post in this military town. The sheer number of clubs and organizations forming suggest that a sense of community was taking root, and the identity of that community was both military and multiracial.

Longtime Seaside resident, Luis Pérez, attributed white attitudes about race in Seaside directly to army life: "The whites in the 1950s and 1960s were very mellow. They were not hostile. The ones here came and stayed because of the army—they had different attitudes. I think they were more accepting and if they weren't you couldn't tell."[99] Pérez's comment encapsulates that what was important about the military during the civil rights era was its commitment to civil rights in policy, rules, and practice, to such an extent that its members reflected a noticeably altered view of race than most other Americans.

REMEMBERING A DIVERSE SEASIDE

Although military towns of the South, such as Fayetteville and Columbia, South Carolina, remained highly segregated in spite of new army policy, in Seaside newer integrated neighborhoods appeared as base life began to have a profound effect on the way people viewed one another. This was especially apparent in the way children saw their world.

For children who grew up in Seaside after 1950 and experienced first-hand the effects of integration on and off base, the city was idealized as a place where racial mixing was routine, and equal treatment was expected. African American, white, Latino, and Asian American children and teenagers recalled Seaside in unconditionally positive terms. Most of them were either part of multiracial families themselves or were on close and familiar terms with people who did not define themselves as belonging to only one racial group. As a result, they viewed their young lives as protected and shielded from the overt racism that had affected their parents and grandparents so deeply and in other parts of the United States. More importantly Seaside children perceived that everyone, while not the same, was equal.

Memory is tricky, however, even "the enemy of history" as recent scholarship on memory clearly shows.[100] Therefore, while the stories about growing up in racially diverse Seaside may very well err on the side of happiness and bliss, they do reveal an important truth about the community. That is, it was considered a normal part of life to live among diverse groups of people in Seaside as far back as the 1950s. There was likely much more conflict, even racial conflict, than is reflected in the fond memories here, but there was also agreement among residents who grew up in Seaside that multiracial spaces were normal and multiracial people were accepted as common rather than unusual.

Former Seaside Mayor Ralph Rubio remembered Seaside in the 1950s and 1960s as a multiracial integrated community: "Seaside was always diverse. In my neighborhood there was a Mexican family next door, a Filipino family next to them, a black family on the other side and [a white family] down the street."[101]

Dave Pacheco (Portuguese/Italian), described neighborhoods in the city in the 1960s and 1970s:

The white area was around Harcourt, what is now City Hall. Some blacks and Mexicans lived there too. The area around Kimball Avenue and Ord Terrace was mostly whites. Most of the blacks lived around Broadway and Noche Buena, but all of these areas had other groups in there. As kids we would play basketball, baseball, football. We organized neighborhood teams . . . No one saw color, different languages. We all communicated effectively. There was no negative anything. Everyone was part of it . . . we had community teams. We all got along, played, and we went home happy. It was really positive.[102]

Mitzi Pettit, who is white, moved from Seaside to San Diego with her parents as a young child but returned in 1970 to attend to middle school and high school in Seaside:

When I went to Fremont Junior High in Seaside . . . I was fascinated with the racial mix. I didn't know anything like that before—blacks, Filipinos, Japanese, Chinese—it was way more diverse than anything I had ever seen. And everybody got along. I don't remember racial tension.[103]

What is most telling about Petit's comment was that she came from San Diego, a city that can also be described as a military town. However, she experienced nothing like the diversity of Seaside there. Seaside was small enough that we can see the impact of the adjacent base as far more significant in terms of race relations than in a larger, much more complex urban center like San Diego.

Anthony Kidd, who is black and grew up in Seaside, agreed:

It was a great place. Everybody was mixed—there were a lot of Filipinos here then [1960s–1970s]. There was racial harmony. There was very little crime or violence—if we had some it wasn't anything we noticed. There were a lot of orchards then and we would all go steal fruit off the trees—that kind of thing. The biggest crime was because we had all the blacks so people figured this was where the crime was . . . The only time we saw racial tension was when we turned on the T.V. We didn't have racial problems out here. None. All of my friends were diverse. No one ever called me "Nigger" or anything like that. We all played basketball, baseball together.[104]

The sensibility in Seaside was that "everybody mixed," that the mixing was normal rather than unusual, which was also reflection of life at Fort Ord or any other military base community for that matter. However, the idea that Seaside was a place of "racial harmony" might be going too far in the opposite direction, and perhaps reflects Kidd's selective remembrance of childhood.

Levelle McKinney, an African American filmmaker who also grew up in Seaside in the 1970s and whose documentary project "Seaside Soul'd Out," found consensus among the African Americans of his age group. According to McKinney and his cohorts, Seaside was a place that was "Beautiful and blessed. You couldn't pick a better place to grow up. It was definitely Black Power. It was the perfect place to be as a kid. We had freedom and we felt like someone was watching over. If you did something wrong your Mother knew about it by the time you got home. This was definitely a real community."[105]

McKinney's use of the term "Black Power" suggests dominance rather than racial harmony, and indicates the extent to which the Oakland-based organization extended to Seaside, which was always deeply connected to other minority communities in California. Many Seasiders traced their family's migrations to Seaside by way of Los Angeles' black communities such as Compton, for example.

Leseandra Roston shared the sense of the city as racially mixed and accepting of everyone. She described herself as part of every group:

The city was very safe. We'd go out and play and walk around. We did a lot of outdoor activities—a lot of things with the community. Everybody knew each other. It was very happy, a very happy place. There were African Americans, Latinos, some Asians. It was really diverse. There were a lot of different races here. That was what I liked. When I went out into the world I was able to appreciate it [Seaside] even more. I appreciated the diversity we have here and how lucky I was to grow up around so many different types of cultures. My father is African American and my mother is Japanese/Filipino and I had a lot of friends who were African-American and Asian ethnicity—Japanese, Vietnamese, Filipino. Strangely, I felt a part of all of the communities—African American, Filipino, even the Latino community because a lot of people would think that I was Latino. So I felt comfortable going to any kind of event, cultural event. It was very comfortable. You didn't have to worry about being judged or anything like that . . . We rode our bikes everywhere. We always felt it was safe.[106]

Nellie West, also described herself in multiracial terms, "It was a strong community. A lot of the families help one another out. Thanks to Fort Ord it was the U.N. I am African American, Japanese, and Caucasian."[107]

Glenn Hanano, who is Japanese and a member of the Seaside Police Department, recalled the city of his youth in the 1970s:

My perception was that the entire city was African American, 75–80 percent. There were only two of us on my baseball team [that weren't black]. But honestly color wasn't an issue when I was growing up. I have to make an effort to remember the ethnicities when I was a kid. As a kid you don't see color. My parents never saw color. There was a major African American population here but I didn't quite understand that until the 1970s when the Black Panther Movement was really popular. A lot of my friends thought it was something to do and something to join. I thought it was too and then I realized I didn't have a chance to be a part of that. I tried to be. I tried to join the Black Panthers. I was about 14 years old. Everything that I studied and learned about the Black Panther Movement was something that I believed in and I thought it was the right thing to do. I very desperately wanted to be a part of it.[108]

Hanano was a teenager and certainly old enough to understand the Black Panther Movement as African American. The fact that he was unsuccessful in his effort to integrate the Black Panthers is not surprising, but it is important that he found this radical African American political organization attractive and wanted to join. His perspective signified that in the local context of Seaside there was a powerful sensibility at work, drawn from the military one, that racial difference did not mean exclusion based on race.

In spite of somewhat romantic memories, these and so many other interviews with residents and former residents make clear that by the end of the 1950s and for the entire century, Seaside had become a place where a Japanese American teenager sincerely could imagine joining the Black Panthers, and African American young people felt the strength of community without the cutting edge of racism. It was a place of racial mixture in the ultimate sense—where someone who was black/Japanese/Filipino felt normal and embraced rather than different and excluded. And, it was a place where young white people became part of the texture of a diverse population rather than standing in opposition to it.

Military families recreated the racial integration of life on base at Fort Ord off base in Seaside, in the context of a vibrant and successful civil rights movement that was sweeping across the country and which they were an integral part of. In spite of all the negative pressures that military life brought, including crime, families with ties to Fort Ord shared values that focused on family, community, and a strong sense of acceptance for people who looked or spoke differently from themselves.[109]

CONCLUSION

In the first years of incorporation, it is possible to see just how important the example of the military policy of integration was in shaping the city into a place that was far ahead of its time in terms of race relations. Most importantly, values of inclusion that Seasiders advocated as integral to the formation of their city were part and parcel of the national civil rights movement, with its widely publicized marches, sit-ins and critical Supreme Court victories. However, there was hard work ahead. Constructing a city meant more than organizing Fourth of July parades or even voter registration drives and running for office. As Seaside grappled with issues of economic development, the city was confronted with the harsh reality that although a military institution could demand and implement both integration and fairness, the rest of the world held fast to racial ideologies that privileged whiteness and promoted white communities over multiracial ones. The following chapter will examine the efforts of Seaside citizens to create the infrastructure and new housing that their city badly needed in a rough political and economic climate in the city and on the Peninsula.

CHAPTER 4

Urban Renewal and Civil Rights

PHOTO 4. Dedication of (former Seaside City Manager) Gordon R. Forrest Library. Pictured are Mr. and Mrs. Gordon R. Forrest. Also shown are, left to right, Councilman Stephen Ross, unidentified, and Seaside mayors Oscar Lawson, Seaside's first African American mayor, 1976, and Glenn Olea, who was the first Filipino mayor in the United States in 1980. Courtesy City of Seaside Archive, Seaside History Project.

"SEASIDE WAS A SOLDIER TOWN and a black city—it was intertwined," stated Morris McDaniel in an interview in 2007. McDaniel had been stationed at Fort Ord in 1959. By 1975, he was ready to retire, "We turned down 22 assignments to get back to Fort Ord—we were coming up on retirement. Finally they offered me a slot at Hunter Liggett. I said that will do fine. We came back in 1975."[1] The McDaniels found that Seaside had changed enormously when they returned. Between 1959 and 1975, Seasiders had undertaken the arduous work of creating housing and infrastructure in an environment that was unique in its close connection to the military and also unique on the Monterey Peninsula for its multiracial demographic makeup. Although in McDaniel's eyes Seaside was "a black city," blacks comprised barely one-third of Seaside's population, and they always had to forge coalitions with other groups, who were rarely organized as racial voting blocs. His perspective, however, was obviously influenced by the fact that almost all blacks in Monterey County lived in Seaside. McDaniel's characterization of Seaside as "a soldier town" by the 1960s was indeed accurate as military families were constantly arriving and replenishing the population of the city.

Seaside shared a secret weapon with other military towns across the country. The federal government extended its support for integration on base to housing off base and tied funding for development to integration of neighborhoods. In November 1963, Secretary of Defense Robert McNamara ordered all local commanders to initiate fair housing practices in civilian communities tied to military bases by creating racially diverse community committees. As with integration generally, the military created change by issuing a mandate, avoiding the contentious issues that surfaced in other, nonmilitary communities.[2]

In an effort to improve cities across the country between 1964 and 1966, President Lyndon Johnson created the Department of Housing and Urban Development and specifically allocated funding for economic development for poorer regions of the country. "I propose that we launch a national effort to make the American city a better and more stimulating place to live," he proclaimed in his inaugural address in 1964.[3] It was a top-down effort that rarely included input from the minority communities that were most directly affected, and as a result, policies meant to improve communities usually disrupted and damaged them by wiping out small businesses and homes and replacing them with massive apartment buildings and transportation systems. In contrast, Seaside's urban renewal and redevelopment efforts always came with enormous community involvement because Seaside residents demanded to be included in the process. As a consequence, the city changed dramatically with the infusion of federal funds during the mid-1960s but escaped the fate of many other municipalities and remained essentially intact as a minority-majority city with most of its culture and community preserved.[4]

Although Seaside was often compared with other California minority-majority municipalities like Richmond, Oakland, and Los Angeles at midcentury, its smaller size and especially its connection to the military made it different in critical ways. In all of these larger urban areas, black residents became activists but had to fight for leadership in city government and civil rights.[5] However, unlike these other places, the army demand for integration on base (and off base too), set the tone for race relations in Seaside, always limiting groups from acting too much as a racial or ethnic bloc. Blacks in Seaside played crucial leadership roles in the planning and decision making that created new neighborhoods, parks, schools, and infrastructure, as did other people, including whites. Seaside remained small enough, never more than 38,000 people, to retain the characteristics of a small town, which allowed constant interaction among people who may have had differences among themselves in terms of race and ethnicity but shared a common bond as military people who had firsthand experience in integration.

The war industries that provided employment and opportunity for women and for minority groups, particularly for blacks, in large metropolitan centers such as Richmond, Oakland, Los Angeles, San Francisco, and elsewhere largely evaporated in the postwar years with the return of military personnel needing employment, leaving individuals and families almost as disadvantaged economically as before the war.[6] In the decades after World War II, however, Fort Ord continued to provide employment for working-class people and an emerging middle class of blacks, whites, and Asians that formed the bulwark of city government and city life. Seaside's story reflects the broader history of America at midcentury, but it also clearly shows important differences from other California municipalities and from other emerging "cities of color" primarily because the nearby military base continued to shape the values, politics, and especially the economy of the city.

The economic and political battles of the 1960s in Seaside were inextricably linked to Fort Ord, which led to urban renewal and development projects that were far more successful and in keeping with the promises of civil rights than in other larger urban areas. Moreover, although redevelopment gave residents an opportunity to confront inequality, the influence of the military helped to create a political environment capable of absorbing racial tension, in sharp contrast to the riots that erupted in cities in California and across the country in these years. Most importantly, Seasiders were closely connected to developments in civil rights nationally and at the county level.

However, as Mark Brilliant ably points out in his work on civil rights in California, the multiple civil rights movements of the 1960s and 1970s in California did not always intersect.[7] As a result, Seasiders like other activists focused on African American civil rights issues such as education and housing discrimination, worked in parallel rather than in close collaboration with, for example, César Chávez's labor movement occurring in Salinas during the same decades. That movement was mostly comprised of Mexican and Filipino civil rights advocates and mostly did not involve African American Seaside activists until the 1980s.[8]

VIETNAM, THE VOLUNTEER ARMY, AND
A NEW SEASIDE DEMOGRAPHIC

For decades since the establishment of Fort Ord, Seaside's population increase was tied to a great extent to the expansion of the troops stationed at the adjacent military base. As the West Coast's most important basic training base for draftees during the Vietnam War, Fort Ord was also a "stopping off point for career officers and noncommissioned officers returning from successive combat tours," according to James McNaughton.[9] In 1964, a school for drill sergeants was opened, and the Silas B. Hayes Hospital was built in 1968. Fort Ord became one of the largest and most important training centers in the United States from 1945 until the mid 1990s.[10] On March 19, 1960, Fort Ord formally dedicated a new $7,000,000 airfield, according to the *Monterey Peninsula Herald*, the "largest Army airfield west of the Mississippi River."[11] The Korean War, then Vietnam, made Fort Ord both a strategic center for basic training and a site for the All Volunteer Army in 1970. Large numbers of veterans who had passed through Fort Ord during training and tours of duty retired on the Peninsula, especially in Seaside. In contrast to earlier depictions of soldiers during World War II, in which only white soldiers are shown actually training for combat duty, as shown in Chapter 3, an extensive yearbook collection from Fort Ord during these decades showed soldiers of all races fully engaged in combat training and a startling diversity in the army population as well.[12]

The Vietnam War greatly accelerated the city's population growth. The "Tet Offensive" of early 1968 escalated the war in Vietnam and increased the number of draftees throughout the United States from 158,000 in 1962 to 299,000 in 1968. At Fort Ord alone in 1968, 71,500 men were trained, with the surge continuing in 1969.[13] According to an official army report on the demographics of Fort Ord in the 1970s, the average length of stay at the facility was about two years for permanent soldiers and eight to sixteen weeks for trainees. The population of Fort Ord in the 1970s included approximately 40,000 permanent soldiers, dependents, and civilian workers. Along with the transient population of trainees, some 100,000 soldiers made up the population of the base in any given year. Moreover, the report emphasized the unique "cosmopolitan community" that made up Fort Ord:

Some 12 percent of the [permanent] military population is black and 3 percent is of Oriental or American Indian origin. The percentage of Mexican-American and Spanish surnamed troops is estimated at 12 percent, which is about three times the percentage throughout the army . . . The training population of Fort Ord is made up of American Indians, Caucasians, Negroes and Orientals. These young men come from highly disparate cultural and ethnic backgrounds— Eskimo, Filipino, Guamanian, Hawaiian, Puerto Rican, Latin American, Mexican, Spanish, Caribbean, Samoan.[14]

At the same time that Fort Ord brought a dynamically new racially and ethnically mixed population to the Peninsula, particularly into Seaside in the 1970s, the antiwar movement strengthened and intensified throughout the country. Fort Ord became one of many sites of protest. An army newspaper and numerous coffeehouses off base in Seaside, Marina, and Monterey served as centers of resistance to the war. In addition, Fort Ord was established by the federal government as the base to conduct criminal trials for draft dodgers, soldiers who were absent without leave (AWOL), and those accused of crimes against the armed services. One of the most famous antiwar court cases to center on Fort Ord during this time was that of Private Billy Dean Smith, an African American accused of exploding a grenade in an officer's barracks in Vietnam with intent to murder his commanding officer Captain Rigby, in retaliation for Rigby's unfavorable discharge based on Smith's objection to the war. The accusation of "fragging" against Smith was to have carried the death penalty.[15] The prominence of this case locally and in the national press stimulated the antiwar movement and further inhibited recruitment. Reenlistment rates fell dramatically between 1967 and 1970 from 21 percent to 7 percent for draftees and 74 percent to 63 percent for careerists.[16]

The diversity of new recruits at Fort Ord was reflected in Seaside's demographics. As discussed in Chapter 3, in an article in the *Seaside Post-News Sentinel* in 1981, community development director Harold Comacho announced that based on new 1980 census data, Seaside's combined minority population had surpassed whites. He stated that Seaside included 9,996 whites, 6,255 blacks, 3,064 Asians or Pacific Islanders, 208 American Indians, and 1,364 others.[17] Although he did not identify Hispanics as a group, according to U.S. Census data, Hispanics constituted 10 percent of Seaside's population in 1980 and 17 percent by 1990.[18] By 1980, Seaside was a minority-majority city.

By the time of the 1980 U.S. Census, Hispanics were counted as a separate group, whites comprised 47 percent of Seaside's population,

TABLE 2

Percentage of Seaside population by ethnicity.

			Year		
	1960	1970	1980	1990	2000
Whites	74%	54%	47%	47%	36%
Blacks	17	20	29	22	13
Latinos	—	8	10	17	35
Asians	7	8	10	13	10
Other	2	10	4	1	6
Total	100%	100%	100%	100%	100%

Source: U.S. Department of Commerce, Bureau of the Census, Census Population Characteristics, California, Association of Monterey Bay Area Governments (AMBAG), Marina, California.

blacks were 29 percent, and Asians and Latinos each made up 10 percent of the rest of the population of the city. Three years later, in 1983, a breakdown of population in Seaside revealed that the city included 18,539 whites, 10,916 blacks, 1,666 Filipinos, 722 Japanese, 584 Koreans, 518 Vietnamese, 320 American Indians, 319 Guamanians, 189 Samoans, 154 Chinese, 132 Hawaians, 49 Asian Indians, 8 Eskimos, and 2,451 "persons of other races," who were likely multiracial and therefore undefined by census takers at that time. Although Latinos had created a large population center and ethnic enclave in nearby Salinas, they had not yet become a visible enough minority group in the rest of Monterey County to figure into a separate category for regional population counts in the mid 1980s. Also with the exception of Salinas, Seaside included the vast majority of minorities in the county as a whole in the 1980s, and, specifically a concentration of blacks (10,916 out of 15,752 in Monterey county), which was reflected in the social and political dominance of African Americans in Seaside in that decade.

According to an economic study of Monterey County conducted for the Bank of America in 1967, the "tension in the Far East" led to a military population of more than "40,000 by far the highest level since 1945 . . . the presence of military dependents in Monterey County contributes substantially to the size of the civilian population . . . Estimates made by local military authorities set the number of military dependents at 40,000." Monterey City Historian Jim Conway estimated that from post-World War II years through the 1970s, "half of the Peninsula's population of 113,500 was military related."[19] According to Sherman Smith, a retired Army Major who successfully forced the integration of Ord Terrace Development and who served as the first president of the Human Rights Commission in Seaside, "The Vietnam conflict has enlarged Fort Ord—and the number of Negro enlisted men, officers and families who want to reside nearby. It is also one of three army posts for the discharge of soldiers with mixed marriages."[20] According to the Johnson report, the military-related population on the Peninsula by 1968 was close to 90,000, which was more than one-third the population of the entire county, many of whom lived in Seaside, the community closest to the base.[21] Although it is not possible to quantify exactly how much of Seaside's population was connected to Fort Ord either as active duty personnel, family members of military personnel, or support personnel who worked as employees at Fort Ord, anecdotal evidence shows a remarkably high affiliation, both direct and indirect. Out of the hundreds of individuals who were interviewed or otherwise participated in The Seaside History Project, all but thirty had some link, usually a direct one, to Fort Ord.

URBAN RENEWAL AND REDEVELOPMENT

The economic development programs initiated in Seaside throughout the 1960s and 1970s were closely linked to and shaped by everything happening at Fort Ord, from constant new immigrations of diverse peoples to needs for housing and infrastructure. A model cities report in 1965 provided a graphic profile of Seaside's underdevelopment:

A typical example of a war time boom town. It had all the classic defects of unplanned and uncontrolled growth. Building codes, while existing at the county level, had never been enforced. There were no sewers, storm drains or sidewalks, few paved streets or street lights and no municipal services. Fremont Boulevard [Seaside's main street], which was kind of a cement artery joining Monterey and Fort Ord, passed through Seaside, and it soon became a long strip expanse of used car lots, beer joints and hamburger stands.[22]

Although this depiction of Seaside was accurate, it must be kept in mind that Seaside was nonetheless prime real estate, located geographically in an environmentally beautiful setting. It was underdeveloped to be sure, but residents and other locals realized its great potential and were determined to make full use of it.

New businesses had proliferated in Seaside in the first decades of incorporation. The city issued 530 building permits worth over $3 million in 1955 alone. In February, 1956, the city council approved a contract with an Oakland consultant to draft a master plan for Seaside that covered land use, including suggestions about which areas of the city should be used for residential, commercial, and industrial sites with an eye toward redevelopment.[23] A series of articles in local newspapers proclaimed Seaside as booming with new business enterprise and promises of industrial and commercial growth.[24] Between 1956 and 1966 a report showed a

55 percent increase in business development in Seaside; by contrast the growth rate was 5 percent in Monterey, 2 percent in Pacific Grove, and 20 percent in Carmel. This did not include small service businesses such as barber and beauty shops or real estate firms, all of which were also increasing in Seaside. By 1963 the city had 241 of these service-related businesses.[25] The Auto Mall, a result of the Gateway Project championed by Mayor Lou Haddad, became a tourist attraction in its own right as it was the first such auto mall in the United States and an enormous asset to Seaside's tax base.

In most other communities across the nation and in California, however, urban renewal in the 1950s through the 1970s was less about a proliferation of new business enterprises and more about public housing projects, often large apartment complexes that kept minorities even more segregated than they had been in the immediate postwar era. In Los Angeles, for example, the Housing Authority of the City of Los Angeles (HACLA) decimated Mexican neighborhoods in Chávez Ravine (to make room for the Los Angeles Dodger's stadium opened in 1962), for example, and created in Watts "a dumping ground for public housing developments that were not welcome in other parts of Los Angeles."[26] City Planners in San Francisco and Oakland likewise demolished neighborhoods and decimated community life in an effort to recreate city space and build massive housing projects, new highways, and the Bay Area Rapid Transit System (BART), effectively wiping out minority-owned small businesses and homes.[27]

Monterey might have tried the same kind of redevelopment with Seaside, but Seaside was by then an incorporated city in its own right. Seaside, because of its high concentration of blacks and minorities, was compared to these larger metropolitan centers even by its own city planners struggling to deal with housing issues. However, Seaside was small in comparison to these large urban centers, but it was an independent corporate entity, and was, first and foremost, a military town that had its own connections to federal funding. Seaside not only had a large proportion of racial minorities but high levels of residential integration as well. Multiracial neighborhoods in the city were just as prevalent as majority black neighborhoods, both attributable to "military clusters" or areas where military personnel lived and congregated off base.[28] Together with the full backing of federal policy in support of racial integration on and off base, it was far easier in Seaside than in other California towns and cities to develop plans for redevelopment that did not focus on relocating blacks, Latinos, or other minority groups or on building large public housing complexes but on investing in and improving what already existed.

Saul Weingarten, who was Jewish, was one of the most important and successful advocates for redevelopment of Seaside. He served as city attorney from 1954 to 1970. According to Weingarten, Seaside in the immediate postwar era was in dire need of development:

Seaside never had any zoning, planning, or even an effective building permit system . . . It had one county building inspector, one deputy sheriff [for the entire area of Seaside, Marina, and Sand City] . . . Gambling parlors were . . . the biggest businesses in town . . . [There was] a sheep ranch above Fremont Boulevard and a duck ranch in the town's residential area . . . the sheep would break out and block traffic and the ranch hands would ride out on their horses and herd them out . . . conditions were pathetic. The area in Del Monte Heights and Hannon was covered with shacks and connected by unpaved sand tracks which were marked as city streets on maps. There were whole blocks which had no utilities of any kind; water, sanitation, or electricity. A lot of shacks were occupied by squatters, many of them soldiers and their families who had come to Fort Ord during World War II and built houses with what few materials were available. Some stayed, so did the shacks.[29]

Weingarten's description of Seaside clearly reflected an urgent need for infrastructure, but once again, it does not do justice to the natural beauty of the town that continued to attract new residents, especially retired officers of color, and particularly African Americans and their families. Fort Ord created "a housing demand not normally found in a normal civilian community," according to sociologist Elaine Johnson. Johnson analyzed population, employment, education, and housing data in Monterey County as a consultant for the Monterey City Planning Commission in 1968.[30] She argued, "The heavy demands for housing have been intensified by the large number of military families who are forced to live off post because of a shortage of military housing . . . This not only causes great hardship on the civilian families of low to moderate incomes but it also creates ill will toward the military."[31]

This situation was commonplace in towns connected to military bases. The Chief of Housing at Fort Carson, Colorado, explained that the military had "no plan to provide enough housing for all its soldiers. The military's goal is to house one-third of the married population on post, leaving two-thirds to live in the community—to support the local community."[32] Still, off-base housing was both scarce and far more expensive, even in Seaside, than it was in most military towns in the country. Even the salaries of officers could not match the demands of the Monterey Peninsula housing market. The situation became so dire that in 1984 one young teenage boy, the son of a sergeant at the fort, committed suicide in a misguided attempt to save his family money. His death focused national attention on the financial crises faced by many U. S. Army families, especially those living in expensive areas such as the Monterey Peninsula.

Although there were repeated headlines in both the *Seaside Post-News Sentinel* and the *Monterey Peninsula Herald* during the 1960s about military investment in housing construction on the base, the Johnson report criticized the army for "showing some concern but little action to alleviate the housing problem except for piecemeal efforts." She argued that the army failed to meet demand "for years . . . As the largest landowner in the county [the military was not] facing up to the responsibility of housing their own people."[33] Her analysis showed that Seaside's military population, like all other military populations in towns near bases, did not stagnate during the postwar years. Instead, as desegregation policy in the armed services matured into a normal state of affairs through the 1960s, military families who experienced that life continued to come to Seaside, reinforcing a norm of multiracial neighborhoods, something that civilian communities in California and the nation still had little to no familiarity with.[34]

Urban renewal and development in Seaside centered on both new housing and on the infrastructure that would make for a modern American city. Eventually this included a modern city hall designed by architect Edward Durrell Stone, whose firm also designed a city logo and flag (a juxtaposition of a seahorse, sun, and sky).[35] Saul Weingarten and the mayors and city councils during this period, along with the newly formed Redevelopment Agency and Planning Commission, spearheaded those ambitious efforts. At the same time, this work took place in the context of redevelopment and urban renewal projects that were common throughout the United States, and in the context of vibrant, often contentious civil rights movements that Seaside residents, just as so many other residents of towns and cities throughout locales in the West, remained an integral part of.

The Seaside Redevelopment Agency was formed in April 1957 to address housing issues first and foremost. J. Hugh Turner was appointed chair of the Redevelopment Agency and was described as "a man of strong convictions" in an article introducing him in the *Monterey Peninsula Herald* in 1958. He made a statement in the interview that sent a strong signal to residents and observers alike—redevelopment and urban renewal in Seaside would follow the model of the civil rights movement and of integrated Fort Ord rather than segregated Monterey, "There is no room or place," he claimed, "for racial discrimination in any housing program. [Housing discrimination] is not only against the law, but against . . . Christian charity."[36] His statement reflected a position and attitude quite different from redevelopment efforts in Oakland or anywhere else in the nation, which justified segregation in redevelopment on economic grounds as an essential way of maintaining property values.[37]

Richard Goblirsch was hired in 1959 as project manager of Seaside's Redevelopment Agency and served as agency head until 1967. He quickly put together a team that was racially diverse.[38] Urban renewal and development was notable in Seaside not only because of the impressive amount of federal funding it generated but also in the multiracial composition of agencies and commissions.

To ensure that future housing would not follow segregated patterns, members of the first agency included Richard Joyce and Sarah Ector, African American political activists. At the same time, a Planning Commission, also multiracial, was appointed to work with the Redevelopment Agency in deciding where to locate new developments, how the city ought to be more appropriately rezoned, and which business and home owners ought to receive restrictive zoning code variances. Their role was to serve as liaisons between the Redevelopment Agency and the Seaside

City Council in their requests for federal funds and in deciding how the city would evolve. According to one of the first Redevelopment Agency officials, "There was no conflict [between the Commission and the Redevelopment Agency]. Nothing was done without their [Planning Commission] support. We worked hand in hand."[39] Seaside residents diverged from other municipalities, which coped with urban renewal by forming racially based interest groups.[40] In Seaside, which was smaller and military, residents expected to work alongside people of different races and get along with them.

Yet, even though Seaside initiated several new housing projects simultaneously throughout the 1960s, many Seasiders feared that the solution would turn out to be worse than the problem; proposed new building developments would deprive them of what they appreciated most about Seaside—it was a place where anyone could build anything they wanted without restriction or restraint. This was a system in place in other regions of the country as well. In Miami, for example, blacks built coalitions with whites and other minorities to challenge Jim Crow housing by utilizing state power in zoning.[41] Most residents cooperated in redevelopment efforts, however, in large part because the redevelopment agency was careful to include them in the planning processes, unlike in San Francisco or Oakland where redevelopment wiped out entire neighborhoods and minority communities without input from the people most affected.[42] In contrast, in Seaside, where minority groups were considered the norm rather than a problem, the focus was on keeping people in their homes and neighborhoods intact.

The agency incorporated infrastructure costs such as curbs, gutters, and sewers into long-term mortgages, rather than making them costly preconditions of bringing homes and businesses up to code.[43] In doing so, they showed a remarkable sensitivity to the economic status of residents who could not otherwise afford new mortgage costs to refurbish homes and businesses. Military personnel benefited the most from this policy. For active duty military families who lived in Seaside for short periods— usually under five years—improving their homes added to their value, and they could be resold long before the added costs of improvement were put in place in mortgage agreements.[44] This was less beneficial to the large number of retired soldiers and families who formed the bulwark of the Seaside community and who lived permanently in the town.

The Noche Buena Project was Seaside's first effort at urban renewal and the Redevelopment Agency's first federally funded grant awarded for redevelopment.[45] A multiracial Citizens Advisory Committee of seventy-five members first formed in 1954, which, after a year of study, led to a recommendation adopted in 1956 by the city council that a 22-block area (66 acres) between Soto and Waring streets and Broadway and Hilby Avenue would be redeveloped and turned into a "garden city of new homes, tower apartments, and landscaping."[46] The city received a Housing and Home Finance Agency loan in 1958 for $949,514. In addition, credit for building additional schools in Seaside and infrastructure needs such as sewers, storm drains, engineering services, and street improvements amounted to an additional $327,640. The city spent $147,118 of its own money on the project and increased the value of the property by 65 percent.[47]

The project was completed in 1964. Pacific Gas and Electric Company, California Water and Telephone Company, and the City of Seaside constructed, moved, and updated water, gas, sewer, and drainage lines throughout the Noche Buena Project area.[48] Noche Buena was considered a "bootstrap operation" and an "improvement" for Seaside, though not the "spectacular one" that was originally promised in 1959 according to an analysis by the *Monterey Peninsula Herald* in 1964 and according to the final report by Seaside's Redevelopment Agency.[49] Richard Joyce, one of the original members of the Redevelopment Agency, deemed it a qualified success: "They could have really widened the streets, made the lots much bigger and eliminated many more substandard residences. We learned a lot from that [experience]."[50] On the other hand, what was most significant about the Noche Buena Project was its early emphasis on restoration and refurbishment rather than demolition, which generated support among Seaside residents who were given funds to renovate their properties rather than being displaced as was the case in the huge metropolitan areas of Oakland, Los Angeles, or San Francisco and many other urban centers in the United States during these years.[51] In most other towns and cities getting rid of "blight" meant bulldozing poor and minority areas rather than granting residents low-interest loans that would maintain neighborhoods.[52] In Seaside, the character of the community was preserved and its value increased because leaders and residents alike learned lessons from nearby Oakland and San Francisco about the consequences of displacement, and they also followed a model that the military gave them to improve rather than destroy multiracial minority neighborhoods.

Carl Williams was hired as a staff member for the Redevelopment Agency in 1965. As a civil rights activist, he paid close attention to how redevelopment affected minorities. According to Williams, what separated urban renewal projects in Seaside from other projects that impacted African American and other minority communities elsewhere in the nation, especially in Los Angeles and Oakland in the mid-1960s, was the combination of diversity on the agencies that controlled development and federal loans that encouraged the maintenance of homes and communities:

My position was called a relocation aid . . . If the agency acquired your property the family had to be provided relocation assistance. They had to be provided with comparable housing. The guy who was my superior, Eldridge Gonaway, [who was also black] had extensive experience in redevelopment in L.A. He was also quite active in African American politics in Seaside. The first redevelopment program was not to tear everything down. We had a heavy emphasis on rehabilitation. Congress made 3 percent interest rate loans to fix up property. That had a very big impact on why there was no wholesale displacement and dislodgement of African Americans. You could really do some wonderful things. A lot of people who were homeowners were able to do a lot to maintain their homes, get them fixed up and modernized. There wasn't that much of that "Negro removal." Maybe that was a way of keeping black folks in Seaside. That was the intention. We [in Seaside] did not have massive dislocation and demolition. Most homes were single family—there were very, very few apartments. You didn't have these huge monolithic type apartment complexes that Oakland had.[53]

Although Williams expressed some skepticism about the reasons for refurbishment rather than relocation, he emphasized that Seaside was a city of aspiring single-family homeowners, many of whom were minorities. The enclaves they created in Seaside resembled the suburban spaces described by Andrew Wiese and Becky Nicolaides and others as common to municipalities in the 1920s and 1930s.[54] In Seaside, rather than leaving for other parts of the Peninsula when they had the opportunity to do so, retired military personnel who were black, white, and Asian were in a position to make their dream of home and community a permanent fixture of their city. The fact that Seaside was a beautiful place made it as desirable a place to live as any other Peninsula community.

Moreover, as Williams makes clear, Seaside was an integral part of a post–World War II urban California deeply impacted by the huge migration of African Americans.[55] It was no accident that individuals like Eldridge Gonaway, who was closely connected to Los Angeles and San Francisco urban renewal efforts, came to live and work in Seaside. Carl Williams eventually worked in urban planning in Oakland.

In April, 1962, Seaside became the first city in the United States to win approval for the special federal loan program funds to which Williams referred.[56] By the time Congress created the loan program in 1962, redevelopment projects across the country were roundly criticized by African Americans as racist, prompting the phrase, "Urban Renewal equals Negro Removal."[57]

According to Williams, "That made a big difference in Seaside by focusing people on improving homes rather than demolishing and relocating."[58] City Attorney Saul Weingarten, Redevelopment Director Richard Goblirsch, City Manager Gordon Forrest, and Mayor Beauford T. Anderson, along with city council members Robert S. Bratt, Jr., Louis Haddad, and African American Stephen Ross, all of whom were former military men forcefully lobbied the Kennedy administration for help in funding redevelopment. After waiting for months for approval, Mayor Anderson sent an urgent telegram to President John F. Kennedy that finally got his attention. President Kennedy sent an emissary to Seaside to assess the city before approving loan funds. As a result, Seaside received the first and only federal 102B loan of a million dollars that allowed for improvements not just in housing projects but also in sewage disposal and storm drainage. It was certainly a coup for Seaside, and a testament to the sophistication of ex-military personnel in manipulating federal policy for the benefit of their city, working together across racial lines to achieve a common goal for Seaside.[59]

Development projects moved forward speedily. The 240 acre, $8 million dollar Del Monte Heights Project was planned by the city council in August 1958. A year later the council granted $29,000.[60] Public hearings were held in December 1962, and by 1964 Del Monte was in its execution stage. Del Monte Heights was located on county land and consisted of approximately 240 acres, bordered by LaSalle and San Pablo avenues to the north and to the west by Soto and St. Helena streets and by Hilby to the south. Del Monte Heights bordered Fort Ord to the east.[61] As part of the Del Monte Heights Development Project, a coalition of citizen's organizations headed by Saul Weingarten and supported by Reverend H. H. Lusk, a prominent member of the Ministerial Alliance, applied for a federal loan of $800,000 to build an 80-unit apartment complex for senior citizens adjacent to 165 other units. Reverend Lusk's coalition included the Seaside Rotary Club, Seaside Hatchet Club, Seaside Chamber of Commerce, Seaside Civic League, Seaside Senior Citizens, Victory Temple, Ocean View Baptist Church, Quota Club of Seaside, Seaside Lions and Kiwanis Clubs, and the Fil-Am Club. It could not have been more representative of Seaside's diverse population and shows how active all groups were in city building.[62]

The project was delayed, however, because Ocean View Baptist Church had defaulted on their contract with the city's Redevelopment Agency. The agency awarded a new contract to the Teamsters Union over the strenuous objections of the two black Redevelopment Agency members, Richard T. Joyce and Sarah Ector. Both believed race and racism were used to decide in favor of the Teamsters. Joyce argued that "Further consideration should be given because they [the architect and developer] are Negroes. Who can youngsters look to when you deny their men? I . . . think that the Teamsters are foreign to our problems."[63] Ector agreed: "We should do anything we can in this community to encourage our Negro children . . . we are working to give the minority a chance."[64] This episode showed just how readily racism was challenged head-on in Seaside by individuals who expected fairness, both because of the gains of the national civil rights movement and because of the political environment of Seaside that empowered everyone.

When Joyce's term expired in the summer of 1967, Mayor Haddad replaced him with Guillermo P. Bautista, a Filipino former army veteran

who had survived the Bataan Death March. African American City Councilman Stephen Ross objected to the replacement as racially motivated
because Joyce was black and Ross believed he should be replaced with
another African American.[65] However, Bautista was Filipino, not white,
and Haddad was of Middle Eastern descent. Bautista, Haddad, Ross, and
Joyce were also all army veterans. Theirs was an argument among equals
about race and racism rather than a confrontation between an embedded
white power structure and oppressed minorities, scenarios that played
out in other California towns and cities in the 1960s.

African Americans were not isolated as a minority bloc in Seaside.
Filipinos played a major role in city politics throughout the period of city
building. Former military officer, Glenn Olea, city councilman from 1971
to 1978 and Seaside's mayor from 1980 to 1982, was the first Filipino
American mayor in American history. Olea, through the Fil-Am Community Club and other civic organizations, spearheaded the fund-raising
effort for a city ambulance called "Project Mercy." Filipino community
leader Emerson Reyes, also retired from the United States Army, was
a member of the Seaside's Economic Implementation Commission under Mayor Stephen Ross (1978–1980). Reyes was also the 4th District's
representative to the Monterey County Affirmative Action Commission
and the first Filipino American to be elected president of the Seaside's
Boys and Girls Club. He was also the first Filipino American to hold the
Monterey Peninsula College's Director of Veterans Affairs, a position
he held during the Vietnam War era. Filipinos were consistently active
in city government and social and political life in Seaside throughout its
history. Filipino women, wives of military personnel, found work in the
agricultural fields of Salinas and as nurses in Salinas hospitals when they
were refused employment in Monterey. Unlike most other Seasiders, these
women subsequently became committed members of the labor struggles
in Salinas during the 1970s.[66]

Although more successful in Seaside than elsewhere, urban renewal
eventually displaced some people by rezoning former residential areas for
commercial use. This policy affected Mexican American and white residents
the most. The $6 million Hannon Project, for example, was supposed to
alleviate housing pressure in Seaside. However, according to the Johnson

report, by 1967, "Housing [was still] one of the most critical needs on the Monterey Peninsula. The vacancy rate is nil . . . there is great competition on the Peninsula for rentals for low income groups displaced by urban renewal . . . with their hundreds of demolitions . . . there has been little or no building activity to replace the residential units eliminated."[67] Johnson claimed that 1,100 demolitions were carried out in the Hannon Project and 250 families and 82 individuals were displaced as a result. Her claim was contested by Agency head Richard Gorblirsch who stated that it was "nonsense." According to Goblirsch, the city worked closely with residents in either bringing residences up to code or in purchasing them for a fair market value and relocating the owners.[68]

According to a report by the Seaside Redevelopment Agency in 1970, all of the projects were largely successful in terms of revitalizing the city. "Of 1,155 single family homes remaining within the project areas, 826 property owners have participated with the Redevelopment Agency in bringing their homes up to standard. Direct grants totaling $225,344 have been given to 110 property owners (of whom 62 are black). Direct loans totaling $309,050 (at 3%) have been given to 128 property owners (of whom 68 are black)."[69] One important and unintended outcome of Redevelopment Agency work in the mid-1960s was that it revealed shady practices in deeds of sale. According to Carl Williams, mostly African American first time home buyers signed contracts that they thought were deeds of sale. They were not.

There was another interesting situation with the properties in Seaside that I found out with the loan program. A lot of people at that time, particularly blacks, were living in their homes under what was known as a contract of sale arrangement. The true owners of the property were, in many cases, whites in Monterey . . . They in effect owned the property. [Blacks] thought [they] were buying the property [as a] traditional deed of trust [arrangement]. In effect, [they] had all of the incidents of ownership, but not the actual ownership . . . One of the unintended consequences of the rehabilitation program was to bring that arrangement to the surface. It made a lot of people realize the illusion they were living under and what they could do to change it. We [staff of the Redevelopment Agency assigned to relocation] told those owners—either you fix up the

property or you give these people a deed of trust . . . I don't know of any incidence where one of these owners refused to sell. These owners had no interest in
fixing up the property and facing the problem of relocating the people. Looking
retrospectively, that program had a mixed blessing. For sure there wasn't a massive relocation and demolition in the . . . community.[70]

According to Mike Harston, advisory title officer for Stewart Title Company, which handled most real estate transactions in Monterey County
during this period, the contract of sale was a popular way of financing
homes for the working poor or anyone who could not qualify for a regular bank loan in the 1950s and 1960s. This indeed included minorities,
especially African Americans. Harston claimed that:

The contract of sale was an installment loan, a financing vehicle for people with
no credit or poor credit. The buyer is accumulating equity, but not very much.
It was used commonly until the mid-1960s, but the catch was that it allowed for
foreclosures without due process. That violated both the United States Constitution and the California State Constitution. After several lawsuits in the 1960s
it was not used without a clause to protect buyers from foreclosure without due
process.[71]

Harston agreed that although a contract of sale was not created to be used
specifically against blacks or other minority groups, realtors in the 1960s
throughout Monterey County (but also all over California and the nation)
used it when dealing with a predominantly African American or military
population they assumed would not qualify for a bank loan.[72] Indeed, at
the outset of the redevelopment efforts federal funding was held up because
the entire city had been redlined, which affected the ability of all Seasiders to get loans. "I had a contract of sale on my house," recalled Richard
Goblirsch who is white, "It was hard to get a mortgage because the city [of
Seaside] was red-marked."[73] City Engineer Don Drummond recalled, "All
of Seaside was redlined. No one could get a FHA or VA loan in the whole
city until we pushed through Del Monte Heights development in 1964."[74]

Although blacks were not displaced by urban renewal in Seaside in
the same way that they were in Oakland, San Francisco, and elsewhere,
Mexican Americans and whites who lived in the area of the new Gate-

way Project Auto Mall were not so lucky. There was no effort to remodel and rebuild here; the city was determined to replace the self-built shacks and small businesses between Del Monte Boulevard and Fremont Avenue with commercial development and the nation's first auto mall. Residents of Seaside during the redevelopment years in these areas were enraged. Gateway was first proposed in December 1965 by Richard Goblirsch who did a feasibility study funded with a federal planning grant. According to Saul Weingarten, "Seaside had the lowest tax valuation of any city of its size in the State of California [at incorporation in 1954 with a population of 14,000] . . . The concern was how to build the tax revenue to relieve the residents of some of the burden . . . of having to support all of the activities of the city . . . one thing that appeared to have a means was providing facilities for automobile dealers . . . because automobiles are a big ticket item [generating] lots of sales tax revenue."[75] The idea was enthusiastically supported by Mayor Haddad, Councilman Bud Houser (who was Sicilian), Councilman Steven Ross, and the Redevelopment Agency.

Gateway removed eighty homes and twenty businesses in the area around Del Monte Boulevard. The area was rezoned for commercial use, new and used car lots, and other large scale businesses. The project was estimated to bring Seaside $174,000 in needed tax revenue, as compared to the $27,000 in taxes before the project. Although Seaside was fast becoming the Peninsula's largest city, its assessed valuation was only $7 to $8 million dollars, compared to the $80 to $90 million dollar valuation of Monterey whose population in 1968 was approximately 10,000 less than Seaside (25,000).[76]

By February 1966, the Seaside City Council not only approved Gateway but also Del Monte Heights and Hannon. It was reported by the *Monterey Peninsula Herald* that the action was "so sweeping it will change the character of the community." City council chambers were packed with people in opposition. Several residents expressed discontent, almost all of whom were either white or Mexican American. Angelo Manzo told the council that they "ought to be ashamed [of themselves]" for taking property away from "little people" and giving it to car dealers. Fred Griffith, white owner of Griffith's Furniture Store concurred, "For the city to take a little man's business and turn it over to a big business seems very unfair."[77]

Frances Soria, who was described as a granddaughter of Mrs. Juan Avilo de Bunce, born in Monterey County in 1839 and a descendant of Governor Pico, the last governor of Mexican California, asked city council members who were native Californians to raise their hands—only one, Emil Schmidt, did so. "If only some of you immigrants would get out of California we would be a lot better off," she said.[78] Mayor Lou Haddad responded to the criticism by arguing that the area was "blighted." Councilman Stephen Ross, who became mayor in 1978, supported Gateway, as did both the Planning Commission and the Redevelopment Agency. Nonetheless, Ross was the only member of the city council at the time who expressed discomfort at displacing residents. Ross said it was "distasteful" to refer to people's homes as "blighted" and that it was his painful duty to vote for the project, "There is no way to value a person's home, for each person's home is his castle and you can't put dollars and cents on it. Nevertheless, the time comes when something has to die for something to live."[79]

Mitzi Petit remembered how painful and traumatized her grandparents were by the Gateway Project that cost them both their home and plumbing business, Nielson's Plumbing, a business landmark in Seaside since the 1930s:

I knew the word "urban renewal" even as a little girl before I knew what it meant. I knew it wasn't good. Any time my grandmother would talk about her time there [on Alpine Street in Seaside] she would say her happiest time was in that house that had been razed. She was always saying, "Well of course that was before the urban renewal" then her voice would sort of trail off. Her house was taken from her and she never got over it. Her home, her neighborhood, her business. There were serious financial concerns that weren't being addressed. Mortgage payments for people who had owned homes free and clear like my grandmother suddenly had to pay rent. Businesses were lost. That area was a nice community in the 1950s and 1960s she used to say. After urban renewal, by the late 1970s it was a mess.[80]

Although former residents such as the Nielsons certainly felt the effects of urban renewal quite deeply, their experience was nothing like that of Oakland or San Francisco in which entire communities, particularly minority communities, were significantly disrupted and even destroyed in an effort to remove "blight."[81] Haddad and most of the members of the Seaside City Council expressed the naiveté of the times that everything new was an improvement and that the demolition of neighborhoods and businesses was worthwhile when that action served the larger purpose of building a modern city.

Most importantly, the common denominator on the Seaside City Council and on the agencies and commissions it created was both military and minority, mirroring the racial composition of Fort Ord and the city itself. This did not mean that racial tensions did not exist. Seaside residents were acutely aware of race and sensitive to any hint of racial bias, but they did so in an environment that was much different from the one groups faced elsewhere. Here whites were not the entrenched power on the city council demolishing black or minority neighborhoods; they were one of many groups struggling to modernize their city while keeping as much of its community and character as intact as possible. In Seaside, no one was entrenched; the city was new, almost everyone was military, and most likely a member of one minority group or another.

CIVIL RIGHTS 1960–1970

The pressing effects of housing shortages coupled with housing discrimination drove redevelopment projects but also contributed to activist politics and an increasingly vibrant civil rights movement in Seaside. Seasiders of all ethnicities often found themselves on opposing sides of city government when it was related to employment and race rather than development, which, with the exception of Gateway, they generally and collectively supported. Yet, the civil rights movement in Seaside remained essentially centrist in its aims and actions. The city experienced sporadic violence but never erupted into widespread rioting that was the case almost everywhere else in American metropolitan centers in those years.

America was engulfed in racial strife, ironically, soon after the signing of dramatic new civil rights legislation in 1964. Between 1964 and through the 1970s, white backlash was expressed in the form of police harassment that triggered violence throughout the country. Probably the most famous moment came in August 1965 in Los Angeles after a young black man was arrested by police, and the Los Angeles subdivision of Watts erupted in sustained violence that was nationally televised live, riveting the American public and worsening race relations.[82] Newark, New York, Chicago, Detroit, and Philadelphia, among many other cities, were also the sites of rioting between mostly white police officers and black citizens. In Oakland, blacks organized a branch of the Black Panther Party, which became a symbol of black empowerment and community building, according to historian Robert O. Self. Self explained the response to the Panthers by white police officers, "The Oakland police department, long a bastion of both racial paternalism and virulent racism, responded to the Panthers with nothing short of guerilla warfare."[83] The racial violence of the late 1960s was not limited to blacks and whites. In nearby San Jose and in Salinas, where Mexican Americans had long been targets of discrimination and police brutality, the Chicano movement and "Brown Power" proponents openly challenged white backlash to civil rights initiatives.[84] Against this backdrop of serious racial conflict in the United States and in California, it is all the more remarkable that Seaside achieved the success that it did in building political coalitions across racial lines. Blacks in Seaside turned conflict into common ground.

According to the Johnson report, "ghettoization" had occurred on the Peninsula and would "spill over to threaten other communities." Comparing Seaside to other cities of color in California in the late 1960s, Johnson warned, "The segregation of Negroes in East Palo Alto, Marin City, and Seaside have a combustible quality which from time to time explode in racial 'incidents' and violence in their nearby communities."[85] She was right about those other places, but in Seaside the fear was hyped and largely unfounded. Noted *San Francisco Chronicle* columnist Herb Caen wrote a column on May 15, 1967, drawing attention to the racism of the Monterey Peninsula and tying the politics of Seaside to the presence of the military and Fort Ord.

Surprise: the No. 1 racial trouble spot, potentially, is not Oakland or Watts—but beautiful Monterey. The reason: Fort Ord which is now handling more troops than it did during World War II, many of them Negroes who bring their families. The problem is familiar: housing and jobs, both in such short supply that tension is building dangerously.[86]

To equate the small town of Seaside with Oakland or Watts was a bit far-fetched, although what Caen failed to note was that it was not only the increase of minority populations in Seaside, especially blacks, due to Fort Ord, but also the model of integration that made inequity off base unacceptable to all Seaside residents, blacks as well as whites and other minorities. Seaside residents of all races, but especially blacks, had strong ties to national and regional civil rights movements and, perhaps because of their backgrounds as military people who had traveled the world, maintained the more centrist and progressive ideals of the 1950s and early 1960s, as opposed to the more extremes of the late 1960s and 1970s.

Three days later, Caen received a response from then Monterey Mayor Minnie Coyle who disputed the findings and questioned Caen's sources. In defense of his claims Caen argued:

The same day Mayor Minnie issued her denial, I rec'd this memo from a Monterey area writer and investigator: 'Don't let Mayor Minnie fool you. It's a trick. There are 130,000 people in this area but not ONE town. There are nine little back-biting and buck-passing communities. When she says Monterey, she means only her locality. The center of the Negro trouble is in Seaside, right next door. There have been several near riots in the last few months. Store looting, and so on. The mayor [Lou Haddad] has told his police to shoot if necessary. The violence spills over into Monterey and elsewhere on the Peninsula, and would again."[87]

Although Caen was correct that housing shortages and housing discrimination along with widespread discrimination in employment for African Americans, Mexican Americans, and Filipinos created much frustration that would erupt into some violence, it was nothing like Watts or Oakland or even Salinas or any of the other big urban centers that experienced race riots and mass protests in the late 1960s. The violence that did occur in Seaside was condemned by the majority of Seaside residents who were imbued in a military culture that demanded discipline and respect for authority, first and foremost. It also tended to be centrist, progressive, and cautious. The Seaside City Council was centrist, too, and even though led by a mayor who was outspokenly racist, the racial tension in Seaside throughout the 1960s and into the 1970s was mitigated by the fact that the city council always included minorities. Blacks such as Pearl Carey, Stephen Ross, Oscar Lawson, and Filipino Glenn Olea and many others participated actively and equally in city government.

However, Mayor Haddad and the Seaside City Council used the potential of violence brought on by racial conflict as leverage to annex parts of Fort Ord in order to add to the city's tax base. According to a report by the Seaside City Council in 1967, under the heading "Benefits Jointly to City and Military," the city council (ignoring the labor strikes in Salinas) exaggerated its role in preventing rioting on the scale of Watts: "Only through Herculean efforts has the City of Seaside been able to keep racial tensions from exploding in an area with substantial racial minorities. City efforts to cope with racial problems through recreational programs and the creation of job opportunities can be expanded with more funds." Presumably these were funds that would be made available with the increased tax revenue that annexation would bring about. The report argued further that "any additional effort in this field will benefit the community, the military, and the nation."[88] This assertion is also notable for its assumption of common purpose. Seaside leaders believed that what was good for Seaside would be good for the military base and vice versa. They viewed the institution of the military base and the city as interlinked. The army, on the other hand, was far less interested in Seaside than Seaside was in the army. Although records for Fort Ord have been scattered and lost when the base closed, there is little in the records that do exist to show that the army was at all focused on what was going on in this relatively small base community.

Nonetheless there were occasions when violent confrontations occurred. In January 1966, for example, approximately thirty young African Americans confronted a police officer who used his dog as a threat against them. Enraged parents in Seaside forced Mayor Haddad to "retire" the dog from the police department. Five months later, in June 1966, arsonists who were assumed to be African American set fire to three stores and

a school, causing $65,000 in damages. On January 26, 1967, a white re-
serve police officer was accused of clubbing a 13-year-old African American girl. In retaliation, two days later, black youths apparently clubbed a
service station attendant. In April 1967, a near riot occurred when police
officers appeared at a party and began making arrests. Twenty-two out-
raged young blacks responded by looting a gas station and liquor store.[89]

What is notable about these incidents is what did not happen next. In
so many other cities across the country any one of these events might have
triggered widespread rioting and looting. In Seaside, however, the military
emphasis on discipline, order, and respect for authority was inherent, and,
coupled with Seaside civil rights activists who valued the more progressive ideals of Dr. Martin Luther King Jr., led to remarkable restraint on
all sides. For example, on February 27, 1968, twenty-five "angry Seaside
Negro youths" came before the Seaside Human Relations Commission
and "demanded that city officials be more responsive to their needs."
They complained of continued police harassment, lack of employment,
or recreational activities for young people in Seaside and demanded that
the Seaside Youth Center be made available to them on weekends. According to one youth, "We want someplace to go to avoid the trouble we
get into while loitering in 'The Pit' [an area known for drugs and prostitution located on the corner of Noche Buena Street and Broadway]. We
have tried to take our problems to city officials . . . Now if Seaside has
trouble it will not be our fault it will be your fault," he said as he pointed
to Mayor Lou Haddad.[90] Instead of igniting the community and instigating
a Watts style riot, these young people took their complaints to the Seaside Human Relations Commission, chaired by respected Seaside leader
and former Tuskegee Airman Sherman Smith. The commission and city
council were respectful enough to allow the young people to voice their
concerns rather than shut them out or simply arrest everyone.

Lou Haddad, in another example of racism and of being tone deaf
politically, responded to the group by offering blacks jobs picking fruit in
Salinas, demonstrating an obtuseness about the real and critical problem
of off-base employment opportunity for African American young people
in the mid-1960s. According to Haddad:

Lee Toler headed up a group called "Young Adults for Action" (YAFA). He no-
tified me that [they] wanted to meet with me. A dialogue ensued and demands
were made. There wasn't enough recreation. There were no jobs. I asked how
many wanted a job. About 10 of the 20 hands went up . . . I said "You meet me
at the Chamber tomorrow morning and I'll have a bus waiting for you to take
you to the job. You'll be picking strawberries and the pay is $1.75 per hour plus
10 cents per box . . ." "Shit, would you work for $1.75 an hour?" one youth re-
sponded . . . when I was a teenager I worked for 25 cents a day [said Haddad] . . .
the bus appeared [the next morning], but not one youth showed up."[91]

Haddad explained his position regarding jobs:

The city's budget was in deplorable state. There were no funds available to increase recreational outlets, nor funds available to hire more people to work in
the parks and streets and other areas that needed attention. I devised a program
whereby those who desired to be mechanics could learn a trade . . . Somehow
the program never caught fire and was ultimately cancelled.[92]

The program that Haddad referred to was called "The 44 Club" which
sponsored a group of black teenagers to work summers and weekends.
In addition, the city hired "six young black students as trainees during
the past six years [1963–1970]."[93] At that point, Haddad decided that he
had given African American young people enough attention.

Haddad expressed bewilderment about the subsequent violence in Seaside partly as a result of the frustration over discriminatory employment
and housing practices on the Monterey Peninsula.[94] He blamed Seaside's
problems on the Watts riots and on black residents:

Race riots broke out in areas like Watts and Detroit. They spilled over into Seaside. A few fire bombings occurred; mostly in the business section . . . There was
general unrest in the community. An army staff sergeant who one day was to
become mayor [Oscar Lawson] made inflammatory statements . . . and the next
night several fire bombings occurred.[95]

Again, this is an exaggeration. Seaside never exploded in violence
the way other cities across the nation did during these years. Moreover,
former mayor Oscar Lawson insisted that he made no inflammatory

statement because he was still on active duty. It would have been against army regulation for military personnel to become political activists: "I could not speak out while I was still in the service and I was at that time. I didn't retire until 1971. It was after that that I got into politics."[96] Lawson served on the city council from 1972 to 1976, was Mayor Pro-Tem from 1974 to1976 and Mayor from 1976 to 1978.

Haddad again raised a red flag when he overreacted on April 11, 1967, and asked the city council to approve a "get tough [policy] even if it becomes shoot if necessary policy for lawbreakers who cannot be apprehended in any other way."[97] This comment infuriated African Americans and a great many other residents of Seaside who recalled the violent police actions in the American South a few years earlier in response to peaceful civil rights demonstrations. They were determined to create coalitions that would solve the problems of segregation and jobs on the Peninsula and remove Haddad from office.

SCHOOLS AND CIVIL RIGHTS

Seaside residents tackled the problem of segregation on the Monterey Peninsula by challenging racism directly. It was over the issue of racial segregation in the schools that blacks, particularly black women in Seaside, demonstrated both their vigorous commitment to political activism and, equally important, to their values as members of the culture of the military. They were not alone. Black women, particularly black professional women, were front and center in the civil rights movements going back to the nineteenth century and certainly carrying on the important race work of the twentieth.[98] Black professional women in Seaside were in the forefront of change on the Monterey Peninsula and deeply connected to their counterparts elsewhere in the country.

The 1954 *Brown v. Board of Education* decision by the United States Supreme Court was supposed to create racially integrated schools. Despite this precedent-setting decision, racially segregated school districts were maintained throughout the 1950s and later because schools were established in neighborhoods that remained segregated. In order to address the problem of school segregation, the 1964 Civil Rights Act stipulated that no public institution that remained segregated would be allowed to receive federal funding. Moreover, in 1965, the Elementary and Secondary Education Act required that segregated school districts had to supply a timely plan for desegregation to the Department of Health, Education, and Welfare (HEW) before they could receive federal funds. This new legislation triggered vicious backlashes by whites, not just in southern states, but in cities throughout the country, notably in Boston, Chicago, Minneapolis, and elsewhere. Violence against blacks, even rioting, broke out over what was considered by whites to be forced desegregation.[99]

In California, busing included Mexican Americans. According to Stephen Pitti, the issue of school segregation was taken up by the Community Service Organization in San Jose, a Mexican American group of political activists that worked to integrate local schools and hire teachers who could "deal effectively with the problems of the Mexican American child." They were met with strong resistance from whites who defended segregation in neighborhoods and schools.[100]

In Los Angeles, the threat of busing to integrate schools created a groundswell of opposition from whites, and their response was to send their school-age children to private schools or to flee the city altogether for nearby all-white suburbs. The Watts riots exacerbated the problem by reinforcing the misguided impression of whites that all blacks (and Latinos) were poor, violent, lazy, and would collectively lower education standards in formerly all-white schools.[101] The suburban community of South Gate formed the South Gate Education Committee to vigorously oppose busing black children from overcrowded schools in Watts into their community.[102]

In Oakland, the Office of Economic Opportunity (OEO) attempted to improve schools and access to schools in what had become a black ghetto by the mid-1960s in the wake of redevelopment programs that isolated poor blacks from their middle-class counterparts. With federal funding support, the OEO began teacher-training programs, summer school remedial education, and Head Start programs rather than focus on integrating schools through busing. The issues that drove civil rights activism in Oakland were employment and housing more than education.[103]

To some extent, the Monterey Peninsula mirrored what was happening in these California cities and towns and throughout the western United

States, as whites who could afford to send their children to private schools did so in droves.[104] But there was no comparable white flight from Monterey, Carmel, or Pacific Grove when the prospect of busing and school integration occurred, because there were no all-white suburbs nearby to flee to. The closest town was Salinas, which had more minorities than either of these communities, or Santa Cruz, which was also populated by minority groups.

The schools in Monterey County simply were not prepared for the surge in enrollment or the diversity of students that was brought about by the expansion of Fort Ord in the 1960s and 1970s. Seaside schools quickly became overcrowded. They also reflected the de facto segregated housing practices of cities throughout the county. The Johnson report applauded the Monterey Peninsula Unified School District (MPUSD) in 1968 for making a "valiant attempt to bring about integration," but called the effort "almost insurmountable" due to housing discrimination.[105] Efforts to establish some semblance of educational equity included the building of a new elementary school in Seaside in 1967, Manzanita School, and, according to Johnson, "brought down the non-white enrollment at Highland [elementary school] by 8 percent." Johnson identified San Francisco, Oakland, and Richmond as other cities in California with racially imbalanced school populations (enrollment of 50 percent or more blacks). A 1966 measure by the California State Department of Education required school districts to conduct "ethnic surveys" and use the results of the surveys to enforce affirmative action in order to achieve better racial and ethnic balance in California schools. Johnson used the results of this survey for Monterey County to present a racial and ethnic snapshot of the area for 1966. Although the transient population from Fort Ord complicated findings, Johnson identified a clear pattern of racial imbalance in Seaside. She found that one-third of Seaside's school-age population of 12,136 were minorities (about 15 percent were black in 1967 and 1968). Three Seaside schools had 62 percent or more minority students (50 percent of the student bodies at Noche Buena and Manzanita schools were black). Highland School was 75 percent minority enrollment (62 percent African American), and the formally all-white neighborhood of Ord Terrace was 48 percent minority (three out of five students were black). In Monterey, by contrast, there were three schools with white enrollments of 94 to 96 percent, while almost all of the other schools had only "token" minority representation (from 0.4 percent to 4.3 percent African American). Johnson found similar patterns at the junior high school level (Martin Luther King Junior High had a 61 percent minority population, 42 percent of whom were black), while at Colton Junior High in Monterey, 83 percent of students were Caucasian. There was more equity at the high school level, particularly after Seaside High was built in 1965; 41 percent of the students were minority, of whom 19 percent were African American. Monterey High's minority student body comprised 24 percent of the enrollment in 1965–1966, of which 10 percent was black.[106]

It was not city government but the county that strove to correct racial imbalances in public schools. To its credit, the MPUSD took integration seriously, even though it faced great odds in solving the problem in the face of city councils on the Peninsula that supported segregation. Like every other district in California and across the country in those years, school boards focused on busing and on integrating student bodies, but they complained that integrating faculties could not be accomplished because, they argued, there were no qualified black teachers to hire. Dr. Charlie Mae Knight, an African American fourth grade teacher at the mostly black Highlands Elementary School who came to Seaside as a military wife, played a key role in the situation and helped make the MPUSD a model for other districts in California. According to Knight, in 1965:

I was teaching 4th grade at Highland Elementary school in Seaside when I was asked to become part of the Administration and part of the integration plan that Monterey was required to submit to the federal government . . . The school district needed to demonstrate that they had made real efforts to integrate in order to receive money from Elementary Secondary Education Act Title I. They didn't have any black administrators then and they came to my class to see if I would like to work at the central office to assist with minority education. At that time minority education meant Filipinos and blacks, with blacks in the greatest number. There were few Mexican Americans or other Asians in the district. We had programs that allowed for busing and integrating middle school and high school, but very little at the elementary school level. We had very few black teachers. In 1966, two African American political activists, Lee Toler and Mattye Blakeney (who eventually taught in MPUSD) came before the board, which was all-white with one black member, Sam Brown, who like most ex-military people was very conservative. They vehemently protested [the conditions at] schools with majority black populations but all white faculty, [arguing that] black teachers could relate to and positively mentor black kids in ways that white teachers could not. Don Woodington, who was white, a former boxer, and fairly liberal, convinced the rest of the Board that we had better do something to recruit black teachers. I was given the responsibility of recruiting black teachers in 1966 through 1969.[107]

Knight visited over 125 historically black colleges in the South to recruit nearly seventy African American teachers and administrators in a little over three years. These individuals included Dr. Henry Hutchins and Bertha Hutchins, Billy DeBerry and his wife Rose, Helen Rucker, and Bettye Lusk, all of whom remain prominent both in Seaside and Monterey County. Dr. Hutchins became an administrator and superintendent of schools, as did Billy De Berry. Helen Rucker, who married a serviceman from Fort Ord, served on the Seaside City Council and is now a member of the Monterey Peninsula School Board. Bettye Lusk, married to H. H. Lusk, powerful minister of Bethel Baptist Church, was principal of Seaside High School and also currently serves on the MPUSD Board. These individuals infused Seaside with new residents who were tied directly to national civil rights movements.

The program to integrate the faculty was an unqualified success for the schools. School faculties integrated, and the new teachers and administrators stayed in Seaside and went on to contribute to the community in a variety of ways. However, integration meant the integration of African American faculty. Few Filipino or Mexican American teachers were recruited. In fact, at a meeting of the MPUSD, Tony Sison, who was on an advisory committee complained, "Filipinos are not proportionately represented in racial balance in the teaching positions in Monterey County. And to aggravate this inequality, plans are underway to cut off the funds of the Public Employment Program and pre-school in which most of the Filipino teachers and employees are employed."[108] Although the MPUSD

Board promised to absorb Filipinos into other positions in the county if funding was cut, little was actually done about rectifying the imbalance in Filipino and Latino faculty.

By 1978, MPUSD Superintendent James Harrison identified "racially isolated" schools as a result of a survey to decide if busing programs were needed. Out of the twenty elementary schools in MPUSD, ten had student bodies below the average acceptable ratio of white to minority students, reflecting persistent segregation in housing on the Peninsula. Colton Junior High in Monterey had a 90 percent white student body, while King Junior High in Seaside had an 80 percent minority (mostly black) student body. It was urgent to develop a strategy to remedy the situation because federal funding depended on it. According to Harrison, if nothing was done, "The state board of education could remove the entire local board, including him, for failing to comply [with current integration policies]. He said that approximately $5 million received by the district each year from state and federal funds could also be withheld."[109] Busing policies occurred, but they focused mainly on bringing minority students into formerly white schools rather than bringing white students into Seaside.

The busing controversy was widespread in the United States by 1972, sometimes erupted into violence, and was met in varied ways by communities across the country and particularly in the South.[110] Black political activists in Seaside chose the less controversial strategy of integrating the faculty of already black public schools rather than attempt to force full integration of faculty or student bodies of white ones, just as coalitions of white liberal women pursued strategies of limited desegregation in Atlanta, Georgia. Theirs was an approach that did not threaten white hegemony on the rest of the Peninsula, just as one-way busing strategies in northern and northeastern suburbs allowed some black students in but kept white ones in their own neighborhood schools.[111]

The policy of faculty integration that focused almost entirely on hiring black faculty for all-black schools may have been largely successful in changing the face of education in Monterey County. However, this was the more cautious approach, in keeping both with African American civil rights ideology of the early 1960s, which was more measured and careful than the movements that emerged in the later years of the 1960s and

1970s, and also with conservative military culture, which was infused in Seaside, especially among black political leaders.

Black women took leadership roles in creating equity in education, just as school politics elsewhere drew women into activism, and just as black women always did for their communities.[112] Active duty military personnel were forbidden from taking a role in local politics, but even with that caveat, it is striking that Dr. Charlie Mae Knight and the women she recruited to teach and to work in school administration who were wives of officers and higher ranking enlisted men became the leaders and champions in the hard work of making a political change through education. While Knight and others accomplished a great deal in terms of integrating faculty, there was little that could be done to integrate schools as long as housing remained segregated.

Powerful housing restrictions led to frustration and to the development of an organized, successful joint civil rights effort by African Americans and other groups in Seaside to desegregate neighborhoods on the Monterey Peninsula, starting with the city of Seaside. However, what was happening on the whole of the Peninsula was similar to what other cities across the nation that included large populations of minorities experienced in the 1970s. "White flight" from urban areas was a well-documented phenomenon that led to elite, all-white suburbs outside of cities.[113] White elites and upper-middle-class whites remained in Pebble Beach or Carmel and increasingly sent their children to one or more of the several private schools in the area when integration in housing in Seaside and Monterey increasingly succeeded in integrating public schools.

CHALLENGING BOUNDARIES IN NEIGHBORHOODS

Charlotte Brooks, in her excellent analysis of racially restrictive housing in California, linked foreign policy efforts in the United States in the post-World War II decades to a gradual shift in attitudes with regard to race and segregation. Efforts by American policymakers to woo Chinese from communism in the Cold War years and, a decade later, during the Vietnam War to win the hearts and minds of Southeast Asians, led to changed views of all Asians on the part of whites. "The government's message to white Americans," Brooks argued, "was that some people were worth fighting for and some were not. In California, the deserving increasingly included Asian Americans, while the undeserving, were, more often than not, blacks and Mexican Americans."[114] Thus, in California after World War II, a shift occurred in neighborhoods as whites began to allow previously excluded Asians (and Jews) into restricted neighborhoods, even as they resisted incursions by blacks and Mexicans.[115]

In Seaside, residential segregation affected African Americans in particular. Data from the OEC in 1966 showed a systematic pattern of racial segregation in Monterey County, with Seaside designated for black families and Salinas for Mexican and Mexican American families. The Johnson report concluded that "the Monterey Peninsula has a pronounced pattern of racial segregation . . . the majority of non-whites reside in only one city—Seaside. The city of Seaside estimates that approximately 18 percent of its population is non-white (predominantly Negro)."[116]

By 1968, Johnson found that even though racially restrictive real estate covenants were illegal, "discrimination [was] apparent since all white communities developed," which she attributed to "subterfuges" by realtors in Monterey County who had overwhelmingly supported California Proposition 14, a measure designed to "nullify existing housing laws" that discriminated based on race. That measure passed "by a sizeable majority" in Monterey County but was ruled unconstitutional by the California Supreme Court in May 1966.[117]

"We were packed in here [Seaside] like sardines," lamented Redevelopment Agency member Sarah Ector.[118] According to Mae Johnson, who moved to Seaside in 1961, "We were taken to see homes in Seaside—only in Seaside. And then we saw streets that had no blacks, such as Kimball Street. There were specific streets where blacks did not live."[119] Johnson advocated public awareness and education campaigns to put an end to housing discrimination, arguing that "the time is near when the patterns of discrimination will evolve into two separate racial ghettoes."[120]

Monterey County realtors and residents were hardly alone in their support of segregated spaces, especially for blacks and Mexicans. Segregation was common practice throughout the country and fiercely defended by whites.[121] In California, Proposition 14 generated widespread support. According to Robert Self's analysis of Oakland, the California Real Estate

Association (CREA), which sponsored Proposition 14, left "little doubt that race was central" in the fight over housing. Self argued that Proposition 14 was "the first evidence of an emerging white political backlash against the civil rights movement." Although California supported the election of Lyndon Johnson in 1964 by a significant margin, "65 per cent [of California voters] approved Proposition 14. The results in Oakland confirm that large numbers of white homeowners opposed desegregation and racial liberalism."[122] Becky Nicolaides found a similar pattern of fierce resistance to integration in Los Angeles suburbs over the issue of Proposition 14.[123] Stephen Pitti's analysis of San Jose showed that the use of racially restrictive covenants effectively confined Mexican Americans to the barrio in East San Jose as all-white suburbs grew around the city.[124] In Salinas, the Mexican American Political Association (MAPA), a more radical Mexican American civil rights group than the CSO, staged marches and protests against Proposition 14, as Mexicans and Mexican Americans were confined to specific neighborhoods of Salinas.[125] At the same time, housing was opening up for Asians of any nationality, even in the most conservative white suburbs.[126]

Nonetheless, with the full backing of the federal government, which responded to the heroic efforts of civil rights activists in these years to open neighborhoods to all people, and as a result of the clear discrepancy between life on and off base in Seaside, African Americans were poised to challenge unfair housing practices head-on, just as they did in other parts of California and the West. The difference in Seaside was the reaction from whites. There were no cross burnings, riots, or violent backlash, as other towns and cities throughout the country experienced.[127]

Sherman and Elizabeth Smith fought and won the right to live in Ord Terrace in Seaside in 1968, a previously segregated neighborhood, simply by moving in. There were others who did the same. In 1968, in the wake of federal legislation prohibiting discrimination in housing, a lawsuit by a black couple made clear how segregated the Peninsula had become as a response to African American immigration to Seaside through Fort Ord, but also how determined blacks, whites, and other minorities were to erase all vestiges of restricted housing, and how they did so without the usual violent backlash that other brave civil rights activists encountered. This also shows, as was the case in Los Angeles and San Francisco, that racist housing restrictions were not practiced only by whites.[128] Mr. and Mrs. Bradford Vaughn, black school teachers in Seaside, attempted to rent a house at 2015 Mendocino Street in Seaside from Dr. and Mrs. Ting Su who were Chinese. Dr. Su was an instructor at the Defense Language Institute in Monterey and lived nearby. The Vaughns contacted Dr. Su through a newspaper advertisement for a rental home. Dr. Su invited them to see the house, but when the Vaughns arrived, Dr. Su "abruptly refused to rent the house to them, permit them to view or examine said house, enter the premises of the landlord other than to stand at the door [who] stated that the house was not for rent." However, when Mrs. Vaughn called Dr. Su two hours later "pretending to be other than a Negro," she was told that the house was available. A week later, a Caucasian couple called the landlord who told them not only that the house was available but also that it was located "in an area free of Negroes."[129]

In his thorough analysis of housing practices in Monterey County, J. Morgan Kousser documented hundreds of instances of racially restrictive deeds as well as in advertisements for rental housing.[130] An attorney for the Vaughns stated "Due to a pattern of racial discrimination throughout Monterey County and a virtual absence of decent housing available to Negroes persons such as [the Vaughns] are compelled to accept inferior substandard housing at inflated values . . . [after a] comprehensive search [of many weeks] each personal appearance of the [Vaughns] was met either by a total rebuff, a statement that the available house was not available for rent or an astronomical raise in rent calculated to totally discourage plaintiffs from entering into any rental agreement." The Vaughns asked for and won the right to rent the house in question and were awarded a settlement of $12,000 for "emotional and mental distress and loss of dignity and pride as Americans and as Negroes."[131] Interviews with African Americans who came to Seaside in the 1950s and 1960s confirm that the Vaughn's experience was common. However, many people demanded and won the right to live in white neighborhoods in Seaside and throughout the Peninsula, often with the help of whites and other minority groups, without having to contest the issue in the courts.[132] According to Janna Ottman, a white political activist in Seaside, white activists routinely bought homes on the Peninsula, then immediately resold them to African Americans, who were able to move in and remain in them, thus effectively desegregating neighborhoods in Seaside, Monterey, and Monterey County between 1960 and 1970.[133] This was common practice throughout California and the West as white liberals aligned with blacks and other minorities to push for equal rights and integration.[134]

EMPLOYMENT AND EQUAL OPPORTUNITY

At the same time blacks were fighting for equal housing, they and their supporters opened a second front against employment discrimination. The 1959 California Fair Employment Practice Act forbid discrimination in employment on the basis of race, and it stipulated that the Fair Employment Practices Commission (FEPC) would enforce the policy. In 1964, Title VII of the Civil Rights Act of 1964 created a sweeping, national prohibition on discrimination and created the Equal Employment Opportunity Commission (EEOC) to oversee and enforce antidiscrimination laws and policies. Both agencies were severely tested in cities throughout the country as activists sought to open economic opportunities for minorities and women.[135] The new civil rights legislation coupled with the antidiscrimination policies were cornerstones of Lyndon Johnson's "Great Society" and the hallmark of his administration in the mid-1960s.

According to Reverend Welton McGee, "It was terrible to live here. The blacks could hardly get jobs. I worked for a dollar an hour [in] construction it was so prejudice here . . . 1950, '51, '52 blacks couldn't hardly *buy* a job."[136] Although McGee referred to the 1950s, conditions had not improved much in the next decade. The Monterey County NAACP was at the forefront of challenging discrimination during the 1960s and had a membership of over 1,000 people of all races at that time from throughout the Peninsula. Cecil Bindel, who was white and served briefly in the armed services during the war, joined the organization in 1951 at the behest of his friend, realtor John Bean, also an ex-military man. In 1962 Bindel became president and served two terms.[137] Bindel and the NAACP focused on equity issues, especially on employment on the Peninsula. The service industries, in particular, had a history of excluding blacks both in employment and as guests. Bindel threatened to take motel owners on the

Monterey Peninsula to court in 1962 to force them to "take down racial barriers." They complied. He and other representatives of the NAACP met with business owners and bank managers to encourage the hiring of African Americans; they met with only limited success and many excuses. As Bindel recalls, "One bank manager came up with the excuse that he couldn't hire any blacks because the union wouldn't let him do it."[138]

Pearl Carey was a military wife who challenged racial bias in employment in Monterey with the fierce determination of someone who had the lived experience of integration and fairness of military life coupled with her deep involvement in the broader civil rights movement to empower her. She was Seaside's first African American city councilwoman and the first African American woman to challenge the Hatch Act of 1939 and later, in the 1990s, racial gerrymandering in Monterey County in the federal courts. Carey was tasked with finding employment for blacks through the Department of Employment, a federal agency in Monterey. Carey recalled:

In 1964 I was in charge of all federal training programs for the area. Through those programs I was able to give those disadvantaged an opportunity to up-grade themselves. Many were placed in meaningful jobs, including jobs in labor unions; jobs that had been previously denied them because of the Grandfather Clause . . . I challenged that practice and was successful in placing men in union jobs . . . under my federal programs I certified black people for business loans and special courses in school if they met government guidelines . . . one of my duties was in securing jobs for qualified applicants with private employers. The government [paid] part of the employees wages [provided] the employer had at least 50 employees with 10 percent minorities and agreed to hire the employee permanently after 6 months. Several employers . . . let them [subsidized employees] go after 5 and a half months. I assured them that they would have to pay the government back . . . these employers were somewhat bent out of shape but they knew they would lose.[139]

Conditions had not changed much by 1967 when Elaine Johnson conducted her sociological analysis of Monterey County. She examined unemployment figures for 1967 and concluded:

The Monterey Peninsula has a very high rate of unemployment. Whereas within the total United States, unemployment is presently 3.6 percent, on the Peninsula it is 7 percent for whites, 26 percent for Negroes, 8.3 percent for Orientals, 9 percent for Mexican Americans, and 12 percent for American Indians. At the national level Negro unemployment is double the white unemployment rate. On the Peninsula Negro unemployment is almost four times the white rate.[140]

Johnson expressed outrage at the level of local racial discrimination in employment: "With the passage of a number of civil rights bills in recent years it is now illegal to discriminate in employment . . . However . . . it is obvious to the writer [Johnson] that few Negroes are being hired in Monterey in other than menial, traditional occupations."[141] She criticized several federal antipoverty and employment programs, such as the one run by Pearl Carey, because although they offered subsidies to businesses to hire African Americans and created training programs, they had proven largely unsuccessful when it came to actual hiring practices, "One of the big problems on the Peninsula is that so much has been spent on training and recruiting minorities and yet there are so few successes . . . the major problem is that there are four or five different programs working in job training and placement. There seems to be so much overlapping and so little coordination."[142] Johnson and others feared that limited mobility based on job discrimination could lead Seaside to the type of violence that was prevalent in urban America by the end of the decade. Seaside's strong connection to the military, however, was a deterrent to widespread racial upheaval. African American activists like Pearl Carey, Sherman Smith, and many others drew on the example of integration and opportunity on base to sustain them with a model of success through this difficult period. Moreover, although Seaside was generally poor, a stable black middle class was largely responsible for creating a city culture similar to more affluent African American communities in California and elsewhere throughout the country.[143] The black middle class in Seaside was composed of African Americans such as Carey, Smith, retired Colonel Al Glover, Ruthie Watts, and many others who either rose in rank as officers and high-ranking en-listed men or who were married to officers or noncommissioned officers. These individuals and their families depended on Fort Ord for livelihoods, rather than just on the local economy, and could sustain a middle-class life that became the backbone of the civil rights movement in Seaside.[144] This was a critically important reality, as black civil rights activists elsewhere in California and the West faced blackmail, threats against their jobs and businesses, and even bankruptcy as the price of activism.[145] The economic security that the military afforded, even with its constraints on political involvement, meant that black soldiers and their families were free to engage in the important race work of civil rights during a critical moment in American history.

MEXICAN AMERICANS AND ACTIVISM IN SEASIDE IN THE 1970S

The race work of middle class civil rights activists in Seaside occurred in the context of one of the most important and well-known civil rights labor movements in the country beginning in 1967 and through the decades of the 1970s and 1980s: the César Chávez labor movement in Salinas. Yet, there is very little evidence that Seaside residents became part of that extraordinary labor movement, aside from the fact that Seaside Filipino women were engaged in fieldwork and participated in protests and strikes.[146] With some notable exceptions, such as with Mel Mason, Dr. Charlie Mae Knight, and Assemblyman Bill Monning, all of whom were actively engaged in labor struggles, the mostly African American activists who were fighting segregation in Monterey County did not get involved in developments in Salinas. As Mark Brilliant has shown, California and the West experienced multiple civil rights movements that rarely collaborated, focused as they were on entirely different goals based on race and ethnicity.[147] This is not to say that groups did not support one another. Salinas MAPA activists, for example, staged protests over labor and equity issues throughout Monterey County, including at the U.S. Post Office in Monterey for discrimination against a Mexican American postal worker.[148] However, it is striking how little interaction occurred between the two neighboring cities. Mexican Americans in Salinas and African Americans and others in Seaside were engaged in different battles in the same struggle.

Mexican Americans in the Seaside civil rights movement tended to be as centrist and middle class in values and beliefs as other Seaside residents. Unlike those other groups however, Mexican Americans were rarely part of military culture. Rodolfo Nava, a professor at Monterey Peninsula College, along with a handful of other Seaside Mexican American families, including the Pérez and Rubio families, formed the Asociaciòn Cultural Hispano Americano (ACHA) in 1976 to promote Mexican music, dance, and art in Seaside. Alfredo Nava, Rudolfo Nava's older brother, had left South Texas to teach on the Monterey Peninsula in 1964, and Rudolfo followed five years later. He was familiar with anti-Mexican racism in Texas but was surprised to find these attitudes in California when he arrived. He recalled:

When I arrived [in Monterey] with my diploma [in 1969] . . . I was [told] this is a resort area. You are not going to find anything here. [The interviewer from MPUSD] said you should go to Salinas or San Jose. You might even become a foreman in some [fruit] packing shed over there. Those were his words.[149]

This comment from the MPUSD interviewer is evidence that Mexican Americans were as isolated in Salinas and San Jose as African Americans were in Seaside. In spite of this demeaning encounter, Nava became the Language Lab Director and taught Spanish at Monterey Peninsula College (MPC) until his retirement in 2004. He became faculty sponsor of the local chapter of the Movimento Estudiantil Chicano de Aztlan (MECHA), the Chicano student organization, in 1969, and supported the invitation they extended to Dolores Huerta to speak at MPC. However, the administration refused their request, willing to relent only if "she [was] coming to MPC to talk about growing tomatoes . . . They were afraid that the students would be inspired by her words and cause some kind of disruption. Then they said we don't have parking. That was ridiculous. We had all kinds of guest speakers and we were able to accommodate them." Nava ensured that Dolores Huerta did speak, but in Seaside, at Martin Luther King Junior High School on October 20, 1976.

Although Dolores Huerta personified civil rights for Latinos linked to the labor movement every bit as much as César Chávez, no other Seaside

activist mentioned her visit to Seaside. On the other hand, almost everyone recalled Dr. Martin Luther King Jr.'s visit to Seaside in 1962.

The activism by Mexican Americans in Seaside the late 1960s centered
on making sure that Mexican culture was given fair representation in the
city, rather than the more confrontational politics that centered in Salinas
over farm worker issues. That would change in the late 1970s and in the
1980s under the leadership of Dr. William Meléndez, a Puerto Rican who
came from New York to teach in Salinas schools in 1970, and who became
President of the League of United Latin American Citizens (LULAC). As
a teacher in Salinas, Dr. Meléndez was struck by the damage done to students through language bias: "I saw teachers relegating Spanish speaking
children to lesser education . . . I saw that it was through community action that you could make significant change. I reached out. To Fernando
Armenta, Juan Martínez, Jesse Sánchez, Phillip Tabera . . . the Latino
community coalesced in the 1970s around LULAC . . . the issues were
farm worker issues, education, housing, jobs."[150] By the 1980s, Latinos and
blacks would join together in new civil rights efforts directed primarily at
the police departments of Monterey County. However, it must be noted
that Latino civil rights issues of language and labor did not resonate with
African American activists who whose efforts in education, housing, and
employment were directed at inclusion into the white mainstream rather
than bilingual education or for workers' rights in agriculture.

CITY POLITICS 1970–1980

The city council election on April 14, 1970, set the stage for the power
shift that gave African Americans control of city government and allowed
for major change at all levels. It was this election that recalled two white
councilmen who were allies of Mayor Lou Haddad, Berdine (Bud) Houser,
and Emil Schmidt, in favor of the first African American woman on the
city council, Pearl Carey, and Gerald McGrath, a white retired military
man, and a close ally of Carey. Carey described McGrath as "a very,
very nice man. He had a good heart and wanted to do what I wanted to
do for Seaside. He voted black."[151] McGrath was typical of many white
veterans from integrated Fort Ord that extended their understanding of
race beyond the base and into the civilian communities of which they

became a part. They expected the equal treatment off base that they had experienced on base, regardless of race.

According to an interview with Carey in the *Monterey Peninsula Herald* on May 8, 1970, Seaside's problems in 1970 were "not only . . . racial issues. There are a lot of poor white people too. I would like to see an end to the political powerlessness of poor people, which has been part of the structure of Seaside for far too long. It is now time for a change." Her comment not only showed a sensitivity to class divisions, but also indicated that in Seaside, African Americans did not have to form race-based blocs for civil rights.[152]

Carey earned the endorsement of the *Monterey Peninsula Herald* when she ran for mayor in 1972. The endorsement described Carey as "a woman who is committed to something more than the politics of self-aggrandizement [as opposed to Haddad] . . . a proved leader with a demonstrated capacity for working with people—all kinds of people—to get things done."[153] Carey remained a vital part of successful efforts to contest the gerrymandering of county supervisor districts twenty years later in Seaside politics and in county Democratic Party politics for the rest of her ninety-six years. She was elected as a delegate to the Democratic National Convention in 1972 and was the first person in Monterey County of any color to serve on a committee of a national political party. However, she lost her state-funded job as advocate for minorities seeking employment in federally funded projects because government employees were not allowed to actively engage in partisan politics, according to the Hatch Act of 1939. She challenged the Hatch Act, but lost at the U.S. Supreme Court level. The fight was a testament to her strength, perseverance, and sense of fairness, all of which was bolstered by her connection to the integrated world of the American military, where her husband made a career as staff sergeant, as well as her deep involvement in a national civil rights movement that reinforced her work and her purpose.

Mayor Lou Haddad engineered a successful recall drive against council members Carey and McGrath within a year of their election (and an unsuccessful recall of council members Stephen Ross and Oliver Murray). Nonetheless, it was increasingly clear that the political momentum had shifted away from Haddad, and that African Americans were a powerful political force that would not be intimidated. By 1976, Seasiders elected Oscar Lawson, their first African American mayor who, like Carey, McGrath, and Ross ran as a defender of the rights of minorities and of disadvantaged members of the community, and like the rest of the city council, including Haddad, was a veteran of Fort Ord.

The first two African American mayors, Oscar Lawson (1976–1978) and Stephen Ross (1978–1980), served one term each and faced constant bickering and power struggles. According to former City Manager Charles McNeely, "There was a lot of racial tension in votes and views about where the city was going and who was in control [before 1980]."[154]

In 1978 Lou Haddad lost the mayor's race to African American Stephen Ross, but he was appointed to fill the city council seat vacated by Ross by the outgoing mayor, Glenn Olea. Haddad attempted but failed to initiate a recall of Ross in 1979. However, when Theodore Bowser, who was the only other African American on the city council abruptly resigned in 1979, Olea, Haddad, and the rest of the city council voted to appoint Al Lioi over the objections of Mayor Ross, who advocated for an election over an appointment. African American Ministers H. H. Lusk and Ben C. Franklin also raised objections to the appointment of Albert Lioi, who was Portuguese, at a city council meeting attended by over 200 people.[155] This left Mayor Ross as the only African American member of the Seaside City Council in 1979.

Together with the firing of Stan Hall, the first African American city manager in 1980, orchestrated by Haddad and Bud Houser, with lukewarm support from Councilman Glenn Olea, this replacement of a black councilmember by a white one appeared to be both arrogant and racially motivated as reported in the *Monterey Peninsula Herald*:

Haddad, who had moved to fire Hall, was supported by Councilman Berdine (Bud) Houser and Glenn Olea. The dismissal was opposed by Mayor Stephen E. Ross and councilman Theodore Bowser Jr. Haddad and Houser are white and Olea is of Filipino heritage; Ross and Bowser are black, as was Hall, and the dismissal was perceived in the city as a racial issue. Since the Hall firing, Bowser has resigned and his seat was filled last month by the appointment of Al Lioi, who must face election in April.[156]

Again, although this conflict centered on race, it contrasted with other cities embroiled in racial tensions in California that pitted one minority group, blacks or Hispanics, for example, against an entrenched white power elite. In Seaside, the struggle was between individual members of groups who all arrived at about the same time (1950s) as part of a military migration, and who had themselves, in the recent past, faced discrimination and an uncertain racial status as members of ethnic minority groups; Haddad (Lebanese) Lioi (Portuguese) and Houser (Sicilian) were members of groups that were thought of socially as "not quite white," although they were always considered white by law.[157]

The community had had enough of the fighting and of the manipulations of Haddad and his allies by the end of the decade. Planning Commissioner Roy B. Daniels wrote about the period in a front page story for the *Seaside Post-News Sentinel*, likening the council meetings of 1979 to a "three ring circus."[158] Ewalker James, Morris McDaniel, and other African American activists formed the Citizens League for Progress in 1979 and gathered over 2,000 signatures in a petition to reinstate Hall as city manager. When that effort failed, they focused on wresting political control from what they believed was a corrupt and racist clique. Robert Miskimon, who was white and the editor of the *Seaside Post-News Sentinel*, spoke for many in an editorial in the newspaper on January 23, 1980, "Seaside may have been once run politically by a small band of white, male supremacists, but this is 1980 and the public has grown weary of the old style politics. Nixon may be out of the White House, but there are still vestiges of the Babbitt mentality everywhere, even in Seaside."[159]

The editorial staff of the *Monterey Peninsula Herald* concurred in the following day's editorial: "The people of Seaside are not going to have any peace and quiet, any security, any social or economic progress, until the political likes of Lou Haddad and his cronies—on and off City Council—are kept out of office once and for all."[160] In spite of the rhetoric Haddad, Houser, and Lioi were hardly entrenched powers. These were all army veterans, small business owners, and of Southern European, or in Haddad's case, Middle Eastern descent. Importantly, it was not just minorities who were offended by their racism. Whites as well as blacks shared a sensibility that racism would not be tolerated off base any more than it was on base, at a moment in time, the late 1960s and 1970s, when whites, fearful of the rioting and violence on the part of blacks who were targeted by police departments throughout the country, largely withdrew from civil rights efforts in other parts of the country.[161]

The Citizen's League for Progress began an intensive voter registration and awareness drive, which mobilized residents for the next election in April 1980, and also strove to recall Haddad from office immediately. They gathered over 2,137 signatures to recall Haddad, 1,629 of which were deemed valid. The League scrambled and collected 116 more signatures to meet the 1,745 needed to force a recall in a special February election.[162]

Haddad and his allies on the council fought back. As a counterpoint to the Citizen's League for Progress, whites (and some Filipinos) formed the Seaside Citizens for Honesty in Government. They convinced the Monterey County District Attorney William C. Curtis to issue subpoenas and to initiate an investigation of the validity of the signatures on the Haddad recall petition. This was seen as a thinly veiled effort to intimidate blacks into withdrawing their signatures from the recall petitions, according to an interview with Citizens League spokesman Mel Mason published in the *Seaside Post-News Sentinel*:

We . . . question whether this investigation [by the District Attorney's Office] was really used to harass and instill fear in the recall petitioners. I myself had a deputy district attorney come to my job and interrogate me in my office when common courtesy would have dictated to him to come by my house after working hours. A number of other petitioners had similar complaints and one woman in particular stated that while she was being questioned, the deputy unbuttoned his coat so that his gun protruded out in full view. Naturally this shook her up.[163]

Haddad's efforts to halt the recall drive failed. Although the District Attorney's office found no evidence of impropriety in its investigations and therefore did not pursue criminal charges, Haddad took the issue to Monterey County Superior Court where it was dismissed. "That's what I expected," Haddad responded, "[Judge Richard Silver] is a very liberal judge. We made a mistake in getting him in the first place."[164] The recall election went forward and Haddad was removed by a slim margin of 88 votes. In one of his last acts as city councilman before he was forced to leave in the wake of the recall campaign, Haddad and allies Bud Houser and Al Lioi voted to terminate the contract of City Attorney Steve Slatkow in retaliation for Slatkow's willingness to move forward with the recall campaign. According to Citizens League for Progress founder Morris McDaniel, "Once we had all of the signatures on the petitions, the city was required to bring it to a ballot and initiate the removal of Haddad. Slatkow was only doing his job."[165]

There was a question about whether Haddad was entitled to vote as a city councilman on the Slatkow termination. However, the day before Haddad was to be removed from office, the rest of the city council called a meeting to review Slatkow's contract. "I don't understand how this [action] met the test for lawfulness," Morris McDaniel commented, "But Slatkow challenged the decision in court and lost."[166] This time Councilman Olea voted with Mayor Ross to oppose the firing of Slatkow. Although Olea's support was not enough to prevent Slatkow's firing, it gave him some of the credibility he needed as a candidate for mayor in the 1980 election.

One important outcome of African American increased political activism was the initiation of voter registration drives. According to the McDaniels, "In 1977, one of the first acts of the Pan-Hellenic council [an umbrella organization for all of the African American sororities and fraternities in the area] was to organize a voter registration caravan all over the city. We registered about 500 people in one weekend alone."[167] The recall election of 1980 increased voter participation even more. An analysis in the weekly *Seaside Tribune* estimated that the Citizen's League for Progress effort to recall Haddad increased voter registration by 15 percent in one month. According to the article, "More than 3,500 Seaside citizens, or about 40 percent of the city's over 8,000 registered voters cast ballots in the Haddad recall election . . . It was a very good turnout."[168] Clearly the Pan-Hellenic Council was not just focused on African Americans but registered a sizeable number of Seaside residents. In a parallel effort, both the Salinas chapter of The Community Service Organization (CSO) and MAPA also organized voter registration drives, leading to "record highs" in Salinas and Monterey County.[169]

In the election held on April 8, 1980, Glenn Olea won the mayor's race, and Mel Mason won a city council seat. The other three members of the city council were Bud Houser, Al Lioi, and George Austin. Once again, the city council was a mixture of racial groups with the common denominator of military service. The only exception to this was council member Mel Mason, who had objected to the Vietnam War, gone AWOL, and was briefly imprisoned as a result. Mason first moved to Seaside with his mother at the age of thirteen in 1956. Mason was the only Seaside city council member to list membership in the Black Panther Party in Oakland on his resume. He had participated with other Panthers on the picket lines during the Great Lettuce Strike of 1970 in support of Mexican American and Filipino farm workers, before returning to Seaside in the 1970s. Mason stood out in Seaside for his radical views, which the mostly centrist black military community did not share. However, he truly embraced women and all minority groups as part of a collective ideology of civil rights that was valued in Seaside. He also stood out because he embodied a critical connection to other civil rights movements in California, such as the one focused on labor and immigration in Salinas and with the Black Panther Party in Oakland.

Mayor Glenn Olea wanted to demonstrate that Filipinos were as integral to Seaside as blacks were and initiated creating a sister city link between Irga City, the Philippines, and Seaside. However, when Councilman Mel Mason attempted to do the same for the island of Grenada, "a furor erupted." Grenada had a predominantly black population but was a socialist country. According to Mason, "It was okay to have a sister city in the Philippines where the U.S. was backing the Marcos dictatorship [but not in Grenada which] established a socialist government that nationalized industries, made education available to all people . . . established free medical care, [and] guaranteed women equal rights by law." Seaside's military population drew the line at the radical politics that Councilman Mason represented. They were deeply patriotic and shared the military's intense dislike of any government that appeared to be socialist or communist.[170]

Olea also made it a new imperative to staff city hall with minorities. City Manager Roger Kemp (who replaced Stan Hall in 1979) emphasized the importance of minority representation in the government workforce, but he actually only increased minorities by 6 percent during Olea's first term of office.[171] In a presentation to the NAACP, Kemp reported that he had polled department heads and determined that 43 percent of city workers were members of minority groups by 1980. His assessment was supported by a report from the city's affirmative action officer, Clarence Campbell, who found a discrepancy between the ethnic and racial makeup in Seaside's population and the ethnic racial makeup of the city's workforce. Campbell was particularly concerned about parity in gender. He noted that while "the percentage of women in the community is roughly 50 percent; the overall percentage of women employed by the City of Seaside is less than 10 percent. Seaside is probably doing better than many other high minority cities . . . the goal is obtainable but we must continue working on it."[172]

The most problematic departments in terms of affirmative action, according to Kemp, were the police and fire. "The police department," he said, "has a total of four black police, with one in the police academy and not yet on the beat [out of a total of] 32 sworn police officers in Seaside. And there are a total of four black firefighters out of a total of 28 certified firefighters."[173]

Kemp also indicated that the city's boards and commissions were 60 percent minority by 1980. Kemp previously had served as assistant to the city manager of Oakland and was keen to promote affirmative action policies. In September 1980, City Councilman Mel Mason went further and presented a "contract compliance ordinance and minority set-aside provision . . . requiring at least 20 percent minority participation in contracts let through or by the city, on a craft-by-craft basis . . . This means if a contractor has all black janitors that's cool, but they've got [to have] 20 percent minority truck drivers and 20 percent minority concrete mixers too . . . I don't think too many people will vote against equal opportunity in Seaside."[174] Mason's wry comment was accurate. Seaside was a town with the twin sensibility of the military view of justice, and a minority awareness of the need for affirmative action, which was based on an intimate connection to national civil rights work.

Affirmative action programs were initiated to encourage educators as well as employers to value the diversity of the city. Ewalker James, Regional Director of the California Association of Compensatory Education, together with Co-Director Nancy Zane organized annual multicultural conferences beginning in 1970 to promote new, effective methods of educating students from varied cultural backgrounds. The ninth annual conference attracted over 4,000 participants and was held at the Monterey Conference Center on January 7, 1981. The organization also published newsletters and promoted workshops to encourage parents and teachers to achieve a better understanding of "cultures and sub-cultures" in the city.[175]

A Cultural Awareness Day on July 25, 1981 showcased a Parade of Nations to represent the many national origin groups in the city and included workshops that promoted cultural understanding. Among the many presentations was one by the Fort Ord Equal Employment Opportunity (EEO) office, and the Indo-Chinese Resettlement Program, the latter a response to the wave of Vietnamese refugees who came to Seaside in the wake of the Vietnam War.[176] In 1981, Mayor Olea, following the rest of the country, formally instituted Martin Luther King Day and Black History Month (February). He also formally proclaimed March to be Women's History Month.

All of this coincided with efforts on base to encourage cultural understanding. The army's response to its own overwhelming new diversity and to the expanding antiwar, antiarmed services activism was to put in place new training programs that eliminated some of the harsher and redundant practices of the past. For example, the army created seminars to "foster racial harmony" and created services targeted to minorities. In addition, the military began the conversion from draftees to an all-volunteer army, with a target date for ending the draft by July 1, 1973.[177]

According to Lieutenant General Harold Moore and Lieutenant Colonel Jeff Tuten in their analysis of Fort Ord, *Building a Volunteer Army*, in an effort to reach possible recruits from the Seaside and Monterey region, commanders at Fort Ord also tried to "warm the atmosphere and foster community spirit" at the post by initiating a Welcome Center for new soldiers and their families, which included financial assistance and help with loans of household items while they waited for their own to arrive. Wives were given tours of the base and sponsors to help with adjustment. The army built four elementary schools and a junior high on the base (high school students attended Seaside High School), opened up the post to visitors and initiated a guest lecture program, planted trees at Hunter Liggett, and created "vigorous" new policing programs to reduce crime rates on and off base.[178] It was not enough. The 1970s and 1980s were marked by turmoil at Fort Ord and by association, Seaside.

CONCLUSION

Seaside residents utilized the decade of the 1960s to realize the promise made by a vigorous civil rights movement supported by an integrated and expanded military. They shrewdly manipulated federal funding to create housing, commercial development, and infrastructure, adding much needed tax revenue to the city's coffers. In addition, they were able to annex the most valuable parts of Fort Ord, particularly the commissary area, to expand both the population of the city and the city's tax base, making Seaside, by 1970, the most populous city on the Peninsula.

Their efforts at redevelopment and urban renewal called attention to serious civil rights problems, such as segregated housing, which, as activists connected to the civil rights networks across the country and throughout California and the West, they were fully prepared to confront and correct. They created a city council and city government in these years that reflected the population makeup, weeding out anyone who did not adhere to basic values of racial equality.

Most importantly, Seasiders accomplished all of these things without the terrible upheaval and rioting that characterized other towns and cities nationwide with large black populations. Their shared sense of values, which came both from military life and from middle-class America, such as respect for authority, patriotism, adherence to order and following rules, and political progressivism, shaped the community into one that was both socially forward thinking and relatively peaceful, even in such tumultuous times.

The challenges of the 1980s centered on the relationship of Seaside to the rest of the Peninsula. It showed that although Seaside's participation in the civil rights movement and its symbiotic relationship to Fort Ord led to the creation of a new, more integrated and equitable city, the rest of Monterey County was only marginally influenced by the dramatic shifts in racial ideology that were exemplified by the civil rights movement and the base. Seaside was frustrated in its efforts to blend into the economy of the Monterey Peninsula as a result.

CHAPTER 5

Fulfilling the Dream—Almost

PHOTO 5. African American wives of officers and high-ranking enlisted men created a vital cultural community in Seaside. Courtesy of Elizabeth and Sherman Smith, City of Seaside Archive.

MONTEREY BLUES FESTIVAL PRESIDENT Dr. Billy DeBerry encapsulated everything important about Seaside in an interview in August 2007. He was intimately linked to the national civil rights movement before arriving in Seaside and fully prepared to engage in civil rights efforts on the Monterey Peninsula:

I came to Seaside '68, '69. Charlie Knight recruited young people from Alabama State to teach. I participated and am a strong believer in civil rights. I was dean of men on our campus, so when our young people got arrested I got them out of jail.

He might have chosen to live anywhere in Monterey, Carmel, Pacific Grove, or Pebble Beach in the 1970s and 1980s. Even though he might have faced "embarrassment" by being ignored in a restaurant or other public space for being black, other activists were experiencing much worse than that when they integrated neighborhoods in cities in the North and East, and even in the Southwest, such as Phoenix.[1] He continued,

When we first got here in 1969 we came down Del Monte and we passed by Seaside . . . We had never been to California before—the first sign we saw was George Wallace for President in Monterey. So right there we had some doubt in our mind about what the Monterey Peninsula might be like. It was not racism like in Montgomery—here they say you can do it then embarrass you.

In reality it was good that blacks lived in Seaside—the best thing that ever happened to me was buying my home in Seaside—if there is any sun on the Peninsula, it is here. The homes up around Mescal [neighborhoods located in the hills of Seaside with spectacular ocean views] and all of that [Ret. Col.] Al Glover built those places. They were more upscale.

Although DeBerry was not a member of the military attached to Fort Ord, he references Colonel Al Glover, whose economic influence in Seaside was enormous. Glover, and other retired black officers were able to capitalize on their prestige and economic security in the military to transform Seaside economically and maximize its natural beauty for the benefit of the community. Like Glover and so many other African Americans who found life in Seaside advantageous at multiple levels, DeBerry played a critical leadership role, not just in Seaside itself, but throughout the Monterey Peninsula:

I was involved with Citizens League for Progress in 1987–1989. I was the only African American President of the Lyceum of Monterey in 1987. I was a founding board member of Leadership Monterey Peninsula and I was President of the United Way in 1981. I was the first African American Superintendent of Monterey Peninsula Unified School District (MPUSD)—I had the support of the entire community. I was also chairperson Monterey County Equal Opportunity Advisory Commission. I am also on the fairground board of directors and founding President for Community Partnership for Youth (CPY). African Americans moved into leadership positions in Seaside.[2]

This was an understatement, as DeBerry's impressive resume shows. It also reveals exactly why Seaside, a minority-majority black community, remained a desirable place to live and why African American residents stayed there, even when they might have left for other nearby communities when civil rights initiatives in housing opened up neighborhoods in Carmel, Pacific Grove, and Pebble Beach. William Julius Williams, John Kasard, Douglas Massey and Nancy Denton, Paul Jargowsky, and many other scholars identified a trend in metropolitan areas in the United States in the period of the late 1960s through the 1990s that showed an exodus of middle-class blacks from inner cities. This trend led to the formation of urban ghettos made up primarily of the poor.[3] Albert Camarillo and other scholars documented this phenomenon in California too, particularly in Oakland and Los Angeles. This led, in part, to the riots in Los Angeles that erupted in the wake of the Rodney King beating in 1992.

Although Seaside was often compared to these inner cities by residents and outsiders alike, it became a place that blacks migrated to rather than fled from. Seaside kept its middle-class black population because it remained a place of great natural beauty with enormous potential. Its ties to the military base of Fort Ord gave middle classes of all races, but especially blacks, access to secure employment. Middle-class blacks in Seaside provided the backbone of stability and leadership, joining forces with whites and other minority groups to establish programs to give disadvantaged members of their community hope and opportunity, as DeBerry's narrative vividly shows. They encouraged voting, provided access to educational scholarships, and supported health clinics and health awareness campaigns among many other social programs. Moreover, they created cultural traditions that became hallmarks of identity for residents of Seaside. Through their collective efforts, Seaside residents not only forged multiracial, multiethnic political coalitions but also created a haven for African Americans and a center for international culture in the region. According to Planning Commissioner Jackie Craighead, "Seaside has been the city on the Monterey Peninsula where blacks could rent or buy a home. African Americans *invested* in Seaside."[4]

Yet Seaside remained ultimately a military town, one that also had its dark side. The decades of the 1980s and early 1990s saw a spike in crime rates, particularly with regard to violent crime, that prevented the city from realizing its hopes for economic development that went beyond the basic rehabilitation efforts of the 1960s and 1970s. To make matters worse, the city's political leadership, like that of other African American dominated cities such as Detroit, became embroiled in internecine battles that distracted them from the more important work of growth.[5]

Seaside faced huge challenges in the 1980s both in terms of economic development and in its effort to overcome crime brought on by the presence of the military and, most importantly, by the influx of crack cocaine into the area. Seaside was better equipped than either civilian municipalities or other military towns to handle the pressure of both, however, because it continued to sustain a middle-class population associated with Fort Ord. These were people who had both economic resources and time to devote to social and cultural causes. They shared a will to remain in Seaside, to fight crime and to build community. "We came in highly energized and ready to work in the community [in 1975]," retired Lieutenant Colonel Morris McDaniel proclaimed emphatically.[6]

This chapter examines the rich social and cultural life of Seaside in juxtaposition to the economic downturns, high crime and perceptions of crime, and political struggles that defined this military town as much as racial integration did.

AN IMAGE PROBLEM

According to historian Elaine Tyler May, who argued in her Presidential Address at the annual meeting of the Organization of American Historians, April 2010, that even though crime rates in urban America rose beginning in the 1970s the chances of any American actually becoming a crime victim were small, even in the so-called most dangerous cities or neighborhoods: "While dangers were real, citizens responded with exaggerated fear and distrust . . . A poll taken in 1981 showed that while the chance of being murdered was a mere one in ten thousand, and becoming a victim of violent crime was just six in one thousand, fully four in ten Americans polled reported that they were "highly fearful" of assault. More than half said that they dress plainly to avoid attracting the attention of attackers. A majority reported that they kept a gun for protection.[7] She argued that the anticommunist ideology that originated with the Cold War coupled with an increasing lack of faith in the power of government to protect them led to "public service announcements" and a burgeoning security industry in the private sector that made Americans both overly fearful and too eager to acquire private security and even weapons to protect themselves.[8]

Seaside was one of those areas that May alluded to that appeared to be far more dangerous than it actually was, thanks both to media attention that single-mindedly focused on every incident of crime that occurred there and to the readiness of Peninsula residents, like other Americans, to believe that crime was rampant in the 1970s and 1980s. One episode in Seaside in February 1982 is evidence of the complex ways that Seaside interacted with its most important neighbor, Fort Ord, and also how military people responded to incidents of crime, however, that challenges the perception of Peninsula residents that Seaside was fraught with danger or out of control. In Seaside, integration and getting along were the models. Strenuous efforts were made to soothe racial tension and combat crime in innovative and energetic ways. Unfortunately, however, although incidents of crime and violence were widely reported in the local media, the constructive and proactive responses of the community often were not.

When a 5-year-old Vietnamese girl was kidnapped, sexually assaulted, and murdered in February 1982, the Vietnamese community believed that it was racially motivated. But the *Seaside Tribune* emphasized that it was crime, not a hate crime. The Seaside community response was immediate. A Block Parent program was initiated surrounding her school, Highland's Elementary School in Seaside, to ensure protections for all young children. Seasiders also established a trust fund for the family. And the father's employer, fishing boat owner Pierre Mercurio, paid for the funeral.[9]

Ruthie Watts, former local NAACP chapter president and a longtime activist and organizer of cultural affairs in Seaside spoke for many when she commented, "When I came here in '65 whites made it seem like Seaside was crime-ridden because it was black."[10] A white couple, Albert and Gloria Kolb, wrote a letter to the editor in the *Seaside Post-News Sentinel* in 1982, "Seaside does have a crime problem. Everywhere there is a crime problem. It seems to increase with population density. But on the Peninsula, Seaside just seems to get written up more."[11] Seaside experienced the negative media attention common in poor and minority communities, especially if there was a military connection. Catherine Lutz argued that Fayetteville, North Carolina, because it was "blacker and poorer than any other parts of the state" was victimized by unfair media hype "no matter *what* its crime rate." She called crime stories in Fayetteville, especially anything military related as "cannon fodder" for a "voracious" print and television media that had an insatiable "appetite for sensational violence."[12]

The romanticized community that children and teenagers in Seaside recalled in Chapter 3 were not untrue but may have been exaggerated by memories that overlooked events and situations that may have been difficult or unpleasant to recall.[13] Given those fond remembrances, it is somewhat jarring to read through local newspaper accounts that describe Seaside as "scary" and as "a place you just didn't go to."

It must be acknowledged that Seaside did experience enough violent crime that fear of the city was based on reality. Still, crime, particularly violent crime, was mostly confined to specific areas and certain neighborhoods; and these were off-limits to most children and teenagers. A headline and full-page article in the *Monterey Peninsula Herald* (including photographs) likened only one neighborhood in Seaside to a "War Zone." Nonetheless, the general perception was that the entire city was unsafe. One resident described vividly how frightening the situation had become by the 1980s:

Between gunfire, high-speed chases, fights and stabbings, residents of Mingo Avenue in Seaside say they are living in a war zone. Shots often ring through the night air, cars speed up and down the street and people walk the street and stand on the corners at all hours. Drug-related crime on the half-mile residential street has residents and police equally frustrated. Some residents say they do not feel safe in their own homes, much less in their front yards . . . "It's like being in Vietnam," said Ted . . . For fear of reprisals, he requested that his real name not be published.[14]

In April, 1981 residents of Del Rey Oaks, sandwiched between Seaside and Monterey, were so fearful of their proximity to Seaside that they placed physical barriers at the critical intersections of Pumas and Tweed streets to keep Seasiders out. This prompted former Seaside Mayor B. J. Dolan to file a formal protest supported by Seaside attorney Don Freeman charging Del Rey Oaks with "discrimination against Seaside citizens." A year later, Mayor Glenn Olea also sent a letter to the Del Rey Oaks City Council "demanding the removal of the barriers."[15]

Statistics from the Federal Bureau of Investigation Crime reports from 1975 through 2004 showed high levels of crime, especially violent crime, in Seaside. However, it must be kept in mind that Monterey also had high crime rates and high levels of prostitution and drug use, especially in the areas of town near the Monterey Conference Center and the newly built hotels along the waterfront and Cannery Row. Monterey, despite high crime rates in the same decades, did not receive the same kind of negative press that Seaside did however. Because crime in Seaside was often related to either the military or to violence and use of guns, this type of "if it bleeds it leads" media attention on crime in Seaside overwhelmed everything else that was newsworthy. In Monterey, on the other hand, where crimes committed were more than likely crimes of property, crime was reported but it was not emphasized in the media, and it was balanced by much more positive reporting about that city.

Table 3 shows similar rates of violent crime in the two cities of Monterey and Seaside between 1974 and 1989. It also shows a substantial increase in violent crime in Seaside in these years. The years 1980–1989 reflected the impact of crack cocaine on crime rates in both cities. It is important to note that although Monterey's population increased by 4,000, Seaside's increased by almost 8,000 between 1970 and 1989.

Although the local media readily reported instances of violent crime in Seaside, the vigorous response of community leaders and city government, particularly of the police department, went largely unnoticed. The active involvement of Seaside residents showed just how invested they were in

TABLE 3
Population and number of crimes for Seaside and Monterey, 1974–1989.

Year	1974–1975		1982–1983		1989	
City	Monterey	Seaside	Monterey	Seaside	Monterey	Seaside
Population	27,513*	30,076*	29,432	32,174	31,410	37,969
Willful homicide	3	4	3	5	NA	NA
Forcible rape	20	10	11	27	16	19
Robbery	71	63	57	103	41	134
Aggravated assault	72	60	49	115	146	358
Burglary	625	610	453	455	422	359
Larceny/theft	—	139	1670	1169	1469	1239
Vehicle theft	123	70	92	88	178	219
Arson	—	—	7	39	11	27

Source: Crime in the United States, Washington, DC, FBI Annual Report, 1974–1975, 1982–1983, and 1989.

*Population of Monterey and Seaside as of 1970. The FBI Crime Reports did not include population figures for either Monterey or Seaside until the 1980s.

their community. Instead of fleeing for so-called safer parts of the Peninsula, such as Monterey, those with the time and means to do so stayed and joined forces with the city police department to turn the situation around. Billy DeBerry remembered how Community Partnership for Youth was established, even though Seaside already had a Boys & Girls Club: "We started that after one of our athletes at Seaside High School was killed in a dope deal. We started CPY in 1991. We wanted to take back our community and make a safe place for our kids after school. We felt that there was room for both [Boys & Girls Club and CPY]—we can never have too many activities in the community that would support young people."[16]

Under City Manager Charles McNeely and Police Chief Ben Cooper, a "Comprehensive Crime Reduction Program" was initiated in 1983 that added two new police officers and a crime prevention specialist to increase investigations in the area of narcotics and vice. And, importantly, the police department increased contacts with organizations and schools "to curtail delinquent behavior."[17] By the next year the department added a "Juvenile Program" and a "We-Tip Program" to its crime reduction efforts. By the end of 1984, burglaries had been reduced by 17 percent, and in 1985 grand theft reports decreased by 29 percent. There was also a 22 percent decrease in armed robbery by 1985. Correspondingly there was an increase in the rate of felony arrests by 35 percent in one year,

1984–1985.The police department initiated special patrols in both Dave Cutino Park and the Del Monte Manor, two areas of the city hard hit by drugs. Over eighty people were arrested on narcotics charges in 1985 alone due to special undercover "buy" programs initiated by police with the help of citizen volunteers.

By the late 1980s, Seaside's rates of violent crime increased disproportionately—the most glaring example is in the rates of aggravated assaults between the two cities. Although there are no data for homicides in Monterey, the numbers of rapes were comparable in both cities but higher in Seaside. Higher rates of rape, domestic violence, and shaken baby syndrome are found more in military towns generally than in civilian communities, although military personnel are also less likely to engage in criminal activity than civilians.[18]

In terms of violent crime, 1986 was a particularly bad year for Seaside, but as crime rates increased, felony arrests also increased by 29 percent. The Crime Prevention Program was expanded to include more community awareness efforts on local television and radio, Neighborhood Watch programs, and a special "Hotline" by the late 1980s.[19] By 1990, Neighborhood Watch programs had expanded from six in 1988 to fourteen, and according to annual city budget reports, the department organized "segments of the business community into groups for the purpose of fighting against drugs and criminal activity."[20]

One of the most notorious areas of Seaside was the neighborhood known as "The Pit," a section of the city located on the corner of Noche Buena Street and Broadway Avenue which contained bars (where drugs were known to be peddled), prostitution, and violent crime (see map below). Chief Ben Cooper addressed Seaside residents in 1982 after stepping up patrols in that area and in parks around the city. He responded to citizen complaints about drug use and criminal activity in Dave Cutino Park, but also to complaints of police harassment of black youth. He argued that his efforts were justified, challenging African American activists Ewalker James and Josh Stewart:

Come up there and walk with my officers and see what is going on. We have been told to cite anything that is illegal, and when that happens I don't want to see any of you people down here screaming about police harassment . . . We almost had a riot situation up there Sunday evening . . . One thing we are going to do is do the job the law allows us to do . . . those people are up there . . . violating the law . . . if I see them even drop a chewing gum wrapper, they are going to get cited.[21]

Two weeks later, Mayor Olea announced that military police would join Seaside police in patrolling Cutino Park and the Roberts Lake areas.[22]

Chief Cooper was known to be a tough enforcer of the law, which was appreciated by many Seaside residents. However, in 1991, Cooper was accused of inappropriate business and personal associations with known criminals and suspended from the department. He retired from

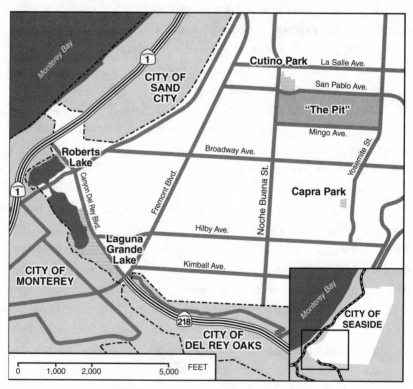

MAP 2. City of Seaside, Former Law Enforcement Focus Areas.

Source: City of Seaside Planning Department

the Seaside Police Department and was replaced by Virgil Epperson, an African American.

The response of Seaside residents to unacceptable crime rates was not to move out but to get involved in solving the problem. The multiracial Seaside Citizens Anti-Crime Patrol, also known as the Yellow Jackets, was formed in 1988 and included as many as sixty Seaside residents and business owners. They walked the streets of Seaside in shifts wearing bright yellow jackets. Typically they started their patrols at the top of Mingo Avenue, which was part of the notorious "Pit" and stood at corners and observed activity. According to organizer and community activist Nancy Amos:

We recorded everything. We wrote down license plate numbers, descriptions of what we saw. We had a police officer either with us or in a van nearby. If he saw something he could act on, he did. We tried not to be confrontational. At the end [of the shift] we would summarize what we observed and turn it over to the community liaison at the police department. They would use that information to get search warrants to help them in their investigations. We helped them build a case. Oftentimes in advance, officers would let us know what they were looking for—at a certain residence, a car license, or sometimes we would give them something completely new. We learned a lot. A lot of us knew people on the streets. Had gone to school with them or knew their kids. Our goal was to get more community awareness. That you could do something and that the police department couldn't do it [eradicate crime] by themselves.[23]

In addition to street patrols, Seasiders formed a nonprofit organization called Citizens Against Drugs and Crime in Seaside in 1988 that met the second Wednesday of each month at Oldemeyer Center throughout the 1990s. They held workshops and invited speakers from local law enforcement agencies as well as ex-offenders to educate citizens in crime prevention and awareness.[24]

A drug enforcement program was initiated in 1988–1989 with the addition of two drug enforcement officers. This led to a nearly 50 percent increase in the number of drug-related arrests from fifty in 1986–1987 to ninety in 1988–1989.[25] The police department added another five officers and investigators to its staff by 1990 and also began a Special Operations Detail in the "war against drugs." Further, the department claimed to have improved response time for emergencies to within four minutes.[26]

By 1992, rates of violent crime in Seaside declined slightly from previous years but still remained high and still surpassed Monterey. Nonetheless, crimes of property in Monterey remained high too. By 1992, burglary rates were three times higher in Monterey than in Seaside. Monterey's rates of aggravated assault quadrupled between 1990 and 1992. Theft was also consistently much higher in Monterey than in Seaside. Despite successful efforts to reduce crime rates, Seaside was rarely given credit and was still considered a dangerous city on the Peninsula in the early 1990s. Twenty-three Neighborhood Watch groups were established in Seaside in 1991 and ten more in 1992. The police department also established a Police Explorers Program for young people between the ages of fourteen and twenty-one in 1991, which became actively involved in community activities. Seven new officers were hired in 1992, all of whom were members of minority groups. A canine unit was added in 1991 to be used for narcotic detection. And a "Critical Incidence Team" was added to respond to high risk, life-threatening situations.[27]

Between 1993 and 1995, there was an increase in crimes of violence for Monterey and still unacceptably high levels of violent crime for Seaside. Crimes of property—burglary, theft, and motor vehicle theft—were all still much higher in Monterey. Monterey had three times the number of burglaries as Seaside by 1995.[28]

By 1998, violent crimes were decreasing but still high enough that mayoral candidate Jerry Smith explicitly ran on a platform of new leadership to address both the perception and reality that Seaside was crime ridden and an unsafe place to visit and to live. Seasiders continued to address high crime by organizing events to counter the problem. For example, neighbors that now included a large proportion of Mexican immigrants and Mexican Americans came together to promote safety in Seaside's many public parks. "We created 'Take Back the Park' [events]," stated Nancy Amos, "[and] invited all the neighbors. Everyone brought a dish, and we invited police officers to stop by. We ran the drug dealers out of Capra Park [and Cutino Park]."[29]

The Seaside Police Department worked hard to build strong relationships with Seaside residents throughout the 1990s. Particularly under the direction of Chief Anthony Sollecito, a Monterey native, various programs were instituted to make community relations a high priority, especially in the wake of new Latino gangs that appeared in Seaside in the mid-1990s. Chief Sollecito was especially effective in bringing an end to drug-related crime in Seaside. Appointed chief in October 2001, he was instrumental in creating an increased community-based policing relationship by expanding the School Resource Officer program, through a federal grant, and implementing the "Mobile Community Substation." His efforts allowed grassroots community organizations such as the Yellow Jackets to disband.

By contrast, in communities associated with military bases such as Fayetteville, high crime was not countered by anything like the collective, grassroots efforts of Seaside residents.[30] In Columbia, South Carolina, the military and the town were at odds over crime rates from the outset of World War II, with nothing like the cooperative efforts base commanders and Seaside residents and city officials made with one another at Fort Ord.[31] Neighborhood Associations that did form in the wake of crack cocaine and violence in the 1980s and 1990s in both military towns and in cities such as Los Angeles, Detroit, or Chicago were created with the clear intention of restricting crime and violence to already black areas, not rectifying the problem or stopping the violence in those places.[32] Seaside was a unique place in this regard. It was military, multiracial, and an environmentally beautiful place. Not in spite of, but because of all these conditions, Seaside was a desirable place for many black, Asian, Latino, and white middle-class retired military personnel to live in and invest in, and many committed to making the city a safe place, rather than fleeing from it when high crime rates might have driven them away.

The early years of the twenty-first century show dramatic reductions in crime rates, especially with regard to violent crime, as is consistent in other cities. According to social scientist Tim Wadsworth:

The early 1990s brought on the beginning of the most precipitous decline in crime that the United States has ever experienced. Between 1970 and 1990, national homicide rates vacillated between 8 and 10 per 100,000. By 1999, they were below 6 per 100,000 According to National Crime Victimization Survey data, the decreases for other offenses were even greater. National robbery victimizations dropped from over 600 per 100,000 in 1990 to less than 200 in 2000, and aggravated assault from about 1,000 per 100,000 in 1990 to about 500 in 2000.[33]

In 2005, for example, Seaside recorded no homicides. However, perceptions about life in Seaside are slow to change despite the reality of lower crime rates. The city continues to shed its past association with crime and to work toward an identity as another Monterey Peninsula tourist destination. "The Pit" and other areas in Seaside that attracted prostitutes, drugs, and alcohol abuse and led to unprecedented violence in the 1970s and 1980s are long gone. The decades of the 1980s through the 1990s did indeed mark a period of unacceptable crime rates. However, the consequence of that was a response by the city and the community that showed how much Seaside meant to them in the long term. Neither whites nor minorities fled Seaside during this period. In fact, the population only increased. The same stalwart middle-class people—black, white, Asian, and increasingly, Latino—who organized themselves to fight crime were the same ones who were involved in the establishment of social and cultural organizations and events that defined the city too.

A STABLE MIDDLE CLASS

Voluntary civic activity that involved Seaside residents regardless of race or ethnicity was in sharp contrast to press reports about violence and social disintegration. Seaside residents of all races and ethnicities contributed to the creation of a bigger community identity by organizing clubs, giving out scholarships, and arranging everything from special events to Debutante Balls. These were also activities that black professionals in Seaside, just as other middle-class and upper-middle-class black communities in California and the nation, did for their communities as part and parcel of the important race work that African Americans, particularly African American women, had been engaged in since the nineteenth century.[34]

Seaside developed a city culture that was grass roots, high energy, and above all, a collective of multiracial people and cultures dedicated to improving the cultural and social lives of residents. Groups in Seaside built their own organizations to promote their respective cultures and, at the same time, became involved in citywide events that celebrated the community as a whole.

Rodolfo Nava, of Monterey Peninsula College, and a handful of other Seaside Mexican American families, including the Pérezes and Rubios, organized cultural events celebrating Latinos:

There was a group [of] about six of us. Luis and Orancio Pérez, Dolores and Nicolas Olivo, my brother Alfredo, Carlos de los Ríos and his wife Guadalupe. They were all teachers in the Monterey Peninsula Unified School District. Also, Roberto Franco, who was the former mayor of Del Rey Oaks. It was his suggestion to name our group Asociaciòn Cultural Hispano Americano (ACHA). Our immediate goals were to have a voice to bring events to the community. We had concerts, theater, dance, lectures.[35]

Japanese American Seasiders celebrated identity through culture too. Japanese Americans returning from internment camps were welcomed back to Seaside, as they often were in predominantly African American neighborhoods in California.[36] Seaside Japanese Americans formed a chapter of the Japanese American Citizens League (JACL), which joined the NAACP in cities such as San Francisco and Oakland to protest racially restrictive housing and fight for civil rights.[37] Unlike in these larger metropolitan centers, however, the Monterey County chapter of the JACL withdrew from organized political activism, although individual members of the JACL engaged in politics and in civil rights actions during the 1960s and 1970s. Instead, the JACL in Seaside mostly coordinated celebrations involving the Buddhist Temple, which was built on Noche Buena Street in Seaside in 1965.[38] The Obon Festival in July was a presentation of Japanese dance, food, and art, notably the spectacular exhibit of bonsai, and is held every July, attracting visitors from all over the region.[39] The de-emphasis on local politics was not unique to Seaside's Japanese American community. For example, in Monterey Park, Asian Americans generally and Japanese in particular stayed out of local politics until the late 1980s.[40]

As discussed in Chapter 2, Filipinos expanded the local Fil-Am Clubs in the 1970s and 1980s and became leaders in Seaside's St. Francis Xavier Catholic Church. In 1970, three Filipino families, the McKenzies, the Niervas and the Lundholms, organized the International Festival at St. Francis Xavier as a counterpoint to the racial tensions of the era. International Day is a celebration of Seaside's richly diverse population, featuring food booths from all of the ethnic communities of Seaside, dancing, and crafts. It remains an important marker on Seaside's calendar today.

Filipinos also created several civic clubs that blended labor activism, Catholicism, and the military. The Monterey Filipino Community Organization was established in 1941. In 1957, the Philippine-American Community Club of Monterey Peninsula moved to Seaside as a response to the increasing population of Filipinos in Seaside and Marina (the social hall was located in Marina). The most important events produced by the Filipino clubs were the crowning of "Queens" and "Princesses," pageants that defined the ideal Filipina woman not only as beautiful, but also as a hard worker, a good Catholic, and a patriot. The Miss Maria Clara Festival is held every December, and the contests for Miss and Mrs. Phil-Am are always held in the spring. Both celebrations involve food, dance, formal native dress, and music. Above all, these events are patriotic moments that serve to connect community identity with the American military and to honor veterans, particularly survivors of the infamous Bataan Death March.[41] In this way, the military once again served as a binding force, the common denominator that linked Filipinos to everyone else in Seaside.

Over the years, as new groups arrived in Seaside, the city added events to reflect the new populations. Vietnamese refugees that arrived in Seaside in the late 1970s and early 1980s had their own city-sponsored event, the important Tet Festival in February to celebrate the harvest. In 1995, the city joined with the League of United Latin American Citizens (LULAC) to create Cinco De Mayo as a way of recognizing an increasing Mexican immigrant community in Seaside. In the first five years of Cinco De Mayo, and under the leadership of Bill and Mariam Meléndez of LULAC, Shari Hastey of Community Partnership for Youth, and Dave Pacheco from the City of Seaside there were over thirty vendors represented on the grounds of Seaside City Hall, several bands, sponsors ranging from local restaurants, radio and television stations, and thousands of people from every ethnic group in the community.[42]

The African American community left the largest cultural imprint on the character of Seaside, especially in the 1970s and 1980s. The social and cultural activities that defined middle-class black life in this period were happening throughout suburbs and cities across the country where blacks formed either a majority or a substantial proportion of the population.[43]

Bobbie and Morris McDaniel were typical of the military retirees who plunged into Seaside civic life both in politics and, importantly, within the context of fraternity and sorority organizations. Retired officers like Morris McDaniel, some as young as forty years old, had the time and resources to devote to community service. Three chartered chapters of African American fraternities were established in Seaside by 1976, all of which remain active today: Omega Psi Phi Fraternity, Alpha Phi Alpha Fraternity, and Kappa Alpha Psi, and two chapters of African American sororities, Delta Sigma Theta and Alpha Kappa Alpha, each with twenty to thirty members at any given time. The McDaniels helped organize the Pan-Hellenic Council of Seaside in 1976 to coordinate activities among the different Greek organizations and ensure maximum participation for each scheduled event. McDaniel explained, "The purpose of the Pan-Hellenic Council was to serve as the coordinating body . . . Once [the council] was in place these social things started to happen."[44]

Two to four events were listed on the Pan-Hellenic Calendar every month, each of which attracted between 200 to 300 people.[45] According-ing to McDaniel, "It was mostly black, but not entirely. It was all about outreach, brotherhood, community service . . . the primary role [of the organizations] was raising money for fund-raising for scholarships. It was all about education . . . The members of the Greek letter organizations represented just a small percentage of the educated blacks in the community."[46]

One of the most impressive of these celebrations was the annual Mardi Gras sponsored by the Seaside chapter of Omega Psi Phi fraternity. It was so popular that in 1977, the first year of the celebration, McDaniel recalled, "I had to stop the Brothers from selling tickets two weeks in advance because we were sold out—700 people came to the first Mardi

Gras. The next year . . . over 600 people attended."⁴⁷ The Mardi Gras celebrations were popular Peninsula-wide events that attracted participants from throughout the region, much like Mardi Gras celebrations elsewhere in the country and like other celebrations of ethnicity on the Monterey Peninsula such as the Santa Rosalia Festa (Italian), the Feast of Lanterns in Pacific Grove (Chinese), the Feast of the Holy Ghost (Portuguese), and Cinco De Mayo (Mexican) to name only a few. It was not limited to participation by blacks.

The Jazz Art Show, also jointly sponsored by the Pan-Hellenic Council and the City of Seaside, featured high school Blues and Jazz groups and included a dinner dance and silent auction to benefit music scholarships for Seaside students, of all races and ethnicities, including whites.

The Monterey Bay Blues Festival stood out among all of these celebrations in its reflection of the culture of Seaside. Blues Festival President Billy DeBerry explained its roots:

We wanted to do something that was authentically American. The Blues are the only original American Art form—everything else derived from it. We were 15 people who had no knowledge [of event organizing] but we wanted to do it right. We put the first festival on for less than $15,000 now it's a 1.5 million dollar operation. The last 10 years we have given over $100,000 away in scholarships. We average about 15,000 people per day for a 3 day event. We absolutely add to the economy of the Peninsula . . . We are able to help aspiring young people and share money with them through scholarships and grants. You may find [another Blues Festival] to equal us, but you won't find one better. We are ranked No.1 in terms of Blues Festivals on the West coast.⁴⁸

The Blues Festival combined all of the important elements of multiracial, multiethnic collaboration in Seaside, with the additional purpose of community service and support for youth education, and without regard for race or ethnicity. The original board directors included blacks, whites, Asians, and Latinos and claimed former military officers and a county supervisor.⁴⁹ The group secured a $10,000 loan from Wells Fargo Bank and a donation of $2,500 from the Pebble Beach Company to produce its first festival event in 1986 with Bobby "Blue" Bland, Millie Jackson, and Taj Mahal as the headliners and popular San Francisco radio talk show host Ray Taliaferro as Master of Ceremonies. Taliaferro continues to serve as Master of Ceremonies today. It was an enormous success from the outset, attracting tens of thousands of people from the region and the state. According to first President Morris McDaniel, "The *Monterey Peninsula Herald,* much to our surprise, proclaimed in headlines 'BLUES FESTIVAL OFF TO A ROUSING START—may there be more' . . . *The Monterey Herald* often downplayed positive aspects of events . . . in the black community."[50]

The Debutante's Ball was another significant marker of African American middle-class sensibility in Seaside. Debutantes Balls had a long history in African American communities. In New Orleans, a black Debutante's Ball had been celebrated continuously as a part of Mardi Gras and sponsored by The Original Illinois Club beginning in 1895.[51] One of the organizers in Seaside, Ruthie Watts, recalled the excitement of organizing, fundraising, and producing the Debutante's Ball:

We started in 1973 . . . Betty Sapp called a group of people together including Betty Mann and myself. The whites had [a Debutante's Ball] in San Francisco, but blacks couldn't participate. It was a motivation for the young people—they had to have a certain grades, good morals, and not have children. It made young ladies think twice. The community was very supportive—at least 200 or 300 people came—it was a sell out crowd. We would have teas and fashion shows for the young people [in advance of the Ball] . . . It was an evening to remember. We put those young ladies in a different class. It was beautiful.

In a similar vein, every year the Pan-Hellenic Council sponsored "Achievement Week" that not only recognized a "Citizen of the Year" but also others in the community: "We wanted to recognize people in the community who were making a difference."[52] Talent shows, Mothers Day celebrations, Halloween parties, the Harvest Ball, the Black & Gold Dinner Dance, Christmas parties for disadvantaged children, golf matches, and Labor Day dances and barbecues were among the formal and informal community events and gatherings that included several hundred people each and were expansive enough to include all ethnic and racial groups.

In 1974, a chapter of The Links, Incorporated was formed in Seaside. The Links, Inc., a national middle-class black women's organization, was

founded in Philadelphia in 1946 to support new African American communities outside of the South. Rose C. Beene was the first president of
the Monterey Bay chapter of Links, Inc. and formed the chapter together
with Elizabeth Y. Smith, Altheia Powell, Mary L. Story, Wilma Campbell, Doris Drummond, Irene Reeves, Gwedolyn Lassiter, Wanda Marshall, Clarise Beene, Jean Drummond, Willie McCoin, Alice Powell, and
Waldene Littleton, almost all of whom were married to military personnel. Their first projects were aimed at helping stay-at-home mothers of all
races reenter the workforce with workshops on interviewing, dress, and
speech. They organized free vision tests for children, created programs
for teenagers and students with learning disabilities, and created "Math
and Reading Are Fun" workshops. None of these was focused only on
blacks but were pointedly inclusive of Seaside's children and teenagers.

Links, Inc., held teas, fashion shows, holiday events, Mother's Day
luncheons, and art exhibits. They awarded scholarships and held benefits
for the American Heart Association and the local symphony and Monterey Peninsula Art Association. The organization was always focused on
raising awareness about the positive aspects of cultural and racial diversity and supporting organizations that were not based on racial identity.
Links, Inc., remains active in Seaside today. Under President Sharon Ray
Gross in 2009, the goal of the organization was embodied in its slogan:
"Linkages to H.E.A.L.T.H.; Empowering Youth to Build Healthy Communities"; it remains oriented toward public service that extends beyond
the African American community.

The work that African American social organizations did to promote
and celebrate community service and cultural awareness included the entire Peninsula. For example, to raise funds for the Jerry Lewis Muscular
Dystrophy Telethon, African American groups from Seaside joined whites
and other ethnic and racial communities in Monterey for a "Gala Evening
of Cultural Exchange" with varieties of food and dress from African and
the Middle Eastern cultures. The *Monterey Peninsula Herald* gave full-
page space in its "Style" section to the event, which featured prominent
Monterey politicians and judges as guests.[53] However, this was reported
as a Monterey event, rather than one that emerged out of Seaside's community of middle-class blacks.[54]

The African American middle class in Seaside was equally committed to political events and voter registration drives. A *Seaside Post-News Sentinel* article in 1978 reported a "Get Out the Vote" campaign sponsored by the Seaside Chapter of Delta Sigma Theta Sorority. In 1988 the sorority also sponsored a much larger "Get Out the Vote" where they created the first "I Voted" lapel stickers (brainchild of Bobbie McDaniel). These are still in use today, in Seaside and throughout the country. The black Sorority members met with the Monterey County Board of Supervisors and then held a press conference at the County Courthouse in Salinas to kick off the campaign in the "Get Out the Vote" campaign of 1988.[55]

Despite the many positive events sponsored by Seaside groups, little news coverage occurred. As an example of the difficulty for Seaside of getting fair press coverage, Morris McDaniel recalled the first Martin Luther King Day March, "The Herald reported a turn-out of approximately 150 participants when it was closer to 1,000. Now, how do you estimate 150 marchers when we were marching eight to ten abreast and when the front of the end of the march reached King Middle School, the end of the march had not even left Friendship Baptist Church (the starting point) some 7 or 8 blocks away? With all of the positives we saw that day, it was very disheartening to have the celebration minimized in that way." The first year Bobbie McDaniel chaired the march under the auspices of Delta Sigma Theta sorority. Subsequently, it was turned over to the Pan-Hellenic Council, which has continued the tradition with as many or more participants into the current day. Over 3,000 people attended the 2007 and 2008 celebrations and marches.[56]

Taken together, the various ethnic and racial groups in Seaside clearly had the wherewithal to form themselves into organizations typically found in middle-class communities throughout the nation. They provided support that the less fortunate among them needed and demonstrated cultural pride of place. In Seaside there were also a slew of collective efforts that brought groups together in citywide efforts to build both military and multicultural community identity and pride.

The Seaside Bed Races and Fourth of July Parade of Champions are two examples of community celebrations that were intentionally multicultural and military. Seaside's Birthday Party in October has been celebrated continuously since incorporation in 1954. The Bed Races, organized by the Seaside Fire Department every summer, gave all Seasiders a chance to dress up, be silly, and play. Teams were organized around every imaginable theme such as prehistoric beds, clown beds, hospital beds, and beds made of hay or other odd materials, often with children in the "beds" themselves (which were equipped with wheels) as adult runners raced down Canyon Del Rey Avenue in front of Seaside City Hall.[57]

The Parade of Champions on the Fourth of July was celebrated even before incorporation and was the most important event on Seaside's calendar. It featured the usual marching bands, floats, and drill teams, and dozens of vintage automobiles driven by Seaside residents who originally came from Dust Bowl states such as Oklahoma and Arkansas and made up a significant part of Seaside's white community. However, the Fourth of July Parade of Champions most clearly reflected Seaside's connection to the military. Fort Ord was always given the most prominent place in the parade, with Buffalo Soldiers, floats from the Veterans of Foreign Wars and the American Legion, military materiel and Avenue of the Flags, drill teams of young people, and representatives of Reserve Officers' Training Corp groups from all over the region. They continue to be the centerpiece of the parade today.

The parade in the 1970s also attracted antiwar groups, people who did not represent the mainstay of Seaside residents. Seasiders, regardless of race, class, or ethnicity, parted ways with many Americans and closed ranks over Vietnam protests. In 1970, for example, at the height of the antiwar movement in the United States, five groups representing peace movements were rejected from participation in the Fourth of July Parade on the grounds that their entries were "adverse to the patriotic [theme of the parade] . . . and that there were threats of violence [against them]."[58] The Women's International League for Peace and Freedom (WILPF) had planned "to march dressed in black accompanied by our children with a banner stating 'Women bear life; War bears death.'" Even when the group offered to include three people "in Revolutionary War costume, carrying fife, drum and an American flag" they were still excluded. The other excluded groups were the Movement for a Democratic Military (MDM), the Peace and Freedom Party, the Monterey Peninsula College Committee for Peace, and Vets for Peace. When the groups publicly protested their exclusions, they were informed by Chief of Police Ben Cooper, who was widely supported by the rest of the community and the city council, that if they tried to march, even on the sidewalk rather than with the parade, they "might be arrested." Some of the women marched anyway and were joined by members of the MDM. According to a written report by the WIPLF, "when the marchers asked for police protection from the physical attack of a horseman also in the parade, they were refused [and left the parade grounds quietly]."[59] Corey Miller, Nancy Wirtz, Diane Sammet, and Janna Ottman were a few of the antiwar activists in Seaside that challenged the military mind-set of Seaside in important ways in the 1970s, joining many other Americans protesting the war in Vietnam. However, what was significant about their protests was how little support was generated in the community of Seaside itself, a quintessentially military town whose residents generally defended all war efforts because they, or their loved ones, were actively involved in them.

The Seaside Birthday Party, organized by city staff every October and held on the City Hall lawn also included an array of food booths and crafts from all groups. Again, this was a pivotal moment on Seaside's calendar, arranged by city staffers and consciously inclusive of all of Seaside's residents. It was an occasion for craft and food displays that not only celebrated Seaside's diverse cultures but emphasized the common ground they all shared as military people and residents of the city. Dave Pacheco, Seaside native and current city recreation coordinator, recalled the sheer number of city-sponsored events that promoted and celebrated ethnicity, the military, and community: "This city sponsors more events and more different events than probably any other city on the Peninsula. It always has. That is where the energy comes from. There has always been great energy here."[60] Throughout the 1970s, for example, the Seaside Jaycees worked closely with the Seaside Parks Department, Recreation Department, and Public Works Department to turn the Youth Center, located on Wheeler Street (where the Oldemeyer Community Center now stands), into an authentic haunted house. According to Pacheco:

Everybody came together and built this thing. They got wood, nails, and hammers and totally transformed the youth center. They did a great job. It was really scary . . . There were over 500 people lined up nonstop for 3 hours to get in. Then they got candy at the end. After the Seaside Jaycees folded 16 years ago the Recreation Department of the city took over. Now we hold the Halloween Bonanza (at Oldemeyer Center). We give out candy bags; we have game booths and a haunted house. This is the only city on the Monterey Peninsula having an event on Halloween night.

In 1984 city manager Charles McNeely appointed an African American, Lewis Jackson, as recreation director for the City of Seaside. Jackson began the tradition of Blues in the Park every Sunday afternoon, a tradition the city of Seaside still maintains. Other events Jackson championed were the Jazz Art Show (September) and the Black History Art Reception (February).

City-sponsored events focused on diversity and also served as an opportunity for community building in unique ways. For example, the Easter Egg Hunt, like the Halloween Bonanza, was no simple egg gathering. The city provided refreshments, gave out candy and hand-dyed eggs, put up a bounce house, and offered pony rides—all for free. It was an effort to bring Seaside residents together in an extended way that served to build community in a city that had to deal with high rates of transience due to its military population. In the same way, the Senior Mother's Day Lunch (May); Summer Music Festival; Sunday Blues in the Park (June–August); Jazz Art Show (September); and the Holiday Snow Festival, parade, and tree lighting (December) were not events that lasted a few hours but were interactive, energetic daylong celebrations that gave residents an opportunity to know one another, quickly and better.[61]

City culture and political activism were intertwined in Seaside. The lessons blacks learned and the alliances they forged in the political arena transitioned into community service and social and cultural events. In the 1970s and 1980s, Seaside's African American middle-class, and the city itself, created an identity as a diverse, middle-class, military community. Although the number of events in Seaside increased, and attendance was impressive, there was little evidence in the media, except in the pages of the *Seaside Post-News Sentinel* and in the private collections and memories of Seaside residents and former residents. As a result, widespread understandings of Seaside during the decades of the 1970s and 1980s were much less positive than the reality of life there. The local news sections contained the usual stories on Seaside City Council meetings and issues about public space, water, and sewage problems that were common to all of the Peninsula communities, but generally failed to notice that for all the crime and violence, a stable middle class emerged that was made up of African Americans, Asians, Latinos, and whites who did not flee the city for so-called perceived-to-be-safer places on the Peninsula, such as Monterey. They stayed, working closely with city government to make Seaside safe and communal in spirit.

Leaders such as Billy DeBerry, Ewalker James, Dr. Charlie Mae Knight, Al Glover, and Ruthie Watts, along with many others who did so much for Seaside culturally, economically, and socially in the 1970s and 1980s were individuals whose integrity was beyond reproach, and who might have been able to overcome the prejudice of the rest of the Peninsula brought on by misunderstandings about what was really happening in this multiracial military town. None of them ran for political office, however. Instead, Seaside's African American mayor for almost all of the 1980s, Lancelot McClair, was continually thwarted in his efforts to encourage investment and growth in the city due to white political leaders at the Monterey County level who still looked down at Seaside as a "minority" military community. His own brash manner and allegations of drug use and corruption did not help. City councils and city government during this period were often diverted from the work of development, embroiled as it was with in-fighting, scandals, and accusations of corruption. Even the powerful Ministerial Alliance was affected when one of their own, Reverend H. H. Lusk, was accused of misappropriation of funds designated for a Head Start program. All of this played a part in limiting the city and undermining the work that groups were doing to improve life there.[62]

There were political successes too, however, as Seaside forced Monterey County to confront racist practices in districting that prevented minority communities such as Salinas and Seaside from equal representation on the

County Board of Supervisors. The Board of Supervisors played a powerful role in deciding everything from water rights to where large-scale development projects would be located. The fact that gerrymandering effectively disenfranchised both Seaside and Salinas was a serious political issue that was rectified by a successful lawsuit brought by the city of Seaside.

AFRICAN AMERICAN POLITICAL
LEADERSHIP IN THE 1980S

"I grew up in this city—in Reverend Martin's Church [Victory Temple]," recalled Lance McClair who went on to become Seaside's mayor for four consecutive two-year terms beginning in 1982. "That was a powerful church." Black churches led by the Ministerial Alliance did indeed lead the way politically for Seaside in the decades of the 1960s through the 1990s. Reverend Welton McGee recalled the vital role black churches under the leadership of the Ministerial Alliance played in Seaside politics in this thirty-year period:

In those days the black churches ran Seaside—Reverend Lusk, Reverend Ellis, Ocean View all those black churches had a lot of folks—and when you called them together, they carried power. We were really together. The churches stuck together then. There was Ocean View Church, Friendship, Victory Temple— these were the churches with black ministers who carried quite a bit of weight . . . They had a pretty good pull. The blacks that were here went to these churches that made up Seaside.[63]

Oscar Lawson, the first black mayor elected in 1976, recalled that his first task in running for election was going to "the Brother Ministers" for their endorsement and support.[64] A few years later, according to McClair, Mayor Stephen Ross utilized the Ministerial Alliance to get elected to the mayor's office too, but McClair questioned the consequences of that support: "When Stephen Ross was mayor, he didn't have to campaign. He depended on the Ministerial Alliance to bring in the votes. That took away his independence."[65]

Lancelot McClair, who had a degree in criminal justice and worked as an investigator for the Public Defenders Office, downplayed his affiliation with black churches, but it was clear that he needed (and received) their support:

I had to get my natural community together—the black community . . . The Ministerial Alliance weren't supporting me at first . . . I went to the church people and [to] citizens one on one. The preponderance of support I got throughout the city made them [the Ministerial Alliance] think 'Well we better look at this guy.' They were about winning."[66]

The power of the Ministerial Alliance was seriously diminished in this period, however. The Reverend Herbert Lusk, Sr. of Bethel Baptist Church, one of Seaside's most important ministers and prominent member of the Alliance, was charged and found guilty of embezzlement, tax evasion, forgery, and conspiracy concerning Operation Shoe String, an organization that he headed. Operation Shoe String was founded in 1968 as part of the federal Head Start program, a nonprofit child care center that received over $70,000 in federal funding and several thousand more in state and county grants. This scandal generated enormous publicity and, fair or not, reflected on the integrity of the Alliance, weakening their political position in the community.[67]

McClair carefully avoided presenting himself as a "black" candidate and attributed his long tenure in office to broad support in a diverse city, which he carefully nurtured. In a somewhat self-serving look back at his first election in 1982 he recalled:

I had to soften the turf first. In my viewpoint there was too much racism on the city council. I felt that the city was bigger than that. Not voting for this guy because he was white/black. I started precinct walking. I asked people 'What do you want out of the mayor?' Everyone said the same thing. We don't care if he's black, white or green—we want someone who is fair not because he was black or white. I said that's a done deal. I could do that. We have the ability . . . but we must win on the basis of fairness. The best thing that can happen to this city is not for a black person to be powerful . . . but to work with everyone—whites, Filipinos, whatever. That's the way it's got to be."

However, what McClair called "racism on the city council" was more like personality conflict (as described in Chapter 3). Although former Mayor

Lou Haddad was an avowed racist, he was also part of an ethnic group himself, and most city council members had ethnic origins as well as military ties. There was no elite white leadership entrenched in Seaside as was the case in Oakland and its surrounding suburbs or throughout the San Francisco Bay Area or in the Los Angeles metropolitan region. In fact, when McClair ran for office, it was against Filipino Mayor Glenn Olea, both of whom were former military men. McClair identified the various political constituencies that made up Seaside in the 1980s:

There was the group from St. Francis [Xavier church]. It was a mixture there—Filipinos, Latinos, military people, whites. There was the NAACP, LULAC. There were the veterans groups—the VFW [Veterans of Foreign Wars], Avenue of the Flags. There were Pacific Islanders and a lot of Vietnamese. There were the [black] elites. It was complicated. Seaside was a tough city [to govern].[68]

What is noticeable here is that although there are identifiable ethnic and racial groups who may have voted together, there were not enough members of any of them to dominate completely. Also, as is apparent, blacks were divided by class and interest group, as were the others. The military organizations and nonblack churches were centerpieces of diversity in terms of their makeup, and they had their own interests to pursue that did not always coincide with the interests of their ethnic or racial group. So although McClair identified St. Francis Church as an interest group, for example, its membership could not have been more diverse and would hardly have voted as a bloc unless perhaps there was some anti-Catholic initiative that threatened them. According to city manager Charles Mc-Neely, "Nobody had dominance. You had to form coalitions—Lance, Mel, T. J. (Theron Polite) had to go out and form alliances with whites and Asians. You could not be a black candidate. You had to work hard at representing the entire community."[69] His comment applied to white, Asian, and Latino candidates as well. The predominantly black Citizens League for Progress, for example, made a point in the 1980 city council election of endorsing both black and white candidates for office when the organization endorsed Mel Mason and Don Likas (white) over black candidates Theron Polite and Reverend Stringer. According to McDaniel, "We sought a diverse slate in preference to focusing on racial exclusivity."[70] In 1982, he stated "We endorsed McClair, Polite and Mel Mason. Our slates would include the city but all elected offices," meaning endorsements at the county, state and national levels too. "We endorsed Sam Farr [for State Assembly then Congress] a number of times, Edith Johnsen and Sam Karas [both for Board of Supervisors, 4th district], and Leon Panetta [for Congress]," all of whom were white.[71]

Theron Polite, who is black, made a point of publicly showing that he was a candidate who would represent all constituents, regardless of race like every other political candidate in Seaside. In his weekly column in the *Seaside Post-News Sentinel* he took a stand against the city council and supported a white family who had built a fence on their property—in conflict with the city's variance codes, but with the support of 200 of their multiracial neighbors. Polite, who lost the previous election for city councilman but won a seat in 1982, argued that councilmen Austin and Houser (both white) "blatantly ignored the desires of the people and flagrantly created an impasse, costing the Plantz family unnecessary expense . . . clearly [indicating] that Seaside needs a change."[72]

Yet, Mayor McClair, and fellow council members Mel Mason and Theron Polite focused on personnel changes in city government in 1983 based on race, including the replacement of City Manager Roger Kemp with African American Charles McNeely, rather than on development or other more pressing issues. Roger Kemp had a solid reputation as a city manager locally and statewide. His doctoral thesis in public administration, "Coping with Proposition 13," which he later published, was widely read and well respected among city administrators throughout California. He was president of the American Society for Public Administration and was actively involved with the League of California Cities and was described by Councilman Houser as "One of the finest city managers [Seaside] ever had."[73] Nonetheless, Kemp left Seaside to work as city manager for the town of Placentia, California, the following year and both the finance director and city attorney resigned. This interrupted the day-to-day operations of city government, which then had to focus on replacing these key staff members rather than on moving forward with development projects.

Mel Mason argued that it was important for this multiracial city to reflect its population and make sure that the highest staff members were minorities. Although he had a point, it was also problematic to dismiss capable employees solely on the basis of race or sex, which created its own set of problems and undercut the argument for affirmative action by appearing to be both high-handed and capricious:

In what racists call 'The Thursday Night Slaughters' we were terminating one person per week. At one point Lance and T. J. asked me if we could stop terminating people so that they could have "a peaceful city council meeting for a change." My response was that there would only be "peace" after we had gotten rid of the folks we needed to get rid of and replaced them with minorities and women . . . I researched and found a way to separate the positions of City Clerk from the City Manager's position. This allowed us to promote Dee Latimore to City Clerk. We then hired Elaine Cass, an activist I knew well, to become City Attorney. [She became] the first woman City Attorney in our history.[74]

Seaside advertised for a new city manager. McClair found one in Charles McNeely. "We were like brothers," said McClair. "We worked well together."[75]

Although Mayor McClair was part of a first ever black majority on the Seaside City Council, it was clear from the outset that African Americans would not form a racially exclusive bloc. The multiracial coalitions black politicians had to form in Seaside carried over in governance. In fact, it was common for Mayor McClair and Councilman Polite, who were centrist politicians, to side with white or other minority members of the city council rather than with avowed socialist councilman Mel Mason. McClair and Polite, like Houser and Lioi and other nonblack city council members before them were ex-military men, who shared strong beliefs that came from military culture such as respect for law and order and authority. According to Mason:

Lance [McClair], T. J. [Polite] and I began to part company over issues . . . the cops being only one. There was one meeting where Al [Lioi] brought forward an ordinance that would have protected tenants from discretionary evictions . . . Lance and T. J. voted against the ordinance along with Lioi and Houser . . .

That same night, I brought forward another proposed ordinance that would have developers hire minority subcontractors . . . Lance and T. J. voted against that along with Houser and Lioi . . . I argued against and voted against [the utility tax]. It passed 4-1 . . . I love Lance as a friend and a Brother but we were different politically.[76]

What is evident here is that a progressive politics that was an integral part both of the early civil rights movement and of military culture trumped race or class in Seaside over issues ranging from tenants rights to unions.

Community activist Ewalker James recalled the bewilderment of many African Americans by a city council that was predominantly black but disagreed on the fundamentals: "We finally got a black majority and they acted just like the [white] ones we replaced."[77]

The whites to which James referred, such as Lou Haddad, Bud Houser, and Al Lioi were all only a generation or less away from being considered "minorities" themselves. Each man had memories of racism directed at them and their families. Lou Haddad's parents came to "Jim Crow" Texas as illegal immigrants from Lebanon in the 1930s. The family was so impoverished that Haddad spent several years of his youth in an orphanage. He, like so many African Americans of his generation, gained upward mobility by enlisting in the U.S. military, and during a tour of duty in Germany in the 1950s, met and married a German woman. Also like so many African American and Filipino contemporaries, after being stationed at Fort Ord, he and his family remained in Seaside after he was discharged from the military.[78] Likewise, Bud Houser was a Sicilian whose father deserted the family when he was a young child. His mother remarried and he was adopted by his stepfather (who gave him his non-Italian name), but he clearly recalled the anti-Italian bigotry of his youth.[79] Most importantly, many of these nonblacks ranked lower than their African American counterparts when they were active servicemen, which was deeply felt. Lou Haddad was a staff sergeant, while Al Glover, for example, was a Colonel, Morris McDaniel was a Lieutenant Colonel, and almost all of the African Americans involved in city politics were officers at the very least, and well educated people. Bud Houser expressed awe of Mayor Stephen Ross. "We used to call him 'the professor,'" he said, because Ross, unlike Houser, who only had a high school education, had been an officer and held several advanced degrees.[80]

Thus, the Council's policy to "shake up City Hall" under City Manager McNeely happened in a far different context than in nearby cities with large populations of minority groups, such as in San Jose or Oakland, which had entrenched white elites who controlled city government. Under McNeely, minorities became both numerous and visible at city hall. Diana Ingersoll, who is Filipino, was hired as the director of public works in 1982. She is currently deputy city manager. She described the climate of city government in the 1980s:

Color was a big issue. Seaside was a champion of minority rights. Blacks were definitely number one [among] the minority groups—they actually counted in Seaside. There was a significant shift in hiring practices . . . in upper management. There were black police chiefs. Minorities had big dibs in city government. [By] 1986 there was a massive retirement. If you looked at the race of those who retired, they were white personnel. They got the "golden handshake."[81]

Seaside City Planning Commissioner Jackie Craighead first applied for the position in 1980 under Mayor Glenn Olea, who denied her the job, she believed, because of race, although once again, she was dealing with a Filipino, not a white mayor, who had the sole authority to appoint commissioners. She was eventually appointed in 1985 and remains in the position today. As in other areas of city government in the 1980s, Craighead argued, African Americans understood the need for activism in a city, "We needed representation on all of the commissions. We needed to be there."[82]

McClair undoubtedly accomplished much for Seaside as head of the Seaside City Council and with the support of City Manager McNeely, but his integrity was repeatedly called into question over ethical and moral issues that white politicians rarely faced. He was prosecuted, but not convicted, for violating the Brown Act. The Brown Act, ratified by the California State Legislature in 1953, was designed to ensure that local and state government officials, commissions, and boards operated openly and with public knowledge, rather than "behind closed doors" or through private, secret meetings. McClair was accused of making decisions about Seaside government without the full participation of the city council or the public. Seasiders realized that black politicians tended to be scrutinized more closely and held to a different standard than white ones. Ruthie Watts, a member of Hays Methodist Church and former president of the NAACP recalled, "Every time the paper came [the *Monterey Peninsula Herald*] they said something negative about elected officials in Seaside but that's okay. The people still put them back in office. We kept putting them back."[83]

Mel Mason left Seaside to run against Los Angeles Mayor Tom Bradley in the race for governor of California in February 1984 and then to run for president of the United States as the candidate for the Socialist Party. The city council was deadlocked and could not decide whether to appoint a new city council member to fill Mason's vacant seat or to hold a special election. As a result, the seat went vacant until the regular election in 1984. Al Lioi lost his seat in 1984 but was replaced by Daniel J. Quinn. Nonetheless, whites were once again a minority on the council. Ira Lively, Theron Polite, and Mayor McClair (all three African American) made up the majority on the city council. Still, McClair found himself frequently at odds with the two other African American council members such as when he became embroiled in a power struggle at city hall with the city clerk, Dee Latimore-Berry, which resulted in her firing in 1991. Latimore-Berry was the ex-wife of city council member Theron Polite and best friend of council member Ira Lively. Far from being allies on the basis of race, one unnamed Seaside pastor commented, "We have a black city council attacking our black city clerk and that don't make sense."[84] It did make sense in Seaside and in other towns and cities in the country that began to include blacks in city government.[85] Seaside leaders coalesced over values and ideology far more than over race.

Darlene Burkleo, who was white and a tough anticrime advocate, replaced Daniel Quinn in the election of 1990, and in 1992 two new city councilmen, both African Americans, replaced Al Lioi, so that between 1990 and 1994 African Americans not only formed a majority on the council but also held four out of five positions. Don Jordan, a former Army Major, was elected to the council in 1991 (he was elected mayor in 1994), along with Helen Rucker, whose husband James was an army veteran, and Darryl Choate. Both Rucker and Choate are African American. The only new white member, Gert Foreman replaced Darlene Burkleo in 1992. Foreman was considered an ineffectual city council member and was replaced in 1994 by Nancy Amos, who is also white. There were no white men on the council until the election of Tom Mancini in 1994.

The political climate of the 1980s showed that coalitions were formed based on issues far more than on race, and that the black community of Seaside was just as divided by class interests and ideology as were white, Latino Americans, and Asian Americans. Furthermore, even in the context of the radical politics of the 1970s and 1980s, Seaside city government reflected the essential progressivism of the early civil rights movement and of the military. Everyone but Mel Mason was a veteran and had been stationed at Fort Ord. Stephen Ross, Lance McClair, and Theron Polite often joined with centrist whites and sometimes Filipinos over issues that put them in opposition to council members, Mel Mason, and city attorney Elaine Cass. For Ross, McClair, Polite, and Olea who built coalitions over issues of development and economics, the problem for Seaside was not racial tension. It was an appalling lack of economic development compared to other communities on the Peninsula, which were rapidly adding hotels and commercial and residential developments to raise their tax bases. What all of these politically progressive leaders shared was their affiliation with the military. They had in common an ideology at Fort Ord in which rank trumped race and, as a result, were less likely to view specific issues in strictly racial terms. Mel Mason, on the other hand, was not part of that sensibility. His roots were with the Black Panthers and Oakland, which began to coalesce with other minority groups over social justice issues such as police brutality and tenant's rights, issues that Mason championed in Seaside.[86]

The one big political success for Seaside came during this period of tumult, however. The most important impediment to development projects came at the level of the Monterey County Board of Supervisors. One of the most important battles Seaside fought and won was over the issue of redistricting at the county level. Minority-majority cities such as Salinas, Marina, and Seaside could not elect minority candidates to the powerful Board of Supervisors if their populations were divided among predominantly white districts, because whites (outside of Seaside) would not vote for minorities regardless of their qualifications. In April 1991, the Monterey County Board of Supervisors approved a redistricting plan that effectively divided the communities of Seaside and Marina. The new districts would create two Latino majority districts as a response to the increase in the population of Hispanics in the county, but they did not address the fact that blacks or Asians were not being represented. According to a report in the *Monterey Peninsula Herald*, "Monterey County's population is 34 percent Latino, but the board has no Latino members. Redistricting is a legal requirement to ensure representation to ethnic groups in line with the 1990 census."[87] The meeting of the Board of Supervisors on April 7, 1991, became so hostile that deputies were posted in the meeting room to keep the peace, a move seen as racist in itself. According to a report by the *Monterey Peninsula Herald*:

Amid flaring tempers and charges of racism from a standing room only audience, the County Board of Supervisors yesterday approved a redistricting plan that could radically change Monterey county politics . . . Arguments were fierce . . . fearing that feelings might run so high as to get out of hand, Sheriff Norm Hicks posted deputies in the hearing room . . . [Seaside] Mayor McClair said the plan should be scrapped because it divides the black residents of Seaside and Marina between two districts.[88]

In 1991, Seaside City Attorney Elaine Cass marshaled evidence from prominent social scientists and attorneys engaged in the same battles over minority representation in Los Angeles County to successfully challenge supervisory districts that discriminated against minorities by effectively neutralizing their political clout.[89] McClair and the City of Seaside along with Marina Mayor Edith Johnsen filed suit against the county in federal court challenging the decision. The mayors argued in court that there was a good reason that there was no minority representative on the Monterey County Board of Supervisors. According to *Monterey Peninsula Herald* reports of the hearings:

City officials [from Marina and Seaside] argue that by putting Marina and Seaside in separate supervisory districts, the map dilutes the black and Asian voting

power in those cities. They said that about 40 percent of the residents in the
cities are members of minorities. While the ethnic demographics of the cities
would not constitute a majority of voters for minorities, splitting the population
discourages potential candidates from seeking county office . . . [McClair said]
"It's a question of opportunity . . . the ethnic breakdown of the supervisory
district appeared prohibitive . . . If the maps were redrawn to include Seaside in
a district with Marina, it would make a difference . . . There would be opportunity. There would be a choice."[90]

In an extensive report on the history of racial discrimination in Monterey County, historian and social scientist J. Morgan Kousser demonstrated how members of the Board of Supervisors (all of whom had been
white going back to the beginning of twentieth century when the board
was created and many of whom had held office for as long as thirty years),
intentionally "whitened" their districts by adding or subtracting cities
based on racial makeup of populations to ensure their own survival on
the board. According to Kousser, "Through-out both reapportionments
[in 1981 and again in 1991], African Americans, Asian/Pacific Islanders,
and . . . Latinos were shuffled around like so many puzzle pieces, according to the self-interest of the Anglos who were doing or ordering the
line-drawing . . . to fashion boundaries to ensure their own reelections."[91]
Kousser cited extensive evidence from demographers, census reports, and
minutes from supervisors meetings to show exactly how boundary changes
created districts that were predominantly white; districts that essentially
fragmented minority populations, and, as a consequence, prevented minorities in Marina, Seaside, and Salinas from consolidating power and
adding their voices to the decisions made at the county level.

Furthermore, the presence of military families complicated the picture. Kousser described the effect of the population of military families
attached to Fort Ord as "dead souls"—people that "supervisors used . . .
to pad the population totals of their districts without threatening their in-
cumbency. As Supervisor Marc Del Piero summed it up 'I think everyone
was aware that they [denizens of Fort Ord] didn't vote much, but could
be utilized to 'bring all five districts to approximately the same 49,000
population.'"[92] This was a misleading generalization. As we have seen,

military personnel, especially retired military personnel and their families, were among the most politically active people in Monterey County, and not only voted, but were in the forefront of voter registration drives. Many of them also ran for, and won, political office.

However, it was this misuse of census data that effectively prevented the consolidation of minority voters at the county level, which would have given Seaside (and Marina) far more power to elect minorities to the Board of Supervisors.

The key witness in the lawsuit, Seaside's Pearl Carey, demonstrated exactly how discriminatory practices in drawing districts worked against minority-majority populations. Carey had enjoyed a long and successful history of political activism in Seaside (and at the county, state, and national levels as well), and she was considered the most qualified candidate when she entered the race for county supervisor in 1981. She narrowly lost that race because, as a black woman, she could not muster enough votes in the rest of the district, outside of Seaside and Marina, an area which was predominantly nonmilitary and white. Seaside won the lawsuit in 1991 and subsequently elected first Edith Johnsen (former Marina mayor) in 1992, then Jerry Smith, who was Seaside's mayor from 1998–2003, and the first Seaside black representative on the Board of Supervisors, in 2004. Supervisor Smith passed away during his term in 2008.

The minority-majority cities on the Peninsula needed something very different from Carmel, Pebble Beach, Monterey, and Pacific Grove. Thus it was absolutely essential for representatives from Salinas, Marina, and Seaside to have a voice in decision making at the county level on the Board of Supervisors. The most critical difference in needs had to do with development. While the other cities already had plenty of development and were most interested in limiting growth, Seaside (as well as Marina and Salinas) needed exactly the opposite. Seaside was on the cusp of enormous change in 1991, poised to acquire vast new lands from Fort Ord that could transform it into the tourist and resort destination it wanted to become.

DEVELOPMENT AND THE LOSS OF THE FEDS

The economic picture of Seaside in the 1970s and 1980s was based on growth that was almost wholly dependent on state and federal funding, described in Chapter 3. When that funding dried up as a result of an economic recession and as a consequence of tough budget cutting by California Governor George Deukmejian and President Ronald Reagan in the 1980s, Seaside was in trouble. Without support from the county to ensure new investment and the imminent closure of Fort Ord by 1990 as an active military base, Seaside faced a crisis. According to an assessment by City Manager Charles McNeely in 1983, as a result of Governor George Deukmejian's budget cuts Seaside lost $722,000 in state revenue for 1983–1984.[93]

Moreover, the city manager stated that Seaside was particularly vulnerable because it had "no significant local revenue source other than the sales tax . . . and has historically been heavily dependent upon State and Federal government funding for its financial survival."[94] The city manager and Mayor McClair outlined projected development that would increase revenue, but only in the long term. For the short term, the city considered a 6 percent increase in utility taxes, a tax utilized by both Monterey and Pacific Grove to increase revenue. This initially created outrage among citizens but was narrowly adopted that year, albeit with an exemption for senior citizens.[95] Among the proposed development projects for 1983–1984 were the Days Inn Motel and a Beach Sub-area Development that proposed a beachfront hotel under Seaside's jurisdiction. In addition, a new business license tax was proposed and an increase in the transient occupancy tax from 8 to 10 percent.[96] Nonetheless, Seaside lagged far behind Monterey in terms of tourist-generated income. According to an interview with City Manager Charles McNeely in *The Monterey Peninsula Herald* in 1992, "In Monterey . . . hotel taxes from the tourist trade alone [brought in] about $10 million a year, equal to Seaside's entire budget."[97] The Days Inn Project was under construction by 1984 and after successful lobbying the Seaside City Council won approval by the California Coastal Commission to develop a hotel on Seaside's 500 feet of beachfront. Seaside planned an expansion of the Gateway Auto Mall as well in 1984.[98]

However, there was more bad news from the national level for Seaside. President Reagan eliminated revenue sharing funds for cities in 1984. This meant a loss to Seaside of nearly half a million dollars; all of it designated for police services at a moment in time when the city was expanding its police department to combat high crime. In response, the city implemented a structural reorganization that cut $250,000 from the city budget and contracted many city services to private vendors and also increased its sales tax, property tax, and transient occupancy tax.[99] In anticipation of the budget cuts, City Manager McNeely reported in early August 1983 that the city faced a loss of 15 percent of the city budget, which would mean possibly cutting thirty-four city jobs "decimating some city services including police and fire protection, public works and recreation."[100]

Lance McClair, supported by Polite and Lioi on the city council, but opposed by Mason and Houser, advocated raising taxes on utilities and on businesses, a move that generated widespread opposition in general in Seaside. In support of the mayor, Lioi argued with businessmen at a packed city council meeting August 18, 1983, "I got no constructive answers [from the business community] . . . just a lot of talk. If we don't adopt this [budget to raise taxes] we'll have to cut government services and lay off workers."[101] Once again, the city council split along ideological, not racial, lines over a contentious issue.

Al Glover, a former colonel in the army who came to Fort Ord in 1971 saw great opportunity for minority-owned local business in the city. Glover, who is black and an active member of the NAACP, partnered with Dean Rockwell, who is white, to form a real estate and construction company in the 1970s that ultimately was responsible for developing Mescal Heights in Seaside. "We bought property in 1974 and bought several of the 24 lots up for auction at City Hall," he said as he described how his company prospered throughout the 1980s. Glover described Seaside in the 1980s as economically "stagnant . . . commercial interest rates were out of sight [at] 22 percent."[102] Nonetheless, he and Rockwell were able to build a thriving business and also helped other Seasiders finance homes and businesses of their own. Most importantly, Glover, Rockwell, James Rucker, and banker and former JACL President Andy Yoshiyama created their own bank, Cypress Coast Bank, which became Cypress Bank, in Seaside in 1990 with an initial investment of $4.6 million dollars. According to Glover, "At one time we had five commercial banks in Seaside. They were all bought out by bigger banks. There was [only] one bank

left—Bank of America [in 1990]. We needed a community bank. We decided to organize one . . . We opened the doors in 1990 with branches in
Seaside and Marina . . . By 1996 [we were able to sell] to Salinas Bank
for $46 million."[103] The ability and will of minority business people to
invest in Seaside, and not just in small ways but in large-scale development, showed their commitment to Seaside and to their economic security.

The environmental organizations on the Peninsula objected strenuously to any development of Seaside's most valuable beachfront. The Sierra
Club and the Audubon Society threatened lawsuits. Charles McNeely,
and the city council came together and negotiated with State Assemblyman Henry Mello to exchange development for the beachfront for the
opportunity for Seaside to develop the area around Laguna Grande Park.
The original plans for Laguna Grande would compliment the Peninsula
aesthetically and were supported by other city governments. However,
this area would eventually become the site of the Embassy Suites Hotel,
a structure that was at odds with new environmentally pleasing development plans the rest of the Peninsula cities were enthusiastically supporting, and therefore it became a serious and controversial issue that
further separated Seaside, rather than bringing it into partnership with
Monterey, Carmel, and Pebble Beach.[104] Efforts were also underway to
initiate a redevelopment project for shopping outlets on Fremont Boulevard. By 1990 the city continued to expand the Auto Center, and also
began redeveloping Lower Broadway, part of "The Pit," for retail sales.
Improvements were made on Del Monte Boulevard and on the corner of
Canyon Del Rey and Fremont.

High incidences of violent crime in the mid-1980s discouraged needed
business investment from outside of the community. The city council
responded by creating a Comprehensive Public Relations Program with
local media. The new City Planning Director, Ernest Franco, promoted
the slogan "Seaside Means Business" and was quoted in a newspaper
article as "fond of saying 'If it ain't quality, it ain't Seaside.'" The city
council rallied together to "lift the city's image to one of a potential high
growth area hungry for a taste of the Peninsula's prosperous lifestyle and
economy."[105] In order to accomplish this goal in the face of increasingly
overwhelming odds, city government promised developers that they would

"cut bureaucratic red tape to speed development." Local and regional developers responded positively, all angling for a chance to develop the city's 90 acres of vacant land, 40 of which was designated for commercial use. "There's a lot of opportunity in Seaside," argued mortgage broker, Paul Foster. One architect/developer from Monterey, Jim Hommes, vice president of Will Shaw Associates suggested that Seaside had "an opportunity to be the front door to the Peninsula . . . Other cities are fairly well built out, and their selection and approval process tends to be extremely lengthy." Another developer, Bill Coffee, who planned a residential project around the more upscale (and mostly white Kimball Street area), argued "While we haven't gotten everything we asked for (from the city), we sure have been treated fairly . . . the responses have been quick and not time-consuming, as in other cases in other [Peninsula] cities."[106] In stark contrast to minority, especially predominantly black, communities across the country, Seaside's natural environment was gorgeous, inviting, and continued to be a promising place for development.

The city hired Camran Nojoomi, who was described as an "economic development specialist" to recruit developers and work with Seaside's Planning Commission in developing a mixed use development plan for the city's future. Nojoomi helped to create a small business center to help guide Seaside small businesses through the Federal Small Business Administration loan process.[107] However, when former Redevelopment Agency Director Richard Goblirsch offered Costco to Nojoomi as Seaside's representative in 1990, he turned it down. Later, Costco proved to be an enormous boon to the neighboring municipality of Sand City. But Nojoomi, like other planners in many cities across the country in this decade, clearly wanted Seaside to be considered an integral part of the communities of the Monterey Peninsula, which meant retaining its flavor as a unique, multiracial, *former* military small town, something that would certainly be threatened by the establishment of big box stores such as Costco.[108]

Image continued to thwart Seaside during the 1980s, however. Developer Bill Coffee argued that his projects would fail to attract new residents: "We've got to get rid of the image that Seaside is a barracks for Fort Ord." Citing the 1980 federal census records of household income, the *Monterey Peninsula Herald* reported in 1984 that at "16,887, [Seaside had] the lowest [average household income] of any Peninsula city." Further, the article argued that Seaside's "eagerness for growth may stem at least partly from an inferiority complex and stagnant economy through the years, as the city watched the vigorous economy of neighboring Monterey with its booming tourist trade and broad business base, and the other Peninsula cities."[109] Charles McNeely summarized the situation of a decade in the 1991–1992 city budgets:

The general economy continues to be uncertain and our dependence on sales tax makes us vulnerable when car sales are down. We also have been battered by the state and county efforts to balance their budgets through extra taxes, fees and charges. The City will have to husband its resources in order to meet these challenges and extra costs.[110]

Indeed, the recession of the early 1980s hit Seaside particularly hard. According to McNeely, "The recession hit us real hard . . . our tourist dollars dropped off and redevelopment efforts just stopped when [federal and state] financing dried up."[111] In order to be competitive with the other economies on the Peninsula, Seaside needed access to resources that would allow for commercial investment especially in the burgeoning tourist industry. Seaside wanted exactly what the other Peninsula cities enjoyed—tax revenues that were generated by motels and hotels, restaurants, and upscale housing. That kind of development required resources such as water, a scarce commodity on the Peninsula, and the support of the other Peninsula cities, just as much as it needed a positive image of the city as safe and secure, and a slow awakening as a postmilitary town. Yet, decisions about development and resource use were made at the county level and through the Board of Supervisors. Seaside's successful lawsuit in 1991 would help with that in the long term, but for the decade of the 1980s, Seaside's needs were secondary, overshadowed by the development projects happening in Monterey, Carmel Valley, and Pebble Beach.

CONCLUSION

The years between 1976 and 1994 held enormous promise for Seaside as African Americans settled into position as a powerful minority-majority group in politics, culture, and economic life bolstered by the economic security of their connection to Fort Ord and the multiple successes of the civil rights movements. The vibrant, sophisticated community that blacks created in these years was based on achieving political leadership through astute coalition building with whites, Asians, and Latinos, who shared common experiences as part of a military community. This in turn lead to a proliferation of cultural and social events that were organized by the community to mark Seaside as one of the most important centers of African American life in California. Even though there were some racially charged political moments, these were mostly due to individual disputes rather than collective group efforts. In Seaside, the political environment mirrored that of Fort Ord, which was one that mandated inclusiveness, especially over important issues such as development.

Yet, much of the positive good that blacks and others did in Seaside was overshadowed by leadership scrutinized intensely by the media and that became embroiled in personal squabbles, as well as high crime rates that the media tended to overreport to the exclusion of everything positive going on in the city. As long as Seaside was associated with African Americans and with the military, its efforts at boosterism and development were thwarted by racism that was pervasive and embedded in the American psyche, and in everything from politics to economics to infrastructure. Therefore, even the best of city managers such as Charles McNeely could do only so much in terms of pushing forward development projects that would allow Seaside to compete effectively with the other "white" municipalities on the Peninsula. Still, middleclass minorities, especially blacks in Seaside, did not leave for more affluent parts of the Peninsula as they did in Los Angeles, Oakland, and in almost every metropolitan center in the United States in those years. Seaside remained an attractive place to live; its natural environment made it desirable and promising.

The connection to Fort Ord did not help Seaside in those decades, however. The idea of a military town as crime ridden and marginal persisted even though the military population that settled in Seaside was centrist, patriotic, and respectful of authority, and believed deeply in law and order. Regular soldiers who trained at Fort Ord (and who gave Seaside its rough reputation) tended to live on base rather than in the city.

Ironically, in anticipation of the closure of Fort Ord, the other Peninsula cities were suddenly very much interested in the military in the early 1990s. The base closure opened up vast tracts of land for commercial and residential development. What was once presumed to be the domain of Seaside was suddenly up for grabs by everyone from Santa Cruz to Big Sur and of interest to developers at the national level. Since the 1990s Seaside struggled to come into its own, to establish a new identity for itself based in part on its history as a minority-majority military town that built unique coalitions across race and class, and in part, on a vision that brought Seaside back to its original place as a resort destination—just like every other Peninsula city.

CHAPTER 6

After Fort Ord: The New Demographic

PHOTO 6. A view of Seaside and the Monterey Bay from Blackhorse and Bayonet golf courses. Both were acquired by the City of Seaside after the closure of Fort Ord in 1994. City of Seaside Archive, Seaside History Project.

THE END OF THE COLD WAR meant changes in military and federal policy that would threaten everything about the relationship between Fort Ord and Seaside and between Seaside and its neighbors.[1] First, in 1988, the Pentagon established the Base Realignment and Closure Commission (BRACC) to close or restructure 451 military bases across the country, including 97 major installations; Fort Ord was among the military bases being considered for closure.[2] Then, in 1990, the United States Environmental Protection Agency marked Fort Ord as a federal Superfund site because of groundwater contamination, making projects for post-Fort Ord development far more complicated. In 1991, Fort Ord was selected officially for base closure by BRACC91. By 1993, the historic 7th Infantry Division (Light) was deactivated, and the soldiers were assigned to Fort Lewis in Tacoma, Washington. Many Seaside businesses and people left with them. Seaside community leaders and residents alike were panicked at the prospect of losing a critical mass of people as well as jobs. They understood perfectly that Fort Ord was integral to the city in everything from city government to its very identity. Fort Ord created Seaside.

By 1990, Seaside was also in the throes of population change as Latinos migrated in large numbers into Seaside from Mexico to work in the service industries of the Monterey Peninsula. By 2000, the city was quickly losing its population of military families of all races, as middle-class blacks and others were able to make huge profits on their homes as many returned to the South to spend their final years in hometowns. The organizations that blacks built from the 1950s through the 1990s no longer attracted new members.[3] Moreover, although many middle-class African Americans in Seaside remained, their children did not. Citizens League for Progress founder Ewalker James expressed frustration over the lack of involvement of young people in the civic organizations that he and others worked so hard to create and build: "Our members are older and dying away. We find it difficult to get young people to join. They say 'That's not my thing.' Well, what *is* your thing? Do you live in this community? How do you think it got to be this way?"[4] James was right to be angered by what he perceived was apathy, but in fact, the problem was numbers. Few children of the black middle class could find employment or affordable housing in Seaside without Fort Ord.

Many other municipalities faced dramatic job loss in this decade as manufacturing plants closed throughout the United States and reopened overseas, leaving entire towns with depleted economic infrastructures. However, the loss of military bases had a qualitatively different impact on towns like Seaside that were intimately connected to them. When the military leaves, it takes its personnel with it, removing a community's consumer base. By contrast, in a manufacturing town, when a company leaves, its employees remain, but without employment. Also, the military is an integral part of the U.S. government, not another corporation making a profit. Military identity formation was intimately American and patriotic. Most importantly, the military exercised a subtle, but important influence on political behavior. Its mandate of equal treatment, regardless of race, supported the values of the civil rights movement, but in a moderate way. As a result, Seaside politics remained both inclusive and centrist rather than radical, even when other minority-majority cities in California and the nation shifted left and toward racial identity politics and even violence, as shown in Chapter 5.

As soldiers in uniform and military families disappeared by 2000, Seaside had to cope with the loss of an institution that had given it much of its identity as a city. Instead of soldiers, or black, Asian, and white ethnic youth, the streets of the city were increasingly filled with families of Latino immigrants who had no connection to the military or familiarity with military towns or military ways. The shops and restaurants of Seaside, once mainly reflective of black, southern white, or East Asian culture now included more Latino markets, restaurants, and small businesses catering to the new demographic of mostly Mexican Americans and Mexican immigrants who came to Seaside for economic opportunity rather than military obligation. Although Seaside's political leadership remained predominantly white, Asian, and African American, it needed to incorporate a nonmilitary Latino populace into its government as well as to reconfigure its relationship to its neighbors. Turbulence and tension ensued.

However, although Seaside, like other cities of color throughout California in the late twentieth century, was deeply affected by large-scale immigration from Mexico, the legacy of Fort Ord and the military had molded the city's culture in ways that allowed leaders and common citizens alike to integrate newcomers in their community without the major problems that characterized other minority-majority cities during the past thirty years, in which groups such as Latinos or blacks formed political and social blocs.[5] This chapter explores how Seaside leaders and residents met the challenges of life after Fort Ord by insisting on the model of both moderation and racial inclusion in politics, economics, and social life. Integration won out.

REALIGNMENT AND REDEVELOPMENT

"I think this community is a better community today [2006]. The military, the loss of the military, has given the community a chance to breathe, to grow," said retired Colonel Al Glover, one of Seaside's most prominent and successful businessmen, about the closure of Fort Ord in the 1990s.[6] His was one of the few voices that were positive about the changes that came about as a result of the military's decision to close Fort Ord. Seasiders spent the better part of the past fifteen years focused on the closure of Fort Ord as a challenge and a loss, rather than as a positive good. The decisions regarding the use of former military lands consumed city managers, planners, and community leaders alike. Seaside aimed for a post-Fort Ord "renaissance" into the twenty-first century but continued to struggle both with its identity and with the legacy of its past.[7] Current City Manager Ray Corpuz, who arrived in Seaside in August 2005, commented on the challenges the city faced:

[Seaside] . . . was a city that was in obvious transition from a military dependent community trying to find its place on the Peninsula where a brand idea defined Carmel, Monterey and Pebble Beach. Seaside was not part of that brand in the eyes of the other communities. The city wanted to move beyond this transition of not being a fully recognized partner and was struggling to find both a direction and a common vision both among the leadership of elected officials and the community at large.[8]

As discussed in earlier chapters, as long as Seaside was viewed as black and minority, and also a military town, it was isolated by the other communities that made up the Monterey Peninsula, which mimicked the postsuburban cities and town patterns that Joel Garreau and Jon C. Teaford described as "edge cities." These were municipalities, like Monterey, Pacific Grove, and Carmel that stubbornly retained their own unique identities and self-governments even as they should have understood that it made more sense to work jointly, creating regional police and fire departments for example.[9] Furthermore, just like the cities of the Monterey Peninsula, which maintained relatively homogenous white communities as counterpoint to minority-majority Seaside and Fort Ord, most of the postsuburban cities Teaford described developed as racially distinct from the urban centers they once depended on. In Michigan, for example, "the increasingly black city of Detroit was socially alien to the predominantly white cities of Oakland [Michigan]."[10] The tension this situation created between Monterey, Pacific Grove, Carmel, and Seaside was exacerbated when the military left the area in the 1990s, pushing Seaside, as City Manager Ray Corpuz argued, to demand to be incorporated into the "brand" of the Monterey Peninsula, even though it remained a minority-majority community.

Just as Seaside struggled to cope with an unstable economy and the huge loss of state and federal funds in the recession of the early 1990s, other military communities across the country were faced with the terrifying prospect of losing their most important employer, asset, and customer base as the Cold War came to an end and the federal government moved to reduce both the size and cost of the military. Forty percent of all military expenditures were located in California, Virginia, Texas, and North Carolina and created interdependent communities around bases, just like Seaside and Fort Ord, which relied heavily on federal spending as the driving force of their economies.[11] In the northeastern states of Connecticut and Massachusetts, one out of every fifteen workers was employed by the military.[12] A colonel at Fort Bragg suggested, "When people start talking about the peace dividend, are [they] willing to give up that much economic impact in their county?"[13] Yet, as recent scholarship shows, this was also a great opportunity to convert the manpower and resources that fed America's military-industrial complex to fight poverty, for example.[14]

City Manager Charles McNeely, writing in 1991, described the "challenges and opportunities" brought about by the base closure:

No other single issue presents the challenge and opportunities as does the closure and reuse of the Fort Ord property. In its worst case, Fort Ord represents a significant loss in revenue to the city not only because of the gas and sales tax revenue, with an estimated loss of 20% to the City in sales tax revenue, but it also represents a significant impact on the city's unemployment rate and loss of housing . . . The city of Seaside has formed its own Fort Ord Economic Development Authority . . . between the cities of Marina and Seaside (with expected county participation) to focus on possible reuse of Fort Ord property that will be disposed of by the military. Clearly, the closure of Fort Ord represents a once in a lifetime opportunity for Seaside's long-term to build a strong economic base that will rival that of other Peninsula cities.[15]

The fact that McNeely was looking to the other cities as "rivals" rather than partners showed how important the postsuburban vision was to Seaside in its effort to retain independence, even though it also wanted inclusion with the Peninsula communities.[16] One year later, however, McNeely was grim: "The city expects that the closing of Fort Ord will mean a 7 percent loss in city revenues—about $740,000 a year."[17]

Although the automobile dealership center generated substantial revenue for the city, revenue was based on sales, not on property taxes. When Fort Ord began the process of closure in 1992, it affected the automobile dealerships and, as a result, city revenues declined sharply. According to former Seaside city councilmember, Tom Mancini, "The soldiers were the ones who bought cars. When Fort Ord closed [and soldiers left] that was a huge loss for the auto center and Seaside."[18] In fact, however, according to automobile dealers such as Don Butts, owner of Butts Acura Dealership in the Seaside Auto Center, the problem was not about poorly paid soldiers (who were less able to afford new cars), who left Seaside as part of military policy than it was about the loss of relatively high-paying Fort Ord jobs that supported the military. In an interview for *The Monterey Peninsula Herald* in 1992, Butts explained, "Most of our cars are too expensive for the post soldiers to afford . . . We sell most of our cars to people who live in this community, and most of the community derives its income from Fort Ord."[19] Many small businesses, also dependent on Fort Ord, were panicked about losing such an important revenue base. "Here we are going fine," explained Jackie Hill who, along with her husband Jack, owned a tax service business, "and, all of a sudden 60 percent of your business is going to be leaving—it's frightening." The Hill's strategy, like so many other business people and individuals dependent on the military for revenue and jobs, was to close their business in Seaside and move with the army to Tacoma, Washington, the site of the 7th Infantry Division's new base at Fort Lewis. "We're camp followers," she said.[20]

McNeely understood how high the stakes were, but he could not have imagined the ensuing battles between the neighboring communities of Monterey, Pacific Grove, Carmel, and even Marina (which was an ally of Seaside, for the most part), as the entire region jockeyed for power, land, and position over the closure of Fort Ord. Under the leadership of then Congressman Leon Panetta, The Fort Ord Reuse Authority was formed in 1994 under the auspices of the State of California to divert the intense rivalry into something more like a partnership. But Panetta and other lawmakers were faced with a collection of cities that deeply distrusted large-scale government control, just as other regional municipalities viewed regional partnerships as threatening, even when it was in their economic and political interest to create them.[21] For Seaside, the problem was also complicated by race. As a minority-majority town without the protection of Fort Ord, Seasiders were wary of losing power over their own development to mostly white neighboring communities.

Seaside felt both the benefit and downside of being intimately associated with the military base but was suddenly in the position of being just another interested stakeholder, equal if not inferior to Carmel or Monterey in terms of dividing the spoils of what was once the largest military training base on the West Coast. It would be the task of the next three city councils and city managers, first under Mayor Don Jordan and City Manager Tim Brown (1994–1998), then Mayor Jerry Smith and City Managers Richard Guillen (acting) and Daniel Keen (1998–2004), and Mayor Ralph Rubio (2004-2010) and City Manager Ray Corpuz (2005–current) to negotiate a good deal for the city, and simultaneously achieve the regional partnership that they had wanted for so many years, but feared at the same time.

Seaside continued to be hampered in its long-term strategies for growth by internecine battles at city hall that threatened to derail any development gains the city so badly needed. Yet, the political crises that ensued over issues of power at city hall also confirmed the fact that Seaside was all about coalition building among races, rather than a city defined in black versus white or black versus shades of brown. Consistent with its political history in recent decades, groups formed and reformed over issues, not along racial and ethnic lines. The power struggles began with the demise of the McClair administration, and the election of Don Jordan as mayor in 1994. He was the fourth African American elected mayor in Seaside history and part of a tradition of minority mayors going back to the 1970s.

Lance McClair dominated Seaside politics throughout the 1980s. He believed that even day-to-day decisions about the city needed to be made in the mayor's office. He had put in place a broad multiracial coalition and had wide support in the city, which allowed him to be reelected four times. His view of governance, however, was at odds with the council manager form of government established at the time of Seaside's incorporation in 1954 in which a professional city manager assumed the duties of managing the city, acting as chief operating officer, with the city council in the role of board of directors. As a response to accusations of improper use of power by McClair, Don Jordan advocated a return to the more traditional council manager form of government with Tim Brown, hired during the McClair administration, as city manager. Jerry Smith, who was elected in 1998, returned to McClair's idea of governance and was frequently accused of "running a one man show" as mayor.[22]

Don Jordan originally won a place on the Seaside City Council in 1991 to fill the vacancy created when Councilmember Al Lioi died in office. Jordan was a retired U.S. Army major and Vietnam War veteran who believed the McClair administration had harmed the image of Seaside on the Monterey Peninsula with highly publicized conflicts and scandals and misuse of power at city hall. Jordan was also frustrated with the seemingly endless negotiations over development issues at a time when an economic recession and the projected loss of Fort Ord made private development an imperative.[23] Jordan, like McClair, was supported by the political establishment that included blacks, whites, and Asians and but was led in large part by the Ministerial Alliance and the NAACP.

By the time Don Jordan stepped into the mayor's office with Tim Brown as city manager in 1995, Seaside was feeling the full effects of the loss of Fort Ord; Jordan and Brown were determined to resolve the financial crisis that they had inherited. Although Lance McClair and the city council of 1994 hired Tim Brown, it was Don Jordan who believed in the importance of a professional city manager having the authority to run the city with the influence of the city council, rather than vice-versa.

Jordan and Brown became the front line in the transition of Seaside from military town to resort community forced by the closure of Fort Ord. A *Monterey Peninsula Herald* article emphasized the opportunity for development in Seaside after Fort Ord: "With the closure of Fort Ord four years ago, Seaside's plans for acquisition of Hayes Park and further development of the nearby Fort Ord golf courses, new homes, dreams, and expectations may soon be realized."[24] According to a report by Brown in July 1995:

The City of Seaside is at a turning point in its history. The progressive forward thinking of the City in the preparation of a long-range economic business development or "Vision Plan" for the Community has taken the initial steps necessary to encourage enhancement of the City economic base, severely impacted by the closure of Fort Ord, and to enhance the City image presented to the public . . . Through the whole process the citizens have been encouraged to participate in the potential transformation of the community.[25]

At first it appeared as though Seasiders would be in a strong position to take advantage of the new opportunities and to forge a new identity separate from its long-standing connection to the military, but it was clear as projects moved forward that there were serious conflicts about the extent to which it would remain a multiracial enclave with a critical mass of African Americans. The tremendous influx of Mexican Americans and Mexican immigrants changed the dynamics of Seaside's population rapidly beginning in 1990. According to Al Glover, "Fort Ord was vital to this community [but] Mexican Americans filled a void left by the military." Far from being a negative, Glover argued, Fort Ord's demise gave Seaside "breathing room . . . the military serves as a magnet for drug dealers, criminals, and prostitutes." After the military population left, Mexican immigrants stepped in and improved the economic infrastructure of the city, according to Glover. "I've been amazed," he said, "at the number of houses that these immigrant workers bought and renovated. They have upgraded their homes, replaced vacant lots with homes . . . there is still a need for housing [but] they are not waiting for the city or county to build for them."[26] Glover serves as a mentor for both black and Mexican immigrant young people, financing their educations and helping them get started in business enterprises. It did not seem to him and to other African American leaders at that time that new populations would dispute the vision they held of Seaside as a city built on the foundation of the African American-led civil rights movement. Like groups before them, new populations were integrated into Seaside and did not fundamentally change the character of the city, one that was always based on both diversity and inclusion.

Notwithstanding Glover's experience and assessment, the loss of the military base to Seaside's economy was real, and it created a genuine crisis for the city economically and also led to a shift culturally and socially. By 1995, the 7th Infantry division had been completely relocated to Fort Lewis, Washington, with the loss of hundreds of jobs by civilians employed at the base; the city's population decreased nearly 20 percent. The construction, retail trade, and service industries also felt the impact of the base closure acutely.[27] According to Seaside City Finance Director and Deputy City Manager Daphne Hodgson, city tax revenues in 1991–1992 were $7.8 million. By 1992–1993, they decreased 9 percent to $7.1 million, and in 1994–1995 revenues were $7.5 million, still not fully recovered to the pre-Fort Ord levels. However, by 1995–1996 tax revenues increased to $8.3 million largely due to the opening of the Embassy Suites Hotel.[28] Hodgson explained further that revenues from the state were based on population. The closure of Fort Ord meant a loss of approximately 10,000 people by 1996. Seaside's population in 1990 was 38,901 and 28,300 in 1996. It gradually increased to 34,194 by 2008, largely due to the Mexican immigrant population. Nonetheless, the years between 1991 and 1998, when the population gradually rose, were challenging ones financially for the city.[29]

The consortium of cities organized by Congressman Leon Panetta, State Senator Henry Mello, Assemblyman Sam Farr, and 4th District Supervisor Sam Karas in 1992 to study the effects of the base closure was turned into the Fort Ord Reuse Authority (FORA), a group charged with creating a master plan for the stakeholders to transform the military base for civilian use. Seaside was included in FORA. From the perspective of Seasiders, efforts by urban planners, government officials, and local environmentalists to weigh in on new development looked suspiciously like an attempt to wrest control of their community that would lead to a loss of its identity as a unique city on the Peninsula, just as so many other postsuburban communities saw federal or state efforts to consolidate regional entities as "coercion" that would lead to their demise.[30] From the perspective of environmentalists and government representatives, however, it was a matter of aesthetics and partnership rather than paternalism or a hostile takeover.

Sam Karas, the Fourth District Supervisor who represented both Seaside and Marina (as well as parts of Monterey, Pacific Grove, and Pebble Beach), refused to allow the two cities of Seaside and Marina to circumvent the county with regard to the control of Fort Ord land, a decision which angered Seaside mayors McClair and Jordan and Marina Mayor Edith Johnsen. However, all of his colleagues on the board of supervisors, Congressman Leon Panetta, State Senator Henry Mello and Assemblyman Sam Farr, as well as leaders of other Peninsula cities supported Karas because they believed in a more holistic approach to development. The other local mayors and city councils also sought to carve out a piece of Fort Ord for themselves, in spite of the possibility that they too would be under the control of a regional rather than municipal agency. Residents and government leaders in those cities wanted to share in the redevelopment plans for the former army base, and framed their critique of Seaside in aesthetic terms, which to many residents of Seaside seemed thinly disguised racism.

Congressman Sam Farr expressed this holistic view of development but also criticism of Seaside and lack of understanding of the deeply felt sensibility of Seaside residents and leaders about the independence of their city:

The Peninsula is one big family and what we ought to be doing is thinking of ourselves as family. What we all have in common is the land. It is the serenity and beauty here that is the economic engine that drives everything else . . . Sam [Karas] and I had the sense that Seaside was really going to take care of Seaside, but in a nice and aesthetic way.[31]

When Lance McClair brought in outside developers to build the Embassy Suites, Farr, Karas, and other residents on the Peninsula were appalled at the scale of the hotel, which Farr described as "detracting" from the beauty of the area. "The turning point was the building of the Embassy Suites Hotel . . . [We all asked the question] Is Seaside going to take that base and turn it into a sea of Embassy Suites?" As a result, when Seaside wanted to make the redevelopment of the former fort an exclusive project for itself and Marina, Supervisor Karas objected. According to Farr, "Monterey and the other cities didn't trust what these towns would do based on the use of developers who came from outside the region and thus had "no long term interest in the community" with the result being the "poorly designed" Embassy Suites.[32]

Seasiders, however, were proud of the fact that the city could now boast that it had a twelve-story hotel with 234 rooms and 8 large meeting rooms. Far from being discouraged, Seasiders were eager for even more development. To many local residents, the widespread criticism and generally negative responses to the Embassy Suites development had the feel of both veiled elitism and racism.

Don Jordan and Tim Brown made an effort to keep Seaside connected to a bigger world, but their efforts generated hostility and suspicion in some part because so many of their connections happened to be African American. Brown had an explanation for these connections:

We (Don and I) were looking for help to rebuild any way we could and had the blessings of the city council to do just that. If it meant we had to go to Southern California we did, if it meant going to San Francisco we did. We met with the Speaker of the House/Mayor of San Francisco Willie Brown. It just so happened that the people we did meet with were African American. The Secretary of Commerce was Ron Brown, the Representative from Economic Development Administration was Leonard Smith, the Secretary of the Army was Togo West and these are the positions you would go to no matter what color or race they were.[33]

Congressman Farr supported affirmative action, but not the use of outside developers with no stake in the long-term life of the Peninsula. However, according to former Mayor Don Jordan, "because of the scale and the cost of the Fort Ord projects, there were no local developers capable that expressed interest. We did an RFP [Request for Proposal] that no local developers responded to."[34] Farr argued "that slick folks come in and negotiate a contract that is all to their advantage . . . what the Peninsula has failed to do was . . . to work with Seaside and Marina by providing brilliant staffing."[35]

It is not clear what Farr may have meant by the term "slick folks," but it suggests that Jordan and Brown were somehow misled or incapable. However, Jordan and Brown, like so many other African Americans engaged in the race work of the civil rights era, had ties with prominent African American business and civic leaders up and down the state of California and in Washington, DC, that clearly indicated they were quite capable of negotiating favorably for Seaside. Also according to Brown, "It was Congressman Farr's idea that we meet with Maxine Waters [D-Los Angeles] to secure that necessary votes to obtain the Golf Courses. We met with the entire [Congressional] Black Caucus to secure those golf courses for the Seaside.[36] As in the 1960s when federal investment in development was needed, Seaside's leaders were sophisticated ex-military personnel and civil rights activists who ably extended their political reach for the benefit of their city.

After FORA was organized, all redevelopment had to go through a master plan. One of the most important components of the Fort Ord Reuse Plan included the creation of a new California State University campus. Both Jordan and Brown enthusiastically supported plans for a California State campus. They wanted Seaside to emerge from its postmilitary identity into a university town as much as they wanted to be perceived as a resort destination. According to Brown, "As the city adjusts to the loss of Fort Ord it has the responsibility to plan for the future with the transition to an educational community base with the opening of the new university campus." Brown emphasized however that Seaside aimed to establish itself as an integral part of the Peninsula: "The location of [Seaside] as the gateway to the Monterey Peninsula puts the city in an ideal situation to capitalize on the economic development of the area." Furthermore, both the new university planners and Mayor Jordan and City Manager Brown were deeply involved in negotiations for joint development of the main gate corridor for the college. After they left office, however, those negotiations were forgotten.[37]

The essential conundrum for Seaside leaders in the 1990s was to balance their need for inclusion brought on by the new reality of the loss of Fort Ord, which promised them what they said they always wanted—to be partners with the other Peninsula communities—with the equally pressing need voiced loud and clear by residents and leaders alike for independence and a unique identity, which in the aftermath of Fort Ord was yet to be determined.

DON JORDAN, TIM BROWN, POWER, AND DEVELOPMENT 1991–1998

By 1995, Seaside made efforts to reform its community identity from that of a military town to one that was both university and tourist oriented similar to the "brand" of Monterey or Carmel. But Seaside continued to draw considerable negative media attention for high crime rates and scandal that made this effort more difficult even than it already was. Most importantly, the nationwide economic downturn of the mid 1990s, together with prolonged and severe water shortages, a perennial problem on the Monterey Peninsula, and the discovery of groundwater contamination at Fort Ord led to water use restrictions and limitations on development throughout the county during the remainder of the 1990s.[38] To make matters worse, the city's budget was in the red for most of the decade, although there was a surplus by 1998. All of this made it difficult, if not impossible, to attract the business investment that Seaside needed to recover from the loss of Fort Ord.

A strong environmental movement led by residents from the other Peninsula cities successfully challenged development projects such as Rancho San Carlos in Carmel Valley with initiatives designed to limit growth. Most of the arguments raised by environmentalists focused on the serious lack of water resources in the county and fears of unbridled development and population growth, which Seasiders believed they desperately needed and generally supported.[39] Unbeknown to environmentalists, the Fort Ord Reuse Plan called for the use of treated water for all external irrigation once it was available. This conflict with the other Peninsula communities made clear to Seaside leaders and residents that they needed to be careful about ceding authority to regional or state organizations such as FORA, and city leaders were tasked with maintaining local control over development at all costs.

The Jordan/Brown administration faced all of these crises simultaneously as they tried to cope with the new reality of Seaside without Fort Ord. At city hall, personnel difficulties as a result of the loss of tax revenue and government support erupted during the mid-1990s. Coupled with personality disputes with the city manager, the city had to deal with a number of lawsuits from former city personnel challenging decisions to downsize staff.[40] In the 1996 budget report, City Manager Tim Brown cut expenditures by "not filling vacant positions, and maintaining [only] basic service levels" at city hall. Brown inherited from the McClair administration a situation limiting staff to thirty-six hours per week and the closure of city hall on Fridays.

The city had contracted with a big five accounting firm, KPMG, to help with Seaside's reorganization, which led to the consolidation of fire and police chief positions, under Police Chief Dave Butler, a move for which Tim Brown was vilified because it was misconstrued as consolidating the departments rather than only the department head. Both the planning and redevelopment departments were contracted out to consultants. This led to serious resentments and new political activism in Seaside by a loose coalition of whites, blacks, and other minority groups against Jordan and Brown. The building of the 255-room Embassy Suites Hotel in October 1996 provided some relief to city revenues. It had taken twenty years both to begin construction and to finish the project in the wake of the sudden death of the developer and conflicts over costs, labor issues, and construction difficulties. Seasiders were enormously proud of the Embassy Suites, which symbolized their unique identity and independence from the other Peninsula cities, which they believed were elitist and arrogant in their condemnation of the project. Estela McKenzie recalled that her husband Patrick "put on his hard hat and took pictures of himself in front of the Embassy Suites. He was so happy."[41]

According to Don Jordan, City Manager Tim Brown should be credited for having "stopped the bleeding" of Seaside as a result of the multiple pressures of the recession, loss of Fort Ord, water shortages, and environmental challenges to development projects. Jordan recalled, "We merged project areas, reorganized staff, moved money into the general fund and kept the city from bankruptcy . . . we ran a lean machine . . . by 1998 we had a [budget] surplus."[42] Jordan and Brown also made "dozens of trips to Washington" to lobby local representatives in Congress and the Clinton administration to give Seaside its share of land, including the golf courses and development rights from the Army property in order to begin the process of economic recovery. They believed that their presence in Washington was the only way for Seaside to prevail in negotiations with the Army. "That's where all the decisions were being made."[43]

Brown and Mayor Jordan took the lead in securing Fort Ord land to develop housing, hotels, and golf courses on the land designated by FORA for Seaside. All became highly controversial. The critical issue was whether the city could provide water for the ambitious and lucrative projects and who should actually be chosen to develop them. Their actions were increasingly criticized in the press. One *Monterey Peninsula Herald* article critiqued Jordan and Brown's strategy of numerous personal visits to Washington, DC, to lobby for the acquisition of the two Army golf courses in 1996:

More than $800,000 has been spent in the past five years by the city on consultants and travel to Washington D.C. to draw up plans, solicit developers and visit politicians and Army officials in the bunkers of Congress and the Pentagon . . . In a special meeting last night, they selected BSL Golf of Houston, Texas as developer—operator of the golf courses . . . the developer is expected to put up the acquisition and rehabilitation funds for the golf courses, perhaps a total of $15 million to $20 million. However, the city would hold title to the property on a long-term lease. The specifics of the acquisition costs are hazy because City Manager Tim Brown does not want to tip his hand to the Army on offers for the golf courses and the adjacent Hayes Park housing area, a total of 477 acres.[44]

Although Brown disputed the $800,000 figure, both Jordan and Brown emphasized that Seaside won over 400 acres of land including the two golf courses as a result of their efforts. The golf courses alone were valued at $17 million dollars. New legislation supported their efforts with the Army. According to a report in the *Monterey Peninsula Herald,* Jordan said Seaside originally sought the golf courses under a contract in which the city would operate the courses for the Army and the revenues would go to the Army's Morale, Welfare and Recreation Fund. Then the BRACC, which had ordered the closure of Fort Ord, directed the Army to sell the golf courses. But the Army issued a legal opinion concluding that the BRACC could not order the Army to sell the courses. The mayor and city manager managed to persuade both Representative Sam Farr (D-Carmel) and U.S. Senator Barbara Boxer (D-California) to write legislation that gave Seaside the right to be the sole bidder for the golf course; the legislation was passed in January [1996] under the Defense Authorization Act.[45]

Although a number of local golf course developers had applied to the city to develop and manage the former Army courses, including the Pebble Beach Corporation, Seaside officials were criticized for choosing a developer from out of state. To be fair, no one in Pebble Beach, least of all the Pebble Beach Corporation, had expressed any interest in developing Seaside prior to the loss of Fort Ord. As a consequence, there was little in the way of incentive or sense of affinity or loyalty on the part of Seasiders to keep development in the hands of local corporations. The problem, however, was one of perception. The process appeared to some residents to be tilted toward BSL Golf, Inc. of Houston.

The city put together a committee of seven individuals who chose BSL Golf, Inc. to finance both the acquisition and needed upgrading of the two courses. The committee members were Larry Arceneax of Katz Hollis, a Los Angeles consultant to municipalities on redevelopment, Vincent McCarley, an investment banker, and Seaside Mayor Don Jordan and City Manager Tim Brown. The other member was Pearl Carey, a well-known Seaside activist and politician who was also quite famous in the world of golf by 1990. She was a committee member of the U.S. Golf Association and Western States Golf Association.[46]

BSL Golf, Inc. was considered suspect, however, because, as one reporter in the *Monterey Peninsula Herald* pointed out, "BSL's financing on other real estate and golf course projects in Houston were the subject of allegations in the early 1990s. According to reports in the *Houston*

Chronicle, the firm had negotiated 'sweetheart' deals with the Houston Public Employees Pension and Houston Police Officers Pension System."[47] Partners Andrew Schatte and Richard Bischoff argued that these were "wild allegations" that had never been investigated either by the Federal Bureau of Investigation (FBI) or the Internal Revenue Service.[48]

More problematic was the issue of water use for the golf courses. Part of the deal reached between BSL Golf, Inc. with the City of Seaside included a guarantee by the city of "free water to irrigate the golf courses" without requiring that the irrigation system be upgraded, according to newspaper reports of the time. However, according to Mayor Jordan, there was indeed a requirement to upgrade the system embedded in the agreement, once treated water was made available.[49]

As water was either rationed or a rationing plan was considered throughout the decade of the 1990s and intense political battles were being waged over the issue of development without adequate water supplies, the willingness of city officials to allow BSL Golf, Inc. to proceed made the front pages of the local newspapers and created outrage among some county residents. According to a report in the *Monterey Peninsula Herald*, "installing new computerized state of the art irrigation equipment . . . could reduce water use by 20 percent to 30 percent [at Blackhorse and Bayonet courses] at a total cost [to the developers] of $2 million . . . Russ Mitchell . . . one of the dominant irrigation designers in Northern California . . . said that almost all of the Monterey Peninsula golf courses have upgraded their irrigation systems to improve playability and reduce water usage."[50] Instead, BSL Golf, Inc. invested a little over $100,000 in upgrades to the irrigation system.[51]

Although average water use rates for golf courses were estimated to be between 200 and 250 acre-feet per year, Fort Ord's courses used approximately 590 acre-feet. An acre foot equals 326,000 gallons or about the amount of water used by four households on the Monterey Peninsula per year. FORA had allocated Seaside 710 acre-feet for housing and development of Fort Ord and another 230 acre-feet for the golf courses. This presented city officials with a potential dilemma about where to get the water they needed to guarantee BSL Golf, Inc. The reports in the *Monterey Peninsula Herald*, however, neglected to explain the long-term plan for the acreage in entirety, which involved a complete overhaul and remodeling of both golf courses that included housing, paths, and roadways and accounted for the installation of two new irrigation systems—one for potable water and another for treated water, as was required by the base reuse plan at a cost of $5 million dollars.[52]

Part of the reason that city officials promised water to BSL Golf, Inc. was in exchange for "favorable rates" (greens fees) to be granted to military personnel, which was a requisite part of the sale on the part of the Army. The cost of acquiring the property, $11 million, was paid to the city by BSL. On October 23, 1996, the city council approved the deal, over the objections of Darryl Choate and Gert Foreman who were absent. What is key here is that although Choate and Foreman were opposed to BSL, they were equally afraid of voting against a measure that was supposed to bring Seaside much needed revenue. In an effort to have it both ways, they just did not show up to the meeting. Their opposition stemmed from their intense feeling that Seaside would lose control over its own development projects by delegating them outside of the community, but at the same time they and the rest of the city council understood that there was no local entity large enough to accomplish what BSL promised.

"Ladies and gentleman," Mayor Jordan announced in council chambers "this is all part of the recovery package of the City of Seaside."[53] Under the provisions of the agreement, Seaside would receive 5 percent of the gross revenue from the golf courses in excess of $5.5 million, which was guaranteed to be at least $100,000 per year. In addition, Seaside residents would receive a 10 percent discount in greens fees, and all military personnel and former military personnel would also receive discounts.

Developing the golf courses was only the first step in revitalizing Seaside in the post-Fort Ord era. The combination of an obvious shortage of housing on the Monterey Peninsula, with the newly available army land, attracted interested developers from across the country, including African American activist Danny Bakewell. Bakewell had organized the Million Man March in Washington, DC, in October 1995 and helped organize the Brotherhood Black United Crusade. He had the support of prominent African American leaders such as Congresswoman Maxine Waters from

Los Angeles and the Reverend Jesse Jackson. Bakewell was known to "bring development to blighted areas" such as in Compton, California, but he was also accused of exploiting the communities he was supposed to be helping. In fact, when he sued *New Times Los Angeles* and columnist Jill Stewart for calling him a "poverty pimp" a judge ruled that the label was valid and ordered Bakewell to pay $25,000 in legal fees.[54]

Bakewell was also known for his campaign contributions to local and mayoral candidates and for hiring ex-convicts as his labor force, giving employment opportunity to an otherwise underemployed population, but also keeping labor costs low and below union wages, which made him suspect in the eyes of labor organizers. In Seaside, it was both the labor issue and also the connection to a giant urban center like Los Angeles that angered (and politicized) labor leaders such as Ralph Rubio, mayor of Seaside from 2005 until 2010, who would be an integral part of the emerging political coalition that sought a new identity for Seaside moving beyond its distinctively multiracial, military one in which African Americans played an especially predominant role.[55]

In spite of these signals that Bakewell might be a controversial figure in Seaside, Tim Brown, who had once been Compton's controller during the 1980s, invited Bakewell "to seek and find a grocery store for the city since he had a relationship with Ron Burkle of Food 4 Less."[56] At the same time, Bakewell toured the Army sites under consideration for development, particularly Hayes Park, which was described in a *Monterey Peninsula Herald* article as "boarded up, with weeds taking over streets and gutters and . . . a developer's nightmare in terms of asbestos removal and replacement of plumbing, sewers and electrical infrastructure."[57] Yet, Bakewell saw the possibility of turning Hayes Park into an upscale residential area that would allow Seasiders to move up into better housing without having to leave the city for Monterey or Pacific Grove. He expected the houses to sell in the range of $200,000 to $300,000, although most homes in Seaside sold for about half that amount. The project was estimated to cost around $100 million, but was expected to be accomplished in phases over eight years.[58] This economic strategy on the part of the Jordan/Brown administration in conjunction with Bakewell is evidence of the commitment on the part of affluent and middle-class

African Americans to the City of Seaside. Rather than leave the city as they acquired wealth and property, which blacks did in an alarming rate in the 1980s and 1990s in inner cities across the nation, many blacks in Seaside were determined to stay, as shown in Chapter 5, to work with the working classes and the poor, and with other groups to improve life for everyone, and especially to improve conditions in the city itself.

By the 1996 election, the city was in an uproar over the deals negotiated by Jordan and Brown concerning Seaside development of both the golf courses and the housing projects, and it brought to a head the ultimate dilemma Seaside faced in both retaining its traditional character and independence and moving into a regional partnership. Integral to those concerns was the issue of power at the city manager level and the conflicting views of how the new, nonmilitary Seaside would be characterized. Both Lance McClair and Darryl Choate ran for mayor against Jordan in the 1996 election along with Felix Bachofner (who is white and a major critic of the golf course deal) on the platform that the city manager wielded far too much power and was using it to make deals to benefit outsiders rather than residents, threatening the local control that meant so much to them. According to one analysis of Seaside politics in the newspaper, the *Coast Weekly*, criticisms of Jordan by the candidates in the mayors race "focus on what the challengers say is Jordan's . . . unwillingness to restrain the power of current City Manager Tim Brown."[59] Bachofner, McClair, and Choate saw Jordan's support for Brown as creating "a vacuum of leadership" on the city council.[60] In support of Jordan and Brown, Tom Mancini was quoted in an article in the *Monterey Peninsula Herald*, "The guy's [Tim Brown] trying to do his job and they're trying to micro-manage . . . I have to give him credit for being an aggressive city manager. I don't believe it's my job to tell him how to do things."[61] Two years later, Mancini, an army veteran himself, became one of Brown's and Jordan's harshest critics and an adherent of the new Seaside that would no longer be defined largely by African American culture and experience or by Fort Ord, but was moving, albeit slowly, in the direction of broader regional identity. The difference was that Jordan and Brown saw the regional connection not just to other Peninsula communities but also to minority-majority cities such as Los Angeles (especially areas like Watts and Compton), which had been crucial in the California civil rights movement.

Jordan easily prevailed in the race against McClair, Choate, and Bachofner and was reelected to a second term as mayor, while Nancy Amos, who is white, and an ally of both Councilmember Helen Rucker and Mayor Jordan, was elected to the City Council, replacing Gert Foreman. Helen Rucker became mayor pro-tem with the highest number of votes counted. Thus, the five member city council included three African Americans and remained predominantly black. Between 1996 and 1998 Jordan was forced again and again to defend his city manager over issues of power and policy at city hall.

The multiracial political coalitions first formed in the 1970s once again prevailed at city hall, but there were sharp divisions between Jordan and his allies and a new coalition of opponents which would include Jerry Smith, Steve Bloomer, and Ralph Rubio, all of whom would eventually serve on the city council themselves, and all of whom shared a new vision of a postmilitary Seaside that was not tied to racial identity politics of the civil rights era or to the military. They envisioned a Seaside that was an equal partner, and perhaps even a leader among the multiple communities on the Peninsula, especially with regard to tourism. Rather than promote their city as a minority-majority postmilitary town with a strong African American cultural identity, they saw Seaside as transformative, a city that had moved beyond racial boundaries and that would continue to be a model for interracial governance.[62]

Seaside might have benefited economically from the establishment of a regionally organized fire and police department, instead of bearing the enormous cost of providing police and fire services by itself.[63] However, when Tim Brown tried to reduce costs in these departments, he was met with a storm of protest that became racially charged. City employees became embroiled in one serious conflict after another with the city manager. In early 1997, police officers picketed city hall as a result of downsizing in the department from forty officers to thirty-four, an impasse over salary increases in negotiations between the city and the police officers union, and efforts on the part of City Manager Brown to consolidate fire and police leadership into one department. Officers blamed ambitious redevelopment costs incurred by Brown for budget shortfalls that adversely affected them. According to Larry Katz, attorney for the officers, Seaside's police (even with a 2 percent pay increase) received less than officers throughout the county. "Seaside has already lost a lot of officers to other cities," he claimed, "And they will lose a lot more . . . Public safety is being ignored . . . we realize that redevelopment is a priority, but it needs to be in partnership with public safety."[64] That night police officers packed council chambers as Mayor Jordan and City Manager Brown presented a State of the City address acknowledging a general fund deficit of $700,000 and formally reported the plan to consolidate fire and police departments under one department. Chuck Streeter, who was president of the firefighters association at the time was outraged and challenged the legitimacy of the report. "I'd like to know if you think we're stupid? Where do you get your expertise?" he asked.[65] Later that month, the city refused mediation and gave the police officers a "take it or leave it" ultimatum.[66] In response, employees claimed that $700,000 was inexplicably "missing" from city coffers.

The dispute intensified to such an extent that the city manager responded to criticisms by writing a lengthy commentary piece in the *Monterey Peninsula Herald* one month later in which he explained the city's financial constraints. Although Seaside had increased in size with the acquisition of land from Fort Ord, he argued, the city had yet to increase its population or tax base and was therefore "unable to pay them [police and fire] what they are actually worth!"[67] This was a call for patience on the part of residents by Brown, as well as strong defense of his job performance. It was meant to calm tensions. It had the opposite effect, however, stimulating the growth of a new political coalition which would prove effective in 1998 in changing the direction and character of the city. It marked a transformative moment in Seaside from one which understood itself as an independent, multiracial military town that was heavily black, to one that perceived itself as both nonmilitary and more integrated into a regional vision that was increasingly both whiter and more Hispanic.

In March 1997, four of the city's unions, with the support of the Central Labor Council, charged the city manager with poor financial management, harassment, and cronyism and demanded that he resign or they would push for a recall, a grand jury investigation, and a class action suit against the city. They were supported in their efforts by Councilman Tom Mancini, who had once been an ally of both Jordan and Brown, and by Councilman Darryl Choate. Mancini in particular recalled how painful it was for him to turn against Jordan and Brown, but he felt he had to acknowledge the real grievances of employees.[68] One city employee expressed the frustration employees felt at Brown's efforts at pragmatism: "He had really stupid ideas like merging fire and police. People just stopped working. The fire chief called a night meeting and recruited Jerry Smith out of nowhere to run for mayor [Smith ran and won in 1998]. They had to get rid of [Don] Jordan because he supported Brown . . . For a while there were no department heads, no city manager. There was no one in charge of this city."[69]

The personal attacks on Brown, disguised as issues over power, were part and parcel of a fundamental disagreement among Seasiders over conflicting views of Seaside's postmilitary identity. The reorganization of staff led to enormous disagreement and debate in the community and to widely attended, often volatile city council meetings in 1997 and 1998. Many of those who spoke out were middle-class African Americans who expressed dismay and distress at the controversy and bad publicity that was being generated about Seaside. At a pivotal meeting in March 1997, sixteen citizens urged the city council to find a way to resolve their differences. All but four supported the mayor and city manager. One woman, Louise Hale "indicated the unions are trying to run the city and she feels that is wrong. We have a city manager and she feels we should be able to . . . work things out."[70] Nonetheless, a growing political movement was forming both in and out of city hall to displace Jordan as mayor and Brown as city manager, and integral to that, to replace their idea of a postmilitary Seaside with a new concept of the city as one still multiracial, but less obviously black, and regionally connected to its neighbors, but only in the loosest form. More than anything, this new coalition feared being subjugated by any entity.

Their anxiety was expressed in the form of organizing against crime and violence, although as shown in Chapter 5, this situation was improving with increased police programs and with the full cooperation by city residents. Nonetheless, Linda Cuttler, a black woman whose son was shot by gang members at the local Jack in the Box restaurant in 1995, joined with Belinda McBirney (white), Jerry and Byrl Smith (black), and Richard Avila (Portuguese) to form the political coalition, Seaside Concerned Citizens Committee (SCCC). The group blamed Jordan and Brown for continued crime in Seaside. Their real aim was to oust both Jordan and Brown: "We basically wanted to drive the mayor insane," said Belinda McBirney.[71] After a shooting incident at Manzanita Elementary School (no one was hurt, but the children were frightened), the group confronted the city council and demanded more police protection, even though Brown had just cut the budget for all city workers. Manzanita was a white majority school at that time, prompting a response from Councilwoman Helen Rucker to the group accusing them of racial bias: "You wouldn't be down here if those were black kids on that school field."[72] This may not have been fair on Rucker's part, but she was right that the controversy was less about child safety and more about politics. The SCCC was clearly a political organization meant to challenge Jordan and Brown. The SCCC adamantly objected to the Jordan/Brown vision of Seaside that it was as regionally tied to urban areas such as Compton, which was considered to be dominated by African Americans, as it was to nearby Monterey or Carmel.

In an effort to put the controversies surrounding Jordan and Brown to rest, Tom Mancini called for an independent third party to investigate Brown's handling of city finances, rather than for an immediate grand jury investigation. The city council tasked Nancy Amos and Helen Rucker to investigate the possibility of using a mediator to resolve the tensions at city hall. In their response to that request, they recommended that the city council accept Brown's responses to the criticisms of his decisions as city manager. Amos argued that "mistakes were made, but they were made by everybody."[73] This enraged employees who felt that it was tantamount to allowing Brown to investigate himself, according to front page *Monterey Peninsula Herald* reports.[74] The alliances on the city council had shifted dramatically over the issue of Tim Brown, who, with some justification, claimed that he was "a political pawn in someone's campaign." He was indeed. The issue of identity for the city was being fiercely contested over local power, and who would wield it, and how Seaside would now fit into the region without its military connection.

The 1997 grand jury investigation sided strongly with the employees. It accused the mayor, city manager, and finance director of behaving inappropriately, but acknowledged that accusations of a missing $700,000 in the budget were unproven. The grand jury report admonished the city manager for poor record keeping, creating a hostile work environment for city employees, and laxness in handling finances, including the failure to submit monthly reports to the city council. The report chastised the city council for failing to hold the city manager accountable and for failing to conduct open bidding before determining which firm would build the golf courses.[75]

At the same time, the grand jury investigation of Seaside concluded that employee unions had valid complaints about the "competence" of city officials and city employees hired under affirmative action policies. This threatened to undermine affirmative action generally. The grand jury had conducted a survey of 120 city employees and found that 77 percent believed that the city was being mismanaged, and that Jordan, Rucker, and Amos appeared to have supported any recommendation made by Tim Brown, whether it was appropriate or not for Seaside, thus enabling Brown to assume too much power.[76]

Mayor Jordan was furious with the report and issued a careful, point by point response, accusing grand jury members of political bias against Seaside and against himself and Tim Brown, demonstrating that the charges against Brown and the city were largely unfounded.[77] Seasiders were divided over the findings, but Jordan and Brown had substantial backing in the community, with unusually high rates of attendance at city council meetings by residents who expressed support for the mayor and city manager. One resident wrote a letter to the editor of the *Monterey Peninsula Herald* that "someone should answer to the false allegations made by Seaside employers who accused their supervisors of financial mismanagement. If the grand jury thought it was important to conduct a survey of 120 city employees, why didn't the grand jury survey an equal number of city residents? I certainly believe the results would have been different."[78] Mancini was the only council member to respond positively to the grand jury's findings, agreeing that the city manager had failed to deliver to them essential documentation of Seaside's financial reports.[79]

Mayor Jordan stood with his city manager. "I support the city manager 100 percent . . . they [the unions] have offered no real evidence of wrongdoing," Jordan said in an interview with the *Monterey Peninsula Herald*.[80] By June when the city budget came up for review by the city council, Brown projected a budget surplus. His proposed $17.2 million budget included $3.7 million coming from federally funded Community Development Bloc Grants meant to assist cities like Seaside with improvements to its infrastructure.[81] However, the atmosphere at city hall had become so poisonous that almost every move made by Brown was criticized as a power play. When he made the appointment of a well-known anticrime activist and former Seaside City Councilwoman Darlene Burkleo (who is white and had served on the city council in 1990) to fulfill the terms of the Bloc Grant with a position as community liaison, he was severely criticized as overstepping his authority once again. Mancini and Choate argued that the appointment should have been made by Police Chief Dave Butler, not Brown.[82] Thus, Jordan and Brown faced opposition not only from a new political coalition with views of Seaside's identity that challenged them, but also from individuals like Choate, who shared the Jordan/Brown vision of Seaside but objected to their power in government and were fearful of the triumph of regionalism over local control.

Both Councilmen Mancini and Choate voted against the proposed budget of 1998, raising questions about the way the redevelopment money was going to be spent. "I'm uncomfortable with the financial health of the city," Mancini was quoted as saying in a *Monterey Peninsula Herald* report. Both men argued that their questions about reorganizing staff at city hall, particularly the merger of fire and police departments, were never answered. Four of the five Seaside city employee associations had demanded Brown's resignation and even offered to pay for his severance package just to get rid of him. Mancini called the employees efforts a "cry for help" and claimed that it was his job as councilman to listen and take action.

Jordan did not acknowledge the real and deeply felt conflict over Seaside's postmilitary identity that was emerging in his administration, and he responded with bewilderment over the turmoil at city hall in 1997 and 1998. Instead, he viewed the attacks and critique as entirely racially motivated and personal: "Look, we are two black men, both of us over six feet tall. Maybe people felt intimidated when we walked into the room."[83] It was a fair assessment given the deep-seated racism embedded in American society, but it failed to acknowledge the fundamental conflict over identity formation in Seaside as a postmilitary city, and that a large number of Seasiders were opposed to the Jordan/Brown assumption that Seaside had as much in common with Compton in Los Angeles as with Monterey or Carmel.

The alliances at city hall and in the community were not neatly divided by race, however, although race and racism certainly played a role. The alliances, which included whites and minorities on both sides, were based on contrasting visions of Seaside. Both Jordan and Brown, with the support of Amos and Rucker, saw Seaside as an outgrowth of the important civil rights struggles that had been part of California's recent history. For Jordan, Rucker, and Amos, it was quite natural to draw prominent African Americans into Seaside's government and infrastructure, as it developed in the wake of the closure of Fort Ord, especially if they came from African American enclaves in San Francisco, Oakland, or Compton. Mancini, on the other hand, together with Jerry Smith, Steve Bloomer, and Ralph Rubio (who were emerging as the new political leaders of Seaside), envisioned Seaside as first and foremost intimately connected to the history and development of the Monterey Peninsula, not to other California minority-majority cities or to a larger civil rights movement or to African American culture or social life. Smith was not a member of the black church community, but of St. Francis Xavier Catholic Church, probably the most multiracial church in Seaside and a cultural and spiritual center for the new Latino population. Both Smith and Rubio were deeply troubled by the importation of staff and the city manager from Compton and suspicious of development from outside the county, particularly that which was connected to Danny Bakewell, who seemed to them to epitomize corruption and the underside of black political and economic life. According to Rubio:

Jerry Smith and I grew up together. His family goes back 100 years in Monterey—so does mine . . . He [Jerry Smith] asked me to run for City Council . . . I got on staff as a field representative and union organizer for the Carpenters Local and began attending City Council meetings [to advocate for] the prevailing wage project [over the issue of] developing the Seaside Highlands . . . It was a social justice issue for me. We needed to protect the citizens of Seaside. I attended meetings when they elected to allow Danny Bakewell and the Brotherhood Crusade to develop the Seaside Highlands without demanding a prevailing wage. He [Bakewell] hires ex-cons at below prevailing wage to work on his developments. He made billions. We got nothing out of that—no local hires, no training, no jobs. It was a total sell-out, a slap to the people of Seaside.[84]

Rubio's comment indicated just how strongly opponents felt about Seaside's economic and political connection to Los Angeles, particularly to Compton, which had become a predominantly black minority-majority city by 1980.[85]

As the plans to develop Hayes Park in Fort Ord moved forward in 1998, a group of Seasiders began to raise objections to the Kaufman/Broad/Bakewell alliance that might drive down the value of housing because homes were projected to list at between $200,000 and $300,000, far less than similar properties elsewhere on the Peninsula. Belinda McBurney, a community activist already involved in anticrime groups in Seaside who was part of Jerry Smith's political coalition, was reported as saying, "Everybody who lives here has put in a lot of hard work into their homes and to watch the value go down overnight because city officials might make a stupid decision . . . is scary . . . everyone is really watching this, and watching it intensely."[86] Her comment revealed the fear that many residents felt about being so closely identified as a minority-majority African American city with permanently low housing values. Many groups in Seaside aspired to create in Seaside exactly the kind of affluent community that defined the other cities on the Peninsula rather than define Seaside as a town of minorities, the poor, and working poor.

By the election of 1998, the new political coalition led by Jerry Smith had emerged as a self-conscious counterpoint to Jordan and Brown. Smith succeeded in mobilizing working-class and middle-class whites, Filipinos,

Latinos, and blacks disaffected by Jordan as his political base—but without the support and even with the opposition of the established African American political activists. This decision would prove to be problematic when he tried to push economic changes through the city council that would link Seaside most closely with Monterey, Pebble Beach, and Carmel. For those, like Helen Rucker, who were staunchly tied to a Seaside that was first and foremost a military city with a significant African American population, a city that reflected the best of the civil rights movement, Smith did not represent Seaside at all. She commented, unfairly, "The whites put him [Smith] in office."[87]

Indeed, Smith, like McClair before him, stated in an interview "I am not a black mayor. I am a mayor." Having been recruited by Chuck Streeter, the former Seaside fire chief, Smith portrayed himself as a champion of fire and police, both groups having made clear their frustration and dissatisfaction with Don Jordan and Tim Brown. Smith ran on a campaign platform that was explicitly about public safety. He pledged "110 percent" support for police, and reiterated all of the issues that SCCC had stood for. He was known to "get in his car and patrol the streets himself."[88] Former Mayor Jordan (backed by FBI crime index statistics) showed a clear decrease in crime between 1995 and 1998, rather than an increase in crime rates as Smith and his supporters claimed. However, highly publicized shootings due to gang activity in these years created the clear impression of Seaside as dangerous, and Smith's campaign benefited from its emphasis on strengthening police and fire as a way to bring Seaside "back to the old [days] when you felt safe."[89] Most importantly, Smith and later Rubio brought the tradition of multiracial political coalitions to a new and different level, and one that would self-consciously include the emerging Latino population of Seaside as the city became less identified as African American and increasingly "diverse."

LOCALISM AND REDEVELOPMENT

Between 1998 and 2000, when City Finance Director Linda Downing left office, the city was without department heads, a chief of police, or fire chief, many of whom had been fired by Tim Brown. In a clear rebuke to so-called lax affirmative action hiring, the city made a lengthy and public search for a city manager that would pass the test for being qualified. Daniel E. Keen, holding a masters degree in public administration and experience as city manager in Las Palmas and Paramount, California, was hired as the new city manager in 2000. Keen systematically installed new department heads, but he left the position in 2004 to be replaced by current City Manager Ray Corpuz, who had served as city manager for Tacoma, Washington.

The political establishment that had commanded leadership in Seaside politics from the 1970s on was losing its political base and formidable power during the Smith administration,. They would continue to lose power in the next administration of Ralph Rubio, as the population of Latinos and whites increased in the new millenium, as shown in Chapter 4, which shifted the demographics of the city from multiracial military and largely African American to a new nonmilitary diversity.

In consolidating power on the city council, Smith embraced Tom Mancini over his cousin, Darryl Choate, appointing him as mayor pro-tem and also to the FORA Board, much to Choate's dismay. Choate threatened a lawsuit, but did not pursue it. Nonetheless, he felt betrayed by Smith on both counts and frequently broke ranks with Smith over council decisions in the late 1990s. He often sided with Councilman Don Jordan in the early years of the twenty-first century.[90]

Smith and Choate came together, however, over issues of development that privileged local interests over regional or national ones—African American based or not. Both wanted to see Seaside businesses benefit directly from the opportunities available from Fort Ord and were deeply suspicious of Danny Bakewell, resisting Kaufman and Broad's (K& B's) efforts to pressure the mayor and into going along with agreements made during the Jordan administration. "Jesse Jackson called me," said Smith recalling that he was fielding phone calls from numerous supporters of Bakewell.[91] "I was angered by the gall of these people," Smith complained in an interview with the *Monterey Peninsula Herald* at the time. "They even called my employer to get them to sway me," he said. The report from the *Monterey Peninsula Herald* confirmed Jackson's call in a front page story on April 8, 1999, entitled "Mayor Smith is no pushover."[92]

In a further effort to challenge the black identity politics symbolized by cities like Compton, which extended to Bakewell and K & B, Smith publicly questioned whether the city was required to pay the costs of protecting the new subdivision, suggesting that Bakewell and K & B ought to pay for the extra requirements of fire, police, and public works and account for additional traffic. In addition, the cleanup of munitions at Fort Ord was beginning to prove costly and time consuming, adding to the development delays. The Salvation Army owned ten transitional housing complexes that were located in the middle of the development area. According to the city's contract with K & B, the developer was required to find a new location for the Salvation Army's housing and pay for its development. Smith suggested that the deal negotiated was not in the city's best interest. According to Bakewell, "If the mayor is saying that three of his colleagues approved an agreement that was not in the best interest of the city that is just not true. We can defend this document to the hilt. When the truth be known, the City of Seaside will rejoice not only in the quality of the development but our commitment to the community at large."[93] In July 1999, Smith and the City of Seaside reached a new deal with the Bakewell Company and K & B that required the developers to pay $600,000 in "impact fees" that would extend fire and police protection to the new residential area and make improvements in public works. In addition K & B were required by law to restore transitional housing for the Salvation Army in the city and to donate $2 million to charity for job training programs for Seaside youth.[94] Smith made it as difficult as possible for Bakewell to continue work in Seaside. He, Rubio, and the rest of the new city council wanted distance between anyone connected to Compton, which seemed too dominated by racial identity politics.

In November 1999, the city council voted to allow DWG Partners/ Pacific Union Ventures, Inc., which was headed by local businessman Al Glover, rather than Danny Bakewell and K & B builders, to develop an $80 million dollar Fort Ord housing project, denying K & B a monopoly on redeveloping Fort Ord and keeping the project local. "It is important that Seaside support local developers," stated Councilman Choate in an article in the *Monterey Peninsula Herald*.[95] Seaside was further helped when the army agreed to give the city $560,000 for public works to help repair streets, buy lawnmowers, and board up dilapidated barracks. The deal was negotiated by Smith with Army Undersecretary Randal Yem.[96] Choate and Smith seemed at this point to share the same interests. Smith had everything to gain by supporting Al Glover over Bakewell. Glover, who gave much to the community financially and in terms of leadership, was enthusiastic about Seaside's new character.

Smith began a public relations campaign designed to show other Peninsula cities that Seaside was changing from a multiracial military town with an important black population to a typical Monterey Peninsula community that also happened to be diverse. He initiated "mayor's walks" through the city and made sure to be in his office at City Hall every day at 3:30 p.m. "I want our city to be looked at not as a bedroom community but a destination point," Smith said in an interview with the *Monterey Peninsula Herald* in January 2000, indicating that Seaside ought to be viewed just like other destination points on the Peninsula such as Carmel or Monterey.[97]

Jerry Smith was handily reelected in 2000 with 100 percent of the vote. No one ran against him except a last minute write-in candidate. Most importantly, Ralph Rubio was elected to the city council, becoming the first Latino to hold public office in Seaside, replacing Nancy Amos who chose not to run for another term. A self-described "Latino and a working man," Rubio received 31 percent of the vote, the highest of all three councilmen running. "I think the people wanted someone familiar with the culture and diversity of Seaside," he said in a postelection interview with the *Monterey Peninsula Herald*. Bloomer also won reelection with 27 percent of the vote. Neither Mancini nor Choate was up for reelection that year.[98] Thus, by 2000 Smith had established a majority coalition on the city council and was prepared for real change, distancing himself from the Southern California connections of Brown and Jordan, firmly concentrating power in the mayor's office, and vigorously working to redefine the city as part of the brand of the Monterey Peninsula.

However, Smith's challenges to the older political establishment that was led by African Americans created a particularly bitter standoff over development issues that prevented him from achieving some important economic goals. It was also during the second term of Smith's administration that conflicts with Congressman Sam Farr over affordable housing in Seaside came to the fore. Affordable housing was something Seasiders generally resented as just another effort to keep the city from achieving the same status as the other communities. Seaside wanted to reinvent itself after Fort Ord but disagreed over what a post-Fort Ord Seaside would look like. Smith and his supporters wanted to create a resort community connected, but not overpowered, by Monterey, Carmel, or Pebble Beach. Affordable housing sounded to these Seasiders as though the rest of the Peninsula wanted to "keep Seaside in its place."[99] On the other hand, a smaller but vocal population envisioned development projects that would retain Seaside's identity as a center for diversity with an emphasis on African American culture, just like many other urban areas in California.

The two sides squared off over the issue of First Tee, which seemed to encapsulate Seaside's new identity as postmilitary and diverse in novel ways. According to Rubio, "It was a rough two years [2000 to 2002]. They [NAACP] didn't think Jerry was black enough. They undermined him . . . First Tee would have been great for the people of Seaside, but they didn't support it."[100] Rubio's comment underscores the real and deep conflict over identity that marked the early years of 2000.

FIRST TEE AND A NEW ERA FOR SEASIDE

First Tee is a nonprofit program for children established in 1997 by the World Golf Foundation and supported by numerous and prestigious golf associations, including the Augusta National Golf Club, the Ladies Professional Golf Association, PGA of America, PGA Tour, and the United States Golf Association. It has 202 chapters nationally and 5 chapters internationally. First Tee is based on a premise of self-help through golf. Proponents argue that improving the lives of young people, especially disadvantaged youth, can be achieved through the values, skills, and character development that learning the game of golf entails. The local chapter was founded by the Monterey Peninsula Foundation, the charity arm of the famous AT & T Pebble Beach National Pro-Am Golf Tournament, held annually on the Monterey Peninsula that generates millions of dollars of revenue for local charities with a particular emphasis on organizations that benefit young people. Supporters included Clint Eastwood, Arnold

Palmer, and many other celebrities and golf professionals. To them, it would seem a great fit for Seaside, which they viewed as a poor military town and minority community in need of economic support.

There was no awareness on the part of First Tee promoters that Seaside included a sizeable population of middle-class black families who might be offended that they had been targeted as a disadvantaged community in need of white intervention and support. First Tee organizers believed that the program would effectively link the city to one of the biggest tourist events on the Monterey Peninsula and, at the same time, provide a positive outlet for Seaside youth. Jerry Smith and Ralph Rubio agreed with them, but they soon faced uproar on the part of long-standing African Americans and other Seaside residents who were insulted by First Tee and opposed to everything about the program.

At first glance, inclusion in the world of high-end tourism was exactly what Seasiders yearned for and proactively sought since incorporation in 1954. However, First Tee could also be described as a quintessentially white elitist program. It seemed paternalistic to many proud Seasiders, heroes of the civil rights movement, who strove for decades to create a middle-class black enclave in the midst of the mostly white Monterey Peninsula and in the face of misperceptions that Seaside was only black and, by association, poor and crime ridden. For them, the focus on Seaside as the economically disadvantaged minority community on the Peninsula only reinforced such misconceptions about the city, and they responded almost viscerally to the program. Their anger and determination to fight First Tee perplexed Jerry Smith, First Tee organizers, and residents of the other Peninsula cities generally.

The First Tee program proposal included an after-school program designed to offer children a community center with four classrooms, a computer lab, a library, and tutoring from California State Monterey Bay students and golf lessons with professionals. According to the Monterey Peninsula Foundation, First Tee offered golf lessons and academics with values lessons in responsibility, courtesy, honesty, and integrity. "Golf is only a hook," argued Ollie Nutt, Executive Director of Monterey Peninsula Foundation, which sponsored First Tee during these tumultuous years, "Values that are inherent in golf transfer seamlessly into life."[101] Black elites in Seaside did not believe that whatever values were being taught by First Tee were values that they wanted their children to be exposed to.

First Tee became a pivotal issue because its attempted implementation in Seaside demonstrated to Seasiders that although they wanted to see themselves as an integral, albeit unique community on the Monterey Peninsula, the rest of the Peninsula still viewed them as an isolated and underprivileged neighbor, not an equal partner. They bristled at the notion that Seaside needed white elites from Pebble Beach to teach their children golf as though they were from a ghetto.

The battle against First Tee became the last effort of the older political coalition spearheaded by African American leaders from the churches and the NAACP to maintain Seaside as a community that reflected their culture and values. It is important to note, however, that this older coalition, although led by African Americans, always included like-minded whites and other minorities. They defeated First Tee, but in so doing they acknowledged that conditions had changed and that Seaside was moving in a new direction. To some extent, their original vision of a community that would embrace all that was good about civil rights was achieved in Seaside by 2000, but Seaside was no longer the multiracial and substantially African American military community imagined in 1970. Ewalker James, a prominent activist and community leader, described Jerry Smith as a "smart, articulate guy who made some boo-boos," First Tee among them. "We challenged First Tee," said James, "The city could not give away 120 acres plus 100 acre feet of water to build yet another golf course. It was supposed to be for kids. But those kids are in school until two o'clock. Let's get some computer company to relocate or build some houses . . . we took it to court and we got First Tee to withdraw."[102]

First Tee organizers expressed naiveté at the resistance by Seaside residents. They had no concept that they were perceived as arrogant and condescending by city residents: "I view golf as a canvas where you can paint a mosaic of life skills with children who are Hispanic, African American, or whatever," said Leon Gilmore, executive director in charge of special projects for the Monterey Peninsula Foundation.[103]

Although negotiations over First Tee began in 1997, the Monterey Peninsula Foundation approached the city in 2000 seriously suggesting that the program be located in Seaside. That year, the Monterey Peninsula Classic golf tournament, sponsored by Bank of America, was held on Seaside's Bayonet Golf course with $450,000 in proceeds that were allocated for First Tee, laying the groundwork for the establishment of the program in Seaside.[104] In January 2003, the First Tee program proposal was first made public at a city council meeting in which it was mostly discussed in closed session. However, opposition to the program quickly became apparent, most notably by city councilmember Darryl Choate, who had become disaffected from his cousin, Mayor Jerry Smith, and realigned with the African American political leadership in the NAACP and the multidenominational churches together with multiracial veterans organizations that opposed Smith. Choate articulated the anger and frustration that many disaffected Seasiders felt at the new concept of the city and its new direction. He was quoted in a news article as arguing, "We don't know if the citizens want a golf course—another one . . . The last 125 acres of prime land [from the acquisition of Fort Ord]. Do you want to make a golf course?"[105] Choate suggested that the land could be better used for affordable housing or a sports complex. The city council meeting of February 12, 2003, was a virtual who's who of representation from minority communities and coalitions in Seaside opposing First Tee.[106]

Ollie Nutt appeared at community forums to answer residents concerns about the issue, particularly emphasizing that First Tee was not merely about golf but about "life skills." Addressing the NAACP, Nutt argued that First Tee was not trying to groom the next Tiger Woods. "This is not about golf . . . this is using golf as a vehicle to get hooked on life." But for many Seasiders it was about golf as an elite white activity, traditionally excluding minorities especially blacks. There were deep suspicions about the stated goal of First Tee as benefiting the community of Seaside. Mel Mason, then spokesperson for the NAACP, supported Darryl Choate's call for a sports complex and presented a resolution to the city council: "The resolution is a response to some 40 residents who attended an NAACP general meeting Tuesday night, who said they would like a revenue-generating development on the site and expressed concerns that some children may not be interested in playing golf."[107] Mason envisioned a sports complex with a pool, weight room, and indoor basketball, among other possible activities. Choate, speaking for many minority groups in Seaside accused First Tee of "targeting minority communities for its own political benefit."[108] These arguments resonated deeply with many middle-class blacks in Seaside who understood First Tee as another example of the myopic vision of well-meaning whites who invariably overlooked the middle class and saw minority communities, especially ones with large populations of African Americans, solely in paternalistic terms.

In the meantime, Ollie Nutt and the Monterey Peninsula Foundation persevered, generating positive press for their dedication to the program in spite of the loss of Bank of America as sponsor and rejecting numerous efforts to "hype" the tournament with famous amateurs. Instead, Nutt kept the tournament focused on kids, inviting juniors in the summer of 2003 to play with the pros, all in an effort to show the people of Seaside that First Tee was serious about improving the lives of kids, and was not about minority exploitation, but genuine good will.

The debate over First Tee took place in the context of the debate over the establishment of affordable housing on former Fort Ord land, an issue wholeheartedly supported by Congressman Farr who wanted at least 50 percent of Fort Ord land dedicated to the construction of affordable housing. The FORA meetings held during the summer of 2003 and 2004 were attended regularly by as many as 200 residents and representatives from groups as diverse as the Sierra Club, the American Association of University Women, LULAC, the NAACP, the multidenominational Communities Organized for Relational Power in Action, and the Citizens for Responsible Decision Making, which formed expressly to oppose First Tee. Residents picketed the FORA meeting holding signs that read "Children of Color Need Affordable Housing Not a Golf Course."[109] But Seaside, Marina, and Monterey County only committed to providing 20 percent affordable housing rather than the 50 percent demanded by the federal government. Requiring Seaside and Marina to bear the brunt of the affordable housing burden over communities such as Pacific Grove, Carmel, or Pebble Beach felt discriminatory, in the same context as First Tee. "We export workers and import debt," stated Marina Planning Commissioner Bob Drake. Ewalker James, a vigorous opponent of First Tee, summed up Seasiders' concerns about so much affordable housing located in their city, which was equated with housing for the lowest socioeconomic levels: "I think Bakewell was good. He was building nice homes. We didn't want Seaside to be poor. We wanted the city to be well-rounded with high end housing too."[110] Seasiders of all groups were united in their sensitivity to perceptions about them as poor, minority, and working class, and they wanted to do everything possible to resist what they saw as efforts on behalf of the federal government (Farr) and powerful economic interests (First Tee) to keep them that way. Many of them increasingly perceived Smith as being co-opted by those forces, particularly after he changed his party affiliation from Democrat to Republican, and they were determined to oppose him.

Opponents of First Tee used the issue of housing to generate resistance to the project and packed city council meetings when it was discussed. At first, the 125 acre site was indeed zoned as residential, but then it was reconsidered as unfit for residential use because of the continued presence of unexploded ordnance. It might have been used for commercial development, but according to Jerry Smith, no commercial firm presented the city with an offer to develop the property. By September 2003 it was clear that Jerry Smith had the support of the city council, with the sole exception of his cousin, Darryl Choate. After a highly charged city council meeting with outspoken comments on both sides, the city council voted to approve First Tee on September 4, 2003. Opponents continued to fight against the project arguing that the additional traffic from First Tee "would flood our neighborhoods."[111]

In October 2003, the Citizens for Responsible Decision Making filed a lawsuit on environmental grounds against the city challenging the decision to allow first Tee to be established. In an article in the *Monterey Peninsula Herald*, the lawsuit "contends the environmental impact report does not sufficiently answer the concerns raised by the project . . . the plaintiffs allege the project will lead to increased traffic conditions, decimate the water supply for projects on Fort Ord, and leave the city liable for any ordnance found on the property." Furthermore, the leadership of the group, which included Helen Rucker and Billy DeBerry, argued that the city did not explore other uses for the property before deciding on First Tee and "does next to nothing to create jobs in a city that needs jobs."[112]

The lawsuit was thrown out on December 6, 2003, on a technicality. But by March of the next year, the group had collected 1,200 signatures in a petition to overturn the city council's decision to approve First Tee, with an aim to get the issue onto the November ballot.

Ollie Nutt and First Tee gave up. By October 2003, First Tee withdrew its offer to Seaside and located its program in Salinas at Twin Creeks Golf Course, where it serves the mostly Mexican American community and boasts a client base of almost 2,000 youth. Jerry Smith left the mayor's office to run successfully for a position representing the Fourth District on the Monterey County Board of Supervisors, opening the way for his friend and colleague Ralph Rubio to become Seaside's first Latino mayor. Rubio shared Smith's vision of a new Seaside that had moved beyond its identity as military, multiracial, and substantially African American and into one that would be characterized as just another tourist destination on the Monterey Peninsula.

MEXICAN AMERICANS IN POSTMILITARY SEASIDE

Hector Azpilcueto, originally from Mexico City, was working in a *maquiladora* factory in Tijuana in 1985 when he made the decision to come to the United States. He recalled life in Mexico City in the 1980s and the economic factors that drove emigration:

The impact of Nafta [North American Free Trade Agreement] really reached everyone. It was not just workers—it was students, professionals, people with businesses who had to close their businesses and move here. Things were harder. Things deteriorated. The pay was not enough. We were poor. From the early 80s we got poorer but it was more varied, a cross section. I had the privilege to finish my college and try to get into the university. My idea when I came here was to make some money and go back to finish school. But I was helping my mother. If I send $200 to my mother she could survive for two months. It was part of my obligation. I had a friend in Seaside who said why don't you come all the way here? Basically I decided that I had to come here because I didn't want to go back to Mexico City with empty hands.

Azpilcueto had lost his job due to labor activism and a declining economy and was eager to start over in the United States, earn money for his family, and return to Mexico City to finish his education. Things did not work out that way, however. Like so many other Mexican immigrants, Azpilcueto remained in Seaside and became active in the hotel workers union. He is now vice president of Local 483 and a leader in the newly established Mexican American community of the Monterey Peninsula who, outside of Salinas, mostly reside in Seaside.[113]

When Azpilcueto first arrived in the mid-1980s, Seaside had very few Latinos. Azpilcueto recalled, "It was mostly men and mostly people from Oaxaca . . . there was one woman for every 10 guys then. There were not many kids around or families. They used to have these dances at St. Francis where most of the Latinos went . . . the center for Latinos in Seaside." Azpilcueto claimed that the new immigrants of the 1980s kept to themselves and did not associate socially with the older, more established Mexican American community of the Monterey Peninsula. He also noted the lack of businesses and support services for Latinos in Seaside in the 1980s. Salinas, not Seaside, was the social and economic center for the small number of newly arrived Latinos on the Monterey Peninsula. "We had to go to Salinas for everything," he said.[114]

However, that demographic changed radically by 1990 and is best reflected in population in the schools. According to records from the Monterey Peninsula Unified School District, between 1985 and 1995, the Latino population of the schools had doubled, while populations of other minority groups declined. The ethnic profile of Del Rey Woods Elementary School is a good example of the demographic transition of Seaside over twenty years. In 1990, the Del Rey Elementary School population was 34 percent white and 15 percent African American; the remainder was a mixture of Asians, Filipinos, Pacific Islanders, and Hispanics. Five years later, in 1995 the Hispanic population of the school had climbed to 42 percent, or 271 students out of a total of 647, and by 2008 Del Rey was 86 percent Hispanic, 7 percent white, "while all other ethnicities account for less than 7 percent of the student body."[115] Moreover, the school profile described a poorer and mostly non-English-speaking student body with 66 percent "designated English learners, and . . . 77 percent qualify for the Federal Free and Reduced Lunch Program."[116] According to Helen Rucker, trustee of the Monterey Peninsula Unified

School Board, "Black people have left Seaside. Right now in the school district there is only 11 percent [African Americans]."[117] In spite of the commitment of black retired military officers and their families to Seaside, the next generation of blacks did not share their parents' economic power and could seldom afford to remain on the increasingly expensive Monterey Peninsula. Coupled with the sudden loss of population in the African American community due to the closure of Fort Ord, the new demographic was stunning.

Mae Johnson, Monterey High School principal from 1986 until her retirement in 1993 remembered a dramatic shift in the population of the high school, which drew students from Monterey as well as Seaside. Johnson recalled, "We had five Hispanic students enroll in the 1990/1991 school year. The next year there was a huge group of Hispanics from Oaxaca. We went from zero to 35 percent Hispanic [between] 1990 and 1993."[118] Johnson believed in inclusion and quickly initiated programs "to make them welcome . . . I asked them what they wanted and they said 'We want a mariachi band. So I organized it and I even danced with them when we put on our program . . . They wanted harps, so I recruited Bill Faulkener [head of wood shop] to teach all the students, white, black, Latino, how to make them . . . we started ESL classes, but that was moved to Seaside High in 1994."[119] Mae Johnson, herself a leader in civil rights who participated in integrating the faculty of Monterey Peninsula Unified Schools in the 1960s and 1970s with Dr. Charlie Mae Knight, was acutely aware of the perils of racially based exclusions and was determined to be inclusive at all costs. Her example and her creative strategies to involve the new Latino population fully into mainstream school activities and culture had the effect of minimizing what might have been serious racial tensions at the high school when so many new students of Mexican origin landed in one fell swoop on what had been a student population of blacks and whites. This is not to say there was no tension, but it is to argue that the lessons African Americans learned in the political arena in Seaside about building coalitions with other groups carried over into other spheres where blacks had assumed leadership roles as well, such as in the school system.

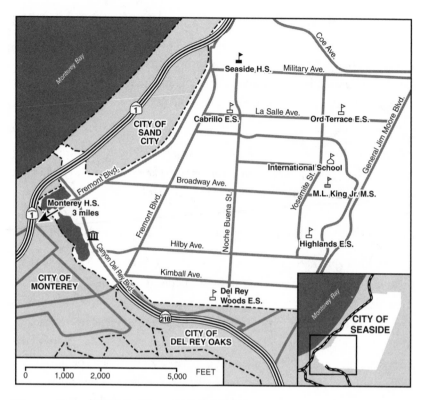

MAP 3. City of Seaside, Map of Public Schools.

Source: City of Seaside Planning Department

Previous immigrant groups had been part of the Fort Ord military social and cultural world. This included most blacks, but also Filipinos, Pacific Islanders, even Vietnamese, all of whom arrived in some fashion under the auspices of the military. The emerging Latino population in Seaside did not immediately feel connected to the rest of the community as the others had because they had no intermediary at Fort Ord to help them adjust. Even with the best of intentions of city leaders and school principals to make them feel included, many Latinos felt isolated and alienated, at least at first. A teacher's aid at Cabrillo Family Center recalled walking the streets of Seaside in 1986, "I felt alone. I was afraid. No one spoke Spanish. There was nobody like me."[120] Sergio Rangel recalled Seaside in the 1980s, "I came alone in 1986 April . . . People didn't understand you. It's worse and you get more discrimination . . . It was so hard until I found a job at Pebble Beach."[121] Another immigrant, Alfredo Valdez, arrived in Seaside in 1985 and became a U.S. citizen under the amnesty program at age eighteen in 1987. He recalled:

I arrived in 1985. I was 17. I came from San Diego. I was born in Tijuana. I came to San Diego in 1978. My parents brought me . . . In 1987 [there were] probably about 300, 400 Mexicans—not many. The main thing was you can't walk around the streets at night. Or you would get killed. You can't be walking in the night. There was no control of the police back then. The drug dealers [were] mostly black. I felt like a stranger—I felt scared to be walking around.[122]

Hector Azpilcueto, who also immigrated to Seaside in the 1980s, described "culture shock" when he first encountered Seaside circa 1986. "The first thing I was told was not to go out on the street because it was dangerous. There were tensions between Latinos and African Americans, so we were afraid of being mugged by black men. But I can testify that I never got attacked."[123] Azpilcueto and Valdez expressed the important truth about the way groups in Seaside were perceived by one another. The census figures show a large population of blacks in Seaside in the 1980s, a high rate of violent crime and drug use, and as Latinos sensed that blacks dominated the city, it produced a high level of fear among many newly arrived Latino immigrants.

Even as early as 1990, the feel of the city had changed enormously. According to Azpilcueto:

By early 1990s we started getting more people . . . and we became more visible in the City of Seaside. I remember riding the bus when there were maybe 5 people [in 1986] from Seaside. By the 1990s it was full of Latinos. They needed more than one bus to bring workers into Monterey. It was still a young population, most people were in their early 20s, and there were still more men but more women were coming too. By 1990 we had already stores, La Morenita [a Mexican owned supermarket]. The Sánchez family [business owners and realtors] is Jalisco's best success—a family coming together and doing things.[124]

Emiliano Garcia Ogarrio graphically recalled the changes in Seaside during his childhood and experience in the schools:

I arrived here when I was 3 years old in 1986 . . . I attended first grade at Bay View [Elementary School]. From what I remember we were outnumbered by African Americans. There were just a few of us . . . Seaside High School was a total opposite than when I went to elementary school. It was very diverse. I met a lot of Hispanic friends. It was balanced. Asians, Vietnamese, African Americans, Americans. I graduated [in] 2002. Sadly our own culture is divided. From my impression the ones who got along were mostly people who had just migrated here and spoke only Spanish. I was trying to speak English. [But] soccer united us.[125]

Former Mayor Ralph Rubio agreed with both Azpilcueto's assessment and Ogarrio's experience, noting that "The shift began in the late 1980s, 1990s. Census statistics [for 2000] show the Latino population at 30 percent, but it's more like 40 or 45 percent. It's hard to define," he commented because of the large number of undocumented residents.[126] The new Latino population of Seaside was highlighted in a series of articles in the *Monterey Peninsula Herald* in the 1990s, which emphasized diversity, rather than the presence of African Americans in the city as was the case in previous decades. Instead, diversity meant the presence of Latinos. For example, an article in November 1995 titled "Seaside's businesses reflect city's ethnic diversity" was almost entirely about the Moreno family and their Mexican market where shoppers could find everything "from *tamales* to *masa* . . . and *chiles* . . . [and] such delicacies as *menudo* and *tripas*."[127] Although the article mentioned Southern home style barbecue as part of Seaside's new landscape of "international" restaurants, African Americans were considered only one of many groups in Seaside by the mid-1990s, rather than the most dominant minority group, in sharp contrast to news stories about Seaside in the past, which depicted the city as first and foremost a black community, although even then it was quintessentially multiracial.

Seaside joins other California municipalities that are coping with a great influx of immigrants from Mexico. However, unlike other cities where political tensions between blacks and Latinos run high, such as in Compton and East Palo Alto, Seaside elected its first Latino mayor in 2005 without focusing on the issue of race as much as on controversial issues of development, and at the same time, continued to keep both blacks and whites on the city council as well as to incorporate other minorities, including Latinos, into city government as visible staff members, if not as elected officials.[128]

Seaside continued its tradition of hosting city events that promoted inclusiveness and made a point of giving prominence to Latinos throughout the 1990s and into the new century. The city incorporated Tet, the Vietnamese harvest celebration, into its calendar in the 1980s to make the refugee Vietnamese population feel at home, but that faded as the Vietnamese population increasingly migrated to Marina. Cinco de Mayo became (and remains) a formal city event in the 1990s and continues to attract hundreds of participants today.[129] September 16, Mexican Independence Day, is also prominent on the city calendar.

Far from resisting or excluding the Latino population, political coalitions formed to include and empower them, in traditional Seaside political fashion, but this did not necessarily mean that Seaside political activists were clear about what that inclusion entailed. For example, in 1992 the Regional Alliance for Progressive Policy (RAPP) brought prominent (and not so prominent) blacks, whites, and Latinos together to confront issues of social justice, primarily concerning immigrants' rights, police brutality, and labor, not only in Seaside, but also countywide (Monterey, San Benito, and Santa Cruz counties), where the majority of new immigrants to Northern California worked in agriculture or service industries. The original group included Mel Mason, Bill Monning, Lily Cervantes, Bill Meléndez (president of LULAC), David Serena, Ana Ventura Phares, and Vanessa Vallarta. It was diverse not only in terms of race and ethnicity, but also in terms of gender, just as most of the political coalitions always were in Seaside. According to Mason:

We [RAPP] were the first organization to express our concern that with the growth in the population of Seaside of Latinos [that] the Border Patrol would begin to carry out actions in Seaside. Even before that happened we were emphatic in our opposition to the Border Patrol coming into Seaside . . . Its [RAPP's] strength was in its ability to mobilize people in the three counties to support struggles and actions going on in communities in those three counties."[130]

Mason then described the important actions of RAPP in the 1990s on behalf of Latinos:

We supported strikes by the United Fruit and Vegetable Workers at . . . Sunrise Mushrooms near Pajaro and United Food and Commercial Workers against Safeway stores and truckers in Salinas and South County. We organized demonstrations against the Border Patrol for its raids in Salinas and Seaside in the early 90s. This led to the removal of a Border Patrol supervisor after he shot at a carload of day workers in Big Sur . . . when the Border Patrol began rousting people on public buses, we organized demonstrations in front of the Border Patrol office in Salinas in which hundreds of people from all three counties came together and blocked the entrance way in and out of the facility. We denounced the raids not only as xenophobic but as racist because they [Border Patrol officers] were not looking for white immigrants but those who one agent said "were Mexican looking." We were able to convince local governments and their police departments, including the County Board of Supervisors and the Sheriff's Department not to cooperate with the Border Patrol in that agency's raid on immigrants.[131]

RAPP officially disbanded in 1997, but the relationships that were created during the 1990s continue today. An example of that is in the formation of the Coalition of Minority Organizations that evolved into the Civil Rights Coalition (CRC) of Monterey County in 2001, which Mel Mason described as "the heart and soul of which are blacks and Latinos. We were told by more than a few folks that such a coalition could not possibly last because 'blacks and Mexicans don't like each other and can't work together.' It has been seven years now and the CRC is still here."[132]

One of the most important efforts by the CRC occurred in 1999 when inmates, almost all of whom were Latino, were forced to endure sheriffs deputies playing the soundtrack of "Full Metal Jacket" at full blast in the very early hours of a Sunday morning. In the soundtrack, a drill sergeant screamed racial slurs at Latino (and African American and Jewish) soldiers, obviously offensive to the inmates. The racial conflicts with police were well documented in the 1990s, and this episode only added to them.[133]

Sheriff Gordon Sonne responded to the incident by accepting the explanation of the deputies that their intention was entertainment rather than provocation, and he suggested that the officers in question be suspended for a year rather than lose their jobs. The CRC objected—loudly and publicly—and took the issue to the Monterey County Board of Supervisors, which supported the CRC and urged strong action against the deputies, including training in racial sensitivity as well as the firing of Deputy Sheriff Louis Comacho, who, notwithstanding that he has a Spanish surname, was responsible for playing the soundtrack. However, because the Sheriff's Department delayed submitting essential paperwork, Comacho was able to challenge his firing and regain his position as deputy sheriff. The CRC again raised a public outcry, and as a result, prompted a response by the editorial board of *The Monterey Peninsula Herald*, which strongly supporting the CRC's position:

Working in a jail requires constant vigilance and guards shouldn't be listening to movie soundtracks . . . his [Sheriff Sonne's] public remarks left the distinct impression that he wasn't particularly troubled by the incident . . . the lax handling of . . . paperwork is yet another example of how county workers treated an act of racism dismissively. Mel Mason [president of the CRC and NAACP] got it right.[134]

Thus, the multiracial political coalition, the CRC, was not only able to advocate as a multiracial coalition for Latinos, it was also able to be effective. The CRC forced policy change and generated support among the public at large in Monterey County. It was an impressive success.

Latinos supported blacks as well. On May 19, 1998, an unarmed, mentally ill, 60-year-old African American resident of Seaside, Charles Vaughn Sr., was shot to death by Seaside police. Seaside police were called to Vaughn's apartment by staff from the Monterey County Department of Mental Health who had decided that Vaughn needed to be hospitalized involuntarily, and Vaughn was shot as he tried to elude police by climbing onto his roof. The entire community of Seaside and countywide organizations as well came together to protest the shooting as an act of racism on the part of the police department. Charles Vaughn's son led groups in a hunger strike that forced a state-sponsored investigation, which in turn vindicated Vaughn and led to policy changes in the police department.

Seasiders believed the police action to be racially motivated because Vaughn was well known and well respected in the community and should not have been considered as though he were a common criminal of unknown origin. Charles Vaughn Sr. came to Seaside by way of military service at Fort Ord in 1958. After he left the military, he attended Monterey Peninsula College and received an Associate of Arts degree, a Bachelor's degree from the University of Santa Cruz, and a master's degree from the Monterey Institute of International Studies. He continued his study towards a Doctorate degree in education administration. While at Monterey Peninsula College, Vaughn played football, earned All-American honors, and was accepted into the college's African-American Hall of Fame. Vaughn was also a leader of various community groups, teaching associations, and civil rights organizations. He was also a volunteer mentor for community youth. Vaughn lived independently in an apartment and received outpatient mental health services from Monterey County Mental Health, from which he received case-management and medication-monitoring services. Local mental health staff and law enforcement knew Vaughn well. Police took none of this into account when Vaughn was shot—only that he was a black man, over six feet tall, who appeared to be resisting arrest. Monterey County mental health workers had deemed Vaughn a danger to himself and others without credible evidence, according to an investigation by the California Protection & Advocacy Protections Unit in May 2000.[135]

Filipinos, whites, Latinos, and blacks condemned the police action as racism, plain and simple. Sal Horquita, representing the Filipino community, Joyce Vandevere, representing the Women's International League for Peace and Freedom, Bill Meléndez, representing LULAC, gay rights coalitions led by Matt Friday and others, and African American activists Mel Mason, Helen Rucker, and Ruthie Watts came together with Vaughn's family and the community at large to press for an investigation by the Monterey County District Attorney's office and policy change. They succeeded. "Because of our advocacy, there was a new level of policy at the county level that trained officers in how to deal more effectively with the mentally ill," said Bill Meléndez. Indeed, the PAI (Protection & Advocacy Investigation) report put in place a new protocol and training for police officers that emphasized specific responses to the mentally ill of any race.

The fact that long-established black civil rights organizations such as the NAACP stood with Latinos, going so far as to create new racial justice organizations such as RAPP and CRC that gave all members equal power, and were reciprocal in nature, made a strong impression on new Mexican-origin immigrants. Hector Azpilcueto reflected on the influence of black activists on the Latino labor movement:

I think since I have been with the union I started connecting with NAACP. We as Latinos have the benefit of their struggle. As African Americans their struggle has been harder [than that of Latinos]. Even as illegals we are not as discriminated against as African Americans. I think it's because historically African Americans were brought into this country as slaves and I think somehow there's this stereotype where people believe they should be kept oppressed. There is not a lot of work offered to them. Even with a lot of African Americans in this city you don't see them working in this hospitality industry, maybe only 1 percent. But when you see Latinos, since we arrived, the industry is more than 50 percent Latinos and we start getting hired as soon as we arrive. I do not know if African Americans resent that.[136]

African Americans and other groups did express resentment, even as they worked to incorporate Latinos into the city's political and social life. By 2004, tensions over language, primarily the increasingly widespread use of Spanish in the schools and public places, the presence of day laborers on the streets of Seaside, and multiple families housed together (evident by numerous cars parked on neighborhood streets), began to dominate Seaside city council meetings. According to former Mayor Ralph Rubio, the tremendous increase in the Hispanic population:

Put pressure on neighborhoods by increasing the density—Hispanics have bigger families, two families in a house, more people in small spaces. [The evidence is reflected in] high school sports . . . Seaside was known for basketball, now soccer is big. Blacks come to meetings complaining about "those people" who have too many kids and chickens in their yards. Excuse me? Those people? They should listen to themselves.[137]

One of the most prominent black activists in Seaside politics, Helen Rucker, explained some of the complications of the 1990s, which created political coalitions of blacks and Latinos, but often kept them at odds over economic and social issues:

The Mexican-Americans just started coming . . . I saw the shift happen. In my mind, the Hyatt Regency down here practically had an all black work force and something happened . . . They [Latinos] broke the union. And they start firing all these black folk. They were the maids, everybody caught the bus and went to the Hyatt. And I looked up and everybody was Hispanic . . . there is a sense that the Hispanics came here and took all the jobs from black folk. Monterey was closing Seaside schools. There were lots of Latinos in Seaside and so yes I was supporting them. But let me tell you about LULAC. For many years I belonged to LULAC. I helped raise money for their scholarships and everything. And Bill [Meléndez—former LULAC president] and I had been friends for many, many years. And then one day Bill said to me, "Helen, you realize your time is over. Just get out the way." Well I helped build this city. I'm not going to get out of the way.[138]

Meléndez explained that he was responding to Rucker who told him that African Americans had been involved in civil rights for decades and he and other Latinos needed to "get in line."[139] Meléndez and Rucker are nonetheless good friends and collaborated frequently over social justice issues. LULAC supported Rucker in her successful bid to become a trustee on the Monterey Peninsula School Board. They differed with regard to bilingual education, however.

Rucker and many other non-Hispanic political leaders did not fully appreciate that for many leaders in the Latino community bilingual education was a civil rights issue. Dr. William Meléndez was not only president of LULAC, he wrote his doctoral dissertation passionately advocating for bilingual education. He argued that the lack of bilingual education in American schools generally put an enormous burden on non-English-speaking students that persisted over time: "Teaching the linguistically

distinct student in a language that is not understood by [them] . . . trau-
matizes, demoralizes, and degrades them during the learning experience . . . this pervasive condition places the student in a disadvantaged
position which becomes increasingly pronounced during the educational
years."[140] Furthermore, he argued, language diversity was a good thing
for the positive development of American society, "The differences among
people . . . could be used to enhance educational opportunities" and make
for "quality educational experiences" in a diverse population.[141] Meléndez's advocacy at the Monterey Peninsula School Board meeting took
place in a context of many years of activism and professional research
with regard to bilingual education in the schools.

For Rucker, and for many other non-Spanish-speaking residents of
Seaside (including whites, Filipinos, and second generation Hispanics),
language barriers in the schools and on the streets were all one issue. "Is
this America, Baby?" Rucker asked rhetorically recounting her experience in preparation for the annual Martin Luther King Day March in
Seaside in 2005:

I went to Highland [school] and I had the flyers for the Martin Luther King
March. I called . . . and said "What is the best way for me to get them to you?"
And this young man said to me, "If they're not in Spanish don't bother." I said
you mean all the kids at Highland are Hispanic? He said no, but all the kids
at Highland get the translation to Spanish. I said "Oh, I thought I was in
America." And I hung up. I was mad. I had not perceived the sheer population
at Highland. What I thought was that the older kids would be able to read
the few little words and I didn't really understand why that poster needed to
be translated . . . It really hurts me if I go to Kentucky Fried Chicken and the
young man doesn't understand my order. I say bring me someone who can
speak English.[142]

Rucker poignantly expressed the social and economic paradox that
Seasiders faced as they worked to build a new identity in a Seaside that
was no longer predominantly black, white, and Asian, but increasingly
Latino and definitely nonmilitary. Although groups continue to form
political coalitions, especially over clear issues of racial justice, getting
together over economic and social problems is trickier. Yet, at the same

time, and in spite of mixed feelings, many black leaders such as Helen Rucker are also at the forefront in helping Latinos with issues that go beyond politics, such as just coping with American bureaucracy. For example, Rucker personally intervened on behalf of restaurant owner Rosa Sánchez to help Sánchez's daughter overcome bureaucratic red tape at her school. Rucker was supportive, compassionate, and made sure that the situation was brought to a satisfactory resolution for all sides. Al Glover and the leadership of the NAACP has also mentored both black and Latino children and given them financial support through college.

One incident, and its outcome, made clear just how Seaside, as a city, handled the challenge of difference brought on by a new population. In the summer of 2004 approximately one hundred mostly undocumented Mexican immigrants marched on City Hall. They were frustrated by what they believed was continued police harassment of them for standing in front of a local convenience store waiting to be chosen for a day's work. It was the first time anyone in the police department or in city government remembered collective action taken by undocumented immigrants for any reason. The police captain, Carl Little, attributed the march on city hall by the day laborers to the recent election of Ralph Rubio, the first Latino mayor in Seaside's fifty year history as an incorporated city. Captain Little explained: "It was 2004 and Mayor Rubio was just in office a few months. I think that they thought since he was the mayor he could do something for them. That's why they came to city hall. In Mexico the mayors have all the power—not like here—but they didn't know that. I don't remember anything like this before Rubio."[143]

Although Ralph Rubio is Mexican American, he is not a new immigrant. His large extended family, part of a long established Mexican American community in Monterey County, has lived in Monterey, Carmel Valley, and Seaside for over a hundred years. Nonetheless, his election in 2004 sparked a new political activism and organization among more recent Mexican origin immigrants and Mexican Americans in Seaside, especially among business owners. The politicization of Mexican American residents of Seaside is notable because although it is a self-consciously racial/ethnic political mobilization, it is also an initiative by an ethnic group working to include itself in, rather than just challenge, the political establishment of Seaside. In the summer of 2004, however, it appeared that racially charged tensions might erupt into open conflict.

Patty Pérez, then a twenty-three-year-old police trainee who served as interpreter for the Seaside Police Department, accompanied Captain Little that summer day in 2004 to translate his message to the day laborers. She recalled:

I remember that day Captain Little called me in. I parked my car and I drove with him. He said "You're going to go with me and we're going to talk to the day laborers and I need you to tell them that they are blocking businesses and they have to move." I introduced myself. I introduced him. It was friendly. In Mexican culture we talk friendly to one another. We respect each other. If you talk mean they're not going to let you tell them what you want them to do. So then I said we're here from the police department and we're not here to cause any harm to anybody. I told them they had a right to be there if they wanted to be there but they could not lean on cars that did not belong to them, or to stand on the street or block the sidewalk—those were the main things. That was mid morning. So there were a few people that spoke out and said stuff like "We're not doing anything wrong, we need to work—we are not doing a crime." I said you are not doing a crime, you just can't block traffic or businesses and you're intimidating people from buying. Many of them were nodding and saying "Okay you're right." Right away they threw their coffees away and moved to the back [of the alley]; they were pretty good like that.[144]

Two hours later, much to the surprise of Pérez, Captain Little informed her that about a hundred day laborers had gathered on the steps of city hall. This spontaneous march was precipitated by Mexican origin workers concerned about harassment that affected their ability to find work. According to Pérez,

"They felt discriminated against—they said it's not right what's going on and why can't we be there. They were not angry they just wanted an explanation—all they were doing was finding work—they wanted to know where they could be without being bothered by the police. They kept asking 'Where else can we go?'" The gathering of day laborers quickly diffused as Pérez described again to them in Spanish that the police department did not intend to harass them but merely to ask them to move from the busy parking lot to a nearby location.[145]

Patty Pérez believed that the marchers did not perceive police intervention as racial discrimination but as an employment issue. However, according to a spokesperson for the Seaside Police Department, many Seaside residents do harbor racist attitudes toward the new immigrants. This spokesperson recalled that the police department began receiving frequent, even daily, racially charged complaints about the presence of Mexican day laborers in front of that particular 7-11 store since at least 2000, and almost all of these complaints came from Seaside's African American community.[146] "I have to tell you that the most biased group in Seaside is African American. One man called . . . and said his wife was intimidated and [demanded] that I should 'get those Mexicans off the street.'"[147]

The police department responded to the repeated and often angry demands of citizens by sending officers to the store to move the men away from the front entrance and parking lot to the back area, where they could not be seen from the street. The constant visits by police officers, considered harassment by the workers, prompted them to march on city hall. Although the march had the potential for open racial confrontation, this did not happen in Seaside. A compromise was eventually worked out in June 2006. Mexican American businessmen in Seaside acted as mediators. The day laborers agreed to move to an area in the shopping center that was not visible from the main entrance to Fremont Avenue, but they were nonetheless allowed to congregate as a way of gaining access to potential employers who continued to stop there and pick up workers for jobs.

Unlike other California cities in demographic transition, the politics of inclusion prevailed over racial identity politics even though new non-military population shifts of the 1990s brought extraordinary economic and social challenge and change to Seaside. Seasiders over the past two decades focused much less on the new population of Mexican origin immigrants than on fighting hard for economic growth and investment in the wake of the closure of Fort Ord, aspiring to reverse the effects of marginalization on the Peninsula that had been in place for many years.

Unfortunately, they were as much at odds with one another as they were in solidarity against outside forces on the Peninsula that would prevent them from taking their place as an equal partner in the tourism and real estate industries. Newly politicized multiracial coalitions challenged the hegemony of older and also multiracial coalitions at a critical moment in time for economic development. "No one gives up [political] power without a fight," commented former Mayor Ralph Rubio in something of an understatement.[148] Yet, even the struggles reflected the influence of an ingrained culture of inclusion and integration brought initially into Seaside by the military, which included dedicated activists in the midcentury civil rights movement. This culture of inclusion and integration persisted, even without Fort Ord, and with a newer population of nonmilitary folk.

The 1990s may have been notable as much for turmoil, confrontation, and scandal as for redevelopment, expansion, and growth. However, by 2001, Seaside city councils and City Manager Ray Corpuz would achieve new levels of development sustained by investment from the private sector, rather than just the federal government or the state.

CONCLUSION

Seaside was created and shaped fundamentally by the twin forces of the United States military, represented by Fort Ord, and the civil rights movement, led by African Americans and others who played active roles in the race work of the twentieth century. The model of integration and multiracial, multicultural demographics that the civil rights movement and the military gave Seaside was never more apparent than when Fort Ord closed, and large numbers of military-affiliated residents left the city. The impact of the loss was profound and exacerbated further when a new flow of nonmilitary immigrants from Mexico arrived in the 1990s, challenging Seaside to come to terms with a new identity as a minority-majority Latino city like so many others in twenty-first century California and the nation.

Seaside's new identity was contested in the 1990s and into the new millennium as residents fought to retain what they saw was the best about the city—its multiracialism, acceptance of differentness, and military values—and relinquish aspects that they saw as detrimental. The problem was that people did not always (or often) agree about what characteristics ought to be retained and which ones needed to be gotten rid of. Many middle-class African Americans such as Don Jordan, Helen Rucker, Mel Mason, and others appreciated Seaside's similarities to African American communities such as Oakland and Compton. Others such as Jerry Smith, Ralph Rubio, and Tom Mancini did not, and they wanted more than anything to distance their city from those locales.

In spite of the serious economic downturn of 2008, Seaside is in the throes of redevelopment and gentrification, bustling with projects ranging from golf courses; 5-star resorts; conference facilities; new residential and commercial development; and plans for a mixed use, transit-oriented, urban village that would transform the downtown. But Seaside, in the twenty-first century, is still far from becoming the resort destination of its neighbors on the Monterey Peninsula. The civil rights movement bolstered by the military directive of integration empowered the people of Seaside to build coalitions across racial and ethnic lines and achieve political, social, and economic successes. They did not always overcome racial politics, but the civil rights movement and the military gave them a model that outlasted the presence of Fort Ord. The coalitions of the post–Fort Ord years were built on issues, not race. They serve as a model too for other California cities currently struggling with racial tensions and conflicts due to similar population shifts.

Communities in demographic transition from white or black to Latino or Asian throughout the Los Angeles area such as Compton and South Gate and even Monterey Park, and north of Seaside such as Salinas, East Palo Alto, San Jose, and Oakland have encountered open conflict, mistrust, and even violence between groups as Latinos or Asians gradually assumed majority status over blacks. Seaside, on the other hand, largely escaped the open racial conflict of these other minority-majority cities because of its long tradition as a multiracial community, without any one group having numerical ascendancy, and with the common denominator of military experience. All of these factors made it advantageous, even imperative, for groups to get along.

Everyone shared in the economic distress brought on by the loss of Fort Ord in Seaside, and all had a vested interest in recovery. This did not mean that there were no racial or ethnic tensions or that everyone agreed on a plan of action to recover from the loss of Fort Ord, much less on what a new Seaside was going to look like. It did mean, however, that differences were based on conflicting views of the city and played out politically over issues of power at city hall and over development projects rather than simply over racial identity politics that pitted one racial group against another. Seaside shows that integration can work quickly, especially when experience, persuasion, and legislation are accompanied by a mandate.

Notes

INTRODUCTION

1. Interview by Carol McKibben, Seaside November 1, 2010. The narrator wished to remain anonymous.

2. See Richard White, "It's Your Misfortune and None of My Own": A New History of the American West (Norman: University of Oklahoma Press, 1991); Patricia Nelson Limerick, "The American West: From Exceptionalism to Internationalism," in The State of U.S. History, ed. Melvyn Stokes (Oxford, UK: Berg, 2002)

3. See Stephen Thernstrom and Abigail Thernstrom, America in Black and White: One Nation, Indivisible; Race in Modern America, (New York: Simon and Schuster, 1997); Howard Winant, "Race and Race Theory," Annual Review of Sociology, Vol. 26 (2000), 179. According to Winant, post-World War II theoretical approaches to race proved inadequate as a way of explaining persistent discrimination, particularly ethnicity-based theories, which suggested that contact, integration, and assimilation did not lead to better relationships but "devolved into neo-conservativism" on the part of whites and increased race consciousness on the part of minorities who had no desire to assimilate into "white cultural norms," 178–179.

4. Winant, "Race and Race Theory," 181; Tomas Almaguer, Racial Faultlines: The Historical Origins of White Supremacy in California (Berkeley: University of California Press, 1994).

5. There is very little scholarship on integration that worked. See I. G. Ellen, Sharing America's Neighborhoods: The Prospects for Stable Racial Integration (Cambridge, MA: Harvard University Press, 2000), and P. Nyden, J. Lukehart, J. Maly, and W. Peterman, eds., "Racially Diverse and Ethnically Diverse Neighborhoods," in Cityscape Vol. 4, No. 2: 1–28, 261–69. Washington, DC: U.S. Department of Urban Development.

6. For a thorough analysis of this phenomenon see David M. P. Freund, Colored Property: State Policy and White Racial Politics in Suburban America (Chicago and London: University of Chicago Press, 2007).

7. See Morris J. MacGregor, Jr., Integration of the Armed forces, 1940–1965 (U.S. Army Center of Military History: Washington, DC, 1985), 34–40, 428–449.

8. For a detailed and thorough analysis of the impact of both legislation and court cases regarding racial discrimination in California see Mark Brilliant, The Color of America Has Changed (New York: Oxford University Press, 2010). The major cases referred to here are as follows: Pérez v. Sharp (1948) overturned miscegenation statutes in California; Oyama v. California (1948) overturned the Alien Land Law and allowed full citizenship for excluded Asians; and Mèndez v. Westminister School District of Orange County (1947) overturned school segregation policy in California.

9. Carey McWilliams, California, The Great Exception (New York: Current Books, 1949); Mark Wild, Street Meeting: Multi-ethnic Neighborhoods in Twentieth Century Los

Angeles (Berkeley, Los Angeles, London: University of California Press, 2005); Quintard Taylor, *In Search of the Racial Frontier: African Americans in the West, 1528–1990*, (New York: W. W. Norton, 1998); Josh Sides, *L. A. City Limits: African American Los Angeles from the Great Depression to the Present* (Berkeley, Los Angeles, London: University of California Press, 2003); Kevin Allen Leonard, *The Battle for Los Angeles: Racial Ideology and World War II* (Albuquerque: University of New Mexico Press, 2006).

10. Mark, Brilliant, *The Color of America Has Changed.*

11. Roger W. Lotchin, *Fortress California 1910–1961: From Warfare to Welfare* (New York: Oxford University Press, 1992); "The City and the Sword: San Francisco and the Rise of the Metropolitan Military Complex, 1919–1941," *Journal of American History*, Vol. 65 (March 1979), 996–1020; "The Metropolitan Military Complex in Comparative Perspective: San Francisco, Los Angeles, and San Diego, 1919–1941," *Journal of the West*, Vol. 17 (July 1979).

12. See Jacqueline Dowd Hall, "The Long Civil Rights Movement and the Political Uses of the Past," *Journal of American History*, Vol. 9, Issue 4 (March, 2005) 1233–1263; Matthew C. Whitaker, *Race Work: The Rise of Civil Rights in the Urban West* (Lincoln: University of Nebraska Press, 2005). According to Whitaker, African American business people active in civil rights were vulnerable to financial blackmail from the white business community.

13. Polly J. Smith, *The Impact of Military Desegregation on Segregation Patterns in American Cities: A Case Study of Colorado Springs, New London, and Fayetteville* (Lewiston, NY and Queenston and Lampeter, UK: The Edwin Mellen Press, 2007), 25; Charles C. Moskos and Sibley Butler, *All That We Can Be: Black Leadership and Racial Integration the Army Way* (New York: Basic Books, 1996); John R. Logan, Brian Stults, and Reynolds Farley, "Segregation of Minorities in the Metropolis: Two Decades of Change," *Demography*, Vol. 41, No. 1 (2004), 14.

14. Ibid.

15. Ibid.

16. Kenneth T. Jackson, *Crabgrass Frontier: The Suburbanization of the United States* (New York and Oxford: Oxford University Press. 1985); Dolores Hayden, *Building Suburbia, Green Fields and Urban Growth, 1820–2000* (New York: Vintage Books, 2004); Becky Nicolaides and Andrew Wiese, eds., *The Suburb Reader* (New York and London: Routledge, 2006). For African American suburbanization see Andrew Wiese, *Places of Their Own: African American Suburbanization in the Twentieth Century* (Chicago and London: The University of Chicago Press, 2005).

17. Catherine Lutz, *Homefront: A Military City and the American 20th Century* (Boston: Beacon Press, 2001). Andrew H. Myers, *Black White & Olive Drab: Racial Integration at Fort Jackson, South Carolina and the Civil Rights Movement* (Charlottesville and London: University of Virginia Press, 2006).

18. Beth Bailey and David Farber, *The First Strange Place: Race and Sex in World War II Hawaii* (Baltimore and London: The Johns Hopkins University Press, 1992).

19. MacGregor, Jr., *Integration of the Armed Forces, 1940–1965*; Sherie Mershon and Steven Schlossman, *Foxholes and Color Lines: Desegregating the U.S. Armed Forces* (Baltimore and London: Johns Hopkins University Press, A RAND Book, 1998); Lee Nichols, *Breakthrough on the Color Front* (Colorado Springs: Three Continents Press, 1993); Jack Foner, *Blacks and the Military in American History: A New Perspective* (New York: Praeger, 1974); Richard Joseph Stillman, *Integration of the Negro in the U.S. Armed*

Forces (New York: Praeger, 1968); Leo Bogart et al., *Social Research and the Desegregation of the U.S. Army; Two Original 1951 Field Reports* (Chicago: Markham Publishing Company, 1969).

20. Smith, *The Impact of Military Desegregation on Segregation Patterns in American Cities.*

21. Albert M. Camarillo, "Cities of Color: The New Racial Frontier in California's Minority-Majority Cities," *Pacific Historical Review*, vol. 76, No.1 (February 2007), 1–28.

22. David Freund, *Colored Property: State Policy & White Racial Politics in Suburban America* (Chicago and London: University of Chicago Press, 2007).

23. Mershon and Schlossman, *Foxholes and Color Lines*, 273–294.

24. Brilliant, *The Color of America Has Changed*; Shana Bernstein, *Bridges of Reform: Interrracial Civil Rights Activism in Twentieth-Century Los Angeles* (New York: Oxford University Press, 2011); Scott Kurashige, *The Shifting Grounds of Race: Black and Japanese Americans in the Making of Multi-Ethnic Los Angeles* (Princeton, NJ: Princeton University Press, 2008); Leland T. Saito, *Race and Politics: Asian Americans, Latinos, and Whites in a Los Angeles Suburb* (Urbana and Chicago: University of Illinois Press, 1998); Charlotte Brooks, *Alien Neighbors, Foreign Friends: Asian Americans Housing, and the Transformation of Urban California* (Chicago and London: University of California Press, 2009); Stephen Pitti, *The Devil in Silicon Valley: Northern California, Race, and Mexican Americans* (Princeton, NJ, and Oxford, UK: Princeton University Press, 2003); Mark Wild, *Street Meeting: Multi-ethnic Neighborhoods in Early Twentieth Century Los Angeles* (Berkeley and Los Angeles: University of California Press, 2005).

25. Brooks, *Alien Neighbors, Foreign Friends.*

26. Bernstein, *Bridges of Reform*

27. Brilliant, *The Color of America Has Changed*; Whitaker, *Race Work*, 174–199; George Sánchez, "What's Good for Boyle Heights Is Good for the Jews: Creating Multi-Racialism on the East Side During the 1950s," *American Quarterly*, Vol. 56, No. 3 (2004), 633–651.

28. Whitaker, *Race Work*; Taylor, *In Search of the Racial Frontier*; Albert S. Broussard, *Black San Francisco: The Struggle for Racial Equality in the West, 1900–1954* (Lawrence: University of Kansas Press, 1998).

29. Michael Katz, ed., *The Underclass Debate: Views From History* (Princeton: Princeton University Press, 1993); William Julius Wilson, *The Truly Disadvantaged: The Inner City, the Underclass, and Public Policy* (Chicago: University of Chicago Press, 1987); Ken Auletta, *The Underclass* (New York: Vintage Books, 1983); Paul A. Jargowsky, "Ghetto Poverty Among Blacks in the 1980s," *Journal of Policy Analysis and Management*, Vol. 13, No. 2 (Spring, 1994), 288; John Kasard, "Urban Industrial Transition and the Urban Underclass," *Annals of the American Academy of Political and Social Science* (January 1989), 26–47; Douglas S. Massey and Nancy A. Denton, "Trends in the Residential Segregation of Blacks, Hispanics, and Asians, 1970–1980," *American Sociological Review*, 52 (1987), 802–825.

30. Thomas J. Sugrue, *The Origins of the Urban Crisis: Race and Inequality in Post-War Detroit* (Princeton: Princeton University Press, 1996).

31. William Julius Wilson, *When Work Disappears: The World of the New Urban Poor*, (New York: Vintage Books, 1996).

32. Wiese, *Places of Their Own*; Shirley Ann Wilson Moore, *To Place Our Deeds: The African American Community in Richmond, California, 1910–1963* (Berkeley:

University of California Press, 2000); Robert O. Self, *American Babylon: Race and the Struggle for Postwar Oakland* (Princeton and Oxford: Princeton University Press, 2003).

33. Douglas S. Massey and Nancy A. Denton, *American Apartheid: Segregation and the Making of the Underclass* (Cambridge: Harvard University Press, 1993).

34. Beryl Satter, *Family Properties: Race, Real Estate, and the Exploitation of Black Urban America* (Metropolitan Books/Henry Holt & Co., 2009).

35. Karyn R. Lacy, *Blue Chip Black: Race, Class and Status in the New Black Middle Class* (Berkeley: University of California Press, 2007).

36. For a thorough analysis of this phenomenon of localization among regional suburbs at midcentury see Jon C. Teaford, *Post-Suburbia: Government and Politics in Edge Cities*, (Baltimore: The Johns Hopkins University Press, 1996).

37. Whitaker, *Race Work.*

38. Sherman Smith Editorial, *Citizen Observer*, February 22, 1968.

CHAPTER ONE

1. David M. P. Freund, *Colored Property: State Policy & White Racial Politics in Suburban America* (Chicago and London: University of Chicago Press, 2007); Andrew Wiese, *Places of Their Own: African American Suburbanization in the Twentieth Century* (Chicago and London: University of Chicago Press, 2005).

2. Malcolm Margolin, *The Ohlone Way: Indian Life in the San Francisco–Monterey Bay Area* (Berkeley: Heydey Books, 1978), 58

3. Consultation with Linda Yamane, Rumsien Ohlone Scholar, May 15, 2007; A. L Kroeber, *Handbook of the Indians of California* (Berkeley: California Book Company, 1953), 883.

4. Miguel Costanso, "Diario historico de los viages de mar, y tierra hechos al norte de la California, escrito . . . en el ano 1770," from Sylvia. M. Broadbent, "The Rumsen of Monterey." *An Ethnography of Historical Sources Contributions of the University of California Archaelogical Research Facilities*, Vol. 14 (January 1972), 50–51; Linda Yamane, Rumsien Ohlone scholar.

5. Broadbent, "The Rumsen of Monterey," 51.

6. Ibid.

7. Ibid.; Donald Thomas Clark, *Monterey County Place Names* (Carmel Valley, CA: Kestral Press, 1991), 457.

8. Albert Camarillo, *Chicanos in a Changing Society: From Mexican Pueblos to American Barrios in Santa Barbara and Southern California, 1848–1930* (Dallas: Southern Methodist University Press, 1996).

9. Mary Tucey and David Hornbeck, "Anglo Immigration and the Hispanic Town: A Study of Urban Change in Monterey, 1835–1850," *Social Science Journal*, Vol. 13, No. 2 (1976), 1–7; Tucey and Hornbeck, "The Submergence of a People: Migration and Occupational Structure in California, 1850," *Pacific Historical Review* (1977): 471–484. See also Doris Marion Wright, "The Making of Cosmopolitan California: An Analysis of Immigration, 1848–1870," *California Historical Society Quarterly*, Vol. XIX, No. 4 (1940), 323–343

10. *Monterey Weekly Cypress, 1897–1901; Monterey New Era 1896–1909; Monterey Daily Cypress, 1907–1911.*

11. *Monterey New Era*, Vol. 15, No. 7 (November 23, 1904), 1.

12. Kenneth T. Jackson, *Crabgrass Frontier: The Suburbanization of the United States* (New York and Oxford: Oxford University Press, 1985), 22; Robert Wiebe, *The Search For Order, 1877–1920* (New York: Hill and Wang, 1967); Dolores Hayden, *Building Suburbia, Green Fields and Urban Growth, 1820–2000* (New York: Vintage Books, 2004), 71.

13. Jackson, *Crabgrass Frontier*, 22.

14. Thomas C. Butterworth, *Seaside: Monterey County California* issued by Monterey Realty Syndicate, Monterey, California, 1910, 7.

15. Ibid., 17.

16. Hayden, *Building Suburbia*, 8.

17. Ibid.

18. Harry D. Barrows and Luther A. Ingersoll, *Memorial and Biographical History of the Coast Counties of Central California* (Chicago: The Lewis Publishing Company, 1893), 280.

19. Freund, *Colored Property*, 8.

20. Donald M. Howard, *Rancho to Roberts Land*, Vol. 2, 441, unpublished ms.

21. Freund, *Colored Property*, 32–34;See also Robert O. Self, *American Babylon: Race and the Struggle for Postwar Oakland*. Princeton, NJ, and Oxford, UK: Princeton University Press, 2003

22. Major Rolin C. Watkins, *History of Monterey and Santa Cruz Counties, California* (Chicago: The S. J. Clarke Publishing Company, 1925), 25.

23. Jackson, *Crabgrass Frontier*, 136.

24. Howard, *Rancho to Roberts Land*, 338.

25. Nellie Imwalle Heneken, interview with Dr. John Roberts, "This Area's 'First Citizen' Recalls Early Days Here" *Monterey Bay News-Seaside California*, Friday, April 16, 1948, 8.

26. Historical and Architectural Reports for Fort Ord, conducted for the Office of Environmental Programs Conservation Division, Keith Landreth, Principal Investigator, September 1993, 4.

27. Carol McKibben, *Beyond Cannery Row: Sicilian Women, Immigration, and Community in Monterey, California, 1915–1999* (Chicago: University of Illinois Press, 2006); John Walton, *Storied Land: Community and Memory in Monterey* (Berkeley: University of California Press, 2003); Connie Chiang, *Shaping the Shoreline: Fishing and Tourism on the Monterey Coast* (Seattle: University of Washington Press, 2008); *Monterey Peninsula Herald*, Saturday, August 27, 1949, 14–15.

28. Kibby M. Horne, "A History of the Presidio of Monterey," Defense Language Institute West Coast Branch, Presidio of Monterey, California, 1970, 44.

29. Sherie Mershon and Steven Schlossman, *Foxholes & Color Lines: Desegregating the U.S. Armed Forces* (Baltimore and London: The Johns Hopkins University Press, 1998), 2–5.

30. Interview with Betty Dwyer Mahieu, 92, California Room Monterey Public Library, February 24, 2007.

31. James C. McNaughton, "Fort Ord, A Working History," unpublished ms., December 1996, 3.

32. *Carmel Pacific Spectator Journal*, "Urchin With Muscles," December 2, 1955, 51.

33. *Monterey Peninsula Herald*, June 1, 1970, 12D.

34. McKibben, *Beyond Cannery Row*; Walton, *Storied Land: Community and Memory in Monterey*.

35. The best evidence for Seaside's diversity of ethnic groups and the increasing poverty of its population comes from the collection of photographs and oral histories, particularly of school children from this era. See Carol Lynn McKibben, *Seaside* (Mount Pleasant, SC: Arcadia Publishing, 2009), 27–29.

36. Howard, *Rancho to Roberts Land*, 421.

37. Walton, *Storied Land*; *Monterey Peninsula Herald*, *Peninsula Life*, "Black History Spans Two Centuries on the Peninsula," Sunday, February 17, 1985, 1D.

38. 1900 U.S. Census for Monterey.

39. John Walton, *Storied Land: Community and Memory in Monterey*. .

40. Mark Wild, *Street Meeting: Multi-ethnic Neighborhoods in Early Twentieth Century Los Angeles* (Berkeley, Los Angeles, London: University of California Press, 2005), 9–37.

41. Camarillo, *Chicanos in a Changing Society*, 139; Stephen Pitti, *The Devil in Silicon Valley: Northern California, Race, and Mexican Americans* (Princeton and Oxford: Princeton University Press, 2003), 57.

42. United States Manuscript Census, 1910.

43. United States Manuscript Census, 1920.

44. McKibben, *Beyond Cannery Row*.

45. Polk's Monterey City Directory, 1930, R. L. Polk Company of California, 183.

46. Freund, *Colored Property*.

47. *Monterey Peninsula Herald*, Weekend Magazine, February 25, 1979.

48. Interview with Rudy Martin, son of Reverand S. R. Martin, founder of Victory Temple, May 7, 2008.

49. United States Manuscript Census, 1930.

50. Ibid.

51. Interview with Sara Souza, daughter of Mr. and Mrs. Manuel Freitas, February 1985, by Historical Commissioner Emily Ventura.

52. Ibid.

53. Howard, Rancho to Roberts Land, 617.

54. McKibben, *Beyond Cannery Row*.

55. United States Manuscript Census 1920, 1930.

56. Interview with Evangelina Pérez, August 25, 2009, Seaside by Carol McKibben.

57. Interview with Luis Pérez, April 2, 2007, Seaside by Carol McKibben.

58. Lopez v. Monterey County MO944, Box 1, Vol. 1–3, 1879–1909; Box 2 Vol. 4, 2/3/1910–12/23/1941.

59. *Salinas Weekly Journal*, 2/24/1900, p. 1, col. 3 in Lopez v. Monterey County MO944, Box 1 Vol. 3, 1879–1909.

60. *Salinas Weekly Journal*, 8/26/1909 p.1 col. 2 in Lopez v. Monterey County MO944, Box 1 Vol. 3, 1879–1909.

61. Lopez v. Monterey County MO944, Box 1, Vol. 1, 1879–1909 *Salinas Valley Settler*, 9/19/1889, p. 1, col 4; *Salinas Valley Weekly Index*, 9/19/1889, p. 2; *King City Settler*, 9/26/1889, p. 3; Box 2 Vol. 4, 2/3/1910–12/23/1941.

62. *The Monterey Daily Cypress*, Vol. 6, Thursday, January 17, 1907, 1.

63. Ronald T. Takaki, *Strangers From a Different Shore: A History of Asian Americans* (Boston: Little, Brown, 1998); Quintard Taylor, *In Search of the Racial Frontier: African Americans in the West, 1528–1990* (New York: W. W. Norton, 1998).

64. Nayan Shah, *Contagious Divides: Epidemic and Race in San Francisco's Chinatown* (Berkeley: University of California Press, 2001), 66; Charlotte Brooks, *Alien Neighbors*,

Foreign Friends: Asian Americans, Housing, and the Transformation of Urban California
(Chicago and London: University of Chicago Press, 2009), 11–15.

65. Nayan Shah, *Contagious Divides*, Chapters 1–3.

66. Sandy Lydon, *Chinese Gold: The Chinese in the Monterey Bay Region* (Capitola,
CA: Capitola Book Company, 1985), 360–377.

67. Michael P. Rogin and John L. Shover, *Political Change in California; Critical
Elections and Social Movements*, 1890–1966 (Westport, CT: Greenwood Publishing
Corporation, 1970).

68. David M. Kennedy, *Freedom From Fear: The American People in Depression and
War, 1929–1945* Oxford History of the United States v. 9 (New York: Oxford University
Press, 2005), chapter 12.

69. McKibben, *Beyond Cannery Row*; John Walton, *Storied Land: Community and
Memory in Monterey*.

70. Interview with William A. "Tex" West and Vivian Ruth West, February 24, 1989
by Seaside Historical Commissioners Emily Ventura and Henry Hopkins, Seaside.

71. Interview with Lois Bratt by K. Crain, n.d. Seaside Historical Commission, Seaside.

72. Interview with William A. "Tex" West and Vivian Ruth West, February 24,
1989 by Seaside Historical Commissioners Emily Ventura and Henry Hopkins, Seaside.

73. McKibben, *Beyond Cannery Row*; John Walton, *Storied Land: Community and
Memory in Monterey*.

74. Interview with Sara Souza, daughter of Mr. and Mrs. Manuel Freitas, February
1985, by Historical Commissioner Emily Ventura, Seaside.

75. Interview with Vi Drake by K. Crain, Seaside Historical Commission, n.d., City
of Seaside Archives.

76. Letter from Adeline DeSilva, April 19, 1988, City of Seaside Archives.

77. Herman D. Ruth, City and Regional Planning Consultant, Population and Employment Survey, 1956, City Planning Commission, Seaside, California, City of Seaside Archives.

78. Donald Thomas Clark, Monterey County Place Names, A Geographical Diction-
ary (Carmel Valley, CA: Kestrel Press, 1991), 519.

79. Jackson, *Crabgrass Frontier*, 193; Freund, *Colored Property*, 89.

80. Freund, *Colored Property*, 92

81. Jackson, *Crabgrass Frontier*, 196–197.

82. This term was coined by Albert M. Camarillo to describe urban areas with mi-
nority/majority populations.

83. Wild, *Street Meeting*.

CHAPTER TWO

1. Interview with Richard Woods at Kiwanis Club Meeting, Seaside, March 13, 2007.
by Carol McKibben. Hereafter referred to as Woods Interview.

2. Woods Interview.

3. Roger W. Lotchin, *Fortress California 1910–1961: From Warfare to Welfare* (New
York: Oxford University Press, 1992); Gerald D. Nash, *The American West Transformed:
The Impact of the Second World War* (Bloomington: Indiana University Press, 1985) and
World War II and The West: Reshaping the Economy (Lincoln: University of Nebraska
Press, 1990; Robert Self, *American Babylon: Race and the Struggle for Postwar Oak-
land* (Princeton and Oxford: Princeton University Press, 2003); Becky M. Nicolaides, *My
Blue Heaven: Life and Politics in the Working Class Suburbs of Los Angeles, 1920–1965*

(Chicago and London: The University of Chicago Press, 2002); Mark Brilliant, *The Color of America Has Changed: How Racial Diversity Shaped Civil Rights Reform in California, 1941–1978* (New York: Oxford University Press, 2010).

4. Report on the United States Census, City of Monterey, Population Folder Two, Verticle File, California Room, Monterey Public Library, Monterey, California. N.d.

5. Ibid.

6. Ibid.

7. Roger Lotchin, "The City and the Sword: San Francisco and the Rise of the Metropolitan Military Complex, 1919–1941," *Journal of American History*, Vol. 65, March 1979, 1006; and Lotchin, *Fortress California 1910–1961*; Self, *American Babylon*, 44; Nicolaides, *My Blue Heaven*, 188; Arthur C. Verge, *Paradise Transformed: Los Angeles During the Second World War* (Dubuque, IA: Kendall Publishing Co., 1993, 85–88; Nash, *The American West Transformed*.

8. Stephen Pitti, *The Devil in Silicon Valley: Northern California, Race, and Mexican Americans* (Princeton and Oxford: Princeton University Press, 2003), chapter 6; Self, *American Babylon*, 59; Nicolaides, *My Blue Heaven*, 187.

9. See David G. Gutiérrez, *Walls and Mirrors: Mexican Americans, Mexican Immigrants, and the Politics of Ethnicity* (Berkeley: University of California Press, 1995), 125–130; Eduardo Obregón Pagán, *Murder at the Sleepy Lagoon: Zoot Suits, Race & Riot in Wartime L.A.* (Chapel Hill: University of North Carolina Press, 2003), 145–147; Lori Flores, "Converging Communities in the 'Valley of the World'": Mexican Americans, Mexicans, and the Chicano Movement's Evolution in Salinas and California, 1940–1970," Ph.D. dissertation, Department of History, Stanford University, chapter two, 44–54, 2011.

10. Pitti, *The Devil in Silicon Valley*, chapter 6; Self, *American Babylon*, 59; Nicolaides, *My Blue Heaven*, 187.

11. Charlotte Brooks, *Alien Neighbors, Foreign Friends: Asian Americans, Housing, and the Transformation of Urban California* (Chicago and London: The University of Chicago Press, 2009).

12. Gutiérrez, *Walls and Mirrors*, 125–130; Pagán, *Murder at the Sleepy Lagoon*, 145–147; Flores, "Converging Communities in the 'Valley of the World'", chapter two, 44–54;

Shana Bernstein, "Building Bridges at Home in a Time of Global Conflict: Interracial Cooperation and the Fight for Civil Rights in Los Angeles, 1933–1954," Ph.D. dissertation, Department of History, Stanford University, 2003.

13. Quintard Taylor, *In Search of the Racial Frontier: African Americans in the West, 1528–1990* (New York: W. W. Norton, 1998); Albert S. Broussard, *Black San Francisco: The Struggle for Racial Equality in the West, 1900–1954* (Lawrence: University of Kansas Press, 1993).

14. Polly J. Smith, *The Impact of Military Desegregation on Segregation Patterns in American Cities: A Case Study of Colorado Springs, New London, and Fayetteville* (Lewiston, NY, and Queenston and Lampeter, UK: The Edwin Mellen Press, 2007), 70.

15. Monterey Land and Hot Springs Company, July 17, 1941, Ord Terrace Subdivision, Book 734, 66. Courtesy of Stewart Title Company, Monterey, California.

16. *Monterey Peninsula Herald*, January 19, 1940, 1; 11.

17. Ibid., 14.

18. N.a., Headquarters, Historical Sketch, United States Army Training Center, Infantry, Fort Ord, 1969, Fort Ord Archive, 5.

19. Major Park Wollam, unpublished paper, "Fort Ord in World War II," May 1998, 4.

20. Ibid., 5.

21. Harold E. Raugh Jr., *Images of America: Fort Ord*, (San Francisco, California: Arcadia Publishing, Inc., 2004), 7.

22. Wollam, "Fort Ord in World War II," 6.

23. Ibid.; Raugh, *Images of America*.

24. Report on the United States Census, City of Monterey, Population Folder Two, Verticle File, California Room, Monterey Public Library, Monterey, California. N.d.

25. Herman D. Ruth, City and Regional Planning Consultant, *Population and Employment Survey, 1956*, City Planning Commission, Seaside, California, City of Seaside Archives. Hereafter referred to as Ruth Report.

26. Elaine D. Johnson, "Sociological Study of the Monterey Area," prepared for the City Planning Commission, Monterey, California, October 1968, 51. Hereafter referred to as the Johnson report.

27. Ibid.

28. George Hill, Alexis Smith, and Debbie Warshawsky, "Seaside, California: A Case Study of A Minority-Majority City" unpublished paper, Stanford University, March 30, 2006, 25.

29. Flores, "Converging Communities in the 'Valley of the World'," chapter two.

30. Catherine Lutz, *Homefront: A Military City and the American 20th Century* (Boston: Beacon Press, 2001), 50.

31. Andrew M. Myers, *Black, White, & Olive Drab: Racial Integration at Fort Jackson, South Carolina and the Civil Rights Movement* (Charlottesville and London: University of Virginia Press, 2006), chapter 2; Smith, *The Impact of Military Desegregation on Segregation Patterns in American Cities*, 70, 158.

32. Quoted in Beth Bailey and David Farber, *The First Strange Place: Race and Sex in World War II Hawaii* (The Johns Hopkins University Press, 1992), 42.

33. Flores, "Converging Communities in the 'Valley of the World'," chapter two, 44–54.

34. *Monterey Peninsula Herald*, October 16, 1940.

35. Interview with Leon Panetta June 30, 2008, Marina, California, by Carol McKibben. Hereafter referrd to as Panetta interview.

36. Historical Commission Report, 1965, City of Seaside Archives, Seaside, California,

37. *Monterey Peninsula Herald*, June 1, 1970, 12D.

38. Interview by telephone with Rudy Martin, May 7, 2008, by Carol McKibben.

39. Interview with Mr. and Mrs. Ira Beverly by Henry Hopkins, Seaside Historical Commission, City of Seaside Archive, November 30, 1989.

40. *Fort Ord Panorama*, "Fort Ord Grows Up," Vol. III, September 25, 1942, 1.

41. *The Seaside News-Graphic*, August 12, 1941, 8.

42. N.a., "This Is Seaside: Urchin With Muscles," *Carmel Pacific Spectator Journal*, December 2, 1955, 52.

43. *Carmel Pacific Spectator Journal*, "This Is Seaside: Urchin With Muscles," December 2, 1955, 52.

44. Joe Schoeninger, "Incorporation of Seaside as a City Is held 'Feasible,'" *Monterey Peninsula Herald*, April 4, 1951, np. City of Seaside Archive, Seaside, California.

45. Lutz, *Homefront*, 54. Myers, *Black, White & Olive Drab*, 3; Smith, *The Impact of Military Desegregation on Segregation Patterns in American Cities*.

46. N.a., "This Is Seaside: Urchin with Muscles," *Carmel Pacific Spectator Journal*, December 2, 1955, 96.

47. David Freund, *Colored Property: State Policy & White Racial Politics in Suburban America* (Chicago and London: University of Chicago Press, 2007).

48. For a full explanation of the tendency to locate waste dumps and other hazards in minority majority neighborhoods and the response of residents against that trend, see Robert D. Bullard and Benjamin Chavis Jr., *Confronting Environmental Racism: Voices from the Grassroots* (Cambridge, MA: South End Press, 1993); Melissa Checker, *Polluted Promises: Environmental Racism and the Search for Justice in a Southern Town* (New York and London: New York University Press, 2005); Robert D. Bullard, ed., *Unequal Protection: Environmental Justice and Communities of Color* (San Francisco: Sierra Club Books, 1994); Luke W. Cole, *From the Ground Up: Environmental Racism and the Rise of the Environmental Justice Movement* (New York: New York University Press, 2001).

49. Ibid.

50. *Seaside News-Graphic*, Tuesday July 15, 1941, 1.

51. *Ibid.*

52. *Seaside Post-News Sentinel*, September 30, 1954, 1.

53. *Seaside Post-News-Graphic*, August 8, 1941, 1.

54. Ibid.

55. *Monterey Peninsula Herald*, September 11, 1947, 1.

56. Ibid., September 9, 1947.

57. Ibid., April 4, 1951.

58. James McNaughton, Command Historian, "Fort Ord: A Working History," unpublished paper December 1966, 9; Sherie Mershon and Steven Schlossman, *Foxholes & Color Lines: Desegregating the U.S. Armed Forces* (Baltimore and London: The Johns Hopkins University Press, 1998); Myers, *Black, White and Olive Drab*, 76.

59. Mershon and Schlossman, *Foxholes & Color Lines*, 51.

60. Statement of the Adjutant General's Department, 1 December, 1941, quoted in Mershon and Schlossman, *Foxholes and Color Lines*, 22.

61. Mershon and Schlossman, *Foxholes & Color Lines*, 52–92.

62. Ibid., 176–177.

63. Ibid., 258. Quintard Taylor, *In Search of the Racial Frontier*, 251–310.

64. Ibid., 103.

65. Ibid., 187–217. Blacks were not the only group to be segregated in the armed forces during World War II. Japanese Americans fought in all Japanese units, the most famous of which was the 442nd Division of the U.S. Army. Mexican Americans were usually integrated within the services, but not always. All–Mexican American units were created as well. Chinese Americans fought alongside whites, however.

66. Lutz, *Homefront*, 45–47.

67. The Monterey Peninsula had Fort Ord, but not the military industrial base that provided employment for so many minority women during the war years.

68. McNaughton, "Fort Ord, A Working History," 6.

69. *Fort Ord Panorama*, Friday November 13, 1942, 2.

70. *Fort Ord Panorama*, Friday September 18, 1942, 6.

71. Ibid., October 23, 1.

72. Ibid., September 25, 16.

73. Ibid., October 9, 1942, 6.

74. Ibid., October 23, 1942, 1.

75. Lutz, *Homefront*, 66–73.

76. Ibid.; Raugh, *Images of America.*

77. *Fort Ord Panorama.* Vol. III, 1–52. Spanish surnamed soldiers were mentioned once in the entire year of 1942. In 1943, two Spanish surnamed basketball players Joseph C. Torres and Ernest A. Morales were mentioned in an article, Friday April 9, 1943, 7.

78. Craig Scharlin and Lilia Villanueva, *Philip Vera Cruz: A Personal History of Filipino Immigrants and the Farmworkers Movement* (Seattle: University of Washington Press, 2000).

79. *Fort Ord Panorama,* Vol. III, October 16, 1942, 1.

80. Quoted in Mershon and Schlossman, *Foxholes & Color Lines,* 173.

81. Ibid., 183.

82. Telegram Hugh F. Dormody, Mayor of Monterey, California et al., to William F. Knowland July 31, 1948, Seaside History Archive Collection, Seaside, California; McNaughton, "Fort Ord," 12.

83. Quintard Taylor, *In Search of the Racial Frontier,* 253.

84. Telegram Hugh F. Dormody, Mayor of Monterey, California et al., to William F. Knowland July 31, 1948; August 10, 1948, Letter from Kenneth C. Royall, Secretary of the Army, to Senator William F. Knowland.

85. Ibid; Wollam, unpublished paper, "Fort Ord in World War II," May 1998, 4; N.a., Headquarters, Historical Sketch, United States Army Training Center, Infantry, Fort Ord, 1969, Fort Ord Archive, 5.

86. Johnson report.

87. David T. Yamada and Oral History Committee, MP/JACL, *The Japanese of the Monterey Peninsula: Their History and Legacy, 1895–1995* (Monterey, CA: Japanese American Citizens League, 1995), especially chapters 1–3. See also Sandy Lydon, *The Japanese in the Monterey Bay Region: A Brief History* (Capitola, CA: Capitola Book Company, 1997), chapter 4.

88. Yamada, *The Japanese of the Monterey Peninsula,* 176.

89. The first Buddhist Temple was lost in a fire in 1971, then rebuilt and dedicated at the same location in 1977.

90. In Monterey Park a suburb of Los Angeles, for example, Asian Americans and Latinos together comprised 14.5 percent of the population by 1960. See Leland Saito, *Race and Politics, Asian Americans, Latinos, and Whites in a Los Angeles Suburb* (Urbana and Chicago: University of Illinois Press, 1998), 32.

91. Yamada, *The Japanese of the Monterey Peninsula,* 164. Interview with Larry Oda, President, National Japanese American Citizens League, May 29, 2007, Seaside, by Carol McKibben. Hereafter referred to as Oda interview.

92. Oda interview.

93. Interview with William Meléndez January 30, 2007, Monterey by Carol McKibben. Hereafter referred to as Meléndez interview.

94. Interview with Ralph Rubio September 5, 2005, Marina by Carol McKibben. Hereafter referred to as Rubio interview; interview with Nancy Towne August 31, 2005, Seaside by Carol McKibben. Hereafter referred to as Towne interview.

95. The Refugee Services Program of Monterey Bay estimated that 2,500 Vietnamese refugees, mostly fishing families, migrated to the area by 1982. *Marina Seaside Tribune,* February 4, 1982, n.p., City of Seaside Archive. Interview with Bui, Duong, by phone, December 3, 2007, Seaside by Carol McKibben.

96. Mike Mills, "Peninsula Faces Social, Racial Problems," *Monterey Peninsula Herald*, February 5, 1968.

97. Although it is impossible to know for certain how many of these multiracial families lived in Seaside, according to data from the Immigration and Naturalization Service, approximately 66,681 Japanese, 51,747 Filipinos, 28,285 Koreans, 11,166 Thai, and 8,040 Vietnamese war brides entered the United States between 1947 and 1975. See Rogelio Saenz, Sean-Shong Hwang, and Benigno E. Aguirre, "In Search of Asian War Brides," *Demography*, Vol. 31, No. 3, August, 1994, 550. For a thorough analysis of the problems interracial couples faced in American society in this period see Paul R. Spickard, *Mixed Blood: Intermarriage and Ethnic Identity in Twentieth-Century America* (Madison: University of Wisconsin Press, 1989) and Susan Zeiger, *Entangling Alliances: Foreign War Brides and American Soldiers in the Twentieth Century* (New York and London: New York University Press, 2010).

98. Ibid.

99. Study Produced by Bank of America, "Focus on Monterey County," 1967, California Room, Monterey Public Library, Monterey, California, 10; McNaughton, "Fort Ord, A Working History."

100. "This Is Seaside: Urchin with Muscles," *Carmel Pacific Spectator Journal*, December 2, 1955, 96.

101. Smith, *The Impact of Military Desegregation on Segregation Patterns in American Cities*, 89.

102. Ibid., 185.

103. *Monterey Bay News*, February 27, 1948, 1 and 11.

104. Ibid., October 16, 1952, 1.

105. "Wartime Boom Boosted Seaside Population to Over 10,000," *Monterey Peninsula Herald*, June 21, 1950, n.p., from Population Folder 2, vertical files, California Room, Monterey Public Library, Monterey, California.

106. Polk's Monterey-Pacific Grove (Monterey County) City Directory 1954–55 including Carmel, Seaside, and Carmel Valley rural routes, R. L. Polk & Co., Publishers, San Francisco, California, 1955.

107. Interview with Joe Cortéz, April 11, 1990, Seaside Historical Commission, City of Seaside Archive.

108. Friendship Baptist Church, 628 Broadway; Memorial Baptist Church, 6th corner Maple Ave; Seaside Methodist Church, 350 Elm; St. Francis Xavier, 1358 Monte Vista Ave; Assembly of God, 506 Maple Ave; Church of God in Christ, 722 Harcourt Ave; Church of the Nazarene, Pine Ave at Kenneth Pl; First Four Square, Maple Ave corner Bay View Ave; Fundamental Seaside Chapel, 262 Del Monte; Hayes Chapel CME, 605 Elm Ave; Kingdom Hall, 50 Park Ave; Pentecostal Church of God, Broadway at Kenneth Pl; St. Seraphin Greek-Orthodox, 667 Del Monte Ave; *Monterey Peninsula Herald*, May 28, 1964, A4.

109. "Seaside's Friendship Baptist Church Has a New Site," *Monterey Peninsula Herald*, August 9, 1953, clipping file, City of Seaside Archives.

110. Photograph with caption, vertical file "Churches," California Room, Monterey Peninsula Library, dated October 10, 1948.

111. Catholic Diocese of Monterey, *The Observer*, March 17, 1962, n.p.

112. Nicolaides, *My Blue Heaven*, 194.

113. Self, *American Babylon*, 100–119.

114. Pitti, *The Devil in Silicon Valley*, 120–136.

115. See Mark Brilliant, *The Color of America Has Changed.*

116. Mark Wild, *Street Meeting: Multi-ethnic Neighborhoods in Early Twentieth Century Los Angeles* (Berkeley and Los Angeles: University of California Press, 2005).

117. Smith, *The Impact of Military Desegregation on Segregation Patterns in American Cities,* 25; Charles C. Moskos and Sibley Butler, *All That We Can Be: Black Leadership and Racial Integration the Army Way* (New York: Basic Books, 1996); John R. Logan, Brian Stults, and Reynolds Farley, "Segregation of Minorities in the Metropolis: Two Decades of Change" *Demography*, Vol. 41, No. 1, 2004, 14.

118. *Monterey Bay News*, October 20, 1950, 3.

119. Ibid., August 1, 1951.

120. Ibid., February 19, 1951.

121. Interview with Richard Joyce April 5, 2007, Seaside, by Carol McKibben. Hereafter referred to as Joyce interview.

122. See Matthew C. Whitaker, *Race Work: The Rise of Civil Rights in the Urban West* (Lincoln: University of Nebraska Press, 2005); Self, *American Babylon.*

123. Pérez Interview.

124. *Seaside Post-News Sentinel*, October 25, 1951, 1 For a detailed analysis of politics of environmental discrimination in minority communities see David Naguib Pellow, *Garbage Wars: The Struggle for Environmental Justice in Chicago* (Cambridge, MA: The MIT Press, 2002).

125. *Seaside Post-News Sentinel*, November 8, 1951, 1.

126. Ibid.

127. Ibid.

128. Ibid., February 7, 1952, 1.

129. Ibid., April 1, 1.

130. Ibid., July 15, 1954, 1.

131. Brooks, *Alien Neighbors, Foreign Friends,* 176; Self, *American Babylon,* 98–99; Nicolaides, *My Blue Heaven,* 156–157; Pitti, *The Devil in Silicon Valley,* 78–102; Taylor, *In Search of the Racial Frontier.*

132. *Seaside Post-News Sentinel*, July 29, 1954, 1.

133. Ibid., August 5, 1954, 1.

134. Ibid., August 26, 1954, 8.

135. Ibid., 1; Interview with Lenora Bean, March 25, 2006, Seaside by Carol McKibben.

136. *Seaside Post-News Sentinel*, August 26, 1954, 8.

137. Ibid., October 7, 1954, 1.

138. Bernstein, "Building Bridges at Home in a Time of Global Conflict"; Brooks, *Alien Neighbors, Foreign Friends.*

CHAPTER THREE

1. Interview with Richard Joyce, Seaside, April 12, 2007 by Carol McKibben. Hereafter referred to as Joyce interview.

2. Robert Self, *American Babylon: Race and the Struggle for Postwar Oakland* (Princeton and Oxford: Princeton University Press, 2003); Matthew C. Whitaker, *Race Work: The Rise of Civil Rights in the Urban West* (Lincoln: University of Nebraska Press, 2005).

3. 1954 Brown v. Board of Education, Montgomery Bus Boycott and the much publicized lunch counter sit-ins 1955–1956, The Civil Rights Act of 1964, The Voting Rights Act of 1965, and The Civil Rights Act of 1968.

4. Quintard Taylor, *In Search of the Racial Frontier: African Americans in the West, 1528–1990* (New York: W. W. Norton, 1998); Whitaker, *Race Work*; Charlotte Brooks, *Alien Neighbors, Foreign Friends: Asian Americans, Housing, and the Transformation of Urban California* (Chicago & London: University of California Press, 2009).

5. Mike Mills, "Peninsula Faces Social, Racial Problems," *Monterey Peninsula Herald*, February 5, 1968.

6. James C. McNaughton, "Fort Ord, a Working History" (unpublished paper), December 1996, 13–14.

7. Taylor, *In Search of the Racial Frontier*; Brooks, *Alien Neighbors, Foreign Friends*.

8. Catherine Lutz, *Homefront: A Military City and the American 20th Century* (Boston: Beacon Press, 2001).

9. Andrew H. Myers, *Black, White and Olive Drab: Racial Integration at Fort Jackson, South Carolina, and the Civil Rights Movement* (Charlottesville and London: University of Virginia Press, 2006).

10. Polly J. Smith, *The Impact of Military Desegregation on Segregation Patterns in American Cities: A Case Study of Colorado Springs, New London, and Fayetteville* (Lewiston, NY, Queenston and Lampeter, UK: The Edwin Mellen Press, 2007).

11. Cynthia Enloe, *Bananas, Beaches and Bases: Making Feminist Sense Out of International Politics* (Berkeley: University of California Press, 1990); Susan Zeiger, *Entangling Alliances: Foreign War Brides and American Soldiers in the Twentieth Century* (New York and London: New York University Press, 2010); Paul Spickard, *Mixed Blood: Intermarriage and Ethnic Identity in Twentieth Century America* (Madison: University of Wisconsin Press, 1989).

12. Charles. C. Moskos, Jr., "Racial Integration in the Armed Forces" *The American Journal of Sociology*, Vol. 72, No. 2 (September 1966), 139–140.

13. See Morris J. MacGregor, Jr., *Integration of the Armed Forces, 1940–1965* (Washington D.C.: Center of Military History United States Army, 1981); Sherie Mershon and Steven Schlossman, *Foxholes and Color Lines: Desegregating the U.S. Armed Forces* (Baltimore and London: The Johns Hopkins University Press, 1998); Smith, *The Impact of Military Desegregation on Segregation Patterns in American Cities*.

14. Smith, *The Impact of Military Desegregation on Segregation Patterns in American Cities*, 2–8; Lee Sigelman and Susan Welch, "The Contact Hypothesis Revisited: Black-White Interaction and Positive Racial Attitudes," *Social Forces*, Vol. 71, No. 3 (March 1993), 781–795; Myers, *Black, White and Olive Drab*; Lutz, *Homefront*.

15. Cornel West, *Race Matters* (New York: Vintage, 1994), 71–90.

16. Smith, *The Impact of Military Desegregation on Segregation Patterns in American Cities*, 25–27; Sigelman and Welch, "The Contact Hypothesis Revisited," 781–795; Charles J. Moskos, *The American Enlisted Man*, New York: Russell Sage Foundation, 1970.

17. Interview with Ruthie Watts, March 10, 2011, by Carol McKibben, Carmel, California.

18. Smith, *The Impact of Military Desegregation on Segregation Patterns in American Cities*, 18.

19. Whitaker, *Race Work*, 103–114; Josh Sides, *L. A. City Limits: African American Los Angeles from the Great Depression to the Present* (Berkeley, Los Angeles, London: University of California Press, 2003).

20. Moskos, "Racial Integration in the Armed Forces," 138.

21. Ibid.

22. Ibid.

23. Email interview with Tom Namvedt July 11, 2010.

24. Albert S. Broussard, *Black San Francisco: The Struggle for Racial Equality in the West, 1900–1954* (Lawrence: University of Kansas Press, 1993); Quintard Taylor, *In Search of the Racial Frontier: African Americans in the West, 1528–1990* (New York: W. W. Norton, 1998); Richard White, *"It's Your Misfortune and None of My Own": A New History of the American West,* (Norman and London: University of Oklahoma Press, 1991; Mark Wild, *Street Meeting: Multi-Ethnic Neighborhoods in Twentieth Century Los Angeles* (Berkeley, Los Angeles, London: University of California Press, 2005).

25. Brooks, *Alien Neighbors, Foreign Friends.*

26. Charles C. Moskos, *The American Enlisted Man: The Rank and File in Today's Military.* New York: The Russell Sage Foundation, 1970.120–121; Charles C. Moskos and John Sibley Butler, *All That We Can Be: Black Leadership and Racial Integration the Army Way* (New York: Basic Books, 1996), 124.

27. *Seaside Post-News Sentinel,* June 10, 1981, 2.

28. Self, *American Babylon,* 59–60, 95.

29. Shana Bernstein, "Building Bridges at Home in a Time of Global Conflict: Interracial Cooperation and the Fight for Civil Rights in Los Angeles, 1933–1954," Ph.D. dissertation, Department of History, Stanford University, 2003, 344–345; Becky Nicolaides, *My Blue Heaven: Life and Politics in the Working Class Suburbs of Los Angeles, 1920–1965* (Chicago and London: University of Chicago Press, 2002) 322–326; Albert M. Camarillo, "Cities of Color: The New Racial Frontier in California's Minority-Majority Cities," *Pacific Historical Review,* Vol. 76, No. 1 (February 2007), 10; Leland T. Saito, *Race and Politics: Asian Americans, Latinos and Whites in a Los Angeles Suburb* (Urbana and Chicago: University of Illinois Press, 1998), 17–19.

30. Stephen Pitti, *The Devil in Silicon Valley: Northern California, Race, and Mexican Americans* (Princeton, NJ, and Oxford, UK: Princeton University Press, 2003), 128–129. Shana Bernstein analyses coalitions of Jews, Latinos, Asians, and blacks fighting for specific civil rights in Los Angeles at midcentury. Charlotte Brooks looks at the ways that Japanese and Chinese groups joined forces with whites and with African Americans to challenge segregated housing. In Seaside, although there were plenty of civil rights issues such as desegregation of housing and finding employment for black youth that brought whites, blacks, Asians, and Latinos into political coalitions, there were many more instances that included multiracial alliances on both sides—urban renewal and redevelopment, for example, which shows how individual members of various races and ethnicities worked together, and also against one another. People engaged with one another as equals, challenging racial ideologies prevalent among Americans that whites should always hold more privileged places in society and government.

31. Lori Flores, "Converging Communities in the 'Valley of the World'": Mexican Americans, Mexicans, and the Chicano Movement's Evolution in Salinas and California, 1940–1970," Ph.D. dissertation, Department of History, Stanford University, 2011.

32. Self, *American Babylon*; Albert Broussard *Black San Francisco: The Struggle for Racial Equality in the West, 1900–1954* (Lawrence: University of Kansas Press, 1993); Whitaker, *Race Work.*

33. Seaside History Project Archives. Numerous clippings and photographs in the scrapbooks of the era show both the inclusion of the military in Seaside events and efforts to control vice by city government.

34. Municipal Code of the City of Seaside, Enacted 1958, City of Seaside Archive.

35. Telephone nterview with Carl Williams, May 23, 2007, by Carol McKibben. Hereafter referred to as Williams interview.

36. Ibid.

37. Interview with Pearl Carey, May 29, 2007, Seaside by Carol McKibben. Hereafter referred to as Carey interview.

38. Ibid.

39. Interview with Morris McDaniel, October 9, 2007, Seaside by Carol McKibben. Hereafter referred to as McDaniel interview.

40. *Monterey Peninsula Herald*, Peninsula Life, n.d., 1. Parker was the church historian.

41. Interview with Cecil Bindel, past president of the Seaside NAACP, December 8, 2006, Monterey by Carol McKibben.

42. Quintard Taylor, *In Search of the Racial Frontier*; Whittaker, *Race Work*; Heather Ann Thomson, *Whose Detroit? Politics, Labor and Race in a Modern American City* (Ithaca, NY: Cornell University Press, 2001).

43. George Sánchez, *Becoming Mexican American: Ethnicity, Culture, and Identity in Chicano Los Angeles, 1900–1945* (New York: Oxford University Press, 1993), 253, 260; Albert Camarillo, *Chicanos in a Changing Society: From Mexican Pueblos to American Barrios in Santa Barbara and Southern California, 1848–1930* (Dallas, TX: Southern Methodist University Press, 1996); Brooks, *Alien Neighbors, Foreign Friends*.

44. Manuel C. Jímenez, "Letter to the Editor" *Salinas Californian*, October 15, 1943, 8.

45. Interview with Emerson Reyes, Segundo Zosa, Violeta Reyes, Tessie Malate, and Estela McKenzie April 4, 2007, Seaside by Carol McKibben.

46. Pearl Carey, autobiography, unpublished manuscript, 2007, n.p., Seaside Archive.

47. *Monterey Peninsula Herald* interview with Reverend Joseph S. Sutton, August 9, 1953. clipping file, California room, np.

48. Interview with Reverend Richard Nance, April 12, 2007, Pacific Grove by Carol McKibben.

49. Interview with Frank Eubanks, March 13, 2007, Seaside by Carol McKibben.

50. N.a. "This Is Seaside: Urchin with Muscles" *Carmel Pacific Spectator Journal*, December 2, 1955, 96.

51. Sample of property deeds covering a cross section of Monterey County, Stewart Title of California. August 8, 1941, Book 734, 66; Declaration of Establishment of Protective Restrictions December 2, 1947, Book 1019, 188, Mayfair Park, Salinas; Del Monte Company "boilerplate format" September 9, 1951, book 1329, 267; Deed recorded September 3, 1958, Book 1894, 274; Deed for property on Del Monte Fairway, September 26, 1952, book 1408, 80; In the section on restrictions for a deed dated July 6, 1964, the part on race is X'd out, and by 1965 there were big blank spaces where racial restrictions had normally been placed as category #4; Elaine D. Johnson, "Sociological Study of the Monterey Area," prepared for the city planning commission Monterey, California, October 1968, 77. Hereafter designated as Johnson report.

52. Interview with Bessie Kramer, *Monterey Peninsula Herald*, clipping, vertical file, California Room, Monterey Peninsula Library, n.d. Monterey, California.

53. Monterey Land and Hot Springs Company, July 17, 1941, Ord Terrace Subdivision, Book 734, 66. courtesy of Stewart Title Company, Monterey, California. "No persons of any race other than the Caucasian race shall use or occupy any building or any lot

NOTES TO CHAPTER THREE

in said protected area, except that this covenant shall not prevent occupancy by domestic servants of a different race domiciled with an owner or tenant."

54. Brooks, *Alien Neighbors, Foreign Friends*.

55. Interview with Anna and Charles Lee, March 12, 2007, Seaside by Carol McKibben.

56. Interview with Estela and Patrick McKenzie, November 10, 2005, Seaside, by Carol McKibben.

57. Kenneth Jackson, *Crabgrass Frontier: The Suburbanization of the United States* (New York and Oxford: Oxford University Press, 1985), 208; Self, *American Babylon*, 105; Nicolaides, *My Blue Heaven*, 156, 157, 210; Pitti, *The Devil in Silicon Valley*, 88–91; Saito, *Asian Americans, Latinos, and Whites in a Los Angeles Suburb*, 30–32.

58. Jackson, *Crabgrass Frontier*, 197.

59. Taylor, *In Search of the Racial Frontier*; Whittaker, *Race Work*, 89–126.

60. *Seaside News-Sentinel*, October 24, 1955, 1.

61. Ibid., *Election Extra*, October 25, 1955, back page.

62. Joyce interview; interview with Lenora Bean, March 25, 2006, Seaside by Carol McKibben. Hereafter referred to as Bean interview.

63. David Freund, *Colored Property: State Policy & White Racial Politics in Suburban America* (Chicago and London: University of Chicago Press, 2007), 115–117.

64. Bean interview.

65. *Seaside Post-News Sentinel*, January 26, 1956, 4 and January 31, 1956, 4.

66. Interview with Lou Haddad, September 2005, Monterey by Carol McKibben.

67. *Monterey Peninsula Herald*, November 18, 1955, 1.

68. Ibid.

69. Interview with Cecil Bindel, December 8, 2006, Monterey by Carol McKibben; Robert Miskimon, "There Are Not Enough White People Involved with Civil Rights," *The Crisis*, May 1976, 152.

70. Seaside City Council Minutes, November 3, 1955, 1.

71. See Whittaker, *Race Work*, for an analysis of the centrist, even conservative politics of civil rights leaders in Phoenix, Arizona.

72. *Monterey Peninsula Herald*, May 28, 1964, A15.

73. Self, *American Babylon*, 95;

74. Interview with Ewalker James, September 12, 2007, Seaside by Carol McKibben. Hereafter referred to as James interview.

75. Interview with Reverend Welton and Margaret McGee, April 17, 2007, Seaside by Carol McKibben. Hereafter referred to as McGee interview.

76. *Monterey Peninsula Herald*, February 15, 1956, 13.

77. Interview with Lancelot McClair September 17, 2008, Pebble Beach by Carol McKibben.

78. *Seaside Post-News Sentinel*, January 16, 1956, 12.

79. *Monterey Peninsula Herald*, February 15, 1956, 13.

80. Ibid., February 6, 1956, 13.

81. Joyce interview; *Monterey Peninsula Herald*, February 15, 1956, 13.

82. Ibid.

83. *Monterey Peninsula Herald*, February 15, 1956, 13.

84. Ibid., February 21, 1956, 2.

85. *Seaside Call-Bulletin*, May 21, 1956, n.d., Amy Stuart Scrapbook, 1956, City of Seaside Archive.

86. *Seaside Post-News Sentinel*, April 10, 1958, 1.

87. McGee interview.

88. Joyce interview, April 12, 2007.

89. Sides, L. A. *City Limits.*

90. Newspaper article from page 5 of Amy Stuart's 1960 scrapbook, titled "Citizen Bounced from Seaside City Meeting" by Fred Sorri, *Monterey Peninsula Herald,* City of Seaside Archive.

91. *Monterey Peninsula Herald*, July 22, 1959, 1.

92. Amy Stuart Scrapbook, Seaside Historical Commission, City of Seaside Archive.

93. Ibid., 1952–1954.

94. Carol Lynn McKibben, *Beyond Cannery Row: Sicilian Women, Immigration, and Community in Monterey, California, 1915–1999* (Urbana and Chicago: University of Illinois Press, 2006) 98–117.

95. *Seaside Post-NewsSentinel; Monterey Bay News*, 1941–1949.

96. *Seaside Post-News Sentinel*, January 25, 1956, 2.

97. Ibid.

98. Bean interview.

99. Interview with Luis Pérez, April 2, 2007, Seaside by Carol McKibben. Hereafter referred to as Pérez interview.

100. Richard White, *Remembering Ahanagran* (New York: Hill and Wang, 1998) 4; Perry K. Blatz, "Craftsmanship and Flexibility in Oral History: A Pluralistic Approach to Methodology and Theory," *The Public Historian* Vol. 12, No. 4 (Autumn, 1990), 7–22; Sherna Berger Gluck, Donald A. Ritchie, and Bret Eynon, "Reflections on Oral History in the New Millennium: Roundtable Comments," *The Oral History Review* Vol. 26, No. 2 (Summer, 1999), 1–27.

101. Interview with Ralph Rubio September 1, 2005, Seaside by Carol McKibben. Hereafter referred to as Rubio interview.

102. Interview with Seaside Recreation Coordinator Dave Pacheco, July 10, 2007, Seaside by Carol McKibben. Hereafter referred to as Pacheco interview.

103. Interview with Mitzi Petit, October 15, 2006, Seaside by Carol McKibben. Hereafter referred to as Petit interview.

104. Interview with Anthony Kidd, March 12, 2007, Seaside by Carol McKibben.

105. Interview with Levelle McKinney, June 26, 2007, Seaside by Carol McKibben.

106. Interview with LaShandra Roston, , October 13, 2006, Seaside by Carol McKibben.

107. Interview with Nellie West, October 13, 2006, Seaside by Carol McKibben.

108. Interview with Glenn Hanano, October 13, 2006, Seaside by Carol McKibben.

109. Moskos and Butler, *All that We Can Be*, 95–102.

CHAPTER FOUR

1. Interview with Morris McDaniel, June 27, 2007, Seaside by Carol McKibben. Hereafter referred to as McDaniel interview.

2. Andrew H. Myers, *Black White & Olive Drab: Racial Integration at Fort Jackson, South Carolina and the Civil Rights Movement* (Charlottesville and London: University of Virginia Press, 2006), 178.

3. Quoted in Rick Perlstein, *Nixonland: The Rise of a President and the Fracturing of America* (New York, London Toronto, Sydney: Scribner, 2008), 6–8.

4. For the effects of urban renewal and redevelopment on American cities see Robert O. Self, *American Babylon: Race and the Struggle for Postwar Oakland* (Princeton and Oxford: Princeton University Press, 2003); Jon C. Teaford, *The Rough Road to Renaissance: Urban Revitalization in America, 1940–1985* (Baltimore: Johns Hopkins University Press, 1990); Howard Gilette, *Between Justice and Beauty: Race, Planning, and the Failure of Urban Policy in Washington D.C.* (Philadelphia: Temple University Press, 1995).

5. Shirley Ann Wilson Moore, *To Place Our Deeds: The African American Community in Richmond, California, 1910–1963* (Berkeley: University of California Press, 2000); Albert S. Broussard, *Black San Francisco: The Struggle for Racial Equality in the West, 1900–1954* (University of Kansas Press, 1993); Josh Sides, *L.A. City Limits: African American Los Angeles from the Great Depression to the Present* (Berkeley, Los Angeles, London: University of California Press, 2003); Self, *American Babylon*.

6. Ibid.

7. Mark Brilliant, *The Color of America Has Changed: How Racial Diversity Shaped Civil Rights Reform in California, 1941–1978* (Oxford: Oxford University Press, 2010).

8. Lori Flores, "Converging Communities in the 'Valley of the World'": Mexican Americans, Mexicans, and the Chicano Movement's Evolution in Salinas and California, 1940–1970." Ph.D. dissertation, Department of History, Stanford University, in progress, chapter 6.

9. James C. McNaughton, Command Historian, "Fort Ord: A Working History," unpublished paper December 1966, 6.

10. Ibid., 9.

11. *Monterey Peninsula Herald*, March 19, 1960 clipping file, City of Seaside Archive, n.p.

12. See the Fort Ord Museum and Archive collection: https://foma.csumb.edu

13. Lieutenant General Harold G. Moore and Lieutenant Colonel Jeff M. Tuten, *Building a Volunteer Army: The Fort Ord Contribution* (Washington, DC: Department of the Army, 1975), 18.

14. Ibid., 118.

15. *About Face! The U.S. Servicemen Fund's Newsletter*, Vol. 2, No. 6, 1, 2005: http://www.sirnosir.com/archives_and_resources/library/articles/aboutface_07.html

16. Moore and Tuten, *Building a Volunteer Army*, 83.

17. *Seaside Post-News Sentinel*, June 10, 1981, 2.

18. United States Census, 1980, 1990, Area of Monterey Bay Area Governments, Marina, California.

19. J. D. Conway, *Monterey: Presidio, Pueblo and Port* (Charleston, SC: Arcadia Press, 2003),139.

20. *Monterey Peninsula Herald*, October 9, 1967, clipping file, Seaside Archives, n.p.

21. Bank of America, "Focus on Monterey County," 1967, 10, California Room, Monterey Public Library, Monterey, CA; Elaine D. Johnson, "A Sociological Study of the Monterey Area," Report prepared for the City Planning Commission, Monterey, CA, 1968, 51–52. Hereafter referred to as Johnson Report.

22. *The City of Seaside California: A Model City*, report Prepared by Development Research Associates (Los Angeles, CA, 1961), Part II, 1.

23. *Seaside Post-News Sentinel*, February 2, 1956, 5.

24. Ibid., 12.

25. *Monterey Peninsula Herald*, May 28, 1964, A16.

26. Sides, *L.A. City Limits*, 119–120.

27. Broussard, *Black San Francisco*, 142.

28. Polly J. Smith, *The Impact of Military Desegregation on Segregation Patterns in American Cities: A Case Study of Colorado Springs, New London, and Fayetteville* (Lewiston, NY, and Queenston and Lampeter, UK: The Edwin Mellen Press, 2007), 90–128, 142.

29. Interview with Saul Weingarten by Kevin Howe, "At Age 25, Seaside Is Peninsula's Largest City; Growing Pains Continue," *Monterey Peninsula Herald*, October 12, 1979, 1.

30. Johnson Report, 71.

31. Ibid.

32. Quoted in Smith, *The Impact of Military Segregation on Segregation Patterns in American Cities*, 120. See also Myers, *Black White & Olive Drab*, 174–178; Catherine Lutz, *Homefront: A Military City and the American 20th Century* (Boston: Beacon Press, 2001), 55.

33. Johnson Report, 72.

34. David Freund, *Colored Property: State Policy & White Racial Politics in Suburban America* (Chicago and London: University of Chicago Press, 2007); Charlotte Brooks, *Alien Neighbors, Foreign Friends: Asian Americans Housing, and the Transformation of Urban California* (Chicago & London: University of Chicago Press, 2009); Becky M. Nicolaides, *My Blue Heaven: Life and Politics in the Working Class Suburbs of Los Angeles, 1920–1965* (Chicago and London: The University of Chicago Press, 2002); Self, *American Babylon*.

35. "Seaside's New City Hall Open Saturday" October 15, 1966, clipping without publication, City of Seaside Archive.

36. "Introducing new chair of redevelopment for Seaside," *Monterey Peninsula Herald*, 1958, clipping file, City of Seaside Archive, Seaside, California, n.p.

37. Self, *American Babylon*, 139–140; David Freund, *Colored Property*.

38. Interview with Richard Goblirsch, April 4, 2008, Seaside by Carol McKibben. Hereafter referred to as Goblirsch interview.

39. Interview with Richard Joyce, April 5, 2007, Seaside by Carol McKibben. Hereafter referred to as Joyce interview.

40. Self, *American Babylon*, 220–255; Stephen Pitti, *The Devil in Silicon Valley: Northern California, Race, and Mexican Americans* (Princeton and Oxford: Princeton University Press, 2003), 148–172.

41. Nathan Connolly, "By Eminent Domain: Race and Capital in the Building of an American South Florida," Ph.D. dissertation, University of Michigan, 2008.

42. Self, *American Babylon*, 139–140; Robert W. Cherney and William Issel, *San Francisco: Presidio, Port and Pacific Metropolis* (San Francisco: Boyd & Fraser, 1981); Chester W. Hartman, *Yerba Buena: Land Grab and Community Resistance in San Francisco* (San Francisco: Glide Publications, 1974).

43. Final Report, Redevelopment Agency of the City of Seaside, n.d., Noche Buena Project California R-27.

44. Goblirsch interview.

45. Planning Commission Report, City of Seaside Archives, 1965.

46. Seaside City Council Minutes, May 7, 1959.

47. Final Report, Redevelopment Agency of the City of Seaside, n.d., Noche Buena Project California R-27. "The project area was inhabited by approximately 1,100 persons and contained approximately 339 dwelling units. Two hundred forty-one of these dwelling

units have been conserved or rehabilitated by being brought up to city standards. Twenty units have been moved outside the project area and seventy-seven which were hopelessly sub-standard have been purchased and removed. One unity was eliminated through code enforcement. The cleared and vacant land was then redivided into larger sized lots."

48. Final Report, Redevelopment Agency of the City of Seaside, n.d., Noche Buena Project California R-27.

49. *Monterey Peninsula Herald*, May 28, 1964, A13; Final Report, Redevelopment Agency of the City of Seaside, n.d., Noche Buena Project California R-27.

50. Joyce interview.

51. Self, *American Babylon,* 139–144.

52. Ibid., 140.

53. Interview by Carol McKibben with Carl Williams by telephone, May 23, 2007, hereafter referred to as Williams interview.

54. Nicolaides, *My Blue Heaven*; Becky Nicolaides and Andrew Wiese, eds., *The Suburb Reader* (New York and London: Routledge, 2006); Wiese, *Places of Their Own: African American Suburbanization in the Twentieth Century* (Chicago and London: University of Chicago Press, 2004); Kenneth T. Jackson, *Crabgrass Frontier: The Suburbanization of the United States* (New York and Oxford: Oxford University Press, 1985); Dolores Hayden, *Building Suburbia, Green Fields and Urban Growth, 1820–2000* (New York: Vintage Books. 2004).

55. Quintard Taylor, *In Search of the Racial Frontier.*

56. Final Report, Redevelopment Agency of the City of Seaside, n.d., Noche Buena Project California R-27.

57. Self, *American Babylon,* 140.

58. Williams interview.

59. Final Report, Redevelopment Agency of the City of Seaside, n.d., Noche Buena Project California R-27.

60. Seaside City Council Meeting Minutes, May 7, 1959, Office of the City Clerk, Seaside.

61. Ibid.

62. Planning Commission Report, City of Seaside Archives, 1965.

63. *Monterey Peninsula Herald*, October 26, 1966, clipping file, Seaside Archives.

64. Ibid.

65. Joyce interview.

66. Interview with Presentacion Larot, Ildefonsa Barron, Brenda Cendaria, and Virginia Nobida, June 16, 2008, Seaside by Carol McKibben.

67. Johnson Report, 71.

68. Goblirsch interview.

69. *Seaside Story: Redevelopment, 1960–1970, Seaside California,* n.p. n.d., brochure produced by Seaside Redevelopment Agency, Merrifield C. Beck, Chair.

70. Williams interview.

71. Interview with Mike Harston, Stewart Title Company, Monterey, California, June 15, 2007, by Carol McKibben.

72. For a recent analysis of this phenomenon see Beryl Satter, *Family Properties, Race, Real Estate, and the Exploitation of Black America* (New York: Metropolitan Books/ Henry Holt & Co., 2009).

73. Goblirsch interview.

74. Interview with Don Drummond, Carmel Valley, June 15, 2006, by Carol McKibben.

75. Interview with Saul Weingarten, by Joel Herzog, July 7, 1988, City of Seaside Archive, Seaside. Hereafter referred to as Weingarten interview.

76. Weingarten interview.

77. *Monterey Peninsula Herald*, February, 1966, clipping file, Seaside Archive.

78. Ibid., December, 1966, clipping file, Seaside Archive.

79. Ibid.

80. Interview with Mitzi Petit, October 15, 2006, Seaside by Carol McKibben.

81. Self, *American Babylon*, 139–140.

82. Perlstein, *Nixonland*, 3–12.

83. Self, *American Babylon*, 229.

84. Albert M. Camarillo, *Chicanos in California: A History of Mexican Americans in California* (Sparks, NV: Materials for Today's Learning, 1990), 85–103; Pitti, *The Devil in Silicon Valley*, 162, 178–185; Flores, "Converging Communities in the 'Valley of the World,'" chapter 6.

85. Ibid, 16.

86. Herb Caen, *The San Francisco Chronicle*, May 15, 1967, clipping file, Seaside Archives.

87. Ibid., May 18, 1967.

88. "Annexation of Family Housing Areas of Fort Ord to City of Seaside," unpublished Seaside City Council Report, Lou Haddad, Mayor, December 1967, 7, City of Seaside Archives. Hereafter referred to as Haddad Papers.

89. *San Francisco Sunday Examiner and Chronicle*, May 28, 1967, 22.

90. *Monterey Peninsula Herald*, February 27, 1968, 27.

91. Interview with Lou Haddad, September 2005, Monterey by Carol McKibben. Haddad Papers, Seaside Archive, 51.

92. Ibid, 52.

93. *Seaside Story: Redevelopment 1960–1970: Seaside California*, back page.

94. Haddad interview.

95. Haddad Papers, 50.

96. Interview by Carol McKibben with Oscar Lawson March 12, 2007, by telephone.

97. *San Francisco Sunday Examiner and Chronicle*, May 28, 1967, 22; Haddad interview.

98. Deborah Gray White, *Too Heavy a Load: Black Women in Defense of Themselves, 1894–1994* (New York: W. W. Norton, 1999), 11–18; Matthew C. Whitaker, *Race Work: The Rise of Civil Rights in the Urban West* (Lincoln: University of Nebraska Press, 2005), 25–61,102; Stephanie Shaw, *What a Woman Ought to Be and Do: Black Professional Women Workers During the Jim Crow Era* (Chicago: University of Chicago Press, 1996), 4–10; Darlene Clark Hine and Kathleen Thompson, *A Shining Thread of Hope: The History of Black Women in America* (New York: Broadway Books, 1998), 205–208.

99. Paul R. Dimond, *Beyond Busing: Relections on Urban Segregation, the Courts and Equal Opportunity* (Ann Arbor: University of Michigan Press, 2005); Joseph T. Durham, "Sense and Nonsense About Busing," *The Journal of Negro Education*, Vol. 42, No. 3, Education in the Black Cities, Summer, 1973, 325–326; Perlstein, *Nixonland*, 133–135.

100. Pitti, *The Devil in Silicon Valley*, 163.

101. Jack Schneider, "Escape From Los Angeles: White Flight From Los Angeles and its Schools," *Journal of Urban History*, Vol. 34, No. 6, 1000–1003; Nicolaides, *My Blue Heaven*, 325; Sides, *L.A. City Limits*, 195–196.

102. Nicolaides, *My Blue Heaven*, 294–302.

103. Self, *American Babylon*, 199–201.

104. For examples of school segregation and efforts by civil rights activists to fight it outside of California, see Whitaker, *Race Work*, 217; Heather Ann Thompson, *Whose Detroit? Politics, Labor and Race in a Modern American City* (Ithaca, NY: Cornell University Press, 2001) 20–21, 45.

105. Johnson Report, 88.

106. Ibid., 137, 138

107. Interview with Dr. Charlie Mae Knight, February 2, 2007, Palo Alto, California by Carol McKibben.

108. *Seaside Metro Reporter*, week of March 12–17, 1973, 1.

109. *Seaside Post-News Sentinel*, May 17, 1978, 1.

110. Matthew D. Lassiter, *The Silent Majority: Suburban Politics in the Sunbelt South* (Princeton: Princeton University Press, 2006); Thompson, *Whose Detroit?* 45.

111. Ibid.

112. Nicolaides, *My Blue Heaven*, 294; Lassiter, *The Silent Majority*; White, *Too Heavy a Load*; Hine and Thompson, *A Shining Thread of Hope*.

113. Kevin A. Kruse, *White Flight: Atlanta and the Making of Modern Conservatism* (Politics and Society in Twentieth Century America, Princeton, NJ: Princeton University Press, 2005).

114. Brooks, *Alien Neighbors Foreign Friends*, 239.

115. Ibid.

116. Johnson Report, 36.

117. Voting in Monterey County was tallied at 36,849 for, 26,593 against—Johnson Report, 78–79, 81.

118. *Monterey Peninsula Herald*, October 26, 1966, clipping file, Seaside Archives.

119. Interview with Mae Johnson, October 15, 2005, Seaside by Carol McKibben.

120. Ibid., 81.

121. John H. Denton, *Apartheid American Style* (Berkeley: University of California Press, 1967); James Kushner, "Apartheid in America: An Historical and Legal Analysis of Contemporary Racial Residential Segregation in the United States," *Howard Law Journal*, 22, (1979).

122. Self, *American Babylon*, 167–168.

123. Nicolaides, *My Blue Heaven*, 307.

124. Pitti, *The Devil in Silicon Valley*, 130.

125. Flores, "Converging Communities in the 'Valley of the World,'" chapter 6, 8.

126. Brooks, *Alien Neighbors, Foreign Friends*, 220.

127. Thompson, *Whose Detroit?* 17–21; Whittaker, *Race Work*, 104–112.

128. Ibid; Sides, *L.A. City Limit*.

129. *Monterey Peninsula Herald*, July 19, 1968, and July 20, 1968, clipping file, Seaside Archives.

130. J. Morgan Kousser, "Tacking, Stacking, and Cracking: Race and Reapportionment in Monterey County, 1981–1992," A Report for *Gonzalez v. Monterey County Board of Supervisors*, September 9, 1992.

131. *Monterey Peninsula Herald*, July 19, 1968, and July 20, 1968, clipping file, Seaside Archive; Interview with Anna and Charles Lee, March 12, 2007, Seaside by Carol McKibben.

132. Interviews with Mae Johnson, Helen Rucker, Ewalker James, Don Jordan, Reverand Nance, Reverend McGee, Richard Joyce, Dr. Charlie Mae Knight, and many others. Also, responses from random interviews at Seaside birthday party, October 13, 2006, and at Seaside Boys and Girls Club Senior Prom, May 19, 2007, with individuals who lived in Seaside in the 1950s and 1960s.

133. Interview with Janna Ottman, April 17, 2009, Seaside by Carol McKibben.

134. Quintard Taylor, *In Search of the Racial Frontier: African Americans in the West, 1528–1990* (New York: W. W. Norton, 1998); Whittaker, *Race Work;* Mark Brilliant, *The Color of America Has Changed: How Racial Diversity Shaped Civil Rights Reform in California, 1941–1978* (Oxford: Oxford University Press, 2010).

135. David M. Kennedy and Lizabeth Cohen, *An American Pageant: A History of the Republic* (Boston: Houghton Mifflin, 2002); Self, *American Babylon*, 198–214.

136. Interview with Reverend Welton McGee, April 17, 2007, Seaside by Carol McKibben. Hereafter referred to as McGee interview.

137. Interview with Cecil Bindel, December 14, 2006, Monterey by Carol McKibben; Carey interview.

138. Robert Miskimon, "There Are Not Enough White People Involved with Civil Rights," *The Crisis*, May, 1976, 153; Bindel interview.

139. Interview by Carol McKibben with Pearl Carey May 29, 2007, Seaside. hereafter referred to as Carey interview.

140. Johnson Report, 66.

141. Ibid., 63

142. Ibid., 66.

143. Wiese, *Places of Their Own.*

144. Interviews with Jackie Craighead January 17, 2006, Carmel; Al Glover, February 2, 2006, Seaside; Ewalker James, September 12, 2007, Seaside; Mae Johnson, October 15, 2005, December 19, 2006, Seaside by Carol McKibben; Don Jordan, October 2005, Seaside by Carol McKibben and Albert M. Camarillo; Knight interview; McDaniel interview; Ruthie Watts interview July 21, 2007, Seaside; Williams interview.

145. Whitaker, *Race Work*, 182–184.

146. Interview with Presentacion Larot, Ildefonsa Barron, Brenda Cendaria, and Virginia Nobida, June 16, 2008, Seaside by Carol McKibben.

147. Brilliant, *The Color of America Has Changed.*

148. Flores, "Converging Communities in the 'Valley of the World,'" chapter 6, 8.

149. Interview with Rudolfo Nava, February 28, 2007, Seaside, by Carol McKibben. Hereafter referred to as Nava interview.

150. Interview with William Meléndez, January 30, 2007, Monterey by Carol McKibben.

151. Carey interview.

152. Interview with Pearl Carey, *Monterey Peninsula Herald* May 8, 1970, clipping file, Seaside Archive.

153. Ibid., April 7, 1972, 18.

154. Interview with Charles McNeely, August 9, 2007, by telephone by Carol McKibben; Seaside City Council Minutes, 1975–1985.

155. Ibid., January 17, 1980; *Monterey Peninsula Herald*, January 18, 1980, clipping file, Seaside Archive.

156. *Monterey Peninsula Herald*, February 6, 1980, clipping file, Seaside Archive.

157. See Thomas A. Guglielmo, *White on Arrival: Italians, Race and Power in Chicago, 1890–1945* (New York: Oxford University Press, 2003).

158. *Seaside Post-New Sentinel*, August 11, 1982, 1.

159. Ibid., January 23, 1980, 2.

160. *Monterey Peninsula Herald*, January 24, 1980, 24.

161. See Whitaker, *Race Work*, 199–221; Thompson, *Whose Detroit?* 98–102.

162. McDaniel interview; petition to recall Haddad and documents, Monterey County Elections office, Salinas.

163. *Seaside Post-News Sentinel*, October 24, 1979, 1; McDaniel interview.

164. Interview with Lou Haddad, *Monterey Peninsula Herald*, January 22, 1980, 1.

165. McDaniel interview.

166. Ibid.

167. Ibid.

168. *Seaside Weekly Tribune*, February 28, 1980, 1.

169. Flores, "Converging Communities in the 'Valley of the World,'" chapter 6, 8.

170. Interview with Mel Mason, October 8, 2007, Seaside by Carol McKibben.

171. *Seaside Tribune*, interview with Roger Kemp and Clarence Campbell, July 10, 1980, clipping file, Seaside Archives.

172. Ibid.

173. *Seaside Post-News-Sentinel*, Interview with Clarence Campbell, February 27, 1980, clipping file Seaside Archives.

174. *Seaside Post-News Sentinel*, September 30, 1980, 1.

175. Ibid., December 30, 1981; interview with Ewalker James, September 12, 2007, Seaside by Carol McKibben.

176. *Seaside Post-News Sentinel*, July 15, 1981, 1.

177. Moore and Tuten, *Building a Volunteer Army*, 48.

178. Ibid., 117.

CHAPTER FIVE

1. Matthew C. Whitaker, *Race Work: The Rise of Civil Rights in the Urban West* (Lincoln: University of Nebraska Press, 2005), 134–136.

2. Interview with Billy De Berry, August 6, 2007, Seaside by Carol McKibben. Hereafter referred to as DeBerry interview.

3. Paul A. Jargowsky, "Ghetto Poverty Among Blacks in the 1980s," *Journal of Policy Analysis and Management*, Vol. 13., No. 2 (spring, 1994), 288; John Kasard, "Urban Industrial Transition and the Urban Underclass," *Annals of the American Academy of Political and Social Science*, January 1989, 26–47; Douglas S. Massey and Nancy A. Denton, "Trends in the Residential Segregation of Blacks, Hispanics, and Asians, 1970–1980," *American Sociological Review*, 52, 1987, 802–825; William Julius Wilson, *The Truly Disadvantaged: The Inner City, the Underclass, and Public Policy* (Chicago: University of Chicago Press, 1987); Albert M. Camarillo, "Blacks, Latinos and the New Racial Frontier in American Cities of Color: California's Emerging Minority-Majority Cities," in Kenneth L. Kusmer and Joe W. Trotter, *African American Urban History Since World War II* (Chicago University of Chicago Press, 2009), 39–59; Robert O. Self, *American Babylon: Race and the Struggle for Postwar Oakland*, (Princeton and Oxford: Princeton University Press. 2003), 211.

4. Interview with Jackie Craighead, January 17, 2006, Carmel, by Carol McKibben. Hereafter referred to as Craighead interview.

5. See Heather Thompson, *Whose Detroit? Politics, Labor, and Race in a Modern American City* (Ithaca, NY: Cornell University Press, 2001), 192–216; Whitaker, *Race Work*, 253–255.

6. Interview with Morris and Bobbie McDaniel, October 9, 2007, Seaside by Carol McKibben.

7. Elaine Tyler May, "Security Against Democracy: The Legacy of the Cold War at Home," OAH Presidential Address, April 10, 2010, Washington, DC. Source: No byline, "Crime: The Shape of Fear," *The Economist*, November 29, 1980, 36. For crime and population, see Bureau of Justice Statistics, *Crime and Justice Data Online*, http://bjs.ojp.usdoj .gov/dataonline/Search/Crime/State/RunCrimeTrendsInOneVar.cfm (accessed February 17, 2010); and Susan B. Carter et al., eds., "Table Aa6–8: Population: 1790–2000 [Annual estimates]," *Historical Statistics of the United States: Millennial Edition Online* (New York: Cambridge University Press, 2006), http://hsus.cambridge.org (accessed March 16, 2010).

8. Ibid.

9. *Seaside Tribune*, February 4, 1982, 1.

10. Interview with Ruthie Watts, July 21, 2007, Seaside by Carol McKibben.

11. *Seaside Post-News Sentinel*, June 8, 1982, 3.

12. Catherine Lutz. *Homefront: A Military City and the American 20th Century* (Boston: Beacon Press, 2001), 208–209. For evidence of the same exaggerated reporting of racial conflict in minority-majority cities see Albert M. Camarillo, "Cities of Color: The New Racial Frontier in California's Minority-Majority Cities," *Pacific Historical Review*, Vol. 76, No.1 (February, 2007), 1.

13. Richard White, *Remembering Ahanagran* (New York: Hill and Wang, 1998) 4; Perry K. Blatz, "Craftsmanship and Flexibility in Oral History: A Pluralistic Approach to Methodology and Theory," *The Public Historian*, Vol. 12, No. 4 (Autumn, 1990), 7–22; Sherna Berger Gluck, Donald A. Ritchie, and Bret Eynon, "Reflections on Oral History in the New Millennium: Roundtable Comments," *The Oral History Review*, Vol. 26, No. 2 (Summer, 1999), 1–27.

14. *Monterey Peninsula Herald*, September 29, 1991, A10.

15. *Seaside Post-News Sentinel*, August 4, 1982, 1.

16. DeBerry interview.

17. City of Seaside Budget for fiscal year 1983–1984, Office of the Finance Director, Seaside City Hall, 3, 58.

18. U.S. Inspector Generals Report, 1979, cited in Lutz, *Homefront*, 295.

19. City of Seaside Annual Budget, 1987–1988, Office of the Finance Director, Seaside City Hall, 104–106.

20. Ibid., 1989–1990, 103.

21. Ibid., May 12, 1982, 1.

22. Ibid., May 26, 1982, 1.

23. Interview with Nancy Amos, September 25, 2007, Seaside by Carol McKibben.

24. Citizens Against Drugs/Crime in Seaside, A NonProfit Organization By-Laws, City of Seaside Archive.

25. City of Seaside Annual Budget, Office of the Finance Director, Seaside City Hall, 1988–1989, 111.

26. Ibid., 1989–1990, 103, 109.

27. Ibid., 1991–1992, 113.

28. According to FBI Crime reports Monterey had 414 burglaries in 1995 and Seaside had 163.

29. Amos interview.

30. Lutz, *Homefront*, 206–209.

31. Andrew H. Myers, *Black White & Olive Drab: Racial Integration at fort Jackson, South Carolina and the Civil Rights Movement* (Charlottesville and London: University of Virginia Press, 2006), 31–42.

32. Polly J. Smith *The Impact of Military Desegregation on Segregation Patterns in American Cities: A Case Study of Colorado Springs, New London, and Fayetteville* (Lewiston, NY, Queenston and Lampeter, UK: The Edwin Mellen Press, 2007), 33; Douglass S. Massey and Nancy A. Denton, *American Apartheid: Segregation and the Making of the Underclass* (Cambridge, MA: Harvard University Press, 1993); Camarillo, "Blacks, Latinos and the New Racial Frontier in American Cities of Color," 39–59.

33. Tim Wadsworth, "Is Immigration Responsible for the Crime Drop? An Assessment of the Influence of Immigration on Violent Crime Between 1990 and 2000," *Social Science Quarterly*, Vol. 91, No. 2, June 2010, 532–533; Alfred Blumstein and Joel Wallman, "The Recent Rise and Fall of American Violence," in Alfred Blumstein and Joel Wallman, eds., *The Crime Drop in America* (New York: Cambridge University Press, 2000).

34. Deborah Gray White, *Too Heavy a Load: Black Women in Defense of Themselves, 1894–1994* (New York: W. W. Norton, 1999), 11–18; Whitaker, *Race Work*, 25–61, 102; Stephanie Shaw, *What a Woman Ought to Be and Do: Black Professional Women Workers During the Jim Crow Era* (Chicago: University of Chicago Press, 1996), 4–10; Darlene Clark Hine and Kathleen Thompson, *A Shining Thread of Hope: The History of Black Women in America* (New York: Broadway Books, 1998), 205–208; Gretchen Lemke-Santangelo, *Abiding Courage: African American Migrant Women and the East Bay Community* (Chapel Hill and London: University of North Carolina Press, 1996), 153–177.

35. Interview with Rodolfo Nava February 28, 2007, Seaside by Carol McKibben.

36. Charlotte Brooks, *Alien Neighbors, Foreign Friends: Asian Americans Housing, and the Transformation of Urban California* (Chicago and London: University of California Press, 2009), 171.

37. The JACL contested the Alien Land Law of 1914 and California's Alien Land Act of 1918, which forbid Japanese, even Nisei citizens, from owning land; the Supreme Court ruling in *Takeo Ozawa v. United States* in 1920 that naturalization would be limited to "free white persons and aliens of African nativity" excluding Asians from citizenship; the 1922 Cable Act specific to Japanese that would force any woman who married an Issei (first generation Japanese immigrant) to lose her citizenship forever, in contrast to Caucasian women who could regain their citizenship on the death or divorce of their noncitizen husbands. The law was amended in 1931, thanks to the efforts of the JACL, to allow Nisei women (second generation U.S.) citizens to retain citizenship even when married to Issei men, then repealed altogether in 1936. The JACL vehemently protested the 1924 Immigration Exclusion Act that barred all immigration from Japan. See Ronald T. Takaki, *Strangers from a Different Shore: A History of Asian Americans* (Boston: Little, Brown, 1998).

38. The first Buddhist Temple was lost in a fire in 1971 then rebuilt and dedicated at the same location in 1977.

39. Interview with Andrew "Andy" Yoshiyama, May 1, 2007, Seaside by Carol McKibben. Hereafter referred to as Yoshiyama interview; interview with Larry Oda,

President, National Japanese American Citizens League, May 29, 2007, Seaside by Carol McKibben. Hereafter referred to as Oda interview; David T. Yamada and Oral History Committee, MP/JACL, *The Japanese of the Monterey Peninsula: Their History and Legacy, 1895–1995* (Monterey, CA: Japanese American Citizens League, 1995), especially chapters 1–3, and 176. See also Sandy Lydon, *The Japanese in the Monterey Bay Region: A Brief History* (Capitola, CA: Capitola Book Company, 1997), chapter 4.

40. Leland Saito, *Race and Politics, Asian Americans, Latinos, and Whites in a Los Angeles Suburb* (Urbana and Chicago: University of Illinois Press, 1998), 32, 64.

41. Interview with Emerson and Violeta Reyes, Segundo Zosa, Patrick and Estela McKenzie, Phil and Tessie Malate, April 4, 2007, Seaside, by Carol McKibben.

42. Interview with David Pacheco, July 10, 2007, Seaside by Carol McKibben. Hereafter referred to as Pacheco interview; lists of vendors, 1995–2000 flyers from Cinco De Mayo with sponsorships, City of Seaside Events Folder, City of Seaside Archive.

43. White, *Too Heavy a Load*; Whitaker, *Race Work*, 103.

44. Ibid.

45. Monterey Peninsula–Salinas Pan-Hellenic Council Calendar of Events, 1977–1978, City of Seaside Archive, Seaside.

46. McDaniel interview.

47. *Seaside Post-News Sentinel* February 15, 1978, 6; McDaniel interview.

48. DeBerry interview.

49. The names of the original board of directors are as follows. Many of them continue to serve on the board today. (e.g., current President is Billy DeBerry): Ltc. (Ret) Morris McDaniel, president, Josh Stewart, vice president, Martin Puentes, secretary, Gus Lewis, treasurer, Warren Williams, legal counsel, Billie DeBerry, Dr. Henry Hutchins, Dr. Elijah Brandon, Supervisor Sam Karas, Elmer Phillips, Jim Manning, Franklin Washington, Col. (Ret) Otis Jones, Ron Harold, William Jackson, and Rubin Simpson.

50. McDaniel interview.

51. Susan Saulny, "No Cinderella Story, No Ball, No Black Debutante," *New York Times*, March 2, 2006. Available at www.nytimes.com/2006/03/02/national/nationalspecial/02debs.html.

52. McDaniel interview.

53. *Monterey Peninsula Herald*, September 8, 1971, 30.

54. Ibid.; Watts interview.

55. McDaniel interview.

56. Knight interview; Watts interviews; observation Seaside History Project.

57. Interview with Jerry Thorne, Bed Races organizer, March 16, 2009, Seaside, by Carol McKibben.

58. Report by Women's International League for Peace and Freedom, 1970 Parade Reject Applications, City of Seaside Parks and Recreation Folder, Box 2 Folder 7, City of Seaside Archive.

59. Ibid.

60. Pacheco interview.

61. Events Folder, Oldemeyer Center Collection City of Seaside Archive; Pacheco interview, Meléndez interview.

62. Jessica Lyons and Andrew Scutro, "Judge Orders Lusk Trial," *Monterey County Weekly*, January 24, 2002, 1.

63. Interview with Reverend Wilton McGee, April 17, 2007, Seaside by Carol McKibben.

64. Interview with Oscar Lawson, March 12, 2007, by telephone by Carol McKibben.

65. Interview with Lancelot McClair, September 17, 2008, Pebble Beach by Carol McKibben

66. Ibid.

67. Joe Livernois, "Pastor admits to theft," *Monterey Peninsula Herald*, May 15, 2003, B1.

68. Ibid.

69. Telephone interview with Charles McNeely, August 9, 2007, by Carol McKibben. Reno, Nevada.

70. McDaniel interview.

71. Ibid.

72. *Seaside Post-News Sentinel*, January 27, 1982, 3.

73. *Monterey Peninsula Herald*, February 4, 1983, 4.

74. E-mail from Mel Mason to Carol McKibben, October 9, 2007.

75. McClair interview.

76. E-mail from Mel Mason to Carol McKibben, October 9, 2007.

77. Interview with Ewalker James, September 12, 2007, Seaside by Carol McKibben.

78. Interview with Lou Haddad, September 2005, Monterey by Carol McKibben.

79. Interview with Bud Houser, February 12, 2008, Seaside by Carol McKibben.

80. Ibid. This is drawn from the Seaside Archive, which contains a collection of campaign literature by city council members in which they list their qualifications, backgrounds, and military affiliation along with their rank. It is filed under each member's name.

81. Interview with Diana Ingersoll, September 2005, Seaside by Carol McKibben.

82. Craighead interview.

83. Watts interview.

84. *Seaside Post-News Sentinel*, June 27, 1991, 5.

85. Thompson, *Whose Detroit?*

86. Mason interview; Self, *American Babylon*, 220–242.

87. *Monterey Peninsula Herald*, April 8, 1992, 1A, 14A.

88. *Monterey Peninsula Herald*, April 8, 1992, .1A, 14A.

89. J. Morgan Kousser, "Tacking, Stacking, and Cracking: Race and Reapportionment in Monterey County, 1981–1992," a report for *Gonzalez v. Monterey County Board of Supervisors*, September 9, 1992, 114; interview with Elaine Cass, March 11, 2008, Seaside by Carol McKibben.

90. *Monterey Peninsula Herald*, September 16, 1992, 1.

91. Kousser, "Tacking, Stacking, and Cracking," 114–115.

92. Ibid., 57.

93. City of Seaside, Annual Budget Message, Office of the Finance Director, Seaside City Hall, August 5, 1983, 5.

94. Ibid.

95. City of Seaside, Alternative Budget Revenue Measures, August 5, 1983, Office of the Finance Director, Seaside City Hall, 4; interview with former City Attorney Elaine Cass, March 11, 2008 by Carol McKibben. According to Cass, the senior exemption was not approved by the finance director but was accidently included in public disclosures of the utility tax proposal. As a consequence, the city council unanimously decided to allow the exemption.

96. City of Seaside, Alternative Budget Revenue Measures, August 5, 1983, 6.

97. *Monterey Peninsula Herald*, July 5, 1992, B4.

98. Letter to the Mayor and City Council from City Manager Charles McNeely, contained in the 1984/85 City Budget, Office of the Finance Director, Seaside City Hall, 4.

99. Annual Budget Message, 1985/86, Office of the Finance Director, Seaside City Hall, 5.

100. *Monterey Peninsula Herald*, August 10, 1983, 21.

101. Ibid., August 19, 1983.

102. Glover interview.

103. Ibid.

104. McClair interview; interview with Congressman Sam Farr, May 29, 2008, Seaside by Carol McKibben.

105. *Monterey Peninsula Herald*, November 4, 1984, 1.

106. Ibid., 1.

107. Joyce interview and Joyce Scrapbook, City of Seaside Archive.

108. Dolores Hayden, *Building Suburbia, Green Fields and Urban Growth, 1820–2000*, (New York: Vintage Books, 2004), 175–179.

109. *Monterey Peninsula Herald*, November 4, 1984, 4.

110. Letter to the Mayor and City Council from Charles McNeely, contained in the 1991–1992 City Budget, Office of the Finance Director, Seaside City Hall, 4.

111. *Monterey Peninsula Herald*, July 5, 1992, B4.

CHAPTER SIX

1. Anne Markusen, Peter Hall, Scott Campbell, and Sabina Dietrich, *The Rise of the Gunbelt: The Military Remapping of Industrial America* (New York: Oxford University Press, 1991).

2. Polly J. Smith *The Impact of Military Desegregation on Segregation Patterns in American Cities: A Case Study of Colorado Springs, New London, and Fayetteville* (Lewiston, NY, Queenston and Lampeter, UK: The Edwin Mellen Press, 2007), 56.

3. Interview with Ewalker James (Citizens League for Progress), September 12, 2007, Seaside by Carol McKibben; interview with Helen Rucker May 12, 2008, Seaside by Carol McKibben; Interview with Ruthie Watts (NAACP), July 21, 2007, Seaside by Carol McKibben.

4. James interview.

5. Albert M. Camarillo, "Blacks, Latinos and the New Racial Frontier in American Cities of Color: California's Emerging Minority-Majority Cities," in Kenneth L. Kusmer and Joe W. Trotter, *African American Urban History Since World War II* (Chicago: University of Chicago Press, 2009), 39–59.

6. Interview with Al Glover, October 3, 2006, Seaside by Carol McKibben.

7. 1995 City of Seaside General Plan, D'Amico and Associates, Inc.; Land Use Associates; Goldfarb and Lipman; Licciardello and Associates; TJKM, Office of the Director of Finance, Seaside City Hall, 5.

8. Interview with Ray Corpuz, October 10, 2007, Seaside by Carol McKibben.

9. Jon C. Teaford, *Post-Suburbia: Government and Politics in Edge Cities* (Baltimore: The Johns Hopkins University Press, 1996), 86; Mark Wild identified the term, *edge cities*, as originating with Tom Wolf, *Electric Kool Aid Acid Test*.

10. Teaford, 124.

11. Catherine Lutz, *Homefront: A Military City and the American 20th Century* (Boston: Beacon Press, 2001), 214

12. Ibid.

13. Ibid.

14. Markusen, Hall, Campbell, and Dietrich, *The Rise of the Gunbelt.*

15. Letter to the Mayor and City Council from Charles McNeely, contained in the 1991/1992 City Budget, Office of the Director of Finance, Seaside City Hall, 1.

16. Teaford, *Post-Suburbia*, 125.

17. *Monterey Peninsula Herald*, July 5, 1992, B4.

18. Interview with Tom Mancini, July 14, 2007, Seaside by Carol McKibben.

19. *Monterey Peninsula Herald*, July 5, 1992, B4.

20. Ibid., B5.

21. Teaford, *Post-Suburbia*, 125.

22. Interview with Jerry Smith September 2005, Salinas by Carol McKibben. Hereafter cited as Smith interview; Rucker interview.

23. Interview with Don Jordan, October 2005, Seaside by Carol McKibben. Hereafter cited as Jordan interview.

24. "L. A. Developer Eyes Seaside's Future," *Monterey Peninsula Herald* June 8, 1997, A1.

25. Annual Budget Letter for fiscal Year 1995–1996, July 21, 1995, 1.

26. Ibid.

27. Report by Association of Monterey Bay Area Governments Draft regional Population and Employment forecast, October, 1991, Marina, California.

28. Interview with Daphne Hodgson, Deputy City Manager and Finance Director, City of Seaside, based on data from the State Department of Finance and Seaside City Budgets, September 19, 2008 by Carol McKibben.

29. Daphne Hodgson, Deputy City Manager and Finance Director, City of Seaside, based on data from the State Department of Finance and Seaside City Budgets, September 19, 2008.

30. Teaford, *Post-Suburbia*, 210; interview with Lancelot McClair, September 17, 2008, Pebble Beach by Carol McKibben; Rucker interview; Smith interview; Jordan interview; interview with Ralph Rubio, September 5, 2005, Seaside by Carol McKibben.

31. Interview with Congressman Sam Farr, May 29, 2008, Seaside by Carol McKibben. Hereafter referred to as Farr interview.

32. Ibid.

33. Tim Brown e-mail to Carol McKibben, August 3, 2008.

34. Interview with Don Jordan, November 1, 2010, Seaside by Carol McKibben

35. Farr interview.

36. Tim Brown e-mail to Carol McKibben, August 3, 2008.

37. Tim Brown, City of Seaside Budget Narrative, Office of the director of Finance, Seaside City Hall, 1995–1996; Jordan interview.

38. *Monterey Peninsula Herald*, June 8 1997, A14.

39. The Sierra Club of Monterey County sponsored a referendum in 1996 called Measure "M," which decreed that neither hotels nor shopping centers could be allowed on Rancho San Carlos land in Carmel Valley, a 20,000 tract that included about thirty homes, a historic "hacienda," and a golf course. After a fierce political battle in which many

Seasiders weighed in opposing the measure, the referendum passed, limiting development to 2,000 acres and leaving 18,000 acres as a permanent wildlife preserve.

40. Annual budget Letter for fiscal Year 1995–96, July 21, 1995, 2.

41. Interview with Estela and Patrick McKenzie April 23, 2007, Seaside by Carol McKibben.

42. Jordan interview.

43. Ibid.

44. *Monterey Peninsula Herald*, June 30, 1996, 1A.

45. Ibid., October 24, 1996.

46. Ibid. June 30, 1996, A18; Jordan interview.

47. Alex Hulanicki, "New golf course owners promise improvements" *Monterey Peninsula Herald*, November 3, 1996, 1A, 11A.

48. Ibid., 11A.

49. Jordan interview.

50. Alex Hulanicki, "Seaside promises free water for Ord golf courses," *Monterey Peninsula Herald*, November 5, 1996, 1A.

51. Ibid.

52. Jordan interview.

53. Minutes Seaside City Council Meeting, October 23, 1996, City of Seaside City Hall.

54. Kevin Roderick, Editor's blog: http://www.laobserved.com/archive/2004/03/danny_bakewell.php.

55. Rubio interview.

56. E-mail from Tim Brown to Carol McKibben, August 3, 2008.

57. "L. A. Developer Eyes Seaside's Future," *Monterey Peninsula Herald* June 8, 1997, A8.

58. Ibid.

59. Richard Pitnick, "Once and Future King?" *Coast Weekly*, September 5, 1996, 9.

60. *Monterey Peninsula Herald*, October 21, 1996, 5A.

61. Ibid.

62. Rubio interview; Smith interview.

63. Paul Lewis, *Shaping Suburbia: How Political Institutions Organize Urban Development* (Pittsburgh, PA: University of Pittsburgh Press, 1996).

64. Alex Hulanicki, "Police to picket for parity," *Monterey Peninsula Herald*, February 6, 1997, C1, C4.

65. Seaside City Council Meeting Minutes, February 6, 1997, 3.

66. Alex Hulanicki, "Seaside makes 'take it or leave it offer,'" *Monterey Peninsula Herald*, February 26, 1997, C1.

67. Tim Brown, Commentary, "Seaside's Fire Police Plans," *Monterey Peninsula Herald*, March 20, 1997, A9.

68. Interview with Councilmember Tom Mancini, July 14, 2007, Seaside by Carol McKibben.

69. This person agreed to be interviewed on condition of anonymity.

70. City of Seaside, City Council Minutes, Oral Communications, March 20, 1997, 3, Seaside.

71. Interview with Belinda McBirney, January 6, 2006, Seaside by Carol McKibben.

72. Rucker interview.

73. Amos interview.

74. Kristi Belcamino, "Seaside may drop review of manager Brown," *Monterey Peninsula Herald*, September 4, 1997, 1; Amos interview; Rucker interview.

75. Monterey County Grand Jury Final Report, 1997, City of Seaside Archive.

76. Ibid.

77. Jordan interview; Grand Jury Report and Response, City of Seaside Archive.

78. Larry Wild, "Seaside charges," *Monterey Peninsula Herald*, January 20, 1998, 1.

79. Mancini interview.

80. Kristi Belcamino, "Lines Drawn in Seaside," *Monterey Peninsula Herald*, April 4, 1997, 1.

81. 1998 City of Seaside Budget Report.

82. Kristi Belcamino, "Seaside Politics Surrounds Post," *Monterey Peninsula Herald*, April 17, 1998.

83. Jordan interview.

84. Rubio interview.

85. Unlike Seaside, blacks maintained a demographic majority in Compton in the 1970s and 1980s. See Albert M. Camarillo, "Cities of Color: The New Racial Frontier in California's Minority-Majority Cities," *Pacific Historical Review*, Vol. 76, No. 1 (February 2007), 5.

86. Kristi Belcamino, "Seaside Project at Next Hurdle," *Monterey Peninsula Herald*, May 2, 1998, B1, B3; McBurney interview.

87. Rucker interview.

88. McBirney interview; Smith interview.

89. Smith interview.

90. Interview by phone with Darryl Choate, April 5, 2006, by Carol McKibben.

91. Smith interview.

92. Kristi Belcamino, "Mayor Smith Is No Oushover," *Monterey Peninsula Herald*, April 8, 1999, A1.

93. Kristi Belcamino, "Seaside Mayor Wants to Revisit Development Deal," *Monterey Peninsula Herald*, April 19, 1999, A1.

94. Smith interview; Farr interview; Jane Haseldine, "Seaside likes new Ord housing deal" *Monterey Peninsula Herald*, July 11, 1999, B1.

95. Jane Haseldine, "Fort Ord project will stay local," *Monterey Peninsula Herald*, November 25, 1999, A1 and A9.

96. Jane Haseldine, "City will get Army funding," July 6, 1999, *Monterey Peninsula Herald*, B1.

97. Jane Haseldine, "Mayor drawing kudos, criticism," January 10, 2000, *Monterey Peninsula Herald*, A1.

98. Cristina Medina, "Seaside elects first Latino," *Monterey Peninsula Herald*, November 7, 2000, B1.

99. James interview.

100. Rubio interview.

101. Sukhjit Purewal, "Project 'More than golf,'" *Monterey Peninsula Herald*, June 30, 2003, B1.

102. James interview.

103. Sukhjit Purewal,"New director ready to fight from the fringe," *Monterey Peninsula Herald*, July 16, 2003, C1.

104. Jerry Stewart, "Bank boosts funding for Buy.com stop," *Monterey Peninsula Herald*, July 9, 2002, C1.

105. Sylvia Moore, "Sports center proposed for Ord," *Monterey Peninsula Herald*, February 13, 2003, B1.

106. Seaside City Council Minutes, February 12, 2003, 3.

107. Sylvia Moore, "Sports center proposed for Ord," *Monterey Peninsula Herald*, February 13, 2003, B1.

108. Sukhjit Prurewal, "Project 'More than golf,'" *Monterey Peninsula Herald*, June 30, 2003, A1.

109. Sukhjit Purewal, "No vote on affordable housing," *Monterey Peninsula Herald*, July 12, 2003, B1.

110. James interview.

111. Richard LeWarne, San Pablo Avenue, Seaside, Seaside City Council Meeting Minutes, September 4, 2003.

112. Sukhjit Purewal, "First Tee study disputed," *Monterey Peninsula Herald*, October 11, 2003, 1.

113. Interview with Hector Azpilcueto, January 8, 2008, Seaside by Carol McKibben. Hereafter referred to as Azpilcueto interview.

114. Ibid.

115. Del Rey Woods Elementary School Profile, courtesy of Monterey Peninsula Unified School District.

116. http://www.mpusd.k12.ca.us/delreywoods/profile.HTML

117. Interview with Helen B. Rucker, January 9, 2006, by Carol McKibben.

118. Interview with Mae Johnson, December 19, 2006, by Carol McKibben. Hereafter referred to as Johnson interview.

119. Ibid.

120. Narrator wished to remain anonymous, Cabrillo Family Day Care Center, December 2, 2006.

121. Interview with Sergio Rangel, March 25, 2008, by Carol McKibben.

122. Interview with Alfredo Valdez, February 19, 2008, Seaside by Carol McKibben.

123. Azpilcueto interview.

124. Ibid.

125. Interview with Emiliano Garcia Ogarrio, August 13, 2007, Seaside by Carol McKibben.

126. Rubio interview.

127. Alex Hulanicki, "Seaside businesses reflect ethnic diversity," *Monterey Peninsula Herald*, November 25, 1995, 10A.

128. Camarillo, "Cities of Color," 18–19.

129. Interview with Dave Pacheco, July 10, 2007, Seaside by Carol McKibben.

130. Interview with Mel Mason, April 25, 2008, Seaside by Carol McKibben. Hereafter referred to as Mason interview.

131. Ibid.

132. Ibid.

133. The clipping files for the 1990s of *Monterey Peninsula Herald* articles located in the Seaside Branch of Monterey County Library documents these and other incidents of police brutality by Seaside police in the 1990s.

134. Editorial, *Monterey County Herald*, 1999, 10.

135. Report of an Investigation into the Death of Charles Vaughn Sr. on May 19, 1998, Precipitous Use of 5150, Protection and Advocacy, Inc. Unit, May, 2000.

136. Azpilcueto interview.

137. Rubio interview.

138. Rucker interview.

139. Meléndez interview

140. William Anselmo Meléndez, "The Effect of the Language of Instruction on the Reading Achievement of Limited English Speakers in Secondary Schools" unpublished doctoral dissertation, The Graduate School of the University of the Pacific, 1980, 3.

141. Ibid., 23.

142. Rucker interview.

143. Interview with Captain Carl Little, Seaside Police Department office, June 26, 2006, by Carol McKibben.

144. Interview with Patty Pérez, July 1, 2006, Seaside by Carol McKibben.

145. Ibid.

146. The 7-11 is located on Fremont Avenue, one of Seaside's two main thoroughfares. The other is Broadway Avenue, which bisects Fremont.

147. Interview with spokesman for Seaside Police department, June 15, 2006, Seaside by Carol McKibben.

148. Rubio interview.

Bibliography

Auletta, Ken, *The Underclass*. New York: Vintage Books, 1983.

Bailey, Beth, and David Farber, *The First Strange Place: Race and Sex in World War II Hawaii*. Baltimore and London: The Johns Hopkins University Press, 1992.

Barrows, Harry D., and Luther A. Ingersoll, *Memorial and Biographical History of the Coast Counties of Central California*. Chicago: The Lewis Publishing Company, 1893.

Blumstein, Alfred, and Joel Wallman, eds., *The Crime Drop in America*. New York: Cambridge University Press, 2000.

Brilliant, Mark, *The Color of America Has Changed: How Racial Diversity Shaped Civil Rights Reform in California, 1941–1978*. Oxford: Oxford University Press, 2010.

Brooks, Charlotte, *Alien Neighbors, Foreign Friends: Asian Americans Housing, and the Transformation of Urban California*. Chicago & London: University of California Press, 2009.

Broussard, Albert S., *Black San Francisco: The Struggle for Racial Equality in the West, 1900–1954*. Lawrence: University of Kansas Press, 1993.

Bullard, Robert D., ed., *Unequal Protection: Environmental Justice and Communities of Color*. San Francisco: Sierra Club Books, 1994.

Bullard, Robert D., and Benjamin Chavis Jr., *Confronting Environmental Racism: Voices from the Grassroots*. Cambridge, MA: South End Press, 1993.

Butler, John Sibley, *All That We Can Be: Black Leadership and Racial Integration the Army Way*. New York: Basic Books, 1996.

Butterworth, Thomas C., *Seaside: Monterey County California* issued by Monterey Realty Syndicate. Monterey, California, 1910.

Camarillo, Albert, *Chicanos in a Changing Society: From Mexican Pueblos to American Barrios in Santa Barbara and Southern California, 1848–1930*. Dallas: Southern Methodist University Press, 1996.

———, *Chicanos in California: A History of Mexican Americans in California*. Sparks, NV: Materials for Today's Learning, 1990.

———, "Black and Brown in Compton: Demographic Change, Suburban Decline, and Intergroup Relations in a South Central Los Angeles Community, 1950–2000," in Nancy Foner and George Fredrickson, eds., *Not Just Black and White: Historical and Contemporary Perspectives on Immigrants, Race, and Ethnicity in the United States*. New York: Russell Sage Foundation, 2004.

———, "Cities of Color: The New Racial Frontier in California's Minority-Majority Cities," *Pacific Historical Review*, Vol. 76, No. 1 (February, 2007) pp. 1–28.

———, "Blacks, Latinos and the New Racial Frontier in American Cities of Color: California's Emerging Minority-Majority Cities," in Kusmer, Kenneth L. and Joe W. Trotter, *African American Urban History Since World War II*, 39–59. Chicago: University of Chicago Press, 2009.

Chan, Sucheng, and Spencer Olin, eds., *Major Problems in California History*. Boston and New York: Houghton Mifflin Company, 1997.

Checker, Melissa, *Polluted Promises: Environmental Racism and the Search for Justice in a Southern Town*. New York and London: New York University Press, 2005.

Cherney, Robert W., and William Issel, *San Francisco: Presidio, Port and Pacific Metropolis*. San Francisco: Boyd & Fraser, 1981.

Chiang, Connie, *Shaping the Shoreline: Fishing and Tourism on the Monterey Coast*. Seattle: University of Washington Press, 2008.

Clark, Donald Thomas, *Monterey County Place Names*. Carmel Valley, CA: Kestral Press, 1991.

Cole, Luke W., *From the Ground Up: Environmental Racism and the Rise of the Environmental Justice Movement*. New York: New York University Press, 2001.

Conway, J. D., *Monterey: Presidio, Pueblo and Port*. Charleston, SC: Arcadia Press, 2003.

Dimond, Paul R., *Beyond Busing: Reflections on Urban Segregation, the Courts and Equal Opportunity*. Ann Arbor: University of Michigan Press, 2005.

Enloe, Cynthia, *Bananas, Beaches and Bases: Making Feminist Sense Out of International Politics*. Berkeley: University of California Press, 1990.

Freund, David, *Colored Property: State Policy & White Racial Politics in Suburban America*. Chicago and London: University of Chicago Press, 2007.

Gregory, James N., *American Exodus: The Dust Bowl Migration and Okie Culture in California*. New York and Oxford: Oxford University Press, 1989.

Gutiérrez, David G., *Walls and Mirrors: Mexican Americans, Mexican Immigrants, and the Politics of Ethnicity*. Berkeley: University of California Press, 1995.

Hartman, Chester W., *Yerba Buena: Land Grab and Community Resistance in San Francisco*. San Francisco: Glide Publications, 1974.

Hayden, Dolores, *Building Suburbia, Green Fields and Urban Growth, 1820–2000*. New York: Vintage Books, 2004.

Hine, Darlene Clark, and Kathleen Thompson, *A Shining Thread of Hope: The History of Black Women in America*. New York: Broadway Books, 1998.

Jackson, Kenneth T., *Crabgrass Frontier: The Suburbanization of the United States*. New York and Oxford: Oxford University Press, 1985.

Katz, Michael, ed., *The Underclass Debate: Views From History*. Princeton: Princeton University Press, 1993.

Kennedy, David M., *Freedom from Fear: The American People in Depression and War, 1929–1945*. Oxford History of the United States. New York: Oxford University Press, 2005.

Kroeber, A. L., *Handbook of the Indians of California*. Berkeley: California Book Company, 1953.

Kruse, Kevin A., *White Flight: Atlanta and the Making of Modern Conservativism* (Politics and Society in Twentieth Century America). Princeton: Princeton University Press, 2005.

Kushner, Sam, *The Long Road to Delano*. New York: International Publishers, 1975.

Kusmer, Kenneth L., and Joe W. Trotter, *African American Urban History since World War II*. Chicago University of Chicago Press, 2009.

Lassiter, Matthew D., *The Silent Majority: Suburban Politics in the Sunbelt South*. Princeton: Princeton University Press, 2006.

Lemke-Santangelo, Gretchen, *Abiding Courage: African American Migrant Women and the East Bay Community*. Chapel Hill and London: University of North Carolina Press, 1996.

Lewis, Paul, *Shaping Suburbia: How Political Institutions Organize Urban Development*. Pittsburgh, PA: University of Pittsburgh Press, 1996.

Lotchin, Roger W., *Fortress California 1910–1961: From Warfare to Welfare*. New York: Oxford University Press, 1992.

——, "The City and the Sword: San Francisco and the Rise of the Metropolitan Military Complex, 1919–1941," *Journal of American History*, Vol. 65 (March 1979), 996–1020.

——, "The Metropolitan Military Complex in Comparative Perspective: San Francisco, Los Angeles, and San Diego, 1919–1941," *Journal of the West*, Vol. 17 (July 1979).

Lutz, Catherine, *Homefront: A Military City and the American 20th Century*. Boston: Beacon Press, 2001.

Lydon, Sandy, *Chinese Gold: The Chinese in the Monterey Bay Region*. Capitola, CA: Capitola Book Company, 1985.

MacGregor, Morris J. Jr., *Integration of the Armed Forces, 1940–1965*. Washington DC: Center of Military History United States Army, 1985.

Margolin, Malcolm, *The Ohlone Way: Indian Life in the San Francisco-Monterey Bay Area*. Berkeley: Heydey Books, 1978.

Markusen, Anne, Peter Hall, Scott Campbell, and Sabina Dietrich, *The Rise of the Gunbelt: The Military Remapping of Industrial America*. New York: Oxford University Press, 1991.

Massey, Douglass S., and Nancy A. Denton, *American Apartheid: Segregation and the Making of the Underclass*. Cambridge, MA: Harvard University Press, 1993.

McKibben, Carol Lynn, *Beyond Cannery Row: Sicilian Women, Immigration, and Community in Monterey, California, 1915–1999*. Urbana and Chicago: University of Illinois Press, 2006.

McWilliams, Carey, *Factories in the Field: The Story of Migratory Farm Labor in California*. Santa Barbara: Peregrine Smith, 1935.

——, *California, The Great Exception*. New York: Current Books, 1949.

Mershon, Sherie, and Steven Schlossman, *Foxholes and Color Lines: Desegregating the U.S. Armed Forces*, Baltimore and London: The Johns Hopkins University Press, A RAND Book, 1998.

Moore, Shirley Ann Wilson, *To Place Our Deeds: The African American Community in Richmond, California, 1910–1963*. Berkeley: University of California Press, 2000.

Moskos, Charles C., *The American Enlisted Man: The Rank and File in Today's Military*. New York: The Russell Sage Foundation, 1970.

Myers, Andrew H., *Black White & Olive Drab: Racial Integration at fort Jackson, South Carolina and the Civil Rights Movement*. Charlottesville and London: University of Virginia Press, 2006.

N. A., *The Bay of San Francisco, The Metropolis of the Pacific Coast, and its Suburban Cities. A History*. Chicago: The Lewis Publishing Company, 1892.

Nankivell, John H., *Buffalo Soldier Regiment: History of the Twenty-Fifth United States Infantry, 1869–1926*. Lincoln: University of Nebraska Press, 2001.

Nash, Gerald D., *The American West Transformed: The Impact of the Second World War*. Bloomington: Indiana University Press, 1985.

———, *World War II and The West: Reshaping the Economy*. Lincoln: University of Nebraska Press, 1990.

Nicolaides, Becky M., *My Blue Heaven: Life and Politics in the Working Class Suburbs of Los Angeles, 1920–1965*. Chicago and London: The University of Chicago Press, 2002.

Nicolaides, Becky M., and Andrew Wiese, eds., *The Suburb Reader*. New York and London: Routledge, 2006.

Pagán, Eduardo Obregón, *Murder at the Sleepy Lagoon: Zoot Suits, Race & Riot in Wartime L.A.* Chapel Hill: University of North Carolina Press, 2003.

Pellow, David Naguib, *Garbage Wars: The Struggle for Environmental Justice in Chicago*. Cambridge, MA: The MIT Press, 2002.

Perlstein, Rick, *Nixonland: The Rise of a President and the Fracturing of America*. New York, London, Toronto, Sydney: Scribner, 2008.

Pitt, Leonard, *Decline of the Californios: A Social History of the Spanish-Speaking Californians, 1846–1890*. Berkeley: University of California Press, 1998.

Pitti, Stephen, *The Devil in Silicon Valley: Northern California, Race, and Mexican Americans*. Princeton and Oxford: Princeton University Press. 2003.

Polk's Monterey City Directory. R. L. Polk Company of California, 1930–1960.

Raugh, Harold E. Jr., *Images of America: Fort Ord*. San Francisco: Arcadia Publishing, 2004.

Roderick, Kevin, *The San Fernando Valley: America's Suburb*. Los Angeles: Los Angeles Times Books, 2001.

Rogin, Michael P., and John L. Shover, *Political Change in California; Critical Elections and Social Movements, 1890–1966*. Westport, CT: Greenwood Publishing Corporation, 1970.

Saito, Leland T., *Race and Politics: Asian Americans, Latinos, and Whites in a Los Angeles Suburb*. Urbana and Chicago: University of Illinois Press, 1998.

Satter, Beryl, *Family Properties, Race, Real Estate, and the Exploitation of Black America*. New York: Metropolitan Books/Henry Holt & Co., 2009.

Scharlin, Craig, and Lilia Villanueva, *Philip Vera Cruz: A Personal History of Filipino Immigrants and the Farmworkers Movement*. Seattle: University of Washington Press, 2000.

Schoenfeld, Seymour J., *The Negro in the Armed Forces: His Value and Status-Past, Present and Potential*. Washington, DC: The Associated Publishers, 1945.

Self, Robert O., *American Babylon: Race and the Struggle for Postwar Oakland*. Princeton and Oxford: Princeton University Press, 2003.

Shah, Nayan, *Contagious Divides: Epidemic and Race in San Francisco's Chinatown*. Berkeley: University of California Press, 2001.

Shaw, Stephanie, *What a Woman Ought to Be and Do: Black Professional Women Workers During the Jim Crow Era*. Chicago: University of Chicago Press, 1996.

Sides, Josh, *L.A. City Limits: African American Los Angeles from the Great Depression to the Present*. Berkeley, Los Angeles, and London: University of California Press, 2003.

Smith, Polly J., *The Impact of Military Desegregation on Segregation Patterns in American Cities: A Case Study of Colorado Springs, New London, and Fayetteville*. Lewiston, NY, Queenston and Lampeter, UK: The Edwin Mellen Press, 2007.

Spickard, Paul, *Mixed Blood: Intermarriage and Ethnic Identity in Twentieth Century America*, Madison, Wisconsin: University of Wisconsin Press, 1989.

Steinbeck, John, *Cannery Row*. London: Heinemann, 1945.

Takaki, Ronald T., *Strangers from a Different Shore: A History of Asian Americans.* Boston: Little, Brown, 1998.

Taylor, Quintard, *In Search of the Racial Frontier: African Americans in the West, 1528–1990.* New York: W. W. Norton, 1998.

———, "African American Men in the American West, 1528–1990," *Annals of the American Academy of Political and Social Science*, Vol. 569, *The African American Male in American Life and Thought* (May 2000), 106–119.

Teaford, Jon C., *Post-Suburbia: Government and Politics in Edge Cities.* Baltimore: The Johns Hopkins University Press, 1996.

Thomson, Heather Ann, *Whose Detroit? Politics, Labor and Race in a Modern American City.* Ithaca, NY: Cornell University Press, 2001.

Verge, Arthur C., *Paradise Transformed: Los Angeles During the Second World War.* Dubuque, IA: Kendall Publishing Co., 1993.

Walton, John, *Storied Land: Community and Memory in Monterey.* Berkeley: University of California Press, 2003.

Watkins, Major Rolin C., *History of Monterey and Santa Cruz Counties, California.* Chicago: The S. J. Clarke Publishing Company, 1925.

West, Cornel, *Race Matters.* New York: Vintage, 1994.

Whitaker, Matthew C., *Race Work: The Rise of Civil Rights in the Urban West.* Lincoln: University of Nebraska Press, 2005.

White, Deborah Gray, *Too Heavy a Load: Black Women in Defense of Themselves, 1894–1994.* New York: W. W. Norton, 1999.

White, Richard, *"It's Your Misfortune and None of My Own": A New History of the American West.* Norman and London: University of Oklahoma Press, 1991.

———, *Remembering Ahanagran.* New York: Hill and Wang, 1998.

Wiebe, Robert, *The Search For Order, 1877–1920.* New York: Hill and Wang, 1967.

Wiese, Andrew, *Places of Their Own: African American Suburbanization in the Twentieth Century.* Chicago and London: The University of Chicago Press, 2005.

Wild, Mark, *Street Meeting: Multi-Ethnic Neighborhoods in Twentieth Century Los Angeles.* Berkeley, Los Angeles, and London: University of California Press, 2005.

Wilson, William Julius, *When Work Disappears: The World of the New Urban Poor.* New York: Vintage Books, 1996.

———, *The Truly Disadvantaged: The Inner City, the Underclass, and Public Policy.* Chicago: University of Chicago Press, 1987.

Yamada, David T., and Oral History Committee, MP/JACL, *The Japanese of the Monterey Peninsula: Their History and Legacy, 1895–1995.* Monterey, CA: Japanese American Citizens League, 1995.

Zeiger, Susan, *Entangling Alliances: Foreign War Brides and American Soldiers in the Twentieth Century.* New York and London: New York University Press, 2010.

Zinn, Howard, *A People's History of the United States.* New York: Harper Collins, 2001.

ARTICLES

Blatz, Perry K., "Craftsmanship and Flexibility in Oral History: A Pluralistic Approach to Methodology and Theory," *The Public Historian*, Vol. 12, No. 4 (Autumn, 1990), 7–22.

Blumstein, Alfred, and Joel Wallman, "The Recent Rise and Fall of American Violence," in Alfred Blumstein and Joel Wallman, eds., *The Crime Drop in America*, New York: Cambridge University Press, 2000.

Broadbent, Sylvia. M., "The Rumsen of Monterey." *An Ethnography of Historical Sources Contributions of the University of California Archaelogical Research Facilities*, January 1972.

Durham, Joseph T., "Sense and Nonsense about Busing," *The Journal of Negro Education*, Vol. 42, No. 3, Education in the Black Cities, Summer 1973.

Gluck, Sherna Berger, Donald A. Ritchie, and Bret Eynon, "Reflections on Oral History in the New Millennium: Roundtable Comments," *The Oral History Review*, Vol. 26, No. 2 (Summer, 1999), 1–27.

Hall, Jacqueline Dowd, "The Long Civil Rights Movement and the Political Uses of the Past," *Journal of American History*, Vol. 9, Issue 4 (March, 2005) 1233–1263.

Jargowsky, Paul A., "Ghetto Poverty among Blacks in the 1980s," *Journal of Policy Analysis and Management*, Vol. 13., No. 2 (spring, 1994), 288.

Kasard, John, "Urban Industrial Transition and the Urban Underclass," *Annals of the American Academy of Political and Social Science*, January 1989, 26–47.

Laverty, Philip, "The Ohlone/Costanoan-Esselen Nation of Monterey, California: Dispossession, Federal Neglect, and the Bitter Irony of the Federal Acknowledgement Process," *Wicazo Sa Review*, Vol. 18, No. 2, *The Politics of Sovereignty*, Autumn 2003, pp. 41–77.

Limerick, Patricia Nelson, "The American West: From Exceptionalism to Internationalism," in *The State of U.S. History*, ed. Melvyn Stokes. Oxford, UK: Berg, 2002.

Massey, Douglas S., and Nancy A. Denton, "Trends in the Residential Segregation of Blacks, Hispanics, and Asians, 1970–1980," *American Sociological Review*, 52, 1987, 802–825.

Miskimon, Robert, "There Are Not Enough White People Involved with Civil Rights," *The Crisis*, May 1976.

Orenstein, Dara, "Void for Vagueness: Mexicans and the Collapse of Miscegenation Law in California," *Pacific Historical Review*, Vol. 74, No. 3, August 2005, pp. 367–407.

Reich, Peter L., "Dismantling the Pueblo: Hispanic Municipal Land Rights in California since 1850," *Journal of Legal History*, Vol. 45, No. 4. October 2001, pp. 353–370.

Schneider, Jack, "Escape from Los Angeles: White Flight From Los Angeles and its Schools," *Journal of Urban History*, Vol. 34, No. 6, pp. 995–1012.

Saenz, Rogelio, Sean-Shong Hwang, and Benigno E. Aguirre, "In Search of Asian War Brides," *Demography*, Vol. 31, No. 3, August, 1994, 550.

Tucey, Mary, and Hornbeck, David, "Anglo Immigration and the Hispanic Town: A Study of Urban Change in Monterey, 1835–1850," *Social Science Journal*, Vol. 13, No. 2 (1976), 1–7.

———. "The Submergence of a People: Migration and Occupational Structure in California, 1850," *Pacific Historical Review* (1977): 471–484.

Wadsworth, Tim, "Is Immigration Responsible for the Crime Drop? An Assessment of the Influence of Immigration on Violent Crime Between 1990 and 2000," *Social Science Quarterly*, Vol. 91, No. 2, June 2010, pp. 531–553.

Wright, Doris Marion, "The Making of Cosmopolitan California: An Analysis of Immigration, 1848–1870," *California Historical Society Quarterly*, Vol. XIX, No. 4 (1940), 323–343.

NEWSPAPERS AND MAGAZINES

Carmel Pacific Spectator Journal. Carmel, California, December 2, 1955.

Fort Ord Panorama. Fort Ord, California, 1942–1990.
King City Settler. Salinas, California, 1889.
Marina Seaside Tribune. Marina, California, 1982.
Monterey Bay News. Seaside, California, 1948.
Monterey Daily Cypress. Monterey, California, 1907–1911.
Monterey New Era. Monterey, California, 1896–1909.
Monterey Peninsula Herald, Monterey, California, 1940–2010.
Monterey Weekly Cypress. Monterey, California, 1897–1901.
Salinas Valley Settler, Salinas, California, 1889.
Salinas Valley Weekly Index, Salinas, California, 1889.
Salinas Weekly Journal. Salinas, California, 1879–1909.
Seaside Metro Reporter, Week of March 12–17, 1973.
Seaside News-Graphic, 1941.
Seaside Post-News Sentinel, 1948–2005.

UNPUBLISHED MANUSCRIPTS AND REPORTS

About Face! The U.S. Servicemen Fund's Newsletter, Vol. 2, No. 6, 2005.
"Annexation of Family Housing Areas of Fort Ord to City of Seaside," *Report to Seaside City Council,* December 1967. Exhibit A-1: The State of California Government Code Title 4 division 2, Part 2, Chapter 1 Article 8, "Annexation of Territory Owned by the Federal Government," Section 35470 and Section 35471 (Statutes 1957).
Bank of America, "Focus on Monterey County," 1967, California Room, Monterey Public Library, Monterey, California.
Bernstein, Shana, "Building Bridges at Home in a Time of Global Conflict: Interracial Cooperation and the Fight for Civil Rights in Los Angeles, 1933–1954," Ph.D. dissertation, Department of History, Stanford University, 2003.
Broadbent, Sylvia. M., *An Ethnography of Historical Sources Contributions of the University of California Archaelogical Research Facilities,* Vol. 14, January 1972.
Carey, Pearl, autobiography, unpublished manuscript, 2007.
Connolly, Nathan, "By Eminent Domain: Race and Capital in the Building of an American South Florida," Ph.D. dissertation, Department of History, University of Michigan, 2008.
DeSilva, Adeline, Letter to Historical Commission, April 19, 1988, City of Seaside Archives.
Final Report, Redevelopment Agency of the City of Seaside, n.d., Noche Buena Project California R-27, City of Seaside Archives.
Flores, Lori,"Converging Communities in the 'Valley of the World'": Mexican Americans, Mexicans, and the Chicano Movement's Evolution in Salinas and California, 1940–1970," Ph.D. dissertation, Department of History, Stanford University, 2011.
Goodchild, Pat, "Seaside's Transit History: The Big Four Link California and Its Cities," Report, City of Seaside Archives, n.d.
Hill, George, Smith, Alexis, and Warshawsky, Debbie, "Seaside, California: A Case Study of A Minority-Majority City" unpublished paper, Stanford University, March 30, 2006, p. 25.
Historical Commission Report, 1965, City of Seaside Archives, Seaside, California.
N.A, Headquarters, Historical Sketch, United States Army Training Center, Infantry, Fort Ord, 1969, Fort Ord Archive.
Horne, Kibby M., "A History of the Presidio of Monterey," Defense Language Institute West Coast Branch. Presidio of Monterey, California, 1970.

Howard, Donald M., *Rancho to Roberts Land*, Vol. 2, unpublished manuscript located in the California Room, Monterey Public Library.

Johnson, Elaine D., "Sociological Study of the Monterey Area," prepared for the City Planning Commission, Monterey, California, October 1968.

Kousser, J. Morgan. "Tacking, Stacking, and Cracking: Race and Reapportionment in Monterey County, 1981–1992," a *Report for Gonzalez v. Monterey County* Board of Supervisors, September 9, 1992.

Landreth, Keith, Historical and Architectural Reports for Fort Ord, Conducted for the Office of Environmental Programs Conservation Division. September 1993.

Mahlon Christianson, "Fort Ord and the Monterey Peninsula During World War II," unpublished manuscript, August 1998.

May, Elaine Tyler, "Security against Democracy: The Legacy of the Cold War at Home," OAH Presidential Address, April 10, 2010, Washington, DC.

McNaughton, James C., Command Historian, "Fort Ord: A Working History," unpublished paper, December 1996.

Meléndez, William Anselmo, "The Effect of the Language of Instruction on the Reading Achievement of Limited English Speakers in Secondary Schools" unpublished doctoral dissertation, The Graduate School of the University of the Pacific, 1980.

Monterey County Grand Jury Final Report, 1997, City of Seaside Archive.

Monterey Land and Hot Springs Company, July 17, 1941, Ord Terrace Subdivision, Book 734, p. 66. Courtesy of Stewart Title Company, Monterey, California.

Moore, Lieutenant General Harold G., and Lieutenant Colonel Jeff M. Tuten, *Building a Volunteer Army: The Fort Ord Contribution*, Department of the Army, Washington, DC, 1975.

1995 City of Seaside General Plan, D'Amico and Associates, Inc.; Land Use Associates; Goldfarb and Lipman; Licciardello and Associates.

Planning Commission Report, City of Seaside Archives, 1965.

Report by Association of Monterey Bay Area Governments Draft regional Population and Employment forecast, October, 1991, Marina, California.

Report of an Investigation into the Death of Charles Vaughn Sr. on May 19, 1998, Precipitous Use of 5150, Protection and Advocacy, Inc. Unit, May, 2000.

Ruth, Herman D., City and Regional Planning Consultant, *Population and Employment Survey, 1956*, City Planning Commission, Seaside, California, City of Seaside Archives.

Seaside City Council Meeting Minutes, 1956–2006, Office of the City Clerk, Seaside.

Seaside Story: Redevelopment, 1960–1970, Seaside California, n.p., n.d. brochure produced by Seaside Redevelopment Agency, Merrifield C. Beck, Chair.

The City of Seaside California: A Model City, Report Prepared by Development Research Associates. 731 South Flower Street, Los Angeles, California. 1961.

Wollam, Major Park, unpublished paper, "Fort Ord in World War II," May 1998.

GOVERNMENT DOCUMENTS

United States Manuscript Census, 1900, 1910, 1920, 1930, Monterey, California.

United States Manuscript Census, 1920, Pacific Grove, California

Statutes of California, 194, Chapter 602, p. 1132, Sections 60 & 69 of the Civil Code

LEGAL RECORDS

Lopez v. Monterey County, 1879–1941.

INTERVIEWS

All interviews were conducted by Carol McKibben in person unless noted otherwise.

Amos, Nancy, September 25, 2007, Seaside.

Azpilcueto, Hector, January 8, 2008.

Barron, Ildefonsa, June 16, 2008, Seaside.

Bean, Lenora, March 25, 2006, Seaside.

Beverly, Mr. and Mrs. Ira, by Henry Hopkins, Seaside Historical Commission, City of Seaside Archive, November 30, 1989 Seaside.

Bindel, Cecil, December 8 and 14, 2006, Monterey.

Bratt, Lois, n.d. by K. Crain, Seaside Historical Commission, City of Seaside Archive, Seaside.

Brown, Charles, March 13, 2007, Seaside.

Brown, Tim by e-mail to Carol McKibben, August 3, 2008.

Bui, Duong, December 3, 2007, by phone.

Carey, Pearl, October 12, 2006 and November 21 and 28, 2006, May 29, 2007, Seaside.

Cass, Elaine, March 11, 2008, Seaside.

Cendaria, Brenda, June 16, 2008, Seaside.

Choate, Darryl, by phone April 5, 2006, Seaside.

Corpuz, Ray, October 10 and 22, 2007, Seaside.

Cortéz, Joe, April 11, 1990, by the Seaside Historical Commission, City of Seaside Archive.

Craighead, Jackie January 17, 2006, Carmel.

DeBerry, Billy, August 6, 2007, Seaside.

Drake, Vi, n.d., City of Seaside Archive, by K. Crain, Seaside Historical Commission, Seaside.

Drummond, Don, June 15, 2006, Carmel Valley.

Eubanks, Frank, March 13, 2007, Seaside.

Farr, Congressman Sam, May 29, 2008, Seaside.

Glover, Al, February 2, 2006, and October 3, 2006, Seaside.

Goblirsch, Richard, April 4, 2008, Seaside.

Haddad, Lou, September, 2005, Monterey.

Hanano, Glenn, October 13, 2006, Seaside.

Harris, Mary Ellen, November 1, 2010, Seaside.

Harston, Mike, June 15, 2007, Monterey.

Hodgson, Daphne, September 19, 2008, Seaside.

Houser, Bud, February 12, 2008, Seaside.

Ingersoll, Diana September, 2005, Seaside.

James, Ewalker, September 12, 2007, Seaside.

Johnson, Mae, October 15, 2005, December 19, 2006, Seaside.

Jordan, Don, by Carol McKibben and Albert M. Camarillo, October 2005, Seaside.

Joyce, Richard, April 5 and 12, 2007, Seaside.

Kidd, Anthony, March 12, 2007, and June 26, 2007, Seaside.

Knight, Dr. Charlie Mae, February 2, 2007, Palo Alto, California.

Larot, Presentacion, June 16, 2008, Seaside.

Lawson, Oscar, March 12, 2007 by telephone.

Lee, Anna and Charles, March 12, 2007, Seaside.

Little, Captain Carl, Seaside Police Department, June 26, 2006

Mahieu, Betty Dwyer, February 24, 2007, Monterey.

Malate, Tessie and Phil, April 4, 23, 2007, Seaside.

Mancini, Tom, July 14, 2007, Seaside.

Martin, Rudy, May 7, 2008 by telephone.

Mason, Mel, September 9, 2006, October 8, 2007, April 23 & 25, 2008, Seaside.

McBirney, Belinda, January 6, 2006, Seaside.

McClair, Lancelot, September 17, 2008, Pebble Beach.

McDaniel, Morris and Bobbie, June 27, 2007, October 9, 2007, Seaside.

McGee, Reverend Welton and Margaret, April 17, 2007, Seaside.

McKenzie, Estela and Patrick, April 4, 23, 2007, Seaside.

McKinney, Levelle, June 26, 2007, Seaside.

McNeely, Charles, August, 9, 2007, by phone.

Meléndez, William, January 30, 2007, Monterey.

Nance, Reverend Richard, April 12, 2007, Pacific Grove.

Nava, Rudolfo, February 28, 2007, Seaside.

Nobida,Virginia, June 16, 2008, Seaside.

Oda, Larry, May 29, 2007, Monterey.

Ottman, Janet, April 17, 2009, Seaside.

Ogarrio, Emiliano Garcia, August 13 2007, Seaside.

Pacheco, Dave, July 10, 2007, Seaside.

Panetta, Leon, June 30, 2008, Marina, California.

Payne, Stephen, May 15, 2007, Fort Ord.

Pérez, Evangelina, August 25, 2009, Seaside.

Pérez, Luis, April 2, 2007, Seaside.

Pérez, Patty July 1, 2006, Seaside.

Petit, Mitzi, June 19, 2006, October 15, 2006, Seaside.

Rangel, Sergio, March 25, 2008.

Reyes, Emerson and Violeta, April 4, 23, 2007, Seaside.

Roston, LaShandra,October 13, 2006, Seaside.

Rubio, Ralph, September 1 and 5, 2005, Seaside.

Rucker, Helen, January 9, 2006, May 12, 2008, Seaside.

Sánchez, Rosa, September 10, 2005, Seaside.

Smith, Jerry, September, 2005, Salinas.

Souza, Sara, February 1985, by Historical Commissioner Emily Ventura, Seaside.

Thorne, Jerry, March 16, 2009.

Towne, Nancy, August 31, 2005.

Valdez, Alfredo, February 19, 2008, Seaside.

Watts, Ruthie, July 21, 2007, Seaside.

Weingarten, Saul by Joel Herzog, July 7, 1988, City of Seaside Archive, Seaside.

West, Nellie, October 13, 2006, Seaside.

West, William A. "Tex" and West, Vivian Ruth, February 24, 1989, Seaside.

Historical Commissioners, Emily Ventura and Henry Hopkins, Seaside.

Williams, Carl, by telephone, May 23, 2007.

Woods, Richard, November 7, 2006 and March 13, 2007, Seaside.

Yamane, Linda, May 15, 2007, Seaside.

Yoshiyama, Andrew, May 1, 20, 22, 2007, Seaside.

Zosa, Segundo, April 4, 2007, Seaside.

Index

San Francisco, California, 5, 8, 20, 24,
235–236, 38, 42, 43, 47, 51, 58, 59,
78, 85, 106, 115, 121, 125, 126–128,
132, 134, 143, 150, 194, 222, 238
San Francisco Chronicle, 136
San Jose, California, 28, 42, 43, 62,
68, 78, 85, 86, 136, 142, 198, 267
San Jose, East, 68, 86, 149
San Leandro, California, 68
Sánchez family, 254
Sánchez, George, 8
Sánchez, Jesse, 156
Sánchez, Rosa, 254
Santa Cruz, California, 143
Santa Cruz, County of, 106, 256
Santa Rosalia Fisherman's
Festival, 105–106, 184
Sapp, Betty, 185
Satter, Beryl, 10
Schmidt, Emil, 134, 156
School Resource Officer program, 179
Seaside: and affirmative action, 151–153,
163–164, 236; and affordable
housing, 62, 244, 248, 249; and
agencies and commissions, 124;
and African Americans, 10, 33,
37, 42, 71, 84, 90, 98, 100–101,
107–110, 115, 119, 169, 179, 180,
191, 208–209; as African American
enclave, 110, 113; and annexation of
Fort Ord, 59, 138; and annexation
by Monterey, 70; and Catholics,
67; and churches, 66–69, 192; city
council, 12, 51, 70, 72, 74, 75, 84,
96, 97, 100–105, 124, 133–135, 138,
141, 145, 158, 162, 198, 216, 218,
247, 249; city of, 184; civil rights,
84, 95, 97, 101, 103, 151, 157, 245;
and closure of Fort Ord, 203, 209,
211–268; commercial growth,
64, 65, 96, 203; commissions, 84;
community culture, 12, 13, 34, 44,
68–69, 91, 114–135, 137, 163, 165,
180, 182, 187; and crime, 7, 12,
97, 98, 111, 172, 173, 180, 205,
206, 234, 254; and desegregation
of neighborhoods, 150–151; and

diversity, 7, 26–34, 37, 51, 59, 75,
81, 108–110, 118–135, 182, 220,
243; and economic development,
18, 63–66, 96, 98, 111, 114–135,
200, 203, 205, 206, 207, 208; and
economic development programs
(federal), 63, 120–121, 151–153, 203;
and employment at Fort Ord, 115,
120; and employment discrimination,
140, 151–153; and environment, 10,
15–16, 20, 25, 27, 30, 37–42, 48–50,
62, 75, 86, 122, 169, 179, 249; and
expansion of, 64, 65, 173, 180; and
Filipino community, 13, 32, 38, 45,
51, 61, 91, 110, 116; and First Tee,
244–250; and Fort Ord, 8, 12, 15,
49–52, 84, 86, 97, 111; and gangs,
179; and Hispanic communities,
61, 233; and Hispanic population,
118, 241; and housing, 96, 148; and
housing discrimination, 72, 140,
148; and identity, 11, 15–16, 29,
65, 69, 83, 127, 179, 187, 105–112,
224–268; and incorporation, 11,
51, 63, 69–76, 84, 96, 111 and
integration, 37, 81, 85, 95, 102, 111,
171; and international culture, 169;
and Japanese community, 59–61,
109–110; and Latinos, 212, 253; as
a marginalized space, 12, 15–16,
23–50, 148, 209; and memories of,
107–112; and Mexican American
activism, 154–156; and Mexican
immigrants, 178, 212, 219, 250–257;
and Mexican settlement of, 17–18,
37, 67, 68, 250–251; middle class,
96, 137, 179, 180, 191, 209, 245;
and military families, 119–120, 127,
212; as a military town, 5, 7, 11,
15, 23–25, 41, 44, 48–52, 69, 76,
83, 85, 87, 102, 114, 128, 170–171,
179, 187, 207, 212–214, 245; as
minority-majority, 5, 15, 75–76,
85, 118, 137, 148, 179, 191, 200,
209, 214, 217; and model cities,
120; as a multiracial city, 66, 69,
83, 95, 106, 107–110, 171, 179,

Taylor, Quintard, 83
Teaford, Jon C., 114–115
Teamsters Union, 129
Tennessee, 67
Tennis club, 10
Tet celebration, 256
Tet Offensive, 117
Texas, 1, 33, 67, 92, 103, 155
Thorne, Jerry, 296n57, 314
Tijuana, Mexico, 250, 254
Toler, Lee, 140, 145
La Tortuga Restaurant, 98
Towne, Nancy, 279n94, 314
Truman, President Harry S.: and civil
   rights, 57–58, 89; and Executive
   Order 9980, 58; and Executive
   Order 9981, 58, 63, 78; and Fair
   Employment Board, 58; and
   integration of armed forces,
   57–58, 78, 87; and President's
   Committee on Civil Rights, 57
Turner, J. Hugh, 124
Tuskegee Airmen, 13
Tuten, Lieutenant Colonel Jeff, 164
"26" Club, 48, 64
Twohig, Thomas, 70
Tyler, Rev J.J., 99

Underwood, Al, 73
United Fruit and Vegetable
   Workers Union, 257
United Service Organization (USO), 55
United States, 146
U.S. Army: and African Americans,
   58, 90; and All Volunteer Army,
   116; and compassionate duty base,
   62, 119; and 1st Filipino Infantry
   Regiment, 45; and 43rd Infantry,
   45; integration of, 58; personnel,
   64; and 2nd Filipino Regiment,
   45; and segregation, 53–55, 78;
   and 7th Infantry, 45, 73, 212;
   and Third Division, 45; and 3rd
   Infantry, 45; and 35th Infantry,
   45; and 27th Infantry, 45
U.S. Army Morale, Welfare and
   Recreation Fund, 227

U.S. Bureau of the Census Census
   Population Characteristics: 1900,
   27–28; 1910, 28–29; 1920, 29–30;
   1930, 29–30; 1940, 29–30; 1950,
   29–30; 1960, 118; 1970, 118;
   1980, 85, 118; 1990, 118, 254;
   2000, 118, 255
U.S. Constitution, 132
U.S. Environmental Protection
   Agency (EPA), 211
U.S. Golf Association, 227, 244
U.S. Navy, 64
U.S. Post Office, 154
United Way, 168
Urban America, 125–127; and African
   Americans, 10; and crime, 179;
   and neighborhood associations,
   179; and white flight, 147, 169
urban crisis, 9, 147
urban renewal, 114, 124–126

Valdez, Alfredo, 254, 302n122, 314
Vallarta, Vanessa, 256
Vaughn, Bradford, 150
Vaughn, Charles Sr., 258–260
veterans, 105
Veterans of Foreign Wars
   (VFW), 105, 188, 194
Vets for Peace, 189
vice, 98
Victory Temple, 31
Vietnam War, 12, 116–130, 147, 162,
   164; and protests, 188; and Tet
   Offensive, 117
Vietnamese Americans, 1, 110, 171,
   194, 253
Vietnamese refugees, 61, 164, 182;
   and Tet Festival, 182, 256
voter registration, 160

Wadsworth, Time, 179
War Against Drugs, 178
War brides, 60, 62, 79, 94
Waters, Congresswoman Maxine,
   223, 229
Watkins, Major Rolin C., 22
Watson, John, 73